The Rights of Adolescents in the Mental Health System

The Rights of Adolescents in the Mental Health System

John P. Wilson
Boston University
School of Law

Lexington Books
D.C. Heath and Company
Lexington, Massachusetts
Toronto

Library of Congress Cataloging in Publication Data

Wilson, John Pasley, 1933-
    The rights of adolescents in the mental health system.

    Includes bibliographical references.
    1. Children—Law—United States. 2. Mental health laws—United States.
3. Insanity—Jurisprudence—United States. I. Title.
KF479.W57   346'.73'013   77-4542
ISBN 0-669-01485-0

Published simultaneously in Canada.

Printed in the United States of America.

International Standard Book Number: 0-669-01485-0

Library of Congress Catalog Card Number: 77-4542

Pages 309-311 constitute a continuation of this copyright page.

Contents

Acknowledgments

This book is the result of the work of many people. Foremost among them is Henry A. Beyer, who for three years devoted his energies full time to coordinating the research for it. The book simply could not have been produced without him, and much of the final result is due entirely to his efforts.

The research project which produced this book was conceived in the first instance by Martha J. Koster, then a staff attorney with the Boston University Center for Law and Health Sciences. Consultants to the project included Dr. Robert Apsler, presently a clinical psychologist with the Drug Problems Resource Center, Cambridge, Massachusetts; Professor Albert R. Beisel, Jr., Boston University School of Law; Professor Gunnar Dybwad, Brandeis University; Professor Stanley Z. Fisher, Boston University School of Law; Associate Professor Stephen J. Morse, Law Center, University of Southern California; Associate Professor Phyllis G. Oram, Boston University School of Medicine; and Professor Joseph C. Speisman, Department of Psychology, Boston University. Professor Morse contributed the chapter on psychological and psychiatric issues (chapter 3), and Professor Fisher contributed the chapter on the right to treatment (chapter 7).

Several students performed invaluable research for the book, working under the direction of Henry Beyer, the consultants, or myself. The work of many of them was outstanding, but special commendation should be given to Richard F. Howard, who devoted two years to the project as a student research assistant. The others, to whom a great debt of gratitude is owed, were: Mary Asbury, David Bakken, Christina Bloom, Jeffrey C. Brazor, Debra A. Chong, Deanna S. Ciccone, Elizabeth L. Coates, Sara A. Dinzes, Linda J. Dreeben, William Fitzharris, Kathleen A. Ford, Anne Hyde, Michael J. Kelly, George A. Kielman, Trudy Kolb, Wendy L. Krasner, Joan Kugelmann, Jan M. Levine, Andrea S. Mintz, Barbara Mitchell, David R. Morris, Ruby Ozur, Tel Putsavage, Georgene I. Robinson, David A. Roush, Austin R. Sherer, Jane C. Snyder, and Michael Sokol.

Grateful thanks must be recorded for the typing, retyping, and patient attention to the details of record keeping and correspondence performed by Lynne K. Resnick, Patricia E. Callahan, Shawn A. Finnegan, and especially Carolyn L. Harrelson, who typed the final manuscript. Tribute must also be given to former Dean Paul M. Siskind, Boston University School of Law, for his support and encouragement through most of the project period.

In a very real sense it should be obvious that this is not my book but the book of many people. I am very grateful to them, and it was a privilege being associated with them in this work.

John P. Wilson

The Rights of
Adolescents in the
Mental Health System

1 Introduction

This book was made possible through the generous support of the Center for Studies of Child and Family Mental Health of the National Institute of Mental Health. Funds to conduct the research and prepare a written report were awarded in late June of 1973. The research was performed under the auspices of the Center for Law and Health Sciences of the Boston University School of Law.

Stated simply, the basic purpose of the project was to explore the extent to which parents or guardians control, or should control, the mental health services afforded adolescent children even though (a) adolescence is a time of rapid maturation and emancipation from parental authority and (b) the perceived mental health problems of adolescents may often be relatively benign results of growth or the products of intrafamily tensions and disagreements. Five years ago it was still novel to question the untrammeled right of parents to admit their children into mental institutions "voluntarily." The impetus to ask such a question may have arisen in part from the spirit of the times, which was characterized by rising distrust of institutions of authority and increasing scrutiny of the potential rights of hitherto ignored minorities. But an equally important impetus was the revelation of abuses in mental institutions throughout the country and the shocking treatment afforded children in some of them. It seemed unjust that, with scanty procedural protections or none whatsoever, parents and guardians could simply consign children to such places.

As a consequence, this project was born. Its initial objectives were fourfold: to determine the legal rights of adolescents seeking or receiving mental health services; to ascertain the actual practices of persons and agencies providing mental health services to adolescents in Massachusetts; to determine from these findings of law and practice some of the major legal problems associated with the provision of mental health services to adolescents; and to recommend changes in laws, regulations, or practices to eliminate or lessen these problems.

The First Phase

For purposes of description, the project can be divided into different phases of work, although in actual practice there were substantial overlaps. Certain tasks were emphasized during these phases, even though others were being performed concurrently. During the first phase, in an effort to determine the most important problems, an extensive review was conducted of both legal and psychological literature related to adolescent mental health services. At the same time, many persons concerned with the provision of care in various settings and representing various viewpoints were interviewed, and approximately five hundred letters soliciting information were written to state mental health departments, law schools, university psychology departments, and various individuals and organizations studying problems of adolescent mental health or advocating solutions thereto.

A more precise definition of the project's scope resulted from this probing. To focus the research effort, certain areas were deemphasized, such as the procedures governing release from voluntary or involuntary treatment; the problems of the mentally retarded as a unique class; and the thorny issues associated with the procedures required for involuntary civil commitment as opposed to voluntary admission. The emphasis was placed instead upon the rights of *mentally ill* adolescents subjected to *voluntary admission*, primarily during the process of *admission* to an institution and during *treatment*. Five broad areas were selected for intensive review:

1. *Access to Treatment.* Under this rubric the project staff attempted to determine the most important impediments an adolescent faces in attempting to obtain mental health treatments without parental consent. Several subissues were thoroughly explored, such as incapacities of minority, parental rights to control their children, informed consent, capacity to contract, emancipation, and liability for payment for services rendered.

2. *Right to Refuse Treatment.* An effort was made to determine an adolescent's rights, if any, to refuse treatment when assigned it by a parent, guardian, school official, juvenile court judge, or other person or institution. As part of this effort, an exploration was made of the advantages and disadvantages of ombudsmen, youth advocates, or special guardians as supplemental, independent protectors of the interests of children subjected to voluntary admission to mental health facilities.

3. *Special Education Laws.* Many states have enacted far-ranging special education laws or have expanded existing laws to include psychological or psychiatric testing and treatment of all children within the state. These statutes attempt to deal with a variety of troublesome issues, such as the rights of a child or his or her parents to appeal decisions of the special education agency, confidentiality of records, and the deleterious effects of early labeling of children "with special needs." A careful review of developments in this area seemed necessary because, if fully implemented, these laws will make the public school system the first place at which most children will encounter their first mental health testing and through which many will receive their first treatment.

4. *Right to Treatment.* In recent years a number of judicial opinions have enunciated a right to treatment or habilitation or a right to be free from harm, for persons or groups of persons in institutions for the mentally ill or retarded. Little has been said, however, about the rights of voluntarily admitted minors to

treatment, whether defined in an individual sense or in the sense of proper staffing, facilities and treatment plans. Research appeared necessary to explore the extent of this right for adolescents and to determine the procedures they or their parents might invoke to exercise the right.

5. *Confidentiality.* Research was conducted to clarify the rights to privacy or confidentiality of an adolescent receiving mental health treatment with respect to his parents, the school system, law enforcement agencies, and others. Questions were posed regarding the advantages and disadvantages of enlarging such rights and the most feasible ways to do so.

With these five major topics in mind, another component of the first phase of the project commenced. A brief check was made of statutes relating to age of majority and voluntary admission of minors to mental health facilities for all fifty states and the District of Columbia. In addition, a careful examination of the statutory and case law on these issues (as well as minors' rights in other areas: consent to medical and other services, contracts, liability for payment, confidentiality, marriage, juvenile justice, education, and so forth) was made by law student research assistants for twenty-eight selected jurisdictions. The following states were chosen as representative of the nation on the basis of their populations, geographic locations, reputed progressiveness or conservatism in matters of mental health, and common law or civil code legal traditions: Alaska, California, Colorado, Connecticut, District of Columbia, Florida, Georgia, Illinois, Indiana, Louisiana, Maryland, Massachusetts, Michigan, Minnesota, Mississippi, Missouri, Nevada, New Jersey, New Mexico, New York, Ohio, Oregon, Pennsylvania, Tennessee, Texas, Virginia, Washington, and Wisconsin.

The Second Phase

The second phase of the project involved a field survey of mental health providers in Massachusetts, which was conducted by Dr. Robert Apsler.[1] The purpose of the survey was to ascertain the types of services actually provided to adolescents; the situations in which services are withheld from them or forced upon them, and the reasons therefor; the degree of confidentiality afforded adolescent patients; the extent of practitioners' knowledge of, and compliance with, laws governing the provision of care; and providers' suggestions for changes in such law.

The survey was conducted in two parts: the first part was a survey of four classes of mental health practitioners whose names appear on statewide master lists—psychiatrists, psychologists, school psychologists, and psychiatric social workers; the second involved a survey of the practices of "nonlisted" providers, including runaway-house counselors, hot-line operators, teen-center counselors, and so forth, which actually account for many of the mental health services provided to adolescents. In view of the breadth and number of respondents, the results of the survey represent the practices and perceptions of a broad cross-section of Massachusetts providers of adolescent mental health services.[2]

Summary of the Results of the Survey of
Mental Health Providers

The survey corroborated many general impressions of work in this field and also produced new and occasionally disturbing findings. For example, both listed and nonlisted respondents indicated, not surprisingly, that their adolescent clients come to them from a variety of sources—on their own or brought or sent by a parent or guardian, by a state or private agency, or by school personnel. They come to the average provider with roughly equal frequency (i.e., "sometimes") from each of these sources except private agencies, where the frequency is somewhat less. For purposes of law reform, it is important to note that a substantial number of providers of many types reported that adolescents "sometimes" seek mental health services on their own initiative. As one might guess, the average nonlisted provider appears to be approached in this manner more often than the average listed provider and less frequently by adolescents brought or sent by parents.

Adolescents coming on their own or being brought to providers for mental health care exhibit a variety of problems. Listed providers cited as the most common problem areas (in decreasing order of frequency): school, antisocial/criminal, intrapsychic, family, drug, interpersonal, and sexual. School-related difficulty is by far the problem most cited by listed providers, with over 70 percent of the psychologists, social workers, and school psychologists listing it first. Slightly less than half of the psychiatrists also mentioned school problems first, but one-third of them listed social/criminal problems in first place. This is at least double the frequency with which other listed providers cited such problems. Nonlisted providers cited family difficulties most frequently.

The perceived severity of adolescents' problems is indicated by the fact that approximately 15 percent of the providers characterized their clients as either all or mostly inpatients. A few providers work with both inpatients and outpatients, but most—both listed and nonlisted providers—service either all or mostly outpatients.

Both listed and nonlisted providers employ a range of services in dealing with the problems of their adolescent clients. Somewhat surprisingly, providers reported that adolescents refuse these services only infrequently. When services are refused, the providers only occasionally override such refusals; when this happens, listed providers are more likely to perform a diagnosis than other services. Similarly, despite a refusal, nonlisted providers are more likely to perform services other than behavior modification. It thus appears that the more intrusive the service, the less likelihood there is that an adolescent's refusal will be overridden.

Because (with very few exceptions)[3] Massachusetts law requires only the consent of a parent or guardian and not that of the adolescent to administer treatment, most providers are clearly according adolescents greater refusal rights than are legally mandated. It is not known whether this is due to ignorance of the law, a perceived moral right of adolescents to refuse, or merely the belief that treatment would be ineffective or too difficult to administer to a patient who refuses it.

Despite the differences between listed and nonlisted providers noted above, both groups have almost identical opinions of the effectiveness of their services. They believe that upon the conclusion of services, their adolescent clients are "sometimes" to "frequently" cured or substantially improved, "sometimes" unchanged, and "seldom" worse off than when services began. However, almost twice as many nonlisted as listed providers acknowledged that they did not know the outcomes.

A very important finding for purposes of law reform is that most practitioners provide diagnosis, initial treatment, and continuing treatment to adolescents, at least occasionally, without obtaining the consent of a parent or guardian. (As might be expected, the likelihood of requesting consent from a parent or guardian varies directly with the extensiveness of the service, and is considerably greater for continuing treatment than for diagnosis.) It appears that almost three-fourths of all providers do not fully comply with the parental consent law.[4] Although the practices of listed and nonlisted providers are quite similar in this respect, the nonlisted group appears slightly more likely to treat without parental consent. (On the other hand, they are also slightly more likely to inform parents that they have done so.) A factor which may be related to the willingness to provide services without parental consent is payment. Thirty-nine percent of the nonlisted providers, and only 28 percent of the listed providers, reported that they charge no fee for services rendered without the consent of a parent or guardian.

When it comes to protecting the confidentiality of their adolescent clients, nonlisted and listed providers' practices are quite similar. Although 4 to 9 percent admitted to releasing information about adolescent clients more readily than information about adult clients, 20 percent claimed to do so less readily, and the great majority (about three-fourths) stated that they treat information on both groups the same. While this last approach would appear to protect adolescent confidentiality rights, it apparently leads many providers to violate the rights of parents and guardians to be told, upon request, whether their minor child is receiving mental health services.[5] Just 4 percent of the listed and 8 percent of the nonlisted providers always answer such parental requests.[6] The rate with which providers answer parental requests for additional information about treatment is even smaller.

A lack of familiarity with the law is undoubtedly a major factor contributing to these low levels of compliance. Many providers recognize and acknowledge their ignorance in this area. But further, the survey results indicate that many providers who claim to know the law are mistaken. On the basis of a measure of *actual* familiarity, no more than about 10 percent of the providers are familiar with the laws related to parental consent or the parents' right to information.

Nonlisted providers professed somewhat less familiarity with the law, and analysis shows them to be somewhat less familiar than listed providers. This difference in familiarity may be related to the different manner in which decisions are made by the two groups when questions arise concerning adolescents' rights. Although over half of each group relies on a group of professional staff members or on institutional policy to resolve such questions, 23 percent of the listed providers make the decisions alone, whereas only 7 percent of the nonlisted providers do so.

All providers were asked if they recommended changes in laws relating to the provision of adolescent mental health services. Despite their great unfamiliarity, over half of the respondents (both listed and nonlisted) expressed a desire for change in the laws relating to the provision of services without parental consent, while only 10 percent or less wanted no change in such laws (the remainder do not know). Almost half would also like to see changes in laws regarding confidentiality, with 15 percent or less opposed. Slightly less than one-third wanted change in laws concerning provision of services against an adolescent's wishes; about half did not know whether they favored change, and the remainder were opposed.

The Third Phase

The tertiary phase of the project was devoted, in substantial part, to compiling the prior research findings and setting them forth in a straightforward style easily readable by both lawyers and nonlawyers. The chapters of this book, however, do not comport exactly with the topics which were selected for particular attention in the first phase. A review after independent analysis of each revealed some to be more important than others, and these determinations are reflected in the final organization. Moreover, the capstone of the book, chapter 9, which details model procedures for a juvenile admissions process, was not prepared chronologically at the end, as its place in the book might suggest. It is without doubt the most intensively scrutinized chapter of the book, and it was prepared over a period of many months—indeed, years—of careful analysis and often heated debate by members of the research staff. In a way it is a distillation, in statutory form, of the research in the chapters before it, and it attempts to provide greater rights and protections to adolescents being admitted to inpatient mental health treatment.

Notes

1. A complete description of the results of the survey was included in the final report of the research project, entitled "The Rights of Adolescents Receiving Mental Health Services" (Grant No. 1 RD1 MH 24934), submitted to the Mental Health Services Development Branch, Division of Mental Health Service Programs, National Institute of Mental Health, 5600 Fishers Lane, Rockville, Maryland 20852.

2. Most listed providers see their clients in settings rather different from those of nonlisted providers. Almost half of the listed group provide services in private practice or public schools, whereas the most popular settings for nonlisted providers are child service organizations and residential treatment facilities. Both groups, however, are substantially represented (10 to 19 percent) at community mental health centers and clinics.

The two categories differ also in the amount of experience they have had servicing adolescents (11.5 years for listed providers; 5.2 years for nonlisted) and in their personal, primary orientation toward the principal causes of adolescent mental disorders: listed providers are more likely to cite psychological causes; nonlisted providers, social causes.

3. See note 4 below.

4. Some portion of the treatment given to adolescent clients without parental consent may have been legal. Massachusetts statutes permit minors 12 years of age or over to consent to hospital and medical care for drug dependency (Mass. Gen. Laws Ann. ch. 112, § 12E), and minors of any age may consent to treatment by a physician for venereal disease (Mass. Gen. Laws Ann. ch. 111, § 117). Another section of the statute relating to drug dependence has for some years permitted physicians and hospitals to render "emergency examination and treatment" without parental consent when delay would "endanger the life, limb, or mental well-being of the patient." (Mass. Gen. Laws Ann. ch. 112, § 12F). In 1975 the legislature expanded this section to include dentists within the emergency provision and to enable certain emancipated minors to consent to certain types of treatment provided by certain categories of providers, even in nonemergency situations. Section 12F now reads:

No physician, dentist or hospital shall be held liable for damages for failure to obtain consent of a parent, legal guardian, or other person having custody or control of a minor child, or of the spouse of a patient, to emergency examination and treatment, including blood transfusions, when delay in treatment will endanger the life, limb, or mental well being of the patient.

Any minor may give consent to his medical or dental care at the time such care is sought if (i) he is married, widowed, divorced; or (ii) he is the parent of a child, in which case he may also give consent to medical or dental care of the child; or (iii) he is a member of any of the armed forces; or (iv) she is pregnant or believes herself to be pregnant; or (v) he is living separate and apart from his parent or legal guardian, and is managing his own financial affairs; or (vi) he reasonably believes himself to be suffering from or to have come in contact with any disease defined as dangerous to the public health pursuant to section six of chapter one hundred and eleven; provided, however, that such minor may only consent to care which relates to the diagnosis or treatment of such disease.

Consent shall not be granted under subparagraphs (ii) through (vi), inclusive, for abortion or sterilization.

Consent given under this section shall not be subject to later disaffirmance because of minority. The consent of the parent or legal guardian shall not be required to authorize such care and, notwithstanding any other provision of law, such parent or legal guardian shall not be liable for the payment for any care rendered pursuant to this section unless such parent or legal guardian has expressly agreed to pay for such care.

No physician or dentist, nor any hospital, clinic or infirmary shall be liable, civilly and criminally, for not obtaining the consent of the parent or legal guardian to render medical or dental care to a minor, if, at the time such care was rendered, such person or facility: (i) relied in good faith upon the representations of such minor that he is legally able to consent to such treatment under this section; or (ii) relied in good faith upon the representations of such minor that he is over eighteen years of age.

All information and records kept in connection with the medical or dental care of a minor who consents thereto in accordance with this section shall be confidential between the minor and the physician or dentist, and shall not be released except upon the written consent of the minor or a proper judicial order. When the physician or dentist attending a minor reasonably believes the condition of said minor to be so serious that his life or limb is endangered, the physician or dentist shall notify the parents, legal guardian or foster parents of said condition and shall inform the minor of said notification. (*Id.* as revised by 1975 Mass. Acts ch. 564).

Although the questionnaire did not ask whether emergency conditions, venereal disease, drug dependency, or indications of emancipation existed in those circumstances when treatment was provided without parental consent, it is believed that the statutory exceptions would apply so infrequently as to have a negligible effect on the results. As corroboration, no respondent mentioned an instance in which a delay necessitated by a requirement for parental consent would have endangered a patient's life, limb, or mental well-being, and the nonemergency provisions did not become effective until October 29, 1975. By that date 87 percent of the completed questionnaires returned by nonlisted providers and *all* of the questionnaires returned by listed providers had already been received. Listed providers, it should be noted, are far more likely than nonlisted providers to fall under the limited coverage of the statute (physicians, dentists, hospitals, clinics, and infirmaries).

Yet another Massachusetts statute permits persons 16 years of age or older to consent to their own admissions to mental health facilities. Once admitted, Department of Mental Health (DMH) Regulations (*See, e.g.*, Mass. DMH Regs. S212.07, S214.04, S220.06(b), and S225.05) appear to accord 16- and 17-year-old voluntary patients the same rights as adult voluntary patients. Sixteen- and 17-year-old adolescent inpatients in DMH-licensed facilities would thus appear to have the legal right to receive treatment without parental consent. Again, however, it does not appear that this exception to the general consent rule significantly affected the results of the survey because (1) the great majority of sampled providers service few or no inpatients; (2) the exception is applicable to only one-third of the class of adolescent inpatients (those 16 and 17, of those age 12 through 17); and (3) the great majority of sampled providers themselves admit to general unfamiliarity with the consent (as well as other) laws regarding provision of treatment.

5. To fulfill their caretaking obligations, parents and guardians are generally understood to have the legal right to be informed of their minor children's activities. This is recognized in statutory provisions such as those granting parents access to their children's school records (*See, e.g.*, Mass. Gen. Laws Ann. ch. 71, § 34E). This parental right to information certainly extends to knowledge of the fact that their minor adolescent child is receiving mental health services (*See, e.g.*, Mass. DMH Regs. S7.03(b) and S7.03(c)). Further, in some states, adolescents do not even enjoy full mental health care confidentiality rights against their school systems. In Massachusetts, for example, a parent who applies for admission to a mental health facility of a child under the age of 16 "shall give written authorization to the . . . head of the facility . . . to provide necessary clinical information to the patient's local school board in order that an educational program can be jointly developed for such patient by the school board and the facility." (Mass. DMH Regs. S214.07). Very few cases have denied parents access to their minor child's mental health records. *See, e.g.,* Application of J.C.G., (Sup. Ct., Law Div., Hudson City, N.J., Oct. 14, 1976), cited in Judicial Highlights, 357 N.E.2d 7 (Jan. 12, 1977). This has been done only in extreme circumstances, such as judicial removal of the child from parental custody, in which case the responsibility for care and treatment becomes vested in the court rather than the parents.

6. Amazingly, not one of the licensed psychologists surveyed reported that he or she informs parents, when requested, of the fact of treatment. Twenty-two percent of the school psychologists claim that they "always" answer such requests, however.

2 Adolescence

Few would argue with the proposition that young children are properly accorded fewer rights and responsibilities than are adults.[1] When a two-year-old toddler is about to step into a busy street, the child's parents most certainly do, and should have, the right to restrain it. Indeed, most would agree that parents have a duty to do so, even though such restraint is obviously an infringement of the child's freedom.

Similarly, we require parents and guardians to provide food, clothing, shelter, schooling, medical care and other "necessities" to their minor children, and, at least for very young children, we impose no requirement that parents obtain their consent, concurrence, or even opinion. Further, we have so structured our social, economic, and legal systems that it is generally impossible for children to obtain such commodities on their own without the consent of a parent or guardian. Again, for very young children, there is no widespread opposition to the existing system of parental control.

There is a growing belief among many social observers, however, that many older children have the physical and psychological capacities to act with some autonomy in many areas in which they are now denied independence, that they have a moral right to such autonomy, and that they should be granted corresponding legal rights. It has been suggested that children receiving mental health services should be accorded greater legal rights at some age or stage of development. Although there is no unanimity regarding the particular age or stage at which such rights should be acquired (nor about which specific rights these are), most recommendations concern that period of life generally described as adolescence. It is therefore appropriate that we consider the findings of various disciplines concerning adolescence; the legal rights possessed by, and disabilities imposed upon, people of that age; and any evidence tending to support or refute the proposition that adolescents have the capacity to properly exercise greater rights in mental health proceedings than they now possess.

Adolescence. That age which follows puberty and precedes the age of majority—
Black's Law Dictionary (1968)

Black's resort to disparate markers—one biological and one legal—to bound this period of human life is illustrative of the problems encountered in considering adolescents and their legal status. Law pays little notice to the physiologically momentous beginnings of the age of adolescence but assigns

11

major import to a chronological point of slight organic significance marking the end of adolescence and minority. Americans gain limited rights and responsibilities in only a few narrowly-defined areas at age twelve, an age frequently identified with the onset of adolescence; but they achieve full civic and personal rights of autonomy at eighteen (twenty-one in a few states)[2] an age of no great importance biologically.

What is the basis of the law's emphasis upon a chronologically determined age of majority? Is eighteen the most appropriate choice for this age? What is the significance of withholding mental health rights from those who have not achieved this age? Do the answers to these questions suggest any changes in present mental health laws? These are some of the issues which will be discussed in this chapter. First, however, it may be useful to examine the general concept of adolescence, some of its physiological and psychological distinctions, and the nature of and reasons for adolescents' general legal status.

Physical and Psychological Significance

Some recognition of the importance of the period of adolescence has existed since ancient times. Plato noted that during the developmental years of childhood through young manhood "more than at any other time the character is engrained by habit."[3] Referring only to males, Aristotle designated adolescence as one of the three distinguishable seven-year stages of development. "The first seven years he called boyhood; and from puberty to twenty-one, young manhood."[4] But "[t]he idea of adolescence as an intermediary period in life starting at puberty and extending to some period in the life cycle unmarked by any conspicuous change but socially defined as 'manhood' or 'womanhood' is the product of modern times.[5] The *Oxford English Dictionary* traces the term to the fifteenth century. Prior to that . . . the notion of childhood hardly existed, let alone the idea of the prolongation of childhood beyond puberty, as the term adolescence suggests."[6] Bakan believes that the term "adolescence" was invented "in order to create a social condition and a social fact."[7]

Yet ample physiological reasons exist for attributing special significance to the adolescent years. Between conception and adulthood, vast changes take place in the human body. For the most part, the changes occur as part of a slow, smoothly continuous process of growth and development. During two periods, however, this development process is so rapid that these intervals constitute almost discrete stages. During the first such period, which encompasses fetal life and the first year or two after birth, the rate of body change is at its maximum. But during this first stage, the subject is not "the fascinated, charmed, or horrified spectator that watches the developments, or lack of developments,"[8] that he or she is during the second such accelerated growth stage, adolescence.

"[A]t puberty,[9] a very considerable alteration in growth rate occurs. There is a swift increase in body size, a change in the shape and body composition, and a rapid development of the gonads, the reproductive organs, and the characters signaling sexual maturity."[10] "In boys the growth spurt may begin as early as 10 1/2 years or as late as 16 years."[11] For the average North American boy, however, this accelerated growth begins shortly before his thirteenth birthday, reaches a peak at about age fourteen, and declines to its former rate at about fifteen.[12] "In girls the adolescent spurt may begin as early as 7 1/2 years of age or as late as 11 1/2,"[13] with the average girl's occurring about two years earlier than the average boy's. Accelerated growth begins shortly before her eleventh birthday, peaking at about age twelve, and falling to pre-spurt rate shortly before thirteen.[14]

"Nearly all the bones and muscles take part in the adolescent growth spurt. . . . The increase in the size of the muscles is much more marked in boys than in girls. . . . Boys also develop a larger heart and lungs in relation to their size than do girls. In addition they develop a higher systolic blood pressure, a lower rate of heartbeat while they are resting, a greater capacity for oxygen in the blood and a greater power for neutralizing the chemical products of exercise . . . , resulting in a faster rate of recovery from physical exhaustion. At the same time the male's shoulders show a proportionately greater spurt in width than the female's, while the female's hips widen more than the male's."[15]

At about the time of the adolescent growth spurt, the reproductive system of both the male and the female begins to mature. In boys the growth of the penis and the testes accelerates. In girls the breasts begin to develop, and enlargement of the uterus, vagina, labia and clitoris occurs. In both sexes pubic hair first appears. Boys experience a growth of hair in armpits and upon the face, a lowering of the voice, and an enlargement of the Adam's apple. Even though girls experience their adolescent growth spurt two years earlier than boys, the sexes are separated only by six months in the initial sexual changes of puberty. Menarche (first mentrual period) is a late event in female puberty and invariably comes after the peak of the growth spurt.[16]

Such biological developments have of course occurred in every generation for millenia. We live, however, in changing times, and these changes are not confined to the political, sociological, and legal spheres. Even in purely physiological pubescent happenings "there has been one considerable change; the events occur now at an earlier age than formerly. Forty years ago the average British girl had her first mentrual period . . . at about her fifteenth birthday; nowadays it is shortly before her thirteenth."[17]

"As the environmental and social conditions of a country improve, the children grow up faster and reach a greater final size. The variation between individuals of different social classes becomes less. This process is termed the secular trend of growth. In Europe and North America the process has been going on continuously for about 100 years. . . . Although the reasons for secular trends are not fully understood, it seems likely that better nutrition, particularly in infancy, is chiefly responsible."[18]

Whatever the cause, this indisputable earlier physical development, the so-called secular trend of growth, is one of the factors to be considered in deciding whether changes should be made in the legal status of today's adolescents.

In contrast to the marked increase in overall height and in the size of heart and lungs that accompanies adolescence, there is little growth in the size of the brain during this period. "Whereas the average child has acquired only about 50 percent of his total adult weight by the age of 10, he has acquired 95 percent of his adult brain weight."[19] This absence of radical physical change in the brain does not, however, indicate a lack of cognitive development. On the contrary, "[i]t is during the years between puberty and adulthood that 'the capacity to acquire and utilize knowledge reaches its peak efficiency.' "[20]

These gains apparently result from not only a "quantitative" increase in an adolescent's ability to assimilate and process information, but also a "qualitative" change in his cognitive capability.[21] Research by Piaget and others has suggested that there are basic differences between the reasoning processes of adolescents and those of younger children. "In Piaget's theory the final period of intellectual development is that of *formal operations*, which begins at about age 12, and is consolidated during adolescence."[22] "It can be said . . . that adolescent thought has achieved an advanced state of equilibrium. This means, among other things, that the adolescent's cognitive structures have developed to the point where they can effectively adapt to a great variety of problems. These structures are sufficiently stable to assimilate readily a variety of novel situations. . . . This does not mean, of course, that the adolescent's growth ceases at age 16. He has much to learn in many areas, and Piaget does not deny this. Piaget does maintain however, that, by the end of adolescence, the individual's way of thinking, that is, his cognitive structures, are almost fully formed. . . ."[23]

Piaget finds that the adolescent's thought processes involve a great many features lacking in those of the preadolescent, "concrete-operational" child.[24] The adolescent is flexible and versatile in his thinking and can deal with a problem in many ways and from many perspectives.[25] He is unlikely to be confused by unusual results, because he has previously conceived of all the possibilities. His thought can proceed in one direction, and then, employing newly acquired formal logical operations,[26] he can use several different methods for retracing his thoughts to return to the starting point.

"The effect of the adolescent's intellectual achievements is not limited to the area of scientific problem-solving. . . . In the intellectual sphere, the adolescent has a tendency to become involved in abstract and theoretical matters. . . . In the emotional sphere the adolescent now becomes capable of directing his emotions at abstract ideals and not just toward people. Whereas earlier he could love his mother or hate a peer, now he can love freedom or hate exploitation. . . ."[27]

"The relentless criticism by many adolescents of existing social, political, and religious systems and their preoccupation with the construction of often elaborate or highly theoretical alternative systems is dependent on their emerging capacity for formal operational thought. The fact that such concerns tend to be most characteristic of our brightest young people appears to be due at least as much (and quite possibly more) to their greater cognitive capability as to their more 'permissive upbringing,' 'affluence,' or other favorite whipping boys of the politicians and the popular press."[28]

Adolescent mental development rates, like physiological development rates, seem to be sex-related. "There appears to be an earlier and more marked growth spurt of mental ability in girls—paralleling their earlier physical growth spurt. . . . But although girls show an earlier growth spurt in mental functioning, boys rapidly catch up as adolescence proceeds."[29]

Exactly what enables the adolescent to achieve this stage of formal operations is not at all clear. Piaget suggests several possibly contributing factors: neurological development occurring around the time of puberty, social environment, education, the intellectual level of the culture, and the individual's experience.[30] Others are less hesitant to assign the development of formal thought to "an interaction of age and intelligence with significant gains being made by adolescents of average intelligence from 12 to 14 and by low-intelligence adolescents from 14 to 16. [Subjects] of superior intelligence show an almost linear development."[31]

Many authorities consider adolescence a discrete and important phase of psychological as well as cognitive development. Sigmund Freud referred to it as the "genital stage," involving a revival of earlier Oedipal attachments and rivalries with a corresponding need to resolve them in the direction of greater independence from parents and a shifting of attachments to new "love objects."[32] Erik Erikson designates adolescence as one of the "eight stages of man," ascribing to it the conflicting basic components of "Identity vs. Identity Confusion."[33] Anna Freud,[34] Kurt Lewin,[35] G. Stanley Hall,[36] Arnold Gesell,[37] Peter Blos,[38] and many others, although differing widely in their psychological views, have all recognized the distinct developmental qualities of the adolescent years.[39]

In addition to cognitive proficiency, however, much decision-making requires the ability to weigh competing values and ethical standards. What do we know of the ability of adolescents to make moral judgments? Research conducted by Lawrence Kohlberg indicates that cognitive development, as measured by Piaget, is an essential component of moral judgment development.[40] Kohlberg does not maintain that cognitive maturity alone provides moral maturity, but only that such cognitive development is necessary for the development of principled morality. He has defined three major levels of moral development: the preconventional, the conventional, and the postconventional or autonomous. Within each level he sees two discernible stages.[41] At the preconventional level he finds: "Stage 1: Orientation toward punishment and unquestioning deference to superior power. . . . Stage 2: Right action consists of that which instrumentally satisfies one's needs and occasionally the needs of others. . . .

"At the conventional level we have: Stage 3: Good-boy-good-girl orientation. Good behavior is that which pleases or helps others and is approved by them. . . . Stage 4: . . . Right behavior consists of doing one's duty, showing respect for authority, and maintaining the given social order for its own sake. . . .

"At the postconventional level we have: Stage 5A: . . . Right action tends to be defined in terms of general rights and in terms of standards which have been critically examined and agreed upon by the whole society. . . . Stage 5B: Orientation to internal decisions of conscience but without clear rational or universal principles. Stage 6: Orientation toward ethical principles appealing to logical comprehensiveness, universality, and consistency. These principles are abstract and ethical (the Golden Rule . . .); they are not concrete moral rules like the Ten Commandments."[42]

Kohlberg maintains that although an individual's moral development may stop at any step and at any age, as long as it continues to change all movement is forward in sequence through these steps and does not skip steps.[43] He finds that "[t]he transition from preconventional to conventional morality generally occurs during the late elementary school years. The shift in adolescence from concrete to formal [cognitive] operations . . . constitutes the necessary precondition for the transition from conventional to principled moral reasoning. It is in adolescence, then, that the child has the cognitive capability for moving from a conventional to a postconventional, reflective, or philosophic view of values and society."[44]

Legal Significance

Physiologically, an adolescent may have attained adult dimensions and biological capabilities; psychologically, he may have developed the cognitive capacity for formal operations; philosophically, he may be entering upon a postconventional level of moral development; psychoanalytically, he may have left behind the id domination of early adolescence to achieve an adult balance of id, ego, and superego; but legally, until he reaches the age of majority,[45] an adolescent is most significantly a minor.[46] And as a minor, the adolescent possesses a legal status quite different from that of an adult.

Constitutions and legislatures have generally denied to adolescents (along with all other minors) rights which are routinely granted their elders.[47] Adolescents, in general, are not able to vote, enter into binding contracts, consent to medical treatment, or purchase alcoholic beverages.[48] Courts have upheld in a number of contexts greater state regulation of children than of persons who have attained the age of majority. In 1944 the United States

Supreme Court noted that "the power of the state to control the conduct of children reaches beyond the scope of its authority over adults. . . ."[49] Courts go even further by denying minors "standing" before the law, so that in general an adolescent may bring suit only through an adult representative.[50]

Underlying such deprivations is apparently an assumption that youths cannot make use of such rights in a mature, competent fashion. Also supporting certain features of their legal status is a belief that, because of their immaturity, adolescents (and all children) require additional legal protections. As one judge has phrased it: "Should children be as equal as people? Certainly not. They should not have equal liberty: they should have less. Neither should they have equal protection—they should have more."[51] Following this rationale, adolescents may not generally be tried for offenses in adult criminal court[52] and cannot usually be bound by contract.[53]

Some argue that these "protections" have, in practice, resulted in further deprivations of young people's rights[54] and should be abolished[55] or drastically revised.[56] Before considering change, however, it would be well to examine more closely the adolescent's present status and some of its origins. Historically, adolescents, like all children, have enjoyed very few legal rights. Aristotle believed that "children require the care and authority of another because they are incapable of wise and effective self government. . . ."[57] In eighteenth-century England "[c]hildren were regarded as chattels of the family and wards of the state, with no recognized political character or power and few legal rights. Blackstone wrote little about children's rights, instead stressing the duties owed by 'prized possessions' to their fathers."[58] In this country, the Supreme Court of Pennsylvania defined a minor's legal position in 1839 with memorable phrasing: "The basic right of a juvenile is not to liberty but to custody."[59] Even that champion of individual liberty, John Stuart Mill, after proclaiming, "Over himself, over his mind and body, the individual is sovereign," felt compelled to add a qualification: "It is, perhaps, hardly necessary to say that this doctrine is meant to apply only to human beings in the maturity of their faculties. We are not speaking of children, or of young persons below the age which the law may fix as that of manhood or womanhood. Those who are still in a state to require being taken care of by others, must be protected against their own actions as well as against external injury."[60]

In our society, the foremost group of "others" who are responsible for the care of minors is, of course, parents, biological and adoptive. A key element in this caretaking relationship is parental control over the child, control which extends to almost every area of the minor's life. Parental power is so broad that it "probably cannot be defined except as a residue of all power not lodged elsewhere by the law."[61] "Some traditional categories of this broad parental power are rights to name the child, to custody and society, to services and earnings, to control of religion and education, and to discipline the child. Categories traditionally viewed as parental duties toward children imply powers necessary to carry out those duties. For example, the duty of support implies a power to make decisions about where the child will live, what he will eat, and how he will dress. The duty to provide a favorable moral environment probably implies a power to censor the books read and movies seen by the child."[62]

Any list of categories such as this cannot begin to exhaust the universe of parental power. Its scope in a particular household "probably is restrained more by the imagination of the parents and the efficiency of the available sanctions than by law."[63] Parents, especially fathers, have long held this great measure of power and more. Abraham came close to sacrificing his son (apparently legally) to affirm his devotion to God.[64] "Before the Conquest, the English father had some power to sell into slavery his child less than seven years old and may have been free to kill his child 'who had not yet tasted food.' "[65] In this country, a line of United States Supreme Court cases beginning with *Meyer v. Nebraska*[66] in 1923 and *Pierce v. Society of Sisters*[67] in 1925 affirmed the primary rights of parents to control their children. The court viewed the right as part of the constitutionally protected "liberty" of parenthood,[68] "[t]he fundamental theory of liberty upon which all governments in this union repose.... The child is not the mere creature of the state; those who nurture him and direct his destiny have the right, coupled with the high duty, to recognize and prepare him for additional obligations."[69]

The child, although perhaps not "the mere creature" of the body politic, is nevertheless one of the creatures for whom the state feels a special responsibility. Under the doctrine of *parens patriae* (the state as father), the state has, since ancient times, viewed itself as one of those "others" whose duty and right it is to care for children. In one of the earliest applications of the doctrine, *Eyre v. Countess of Shaftsbury*,[70] the court reasoned that "the king has a duty to protect lunatics because they cannot take care of themselves, and this reason applies to children as well, so the king has a duty to protect children. *Eyre* seems to found the general duty to protect those incapable of protecting themselves on a duty to protect all citizens so far as necessary."[71]

Down through the years, the state has fulfilled this responsibility in a number of ways. A great many, such as this provision of the 1634 General Laws of Massachusetts Bay,[72] have simply been supportive of parental control:

If any child or children above sixteen years old, and of sufficient understanding, shall curse or smite their natural father or mother, he or they shall be put to death, unless it can be sufficiently testified, that the parents have been very unchristianly negligent in the education of such children, or so provoked them by extreme and cruel correction, that they have been forced thereunto to preserve themselves from death or maiming. . . .

Such state backing of parental power, though clearly less extreme, continues today in state acts such as "wayard" or "stubborn child" or "child in need of services" (CHINS) laws, which enable parents to seek a court's help in controlling a child who, for example, runs away from home or refuses to obey.[73] In these situations, the assumption exists that the parent's interest in child rearing and the child's long-range interests in safe, healthy development are congruent, and that the state's action therefore benefits both.

In addition to supporting parental control, however, the state also imposes its own rules upon children, rules which may or may not be in accord with parental desires. Preeminent of such controls are mandatory school attendance statutes.[74] Although most parents probably support these laws, certainly not all do. For example, in 1971 a group of Amish parents successfully challenged the Wisconsin statute requiring attendance beyond eighth grade as contrary to their religious beliefs.[75] Most such laws have been upheld, however, over parental objections as a proper exercise of state concern for the welfare of children and of society generally.[76] Similarly, state controls over minors' employment[77] have been sustained, even over parents' religiously based objections.[78]

In the most striking application of the *parens patriae* doctrine, the state, acting through its courts, may intervene directly in a particular parent-child relationship to protect the child's interests against a parent. An early example of such state action occurred in the famous custody case of *Wellesley v. Wellesley*,[79] wherein the petition of a father against his deceased wife's sisters for custody of his minor children was denied "because he was living in adultery and was otherwise a poor moral exemplar.[80] Lord Rosedale assumed that parents had rights to their children only by grace of the state, and explained the usual delegation of control over children to parents as a trust, with which parents were endowed because usually they would discharge it faithfully on behalf of the child."[81]

One might expect that this view of the origin of parental power would have been discarded at the time of the American Revolution, along with other notions that ultimate power resides not in the people but in the state. The United States Constitution might be thought to support such an expectation. It does not purport to delegate power to parents (it is, in fact, silent on the subject) but does provide that "[t]he enumeration in the Constitution, of certain rights, shall not be construed to deny or disparage others retained by the people."[82] The Constitution, however, was intended primarily to fix the rights of the federal government with respect to the states and people, not the rights of individual states with respect to their citizens.[83] Thus, the American cases, although frequently stating that parental rights are natural, sacred, and inalienable, do not generally ask where the ultimate power over children resides but simply proclaim, usually with a mention of the *parens patriae* doctrine, that the state must provide children with protection when such is required.

Instances of state intervention in individual families have, however, been relatively infrequent, being restricted generally to quite flagrant cases of parental malfeasance.[84] Dean Roscoe Pound attributed the general failure of courts to enforce parental duties or to limit parental rights over children partly to a judicial commitment to maintaining family unity and partly to "an historical quirk that family law became fixed relatively early when the law was more concerned with family than with individual interests."[85] Recently, a number of critics in both law and the social sciences, growing skeptical of the supposedly beneficent effect of government interference in family affairs, are coming to favor even greater state reticence.[86] Regarding the legitimacy of the philosophical underpinnings of state intervention, Justice Fortas, in 1966, said that *parens patriae* had been used "to rationalize the exclusion of juveniles from the constitutional scheme; but its meaning is murky and its historic credentials are of dubious relevance."[87] It is unclear, however, whether these signs of disillusionment will lead to less judicial intervention, or merely to less use of the Latin phrase justifying it.

It can be seen that adolescent rights are delineated by a three-way balance of power among minors, their parents, and the state.[88] Any description of a particular right of adolescents is therefore incomplete without specifying the party against whom the right is asserted—the state, parents, or others. Since the end of World War II we have witnessed a steady expansion of adolescents' rights with respect to the state, mostly in the context of juvenile delinquency or education.[89] Much slower has been the growth of adolescents' rights against parents. Except in cases of serious and substantial neglect and child abuse, the traditional legal assumption has generally been that the parents' and child's interests are congruent, and that parents should be recognized as speaking for their children.[90]

Today, however, a few courts appear reluctant to recognize parental waiver of children's rights at delinquency proceedings.[91] Other courts have limited parents' right to place their children in mental institutions.[92] And the United States Supreme Court has denied parents' veto power over their adolescent daughters' abortions.[93] These and other recognitions of children's rights in areas quite removed from child neglect and abuse suggest that we may be on the verge of a considerable expansion of rights of adolescents vis-à-vis their parents.

The Age of Majority

An adolescent's lack of full autonomy persists until he or she reaches "the age of majority." That is the age at which a person is entitled to full civic rights and to fully manage his own affairs. But precisely what age is that?

For about eight hundred years this was an easy question to answer. Twenty-one was the age of majority, although why it was chosen as the crucial age is less certain. In northern Europe, between the ninth and eleventh centuries, fifteen seems to have been the age of majority for males, and the reason seems to have been based on their capacity to bear arms.[94] In Rome, the test was: "had the male 'pupil' both understanding and judgement as to acts of law, in particular in relation to property rights? These capacities he was presumed to have at puberty, later fixed at fourteen years. . . . [T] he age of fourteen may have been generally accepted, as a result, as the age of majority for males. However, there is a curious tendency to add a year to ages for capacity. . . . The explanations given are various, such as an additional year for the handing over of the property or livery of seisin, . . . or for better certainty. . . . [or to allow] a certain latitude in calculation. . . ."[95]

"In the absence of any clear authority, it may be assumed that at one time between the ninth and tenth century, fifteen was also the age of majority in England; but by the time of the Magna Carta, [1215], this age had been raised to twenty-one, at least so far as men holding in knight service were concerned. . . . The raising of the age has been attributed to various causes. Some writers have alleged that it was due to the increase in the weight of arms."[96] Another contributing factor may have been "the use of horses in battle by the knight and the added skill required in combat. These would give rise to the need for the more thorough training of the young potential warrior."[97] In support of such theories it may be noted that St. Palaye writes that "though the French nobles attained their majority at seventeen, being then strong enough and sufficiently qualified to cultivate their lands and to indulge in commerce, still 'the profession of arms demanded an ability and strength not to be acquired till the age of twenty-one.' "[98]

The ultimate selection of twenty-one as the age at which knighthood was attained "was probably connected with the age at which infants come out of ward. So far as wardship was concerned, the Duke of Normandy had the guardianship of all orphans within age bound by homage in connection with a fief. Within age is specifically defined, in this connection, as those who have not completed their twentieth year 'and for these one allows another year, according to the customs of Normandy, in which they may apply to the court and claim the property of their ancestors.' Why twenty was selected as the age of emancipation is a question to which there seems to be no answer. It is suggested that the choice is related to the development of the age of chivalry, in the eleventh and twelfth centuries, which required a period of training, for the attainment of the honour of knighthood, not only in the military arts but also in the principles of chivalry."[99]

Whatever the precise original reasons, twenty-one became firmly established as the age of majority in Britain. Although the United States Constitution did not specify an age of majority, leaving the question to the individual states, those states almost without exception held fast to the traditional English rule.[100] This situation persisted practically unchallenged until the middle of this century. Then, in 1942, in both the United States Senate and the House of Representatives, constitutional amendments were proposed to lower the voting age to eighteen.[101] Similar proposals were submitted in 1943, 1954, 1968, 1969, and 1970,[102] but none gained congressional approval. Finally, in the

Voting Rights Act of 1970, Congress enacted, not a constitutional amendment, but a federal statute purporting to lower to eighteen the voting age for all elections.[103]

Reasons put forth for the act by congressional backers included an argument that "the higher educational achievement of today's youth, coupled with their heightened involvement in public issues and their increased service to the nation through agencies such as the Peace Corps and VISTA, justified the conclusion that 18 to 21-year-olds are more mature than previous generations and are ready to accept the responsibilities of the right to vote."[104] At least equally significant in persuading many to support the measure must have been the fact that, at the time, the United States was drafting young men into military service in an unpopular war. Almost 30 percent of the 3.5 million men in the armed forces were under twenty-one, and approximately 50 percent of those who died in Vietnam were under twenty-one.[105] In support of the theory that war and the draft were major factors in the bill's passage, it should be noted that earlier, serious attempts to enact such a constitutional amendment had coincided with World War II and the Korean conflict.

No sooner was Title III enacted, however, than Oregon, Texas, Arizona, and Idaho, supported by thirteen other states, sued to enjoin its enforcement.[106] The states argued that only they, and not Congress, were constitutionally authorized to set voter qualifications. In December 1970, the United States Supreme Court agreed with this argument insofar as state and local elections were concerned, but held that Congress's Act was valid for national elections. Thus, eighteen became the voting age for all national elections, and individual state laws set the age, generally still twenty-one,[107] for state and local contests. The potential confusion inherent in this situation did not materialize, however. Within three months of the Supreme Court opinion, the Congress succeeded in doing what it had been attempting for twenty-nine years; it passed a proposed constitutional amendment lowering the voting age to eighteen in all elections. And in a mere 100 days[108] this proposal was ratified by three-fourths of the states, making it the Twenty-sixth Amendment to the United States Constitution.[109] This speedy ratification (the fastest of any amendment) indicates that the Oregon suit was prompted not by opposition to the lowering of the voting age but by a jealous guarding of state prerogatives. There is no question that in 1971 a very strong national consensus favored exercising the franchise at a lower age.

With the Twenty-sixth Amendment did the age of majority become eighteen in all matters throughout the nation? It did not. Recall that the age of majority concerns two capacities: full civic rights and full management of one's own affairs. The amendment concerned only the first of these. After its ratification persons under twenty-one still generally could not contract, consent to treatment, or legally speak for themselves in many situations. The amendment did, however, serve as a powerful impetus to state legislatures to revise the age of majority downward in nonvoting matters. This movement was so rapid that by 1976 only six states and the District of Columbia still retained the traditional age of twenty-one, and even some of those granted persons under that age the right to enter into binding contracts and other rights ordinarily denied to minors.[110] Three states[111] have set nineteen as the age of majority, while forty-one states have lowered the age of majority to eighteen. A few state legislatures, however, have carved out specific exceptions to the plenary rights ordinarily granted at the age of majority. Kentucky and New Mexico, for example, grant all majority rights at age eighteen except the right to purchase or consume alcoholic beverages.[112] Whether or not it is so labeled, age eighteen in these states is obviously only an age of partial majority; the right to full management of all of one's affairs is reserved until a later age. The statutory ages of majority for all states and the District of Columbia, with a few of the major qualifying provisions in some states, are set forth in Appendix A.

Similarly, in every state the statutory age of majority is really only an age of partial majority, because a person does not gain total civic rights at that age. Because of explicit Constitutional provisions, he or she cannot become a United States Representative until age twenty-five,[113] a United States Senator until thirty,[114] or President until age thirty-five.[115] To be sure, most legal scholars would no doubt consider this observation more semantic than real, but it does point up the fact that many legal rights are accrued incrementally over time at various ages and not in a single lump at a specified age of majority. Much of this accretion of rights occurs before majority is reached; therefore, the following section will discuss some of these pre-majority rights enjoyed by the adolescent in various contexts, alert for their relevance or implications for the mental health field.

Pre-Majority Rights of Adolescents in the Field of Education

Education is one of the two contexts[116] in which the rights of adolescents (and minors generally) have been most litigated, clarified, and expanded in recent years. Here the traditional judicial "hands-off" approach in disputes between school authorities and pupils was almost as rigidly applied as the courts' similar policy in intrafamily disputes. In avoiding intervention, courts usually cited the doctrine of *in loco parentis*. The basis of this doctrine is found in Blackstone's Commentaries:[117]

[A father] may also delegate part of his parental authority, during his life, to the tutor or school master of his child; who is then *in loco parentis*, and has such a portion of the power of the parent committed to his charge, *viz.* that of restraint and correction, as may be necessary to answer the purposes for which he was employed.

"Some commentators have noted that the compulsory attendance law[118] rather than parental delegation provided the school its unusual authority over the child. . . ."[119] Regardless of which of these was the dominant rationale, the fact is that judicial review of school actions has been, during most of our history, quite rare. When it did occur, this review was usually narrowly focused, sustaining "any school regulation unless convinced that it could have no reasonable connection with the successful operation of the school."[120]

In 1961, however, a federal Court of Appeals, in deciding *Dixon v. Alabama State Board of Education,*[121] held that "due process requires notice and some opportunity for hearing before a student at a tax-supported college is expelled for misconduct."[122] The court said it was "shocking to find that a court supports [school officials] in denying to a student the protection given to a pickpocket."[123]

As one commentator has noted, "The opinion . . . had the force of an idea whose time had come and it has swept the field."[124] In the succeeding fifteen years, state and federal courts, including the United States Supreme Court, have been inundated by student rights cases of every variety. As a result, a sizable body of education law has emerged, which has attempted to balance the emerging rights of students against the reasonable needs of schools to maintain order and preserve the climate of the educational process.

"In 1966, the Fifth Federal Circuit faced two cases in which students had been suspended from school for violating regulations against 'freedom buttons' advocating equal rights for black people. It held in *Burnside v. Byars*[125] that the regulation was unconstitutional as an infringement upon the students' protected rights of free expression, but held in *Blackwell v. Issaquena Bd. of Educ.*[126] that the regulation was reasonable. The court distinguished the cases on the ground that in *Burnside*, the buttons caused only mild curiosity among non-wearers (though the principal promulgating the regulation had predicted that they would cause commotion and difficulty in calling classes to order), while in *Blackwell*, button wearers tried to pin buttons on to non-wearers against their will, were boisterous, disrespectful of teachers, and disruptive in class, and threw buttons through windows into classrooms when asked to leave. The pair of cases unequivocally assumes a right of free expression in students. . . ."[127]

Three years later the United States Supreme Court ratified this assumption in *Tinker v. Des Moines School District*[128] when it struck down a school regulation prohibiting the wearing of arm bands (which students had worn to protest the Vietnam War). The Court held that such a regulation, if based only on "undifferentiated fear or apprehension of disturbance,"[129] unconstitutionally interfered with the students' First Amendment right of free expression. Although *Tinker* did not bar regulation of all student conduct, particularly conduct interfering with reasonable discipline, it did affirm that students are "persons" under our constitution, and that they do not "shed their constitutional rights at the schoolhouse door."[130]

Much recent judicial intervention in school affairs has been in response to challenges to suspension and expulsion. Since 1961 the lower federal courts have uniformly held that due process requirements must be satisfied if a public school student is to be expelled.[131] The Supreme Court confirmed and extended these rights in 1975 when it held, in *Goss v. Lopez*,[132] that "[s]tudents facing temporary suspension have interests qualifying for protection of the Due Process Clause, and due process requires, in connection with a suspension of 10 days or less, that the student be given oral or written notice of the charges against him and, if he denies them, an explanation of the evidence the authorities have and an opportunity to present his side of the story."[133] Just a month after the *Goss* decision, the Supreme Court added considerable force to students' rights by holding, in *Wood v. Strickland*,[134] that "in the specific context of school discipline, . . . a school board member is not immune from liability for damages . . . if he knew or reasonably should have known that the action he took within his sphere of official responsibility would violate the constitutional rights of the student affected, or if he took the action with the malicious intention to cause a deprivation of constitutional rights or other injury to the student."[135]

Limits to students' constitutional protections are still recognized, however, by the Supreme Court as well as lower courts. Even in *Goss*, the Court stopped far short of providing students all of the constitutional safeguards which the student plaintiffs had sought. The Court stated that it was *not* ordering "that hearings in connection with short suspensions must afford the student the opportunity to secure counsel, to confront and cross-examine witnesses supporting the charge or to call his own witnesses to verify his version of the incident."[136] The Court felt that the imposition of even truncated trial-type procedures might overwhelm administrative facilities, divert resources, and "cost more than it would save in educational effectiveness."[137]

The *Goss* notice and hearing requirements, though they appear burdensome to some educators, have been criticized by others as providing insufficient protection to many students, particularly racial minority students in newly desegregated school systems. School records show, for example, that during the first seven weeks of the Boston public school term of 1974-75, despite a notice and hearing policy apparently in conformity with *Goss*, the suspension rate of minority students was twenty-nine per thousand whereas that of other students was only thirteen per thousand.[138] Some student and minority advocates[139] claim that this phenomenon, which they see as part of a "student pushout" syndrome, is typical of a national trend in cities that have undergone school desegregation[140] and is attributable to "the insensitivity of many white teachers to behavior patterns and lifestyles" of minority students.[141] Whether or not these claims are justified, they demonstrate that the Court's decision in *Goss* has not laid to rest all of the many issues surrounding children's rights with regard to suspension and expulsion.

In applying the *Tinker* decision, lower federal courts have generally upheld students' constitutional rights in matters clearly involving free speech (such as a refusal to participate in the pledge of allegiance).[142] However, noting the admonition of Justice Fortas in *Tinker* that the case dealt only with "direct, primary First Amendment rights akin to 'pure speech,' "[143] they have taken widely divergent positions on issues which arguably involve symbolic speech, such as school regulation of hair styles.[144] Several courts, including the Court of Appeals for the Fifth Circuit in *Stevenson v. Board of Education,*[145] have failed to find any constitutional merit in students' objections to such rules. "Other courts, such as the Court of Appeals for the Seventh Circuit in *Breen v. Kahl,*[146] have held that a high school student's right to wear his hair as he pleases is fundamental and [applying the *Burnside-Blackwell* test] can be abridged only upon a demonstration that the hair has led to actual disruption of the learning process."[147]

The Supreme Court's most serious limitation of students' rights probably occurred in its October 1975 affirmation of a federal district court's decision in *Baker v. Owen.*[148] The lower court had upheld the constitutionality of a North Carolina statute permitting public school teachers to use corporal punishment to restrain or correct pupils, even over parental objections. Although the opinion required that minimal due process protections be afforded,[149] its overall result may indicate that the growth of student rights, if not at an end, has at least reached a plateau.

The three-way balance of power between parents, their children, and the state is,[150] in education as elsewhere, poorly defined. Even Thomas Jefferson, while recognizing that education was essential to the welfare and liberty of the people, was reluctant to force the instruction of children "in opposition to the will of the parent."[151] This dilemma survives to this day, as illustrated by *Wisconsin v. Yoder,*[152] the Supreme Court case mentioned earlier in this chapter, in which Amish parents successfully challenged compulsory education laws. The Court held that the parents' First Amendment right to exercise their religion freely and the traditional interest of parents in the religious upbringing of their children justified the parents' refusal to send their children to school after graduation from eighth grade. Justice Douglas, however, dissented from the ruling with respect to two of the three children involved (ages fourteen and fifteen).[153] He did so on the basis that *their* religious views on high-school education were not included in the evidence before the courts.[154]

On this important and vital matter of education I think the children should be entitled to be heard. While the parents, absent dissent, normally speak for the entire family, the education of the child is a matter on which the child will often have decided views. He may want to be a pianist or an astronaut or an oceanographer. To do so he will have to break from the Amish tradition.

It is the future of the student, not the future of the parents, that is imperiled in today's decision. If a parent keeps his child out of school beyond the grade school, then the child will be forever barred from entry into the new and amazing world of diversity that we have today. The child may decide that that is the preferred course, or he may rebel. It is the student's judgment, not his parents', that is essential if we are to give full meaning to what we have said about the Bill of Rights and of the right of students to be masters of their own destiny. If he is harnessed to the Amish way of life by those in authority over him and if his education is truncated, his entire life may be stunted and deformed. The child, therefore, should be given an opportunity to be heard before the State gives the exemption which we honor today.

However, Douglas's eloquent call for granting children a greater voice in their own destinies, far from prevailing, was the lone dissent to the decision. Chief Justice Burger, writing the majority opinion, noted that the Court was not deciding whether parents could prevent a child who wished to attend school from doing so; there was therefore no reason to consider the point, and he left the door open to a future decision of the question. "Our holding in no way determines the proper resolution of possible competing interests of parents, children, and the State in an appropriate state court proceeding in which the power of the State is asserted on the theory that Amish parents are preventing their minor children from attending school despite their expressed desires to the contrary."[155]

Merriken v. Cressman,[156] a 1973 federal district court case which upheld the constitutional privacy rights of juveniles, also managed to avoid deciding how much control parents may exercise over those rights. The case concerned a drug abuse program proposed for the Montgomery County, Pennsylvania, public school system. The court held that the proposed administration of the program's questionnaire to eighth-grade students would violate the constitutional privacy rights of both the children and their parents.[157] The court further noted that "the question . . . arises whether parents, as guardians of the children, can waive their children's Constitutional rights. . . . [B]ut the Court does not have to face that issue because the facts presented show that the parents could not have been properly informed . . . and as a result could not have given informed consent for their children. . . ."[158] Thus *Merriken*, by holding that minors have a constitutional right of privacy which will be upheld against the state acting through its school system, followed and expanded upon the reasoning of *Tinker*.[159] However, by not deciding the question of waiver, *Merriken*, like *Yoder*, did little to clarify children's rights with respect to their parents.

To round out the picture of minor's rights in the education context, several other legal developments of the last few years must be mentioned. In 1973 a closely divided United States Supreme Court, in *San Antonio Independent School District v. Rodriguez*,[160] refused to find that education is "a fundamental right or liberty." A converse holding would have required the court to scrutinize strictly[161] the justifications advanced for funding inequalities between school districts within San Antonio. *Rodriguez* weakens the stance of those who advocate that special education is a basic right; it will therefore be discussed, along with other cases and legislation relating to that subject, in chapter 5.[162]

Pre-Majority Rights of Adolescents in Contracting

A major disability of minority, which includes adolescence, is lack of legal capacity to enter into a binding contract. The prevailing rule is that the contract of an "infant" (any person under the age of majority) is voidable by the infant, that is, the minor may "disaffirm" (renounce, tear up) a contract into which he has entered. As a consequence the other party may not enforce it. This right of "disaffirmance" may be exercised by the minor at any time during his minority or within a reasonable period after reaching the age of majority.[163] The minor disaffirms by notifying the other party of an intention to do so, surrendering any article received,[164] and demanding the return of any article or payment transferred by him. Alternatively, the minor may simply raise the defense of "infancy" to any action brought by the other party.[165]

The only contracting party who enjoys this right to disaffirm is the minor (or his spokesman, the parent or guardian). If the infant elects to stand upon the contract, to insist upon its retention, the other party is bound to perform and is liable for any breach of his contractual obligation.[166] The disaffirmance rule's obvious purpose is to keep minors from being bound by unfair bargains entered into imprudently because of their immaturity. The rule's one-sidedness may seem, at first glance, to constitute a tremendous boon, rather than a disadvantage, to an adolescent.[167] The general and natural consequence of the rule, however, is not that minors enter into many advantageous contracts, but that they are able to enter into extremely few. Understandably, merchants are extremely reluctant to enter into an agreement which binds them but not the other party.[168]

There are, however, several classes of exceptions to the disaffirmance rule, the two most common being statutory provisions and contracts for "necessaries."[169] Statutes may expressly provide that persons under the age of majority possess the legal capacity to contract for particular purposes without the right to resort later to disaffirmance.[170] Common examples of these purposes are the right to marry, enlist for military service, acquire medical or dental services or obtain educational loans.[171] Massachusetts permits minors fifteen years or over to make contracts for life or endowment insurance.[172] Colorado, a state in which twenty-one is the age of majority, eliminates the disaffirmance rule entirely for all contracts made by minors eighteen through twenty.[173] Statutes in some states, which permit minors of some minimum age (such as fourteen or sixteen) to apply on their own for admission to mental health facilities, may constitute a most important exception and will be discussed in chapter 4.

So that minors will not be deprived of the necessities of life if they are not supplied by a parent or guardian, courts have long recognized a "necessaries" exception to the disaffirmance rule. In most states, minors may not disaffirm a contract for the necessities of life.[174] In theory, at least, merchants will be willing to contract with an adolescent for the sale of "necessaries" without fear that the contract might later be disaffirmed. The "necessaries" exception derives from principles of "quasi-contract." Where a party lacks the legal capacity to contract, the law ordinarily finds that there exists no enforceable promise to pay. But where the service or article contracted for is deemed to be of such a nature that there would be no reasonable alternative to contracting for it, a binding promise to pay is found to be "implied" even without a party's formal assent. A minor may not disaffirm a contract for "necessaries," because there is an implied-in-law promise that he will pay reasonable compensation for the article or services provided.[175] However, because the "necessaries" exception is quasi-contractual, the minor's liability extends only to the duty to pay reasonable compensation; he is not bound to pay any unreasonable or excessive amount, even if required by the terms of the contract.[176]

"Necessaries" have never been precisely defined, although essential food, clothing, and shelter are uniformly recognized as falling within the meaning of the term.[177] Basic educational expenses have also been deemed to be "necessaries," although courts have not generally extended the doctrine to college or professional school expenses.[178] Legal fees and medical and dental care expenses are generally considered "necessaries."[179] Thus, diagnosis or treatment by a psychiatrist (who perforce is a medical doctor) would undoubtedly be characterized as "medical attention," and a "necessary," by all courts. It is less certain, though still quite probable, that treatment by a licensed psychologist would be so characterized. And there are significant doubts whether much less traditional but quite common "mental health services"—a group rap session, for instance, with a nonregistered, nondegreed drug abuse counselor—would be regarded as a "necessary" by the typical court.

The particular nature of an article or service is not the sole determinant to finding that there is an enforceable "necessaries" contract:

the terms 'necessaries' is a flexible and not an absolute term having relation to an infant's condition in life, to the habits and pursuits of the place in which and the people upon whom he lives, and the changes in those habits and pursuits occurring in the progress of society.[180]

A minor residing with his parents, who support him according to their own economic capabilities, cannot bind himself for things provided in the home.[181] In most cases a minor must be unable to obtain essential items because his parents either are unable or refuse to provide them. Some courts have gone so far as to hold that one seeking to recover against a parent for medical services must, in the absence of express agreement, show that the parent negligently failed to provide such services for the child, although he or she knew that they were necessary for the well-being of the child.[182]

Medical Treatment

One context in which adolescents' rights are expanding rapidly is that of medical treatment. The general rule in most jurisdictions has long been that a person providing medical care to a minor, without obtaining the consent of the minor's parents or guardian, may be civilly liable for committing a battery upon the minor.[183] The essence of battery is an unconsented touching, and any consent of the legally incompetent minor is the equivalent of no consent at all.[184]

Several exceptions to this rule have long been recognized. In emergencies, when parental consent is not readily available and a delay of treatment may result in death or serious injury, courts have traditionally found doctors justified in administering treatment, sometimes employing the fiction that, in such cases, consent is "implied."[185] In addition, courts have generally been reluctant to hold physicians liable when they have treated, without parental consent, minors who have been "emancipated" from parental control.[186] In some states, courts have found physicians justified in relying upon the consent of "mature" minors.[187]

In the past few years, all state legislatures have added new statutory exceptions to these traditional judicial exceptions to the medical consent rule. Statutes in almost all states now permit minors (sometimes of a specific age, such as twelve) to give valid consent to treatment for drug dependency or venereal disease.[188] Several states have enacted laws which enable adolescents of age sixteen[189] (or even fourteen)[190] to apply, without parental consent, for admission to mental hospitals as voluntary patients. And a few legislatures[191] and several courts have given minors means of resisting mental hospital admissions when they are "volunteered" by a parent or guardian.[192]

Probably the most current, active, and controversial area of minors' legal rights to medical treatment concerns birth control and abortion. Some state legislatures have acted to make these services more available to minors,[193] while others have attempted to make them less so.[194] The latter attempts have not always been successful, however. In 1976 the United States Supreme Court, in *Planned Parenthood of Missouri v. Danforth,*[195] struck down a Missouri statute giving parents an absolute right to veto their daughter's abortion, and in 1977 it held unconstitutional a New York law which banned the sale of contraceptives to persons under sixteen.[196]

A few state legislatures have not confined the expansion of adolescents' rights to specific categories of medical care; they have, instead, conferred upon several categories of minors the right to consent to all types of medical services.

Generally such statutes have, in effect, codified and, in some cases, expanded the "emancipation" and "mature minor" criteria which various courts have long applied.[197] The topic of minors' consent and refusal rights for medical care in general, and for abortion and mental health services in particular, are central to the topic of this volume and will therefore be discussed at length in chapters 4 and 6.

Juvenile Justice

As the United States entered the final third of the twentieth century, it also entered the third major phase in the evolution of the American legal approach to the problem of "wrongdoing" by adolescents (and all minors). In its first phase, dating from the colonial period until the latter part of the nineteenth century, there existed nothing which could properly be called a juvenile justice system. Chancery courts in the states dealt with neglected and dependent children and, as heirs to the English chancery court tradition, exercised *parens patriae* jurisdiction to protect minors' property rights.[198] But the criminal courts handled children accused of criminal law violations. Those courts applied the ancient common law rule that a child under seven years of age was presumed incapable of felonious intent and therefore could not be held criminally responsible; a child between seven and fourteen was presumed similarly incapable unless it could be shown that he was able to understand the consequences of his actions;[199] and a child fourteen years or over was held criminally responsible as an adult.[200]

It is uncertain whether the current, separate juvenile justice system resulted primarily from an expansion of chancery court jurisdiction together with a modification and institutionalization of the common law of crimes;[201] from a "recognition of the failure of the older criminal courts to prevent crime" coupled with "experimentation in judicial methods and procedure";[202] or "as part and reflection of the growth of contemporary administrative and quasi-judicial tribunals."[203] Proponents of the last view argue that the *parens patriae* theory is merely an *ex post facto* justification for juvenile court practices and that such courts are special statutory creations rather than direct descendants of chancery.[204]

Whatever its precise genesis, the juvenile justice system was preceded and anticipated by a variety of nineteenth-century reforms. In 1825, New York City established a House of Refuge in which children were to be separated from adult offenders and given corrective treatment rather than punishment. A number of states followed the 1847 lead of Massachusetts in opening reform and industrial schools for juveniles. These schools were aimed at teaching youths discipline and an honest trade and instilling dedication to advancement through hard work.[205] "In 1861 the mayor of Chicago was authorized to appoint a commissioner to hear and decide minor charges against boys between 6 and 17 years, and to place them on probation or in a reformatory."[206] Between 1872 and 1898 separate trial sessions and dockets were established for juveniles in Massachusetts, New York, and Rhode Island.

Finally, in 1899, the Illinois legislature passed the Juvenile Court Act, creating the first statewide court system especially for children. This act (and its early amendments), bringing together under one jurisdiction cases of dependency, neglect, and delinquency, marked the beginning of phase two of America's legal approach to juvenile wrongdoing. Hearings were to be informal and nonpublic, records were to be confidential, children were to be detained apart from adults, and a capable probation staff was to be available. "The goals were to investigate, diagnose, and prescribe treatment, not to adjudicate guilt or fix blame. The individual's background was more important than the facts of a given incident. . . . Lawyers were unnecessary—adversary tactics were out of place, for the mutual aim of all was not to contest or object but to determine the treatment plan best for the child. That plan was to be devised by the increasingly popular psychologists and psychiatrists; delinquency was thought of almost as a disease, to be diagnosed by specialists and the patient kindly but firmly dosed."[207] "[A] child that broke the law was to be dealt with by the State as a wise parent would deal with a wayward child."[208]

"Within a dozen years 22 states had followed the example of Illinois, and by 1925 there were juvenile courts in every State but 2. Today there is a juvenile court act in every American jurisdiction. . . ."[209] In the face of this rapid growth, a few observers dared to ask "How Far Can Court Procedure Be Socialized Without Impairing Individual Rights?"[210] In 1937, Dean Pound noted that "[t]he powers of the Star Chamber were a trifle in comparison with those of our juvenile courts. . . ."[211] As is now widely recognized, the "[d]epartures from established principles of due process . . . frequently resulted not in enlightened procedure, but in arbitrariness."[212] Some critics maintained that when the procedural laxness of the *parens patriae* attitude was followed by stern disciplining, the contrast may have had an adverse effect upon the child, who then felt that he had been deceived or enticed.[213] And there is no gainsaying the fact that, despite the most beneficent motives of the keepers, the disciplining could properly be characterized as stern by the kept.

The fact of the matter is that, however euphemistic the title, a "receiving home" or an "industrial school" for juveniles is an institution of confinement in which the child is incarcerated for a greater or lesser time. His world becomes "a building with whitewashed walls, regimented routine and institutional hours. . . . Instead of mother and father and sisters and brothers and friends and class mates, his world is peopled by guards, custodians, state employees, and "delinquents" confined with him for anything from waywardness to rape and homicide."[214]

The third and current phase of America's legal approach to juvenile wrongdoing can be dated from the 1967 United States Supreme Court opinion in the case of *In re Gault*.[215] Fifteen-year-old Gerald Gault had been committed by a juvenile court to an Arizona industrial school "for the period of his minority [that is, until 21], unless sooner discharged by due process of law."[216] This possible six-year commitment was imposed for the making of lewd telephone calls, an offense for which an adult could have been fined a maximum of $50 or jailed for not more than two months.[217] The Court, recognizing this disparity of consequences and the aforementioned deficiencies of the juvenile justice system, concluded that "it would be extraordinary if our Constitution did not require the procedural regularity and the exercise of care implied in the phrase 'due process.' Under our Constitution, the condition of being a boy does not justify a kangaroo court."[218]

The Court then enumerated the procedural safeguards constitutionally mandated for the juvenile justice system. Timely and adequate written notice of charges, the right to counsel (appointed by the court in cases of indigency), the privilege against self-incrimination, and the rights of confrontation and sworn testimony of witnesses available for cross-examination were all found to be constitutionally required.[219] Thus, the social welfare model of the juvenile justice system was largely discarded for a criminal procedure model. In 1970 the Court continued this movement by requiring the criminal trial's standard of "beyond a reasonable doubt" in juvenile hearings,[220] but the following year it stopped short of finding total congruence between adult criminal court and juvenile court procedural rights in holding that a jury trial is not a constitutionally required element of a juvenile delinquency proceeding.[221] Nevertheless, it is evident that since *Gault* the general trend of courts (followed by legislatures) has been to require in the juvenile justice system the same types of adversary procedural protections provided in the criminal justice system.[222]

Although the court decisions have clearly mandated a radical change of direction in the law, a change which has deemphasized the *parens patriae* philosophy while limiting state power in juvenile courts and recognizing individual rights,[223] neither those nor ensuing Supreme Court decisions elucidated the relative roles of parent and child in wielding these new rights. Implicit in the recognition of a constitutional right is the right-holder's freedom to forgo its exercise in any particular situation. Yet the Supreme Court left unclear precisely who—the child, his parent, or both of them—has the power to exercise or waive the *Gault* rights at various critical stages of delinquency proceedings. This issue has little or no importance where the parent and minor agree upon a course of action. It is critical, however, where they do not join in such a decision.

What does or should happen, for instance, if a parent, over his child's objections, wishes to compel the child to plead "guilty"[224] in a delinquency proceeding so as to receive "treatment" from the juvenile justice system? Although before *Gault* the parent's wishes might have prevailed, it seems clear that now the minor will prevail. The thrust of *Gault*, supported by cases in related fields of law such as *Tinker v. Des Moines School District*,[225] is that the minor personally possesses certain constitutional rights against the state. Because courts regard "pleading guilty" as a waiver of a child's constitutional rights to self-incrimination and confrontation, they undoubtedly would hold that a parent cannot force a child to waive those rights. The "rehabilitative treatment" which the parent wishes the state to administer to the minor would be viewed by the courts as a restriction of a constitutional right, which the minor has a right to resist. Moreover, the parent's contrary view might signify a conflict of interest; if so, it would disqualify him from acting in the minor's behalf, and a guardian *ad litem* might be appointed to advise and assist the minor in the parent's place.[226]

Alternatively, what is or should be the result when an alleged delinquent wishes, without parental consent, to plead guilty and thus subject himself to "treatment"? The contemporary resolution of this situation is less clear. Unfortunately, no statutory or case law seems to govern whether a parent can contest delinquency charges which a minor wishes to admit. Although permitting the parent to do so might harm the minor's ability to conduct the most beneficial "defense" possible—for example, by foreclosing the benefits of "plea bargaining" with the petitioning authorities—this interference with the minor's interests (as defined by the minor and his counsel) must be balanced against the parent's custodial rights, which are jeopardized by the minor's admission of delinquency.[227] A resolution of this difficult problem—balancing the competing interests of parent, child, and state—has yet to occur.

Although there is a paucity of law on a minor's capacity to plead to a delinquency petition, there is an abundance of statutory and case law with respect to his capacity to waive his right to counsel and the privilege against self-incrimination. The classic definition of waiver (as exercised by adults) was announced by the United States Supreme Court in *Johnson v. Zerbst*,[228] as follows:

A waiver is ordinarily a relinquishment or abandonment of a known right or privilege. The determination of whether there has been an intelligent waiver of the right to counsel must depend, in each case, upon the particular facts and circumstances surrounding that case, including the background, experience, and conduct of the accused.[229]

Moreover, the Supreme Court stated that a court must "indulge every reasonable presumption against the waiver of fundamental constitutional rights."[230] Thus a heavy burden of proof is placed on the government to show that an adult defendant's waiver of his rights is knowing and intelligent.[231]

Does a minor ever have the capacity to relinquish voluntarily, knowingly, and intelligently the privileges guaranteed him by the Constitution? *Gault* indicates that a juvenile may waive his constitutional rights, but it leaves uncertain what standards are to be used to measure the validity of his waiver. The Court states:[232]

We appreciate that special problems may arise with respect to waiver of the privilege by or on behalf of children, and that there may well be differences in technique—but not in principle—depending on the age of the child and the presence and the competence of parents. . . . if counsel was not present for some permissible reason or an admission was obtained, the greatest care must be taken to assure that the admission was voluntary, in the sense not only that it was not coerced or suggested, but also that it was not the product of ignorance of rights or of adolescent fantasy, fright or despair.

This statement raises questions about the meaning of waiver in the juvenile context. For instance, what criteria should a court use to determine the capability of a youth to understand his rights and the consequences of waiving them? Must parents be present before or during the custodial interrogation? If they are, is their role that of advisor, or must they join in waiving the youth's rights as well? When must counsel be present, and what are permissible reasons for counsel's absence? Lower courts and legal commentators have struggled to resolve these issues, but no single solution has been consistently followed and approved. The resulting case law has been described as a "kaleidescope of merging yet conflicting decisions."[233]

Three principal approaches have been suggested to ascertain if a juvenile's asserted waiver of the privilege against self-incrimination is valid—that is, made voluntarily, knowingly, and intelligently. A fourth variant suggests that a youth may never waive the privilege out of court, and hence no pretrial statements are admissible against him at a subsequent juvenile hearing.

The first method of testing the validity of a waiver, one used by the majority of juvenile courts, is to look at the "totality of the circumstances" under which the waiver is made.[234] Using this approach, a court will focus on the background, experience, and conduct of the accused, the factors stressed by the Supreme Court in *Zerbst*,[235] the adult waiver case. As part of this approach, a court may also undertake a careful examination of a youth's actual understanding of the consequences of his waiver,[236] as suggested by the high court in *Van Moltke v. Gillies*.[237]

Regardless of the factors used, the "totality" test is based on the assumption that a number of youths are capable of competently waiving their rights without adult presence or advice. But the test has been criticized for several reasons. First, the courts tend to emphasize the voluntariness of a statement rather than a youth's understanding of the consequences of waiver. Most courts fail to determine if a waiver was made intelligently as well as voluntarily.[238]

Further, there is doubt that a juvenile waiver can ever be made freely or with an understanding of the legal intricacies involved in waiving rights.[239] The courts have not delineated precise standards about when and if interrogation may occur.[240] Also, the totality test does not reflect society's concern with protecting young persons from their immaturity and inexperience, as evidenced in other areas of the law such as contracts and consent to medical care.[241] These weaknesses have led some courts, legislatures, and commentators to suggest other approaches to waiver which better safeguard a juvenile's rights.

A second approach, which has recently won new adherents in some state courts and legislatures, requires that, for a youth's waiver to be valid, parents or guardians be present and advised of their child's *Miranda* rights; any statement made by a young person to law enforcement officials is inadmissable as evidence at a delinquency hearing unless this precondition is met.[242] The role of the parent may be to consult with and advise the youth,[243] or it may be to consent to waiver of the minor's rights.[244] By requiring the presence of the parents, the underlying assumption of the totality test (that a child alone may be competent to waive his rights) is rejected, and additional protection is provided for the juvenile.

This standard has been criticized because it fails to consider that often a parent's presence may not in fact be in a child's best interest or best protect a youth's constitutional rights. In the first place, parents may not adequately advise their child, either because they do not sufficiently understand the consequences of waiver or because they may be equally intimidated by the coercive atmosphere of a police station.[245] Furthermore, in many cases there may be a conflict of interest between parents and the child. This may be explicit, such as the case where the parent brings the complaint against the child. It may be more subtle, as when parents feel hostility or embarrassment about their child's involvement with law enforcement officials. This attitude may induce parents to cooperate with the police and require their child to tell all. Also, the child may feel that he must exonerate himself in his parents' eyes by admitting his act (or fabricating a story of guilt, if necessary). Parents may feel their child needs treatment and will encourage him to confess so he may obtain help, or they may simply feel frustrated and overburdened by the youth's recurrent troubles with the law and wish that he be committed to an institution to relieve them of responsibility.[246] If the parents can afford legal services, an additional conflict may arise. The parents may resent paying money for the child's lawyer and encourage him to forego one. In a California case, *In re H.*,[247] the youth recognized the burden that legal fees would place on his family and elected to waive counsel rather than incur a further debt for his parents.

Some commentators, though no courts to date, suggest that no waiver of rights made by a child be effective unless counsel is present to assist the child.[248] This third approach views the protection provided by parents as inadequate to safeguard the rights of a juvenile. It holds that only a rule mandating the presence and advice of an attorney, who supposedly will be well versed in juvenile law and procedure and aware of the consequences of any statement, is sufficient to safeguard a juvenile's rights. But those who support the need for total nonwaiver question whether, given the lack of training of most lawyers in juvenile law, a rule requiring counsel at custodial interrogation will be adequate to protect the rights of a youth and encourage his or her confidence in the judicial process.[249]

These approaches indicate that most courts still believe that juveniles are capable of waiving their rights. However, a trend appears to be emerging which questions the capability of a youth to relinquish rights unless his parents are present. Many jurisdictions may now require the presence of parents at interrogation before an admission will be allowed into evidence at a subsequent trial. The total incapacity of a youth to waive his rights, even in the presence of his parents, has not yet been accepted by the courts. The goals of the juvenile justice system, to protect society as well as to rehabilitate youth, have influenced the courts to date to allow waiver when there is a "certainty" that it is given voluntarily and intelligently.

Other components of the juvenile justice system which are currently undergoing change involve state support of parental control over children. This governmental function has ancient roots. As mentioned previously,[250] Massachusetts Bay Colony law of 1634 prescribed the death penalty for children over sixteen who "smote" their parents, and such state support of parental power persists to this day (with somewhat less extreme sanctions) in juvenile delinquency laws respecting children who are labeled stubborn, wayward, or incorrigible.[251] These laws enable parents to charge their children with offenses such as habitual disobedience and being beyond parental control and, if sustained by a juvenile court, to have them committed to reform schools.[252] A recent movement to eliminate such juvenile "status offenses" has brought about their repeal in a number of states. They have usually been replaced, however, by statutes acronymically known as PINS (Persons In Need of Services, or alternatively, Supervision) or CHINS (Children In Need of Services) laws. The intent of these statutes is to fulfill parents' requests for state assistance in handling "difficult" children without applying stigmatizing labels such as "delinquent." They seek to provide this aid in the form of needed social services rather than through incarceration—a "treatment" rather than a "punishment" rationale.

Advocates of children's rights have argued, however, that both "status offense" laws and their "service" successors grant parents excessive power over their children. Even under the new laws, it is the parents who initiate action to involve the state. A 1975 case,[253] on the other hand, shows that children too may make use of these laws, and in ways that their drafters surely did not foresee. A sixteen-year-old Oregon girl named Cynthia, after being placed in a youth service center by her father, petitioned juvenile court to find her incorrigible, to prevent being returned home. The Oregon Supreme Court held that the testimony of Cynthia and others, and Cynthia's action when she, "in effect, fled her home by filing petitions in Juvenile Court in order that she might be made a ward of the court,"[254] constituted sufficient evidence to support the Juvenile Court's finding that she was incorrigible, even though her parents maintained that she was not. Although cases like Cynthia's may be exceedingly rare, it is striking and perhaps instructive to note that even statutes specifically designed to enhance parental power may sometimes be used by adolescents (with help from a sympathetic judiciary) to further their own autonomy.

A final issue being actively litigated in the juvenile justice area is the system's failure to implement a "right to treatment" as a necessary component of justice for children.[255] This issue will be discussed in chapter 7.[256]

Alcohol, Pornography, Curfews, and Blood Donations

The legal rights of adolescents continue to be less comprehensive than those of adults in a great many other contexts. State legislatures have enacted laws prohibiting minors from purchasing alcoholic beverages[257] or certain kinds of reading material,[258] and restricting the types of motion pictures they may attend[259] and the times at which they may be on the public streets.[260] Below certain ages they may not drive a car[261] or work at particular occupations.[262]

Legislatures have sometimes provided exceptions to these general prohibitions, if such exceptions are sanctioned by a child's parent or guardian. Thus, for example, a Massachusetts statute[263] provides that no person other than a parent, guardian, or spouse may procure an alcoholic beverage for a minor; a Middletown, Pennsylvania curfew ordinance[264] prohibits persons under eighteen from being on the borough's streets between 11 p.m. and 6 a.m. unless one of nine explicit conditions is satisfied, one of which is accompaniment by a parent or an adult authorized by a parent; and a Massachusetts statute[265] prohibits a person under eighteen from operating a motor vehicle between the hours of 1 and 5 a.m. unless accompanied by a parent or legal guardian. It thus appears that, in acting to limit minors' rights, legislatures have attempted to refrain from usurping parental power while using the power of the state to safeguard children's physical and moral well-being. Justice Brennan recognized this aspect of the New York obscenity law when he observed, in *Ginsberg v. N.Y.,*[266] that "the prohibition on sales to minors does not bar parents who so desire from purchasing the magazine for their children."[267]

These statutory provisions may also be viewed as more than mere reluctance of a legislature to interfere with parental control; they may quite properly be viewed as affirmative governmental support of parental power. We noted a historical example of this in the 1634 law of the Massachusetts Bay Colony,[268] and we cited two modern-day parallels in the CHINS laws[269] and the constitutionally questionable laws involving parents in their daughters' abortion decisions.[270] Such legislative support may help not only parents but others standing *in loco parentis*. Justice Brennan took this view in *Ginsberg*. He noted that "[t]he legislature could properly conclude that parents and others, teachers for example, who have this primary responsibility for children's well-being are entitled to the support of laws designed to aid discharge of that responsibility. Indeed [one subsection of the statute] expressly recognizes the parental role in assessing sex-related material harmful to minors according 'to prevailing standards in the adult community as a whole with respect to what is suitable material for minors.' "[271]

Noninterference with parental prerogatives is not an essential element of such laws, of course. In addition to state intervention through child abuse and neglect statutes, legislatures have not granted parents the power to override child labor laws, and the United States Supreme Court has upheld such state limitations of parental power, even where the parents defended their actions on First Amendment religious grounds.[272]

In a few areas, particularly in recent years, statutes have broadened rather than curtailed adolescents' rights. In addition to the statutes already discussed which enable minors to obtain limited medical services, some states now permit minors to make blood donations.[273] Another recognition of minors' rights can be seen in adoption statutes which require the consent of children over a specified age, such as twelve, before the court may issue a decree for their adoption.[274] Such rights-granting statutes, however, are in the minority. It remains a valid generalization that adolescents and other minors enjoy fewer rights under the law than do adults.

Marriage

Because it is recognized as a sign of emancipation, marriage has the effect of conferring many of the legal rights of adults upon persons who have not yet reached the age of majority.[275] As a sign of emancipation, it generally enables minors to consent to their own medical care.[276] Other evidence of the emancipating effect of marriage can be seen in state statutes and court opinions which provide for the termination of any guardianship at the time of marriage,[277] although several courts have held that marriage does not automatically terminate guardianship by a court or state welfare agency over delinquent or dependent children. According to a 1927 opinion, "[t]he underlying reason for [statutes and court opinions terminating guardianship upon marriage] is based upon the public policy that the control by the husband of his wife's property ought not to be denied, or interfered with, or, under some jurisdictions, that the wife, having assumed the marital relation, is of right entitled to control her own property. But such reason does not at all apply to cases where the physical or moral welfare of the child is involved, and where the government has intervened, as *parens patriae*, to secure such physical or moral well being."[278]

Although the "husband's control" rationale is rapidly vanishing from almost all jurisdictions, the court's conclusion remains valid; governmental *parens patriae* controls over a minor are, in most jurisdictions, not automatically removed by marriage. "A person who is under 18 and married is still entitled to the protection or guardianship of the state, and the fact of marriage does not ipso facto thrust that person into majority for all purposes. Rather, marriage removes only those disabilities connected with minority which would impair that person's ability to operate a home and family."[279]

This reluctance to remove all disabilities for minority upon marriage undoubtedly results from the same concerns which gave rise to those disabilities—a general belief that the average young person lacks the wisdom, maturity, and experience to manage his or her own affairs. Similar considerations[280] have, since ancient times, led societies to fix minimum ages at which persons may legally marry.[281] In his codification of Roman law in the sixth century, the Emperor Justinian fixed fourteen as the age at which males could marry, subject to the consent of parents and guardians.[282] "Swinburn, writing at the end of the sixteenth century on 'Spousals,' states that under seven all espousals are void. From seven to fourteen for males and to twelve for females they are voidable. Coke allowed a girl to be dowable once she had attained the age of nine. Clearly, at one time marriages took place at very early ages on occasions and could be consummated as soon as the onset of puberty."[283]

In the United States, the minimum age for entering a marriage contract has sometimes not been distinguished from the age for entering other types of contracts, that is, the age of majority. Marriage is such a special type of contract, however, that minimum ages are now set explicitly by statute in every state and are, in many cases, below the age of majority. These ages, however, differ considerably among states, ranging from thirteen in special circumstances for New Hampshire females[284] to eighteen for both sexes in Massachusetts.[285]

Sex Discrimination in Marriage Statutes and Other Laws Affecting Adolescents

The statutes of many states permit marriages at younger ages with parental consent, and a great many set lower minimum marriage ages for females than for males.[286] One apparent rationale for this sex distinction has been "the belief held by many that generally it is the man's primary responsibility to provide a home and its essentials for the family; and that however many exceptions and whatever necessary and proper variations may exist in varying circumstances, it is a salutory thing for him to get a good education and/or training before he undertakes those responsibilities."[287]

In *Stanton v. Stanton*,[288] a 1975 case striking down sex-related differences in age for the cessation of parental financial support of minors, the United States Supreme Court rejected these "old notions."[289] The court observed that "[n]o longer is the female destined solely for the home and the rearing of the family, and only the male for the marketplace and the world of ideas."[290] Although hardly a radical view in today's world, the opinion demonstrates a drastic change in the Court's position during the past century.[291] In 1873, Justice Bradley, in a concurring opinion, expressed the judicial spirit of that age when he wrote that "the civil law, as well as nature herself, has always recognized a wide difference in the respective spheres and destinies of man and woman. Man is, or should be, woman's protector and defender. The natural and proper timidity and delicacy which belongs to the female sex evidently unfits it for many of the occupations of civil life. . . . The paramount destiny and mission of woman are to fulfill the noble and benign offices of wife and mother. This is the law of the Creator."[292]

In *Stanton*, however, the Supreme Court stressed (as it had four years previously in *Reed v. Reed*,[293] an opinion striking down an Idaho statute favoring men over women as administrators of estates) that the particular discriminatory provisions under consideration did not rest on grounds of difference having a "fair and substantial relation to the object of the legislation."[294] However, would the court assess these discriminatory marriage age statutes differently if it could be shown that their object was to ensure that the contracting parties had achieved the physiological and psychological maturity required for marriage and child rearing? As discussed at the beginning of this chapter, the physical maturation rates of the sexes are different, and this might provide a sufficient rationale for the distinction.[295]

In two opinions issued in 1972, however, the attorney general of the state of Illinois did not subscribe to such reasoning.[296] He found, with respect to a sex-distinguishing marriage age statute in Illinois, that such differentiation between the sexes is "discriminatory and unconstitutional under the Equal Protection Clause of the Federal Constitution, the Illinois Equal Protection Clause . . . , and the guarantee of equal protection to the sexes [in the] Illinois Constitution."[297] In the preceding year a committee, studying the same question at the request of the Illinois governor from a psychological and sociological perspective, had arrived at the same conclusions as the attorney general. "The Committee believes that males require no incremental time period over females in which to prepare for marriage. It urges the equalization of legal ages between males and females wherever possible. The Committee believes that prolonging the age during which males must seek parental consent to marry is tantamount to saying that young men at eighteen are childlike and females are not."[298]

Both the attorney general's opinions and the committee's recommendations, however, related to statutory minimum age of twenty-one, eighteen, and sixteen. It might be argued that sexual differences in maturation rates are no longer significant by age twenty-one or eighteen, and perhaps have largely vanished even by age sixteen. On the other hand, differential maturation rates do exist at age fifteen and below[299] and thus would be highly relevant in considering the rationality of statutes discriminating between the sexes at these younger marriage ages.

The United States Supreme Court has thus far ruled only twice on the constitutionality of laws discriminating between male and female adolescents.[300] One, the *Stanton* opinion, was mentioned above.[301] The other was *Craig v. Boren,*[302] a 1976 case striking down as violative of the equal protection clause an Oklahoma statute which set twenty-one as the age at which 3.2 percent beer could be sold to males, and eighteen as the corresponding age for females. The drunk driving statistics presented did "not satisfy [the Court] that sex represents a legitimate, accurate proxy for the regulation of drinking and driving."[303]

Lower courts have addressed the age differential issue in several other contexts. In 1972, for instance, a federal Court of Appeals considered another Oklahoma statute which gave the juvenile court jurisdiction over females under eighteen years of age and males under sixteen.[304] A lower court had upheld the statute as a "judgment of the Oklahoma State Legislature, premised upon the demonstrated facts of life."[305] The appeals court found such "demonstrated facts" not obvious or apparent. It held the statute to be unconstitutional, because the age distinction (which had required that a seventeen-year-old boy be tried as an adult for theft of an automobile) amounted to invidious discrimination.[306]

A common complaint has been that females are regularly slighted in social services ranging from mental health facilities[307] and foster homes to athletic facilities.[308] "Whenever they talk about needing more locker rooms at the YWCA, or more money for job counseling programs at the Girls' Club, it's viewed as a 'woman's issue'," said a woman on the Allocations Committee of a major charitable fund. "But when they're discussing a YMCA or a Boys' Club, it's never a 'men's issue.' Then it's 'the community.' "[309] Several courts, including the federal Court of Appeals for the Eighth Circuit,[310] have held that rules barring females from participating with males in public high school noncontact interscholastic sports denied females equal protection of the law and were thus unconstitutional. In overturning such rules, these courts found that the schools had failed to demonstrate that the sex-based classification "fairly and substantially promoted the stated purpose of its rule of assuring that persons with similar qualifications compete among themselves."[311] On the other hand, courts continue to hold that, in an otherwise coeducational public school system, maintenance of two single-sex high schools in which enrollment is voluntary and educational opportunity offered to girls and boys are essentially equal violates neither the Constitution's equal protection clause nor the Equal Educational Opportunities Act of 1974.[312]

State Individualized Intervention in
Parent-Child Relationships

The legal rights discussed thus far apply to adolescents *en masse,* and most are fairly explicit in their entitlements and prohibitions. Another category of rights applies to particular families, and these are less clearly defined. This category consists of those rights intended to insure that children are properly cared for by their parents or guardians. It includes the rights not to be neglected, abandoned, or abused—rights which the state attempts to enforce through its *parens patriae* power.

Note that the term "neglect" in this sense does not refer to a *state's* failure to provide a child adequate, essential services such as education or medical care. It refers rather to failure by a parent or legal guardian.[313] It is thus a right which a child possesses against his parents, and their failure to honor that right may cause the state to intervene in the parent-child relationship.

The basis for such individualized state intervention is the parental duty of care owed to minor children. "The obligation of parents to support their offspring rests upon an entirely different foundation from that upon which the law bases the duty of the husband to support the wife. That obligation is at once legal and natural. It springs as necessarily from the law as from the primal instincts of human nature."[314]

Although at common law parents had a duty to support and maintain their children, failure to do so was not a punishable offense.[315] However, in many, if not all, jurisdictions it has been made a criminal offense by statute for a parent to desert, abandon, or fail to support or provide for a minor child.[316] "Such statutes are not intended to change the parent's common-law duties in respect of maintaining and supporting his children, but merely more effectually to enforce the legal duty."[317]

In general, the duty of support obliges parents "to provide such a place of abode, furniture, articles of food and wearing apparel, medicines, medical attention, nursing, means of education, and social protection and opportunity, as comport with the health, comfort, welfare, and normal living of human beings according to present standards of civilization, considering [the parent's] own means, earning capacity, and station in life."[318] A parent who fails to provide such necessaries is guilty of "neglect."[319]

"Medical attention" is included in the necessaries a parent must provide,[320] and a few cases have held that such attention includes mental health services. A 1952 New York case[321] reasoned as follows:

When a child does have a mental or emotional disturbance or whatever the case may be, it is the duty of the community to do everything to prevent the acts which may be only temporary from becoming a permanent state of mind . . . I conclude as a matter of fact, that the mother had been repeatedly informed of the conduct of this child; she was put on notice. She should have done something about correcting this child's state of emotional condition ... I conclude that this mother was informed and she was in duty bound to do something to correct the conduct of this child. I find that the woman neglected the child.

Child abuse may be thought of as an unreasonable imposition of harm rather than a withholding of necessaries, although it may include a failure to act; in such cases it is often difficult to distinguish from neglect. Not all harms inflicted by parents constitute abuse. For example, a parent who spanks his child generally is not guilty of this offense. Parents have long had the legal right to resort[322] to reasonable physical force to control and discipline their children. A father, as head of the household, was recognized in early English and American law as having authority to discipline all the members of his family. He might administer to his wife "moderate correction" and "restrain" her by "domestic chastisement."[323] The altered position and independent legal status of married women in today's society has done away with any such discipline, and physical chastisement of a wife is now everywhere a crime.[324] The early privilege to chastise domestic servants is also no longer recognized.

However, "[a]s to children, the privilege remains, despite any modern theories that to spare the rod is not to spoil the child."[325] A parent, or one who stands in the place of a parent,[326] may use reasonable force, including corporal punishment, for discipline and control.[327] But not surprisingly, the degree of force regarded as "reasonable" is a continuing legal question. Some older cases have said that where the force applied is without malice, and results in no serious injury, the judgment of the parent determines its reasonableness. Later cases have held that, "for the protection of the helpless at the mercy of the merciless,"[328] there should be applied an external standard of reasonableness under the circumstances.[329] All of the circumstances are to be taken into consideration, including the nature of the child's offense, the age, sex, and strength of the child, his or her past behavior, the kind of punishment, and the extent of the harm inflicted.[330]

"The first recorded instance of child abuse in the United States was the case of Mary Ellen. In 1875 she was discovered in New York City, beaten and starved by her stepparents. At that time there were no facilities for caring for abused or neglected children. Concerned citizens persuaded the Society for Prevention of Cruelty to Animals that Mary Ellen, as a 'member of the animal kingdom' was entitled to at least the protection afforded dogs and horses. News of her plight led to the founding of the Society for Prevention of Cruelty to Children and other 'protective' agencies for children."[331] Although such protective services have grown greatly since then, it may be noted that "[s]till, in 1970, the Society for Prevention of Cruelty to Animals in New York City had more contributors than the Society for Prevention of Cruelty to Children."[332]

It is generally accepted that child abuse is a common, widespread problem, but its incidence is not known with any degree of precision. In 1962, Dr. C. Henry Kempe coined the term "battered child syndrome,"[333] a sign of growing recognition of the problem by the medical community. In 1963 the Children's Division of the American Humane Association found 662 cases that were severe enough to be reported in the press that year.[334] Brandeis University attempted to establish abuse rates from numbers of cases reported over two years; their estimates ranged "from 8/year/million population in Arkansas to 59/million in California, 21/million in New York, and 670/million in Nevada."[335] Such vast disparities are apparently attributable more to reporting differences than to real geographic differences in the incidence of abuse.

According to the National Center for the Prevention and Treatment of Child Abuse and Neglect, there were 280 cases of child abuse reported per million population in 1972, 348 in 1973 and 380 in 1974.[336] Dr. Eli H. Newberger, Director of the Family Development Study at Boston's Children's Hospital Medical Center, recently stated that there were 200,000 cases reported nationally in 1975, compared with only 7,000 in 1967. "He feels the true annual number of abused and neglected children is between one million and 1 1/2 million nationally."[337] Newberger further believes that child abuse itself has not increased, and that the growth in cases reported results from new laws requiring those in child-related professions to report occurrences which come to their attention.[338] Holding the opposite view is Dr. Vincent Fontana, head of the New York City task force on child abuse. He believes that the apparent increase in child abuse is real and is attributable to "the stresses and strains that our society is suffering today—the frustrations, the poor quality of life, the increase in drug addiction and alcoholism."[339]

State intervention in cases of child neglect or abuse is usually initiated by a complaint originating with a social worker, teacher, physician, relative, or neighbor.[340] "A case usually reaches . . . court only after weaving its way through a process where numerous officials—including social workers, probation officers, and court personnel—may have had contact with the family."[341] "Unfortunately very little is known about how the discretion of these various officials is exercised."[342] During an investigation some parents "voluntarily" agree to the child's removal from their custody. "In California, for example, the State Social Welfare Board estimated . . . that one-half of the children in state-sponsored foster care were 'voluntary' placements where the parent(s) consented to relinquishing custody without a formal court proceeding. A study in New York City found that 58 percent of the natural parents of foster children had agreed to foster care placement."[343] As one might suppose, "[i]n some of these placements, a significant degree of state coercion is involved; and in some cases, parents' 'consent' is hardly voluntary when judged by standards applicable in other areas of the law."[344]

When a case involving allegations of parental neglect or abuse does reach court, it usually takes the form of a child custody hearing. Obviously, the removal of a child from his family is a drastic step, which the state should take only after other measures have been tried. Probably all states recognize this implicitly, and some do so explicitly. The Massachusetts statutes, for example, declare that it is "the policy of this commonwealth to direct its efforts, first, to the strengthening and encouragement of family life for the protection and care of children; to assist and encourage the use by a family of all available resources to this end; and to provide substitute care of children only when the family itself or the resources available to the family are unable to provide the necessary care and protection to insure the rights of any child to sound health and normal physical, mental, spiritual and moral development."[345] Yet despite this state policy, a 1973 study by a Massachusetts Governor's Commission found that "[v]irtually no effort is made by the Division [of Family and Children's Services] to keep the biological family together and prevent children from being placed into foster care."[346] In fact, by the time the problem reaches a courtroom, any supportive family services available have already been tried.[347] The question most frequently put to the court, therefore is: shall this child be removed from his parents to a foster care placement?[348]

Traditionally, custody hearings have been conducted before a juvenile court or probate court. "Every state today has a statute allowing a court, typically a juvenile court, to assume jurisdiction over a neglected or abused child and to remove the child from parental custody under broad and vague standards. . . ."[349] Most states provide several grounds for assuming jurisdiction. Besides provisions citing "abuse"[350] and lack of "proper" care or attention,[351] many statutes include provisions granting jurisdiction over such categories of children as those "in danger of being brought up to lead an idle, dissolute, or immoral life"[352] or those "living in an environment injurious to the child's welfare."[353]

The test which practically all jurisdictions now purport to apply in deciding whether a child should be removed from the custody of his family is whether that action would be "in the best interests of the child."[354] Although there is little dispute concerning the standard,[355] there is much controversy over what it means and how it is to be applied. Three years ago, Joseph Goldstein, Anna Freud and Albert Solnit published a widely acclaimed book on this topic, entitled *Beyond the Best Interests of the Child.*[356] One of the book's principal themes is that greater importance should be attached to maintaining a continuity of relationships for the child.[357] This position militates against initial removal of a child from his parents, and also against later removal from a foster home for return to his parents. The book also argues that children have a greater need to preserve psychological than biological relationships.[358]

Some *Beyond the Best Interests* proposals have been criticized as unworkable, as likely to create as many problems as they solve,[359] and as failing to recognize that parents also have rights which existing custody laws should and do[360] recognize.[361] But most commentators seem to agree that a child should have a significant voice in any custody hearing. Yet, "[w]hile the best-interests principle requires that the primary focus be on the interests of the child, the child ordinarily does not define those interests himself, nor does he [usually] have representation in the ordinary sense."[362] The authors of *Beyond the Best Interests* and others[363] would correct this situation by granting the child full party status and the right to counsel at any hearing.[364] Some states attempt to have this function performed by a "friend of the court."[365] But Professor Goldstein, among others, believes that what is needed is a "friend of the child" rather than of the court.[366] Elton Klibanoff, while deputy director of the Massachusetts Office for Children, argued that a child needs an advocate at every stage of a state's intervention in the parent-child relationship, if only to cause state agencies to respond with some promptness to the child's needs.[367]

The custodial preference of an adolescent (and of any child above the age of discretion) may be given weight in the court's decision, but it is usually not controlling.[368] According the child's wishes substantial weight may mislead him by raising the false expectation that his preference will be decisive. Since the child's desires are almost always quite mixed, it is frequently extremely difficult for either a court or the child's own counsel, if any, to fathom those desires[369] or to accord them the respect which would be given an adult's. Consider the following recent opinion of the Massachusetts Bar Association's Committee on Ethics:[370]

In light of [ethical considerations] EC 7-9, EC 7-12, and [disciplinary rule] 7-101(a)(3) [of the A.B.A. Code of Professional Responsibility], we believe that when a lawyer is appointed to represent a "child in need of services" who (by reason of lack of education, lack of experience, or other factors) is unable to make an informed judgment as to what is in his or her own best interest, the lawyer (after obtaining "all possible aid" from the child) has an obligation to the child to advocate to the court that disposition of the case which the lawyer believes to be in the best interests of the child, *even if such disposition of the case is not consistent with the expressed wishes of the child.* In any such case, however, we believe the lawyer should inform the court of the contrary views of the child on the matter, and should state his or her own reasons for believing that the disposition of the case desired by the child is not in the best interests of the child.

Under this interpretation of counsel's function, the lawyer becomes, like the social workers and probation officers who preceded him and the judge who follows him in the process, simply one more party trying to decide what is in the child's best interest. It is questionable whether an "advocate" in this role contributes significant additional protection to a child involved in neglect or abuse proceedings.

Other reformers argue that the adversarial nature of the judicial forum in which neglect and custody hearings are conducted unnecessarily injures the parties.[371] It is said that "judges are ill-equipped to make the necessary determinations,[372] and that social workers, psychologists, or psychiatrists should have a more important role in the ultimate decision,[373] perhaps as part of a family court."[374] "Reform" legislation in some states now permits emergency intervention on behalf of an abused child by a court acting without a hearing,[375] and sometimes even without a neglect petition having been filed.[376]

But a number of commentators, rather than recommending improvements in the state's methods of intervening, are now arguing that such intervention should be greatly curtailed. They maintain that, despite the high-minded purpose of child protection statutes, their effect on a great many children is worse than no intervention at all.[377] A range of possible adverse consequences are cited. First, removal from home, even from a very bad environment, may be psychologically damaging.[378] Second, "the ambiguous and anomalous position of a foster child within a foster family may make it difficult for the child to develop an adequate conception of who he is. . . ."[379] "The child often experiences conflict over which set of parents, natural or foster, to trust and rely on when in trouble. Moreover the child may observe [and the older child, especially, may learn to manipulate] power struggles among the natural and foster parents, the social workers, and the judge, each of whom has a reason to be concerned about the child's care and future."[380]

Insofar as possible, a foster home is supposed to provide a normal family environment. However, it is also, in theory at least,[381] a temporary arrangement.[382] Agencies, therefore, often become concerned if the foster parents grow too attached to the child.[383] Some agencies make a practice of removing children from foster homes when they discern an "overly close" relationship developing. There are courts that subscribe to this view. "In one case, the highest state court in New York approved the transfer of a child from a foster home to an unknown alternative because the foster parents 'had become too emotionally involved with the child.'[384] The court upheld an agency determination 'that the child's best interests necessitated her placement in another environment where she would not be torn between her loyalty to her mother and her boarding parents.' "[385] In June 1977 the United States Supreme Court held constitutionally sufficient New York statutory provisions which require ten days' advance notice and an agency conference upon request, but not a full adversary hearing, before such a removal can occur.[386] Even if the court had required a hearing prior to removal, that would not have guaranteed that foster placements would acquire greater permanence.

Third, and most important for the adolescent child, the state is frequently unable to find a suitable foster placement, so the child may spend years in an institution. In the more baleful of such cases, children have been housed in state mental health facilities because of the modern-day lack of state orphanages.[387]

In light of the problems mentioned above, it has been suggested that state intervention on behalf of neglected or abused children should be statutorily authorized only when: (1) the child is suffering, or there is substantial likelihood that he will imminently suffer, a serious harm; (2) coercive intervention to alleviate the harm will, in general, be the least detrimental way of protecting the child; and (3) the court finds that the child's position will be less detrimental as a result of the proposed intervention.[388]

To determine whether the third criterion is satisifed in a particular case, the court would have to consider not only the child's home environment, but also the environment in which he would probably be placed if removed from his home. This approach would have parellels with the one used in *Gault*, where the deplorable conditions in juvenile detention facilities were cited by the United States Supreme Court as justification for limiting the state's right to place juveniles in such facilities.[389] A similar appraisal of the subsequent quality of the living arrangements of children removed from their families would, it is believed, lead to a reduced incidence of state intervention on behalf of children.[390]

Guardianship

In the child abuse and neglect situations thus far discussed we have noted that courts frequently transfer a child from his family to a state agency, which then places the child in the custody of foster parents or an institution. In this procedure, the stage agency is designated either explicitly or implicitly as the legal "guardian" of the juvenile. Guardianship is an inveterate legal mechanism. "A guardian is a person lawfully invested with the power, and charged with the duty, of taking care of the person and managing the property and rights of another person, who, for some peculiarity of status, or defect of age, understanding, or self-control, is considered incapable of administering his own affairs."[391] Guardians have been appointed most frequently for minors or for legally incompetent persons who have material wealth.[392] "A general guardian is one who has the general care and control of the person and estate of his ward; while a special guardian is one who has special or limited powers and duties with respect to his ward, *e.g.* a guardian who has custody of the estate but not of the person or vice versa."[393] Theoretically, a guardian of the person makes only nonfinancial decisions on behalf of his ward, but in practice such a guardian almost invariably controls the ward's estate as well.[394] (As noted above, a guardian is not necessarily a single individual; besides state agencies, who may be made guardians of neglected children, a trust department of a bank may be appointed guardian of a person's estate.)

Like many venerable legal institutions, guardianship has been accused of being unsuited to the needs of our present society. Some find the law respecting it, which was developed in a simpler, more rural society, too restrictive to allow adequate handling of a ward's financial affairs.[395] Others see inadequate control of the competence and behavior of a guardian as the major flaw. They point out that in contemporary society a proposed guardian is less likely to be known personally by a judge, that families are less willing or able to care for their own members, and that there are no longer close knit communities backing up bare legal sanctions with informal social pressure.[396]

In attempting to adapt the guardianship mechanism to particular problems, the law has developed another type of special guardian, the "guardian ad litem." "A guardian ad litem is a guardian appointed by a court of justice to prosecute or defend for an infant in any suit to which he may be a party."[397] Some courts, particularly in the older cases, have required that the minor actually be a formal party to the proceeding before a guardian ad litem can be appointed.[398] However, a growing number of jurisdictions now allow a guardian ad litem to be appointed whenever a minor's interests may be adversely affected, whether or not the child is a formal party.[399]

Some statutes require that a guardian ad litem be appointed in certain proceedings, but usually considerable discretion is left to the judge. For example, a Wisconsin statute allows the judge to decide whether a guardian ad litem should be appointed in neglect proceedings[400] and proceedings to appoint a general guardian.[401] A guardian ad litem is sometimes appointed in adoption proceedings,[402] but at least one court has held that, when not required by statute, such a precaution is unnecessary where the child's mother is the defendant in the proceeding.[403] If a mother has just given up her child for adoption, however, it is questionable whether she is likely to be a good judge of, or advocate for, the minor's interests.

A guardian ad litem is often appointed when there is an obvious conflict between the interests of the child and those of the parent or general guardian.[404] A New Jersey court has held that appointment is mandatory for a general guardian's accounting proceedings.[405] If appointment is discretionary, however, a judge generally has little guidance as to the standard to apply. A Texas court has held that no guardian ad litem is necessary unless there is a "clear and substantial" conflict of interest between parent and child.[406] That case concerned the division of litigation proceeds by the husband and the children of the deceased, but the court seemed to think that the jury could fairly apportion the money without the aid of a separate spokesman for the children.

Even when provided with a clear standard, courts often base their decisions regarding appointment on considerations which have little or nothing to do with protecting a child's interests. The court in *United States v. Noble*[407] was explicit:[408]

Every effort should be made . . . to reduce costs by avoiding the appointment of independent guardians unless there is a substantial probability of conflict of interest and need for protection. . . . This court is permitted by Rule 17 (permitting the appointment of guardians) to rely upon the fundamental assumption on which our society rests, that parents are concerned about the welfare of their children.

Once a court does overcome fiscal and other hurdles and decides to appoint a guardian ad litem, several questions remain. First, what sorts of persons are selected for the role? The answer differs with the jurisdiction and with the court. An attorney is required in some jurisdictions, and at least one commentator sees such a provision as necessary for effective representation.[409] But often the guardian ad litem is a near relative,[410] although courts sometimes suggest that such a guardian "ordinarily" should *hire* an attorney.[411] One study found that in appointing guardians for incompetents, a relative was usually chosen and was scrutinized only if he or she was also the petitioner in the incompetency proceeding.[412] The same study found that a requirement that the appointee be an attorney frequently provided little effective protection, since the candidates were often from a panel who were owed political favors or who had represented defendants without charge in criminal trials.[413]

Another question is: precisely what are the duties of a guardian ad litem? Although the general rule is that he or she should represent the minor's interests before the court,[414] it is not clear how the guardian ad litem should discern those interests. Some courts have found that a guardian ad litem has a duty to vigorously present a minor's case,[415] that he must investigate all questions of law and fact,[416] and that he may not waive important rights.[417] How frequently guardians ad litem are actually held to these standards, however, is another question entirely. At least one court has found a guardian ad litem liable to his ward for negligent conduct.[418] More often, the duties of a guardian ad litem are enforced through court supervision,[419] although confusion sometimes results. The court in *Miller v. Clark*[420] saw the guardian ad litem as an "agent" of the court, with the court itself as the "guardian." One study found such role confusion to be standard, based upon the common view that the guardian ad litem is a neutral fact finder, not an adversary.[421]

Intrafamily Tort Immunity

Similar difficulties exist in ensuring that guardians ad litem and parents properly perform their duties, but the remedy is different in each case. As noted above,[422] a minor has occasionally been permitted to bring suit against his guardian ad litem for personal injuries resulting from the guardian's negligent performance of duty. However, until recently, the general rule in this country was that a minor could not bring such a personal tort suit against his parents.[423]

This rule of parental immunity for personal torts did not exist in English common law. It seems to have originated in an 1891 case, *Hewelette v. George*,[424] decided by the Mississippi Supreme Court. In *Hewelette* the court held that[425]

so long as the parent is under obligation to care for, guide, and control, and the child is under reciprocal obligation to aid and comfort and obey, no such action as this [for false imprisonment] can be maintained. The peace of society, and of the families composing society, and a sound public policy, designed to subserve the repose of families and the best interests of society, forbid to the minor child a right to appear in court in the assertion of a claim to civil redress for personal injuries suffered at the hands of the parent. The state, through its criminal laws, will give the minor child protection from parental violence and wrong-doing, and this is all the child can be heard to demand.

This rule was rather quickly adopted by other courts throughout the country until few, if any, American courts rejected it entirely.[426] It reached an extreme in the oft cited 1905 case, *Roller v. Roller,*[427] in which the Washington Supreme Court denied recovery to a fifteen-year-old girl who had been raped by her father. The ironic judicial rationale in this case, as well as in most of the others, was that of *Hewelette*: that maintenance of suits of this nature would violate intrafamily harmony.[428] Other reasons advanced to justify parental tort immunity are the danger of intrafamily fraud or collusion (against insurance companies);[429] the threat such suits pose to parental rights to control and discipline children; and the danger that permitting a child to recover from his parents "would permit the child, in effect, to deprive all other members of the family of their fair share of the familial assets."[430] Similar immunity rules generally prevent parents from suing their unemancipated minor children, but the underlying reasons are not so clearly stated as those for parental immunity.[431]

Although parental tort immunity has been the general rule, almost from the time of its inception a number of exceptions were introduced, which greatly undermined its effect.[432] Various courts have excepted from the immunity rule torts arising out of parental activities not associated with parental duties,[433] torts resulting in the child's death,[434] and intentional or willful and malicious torts.[435] On this question, as in the matter of consent to treatment,[436] emancipation has been recognized as an important factor. "Where the child, prior to the commission of the tort by the parent, has been emancipated either by reaching his majority, by a lawful agreement with his parents, by the parent's forfeiture of his parental rights by failing to fulfill his parental duties, or by any other legal means within a given state whereby emancipation may be effected, the injured minor may generally file a tort against his parent in the same manner that he would sue a stranger."[437] Generally persons standing *in loco parentis* have been found not to enjoy the immunity of a natural parent,[438] but a number of states have extended the immunity rule to include stepparents,[439] and adoptive parents.[440]

The potential for injustices, the inconsistency of the exceptions, and the unsatisfactory reasoning underlying the entire intrafamily tort immunity rule have been strongly criticized by eminent legal commentators for half a century.[441] As long ago as 1916 Dean Roscoe Pound observed that "family law in general is one of the earliest branches of the law to become fixed and hence preserves traces of an archaic condition in which group interests rather than individual interests were secured. Tenderness of the individual interests of parents, since legal interference in family relations touches individuals in a particularly sensitive spot, has induced hesitation in changing the established rules, even where reasons for change were evident."[442]

Nevertheless, change is now occurring. Beginning with Wisconsin in 1963, about one-third of the states have gone beyond piecemeal exceptions and have either entirely eliminated or greatly restricted[443] the parental immunity rule. Abrogation has been so extensive that "it now seems appropriate to consider the exceptions to what has become in many of these states a general rule of parental liability."[444] These new exceptions fall into two main categories, the Wisconsin "authority and discretion" exception and the California "reasonable and prudent parent" standard. In 1963 the Wisconsin Supreme Court declared that parental immunity would be retained in two situations: (1) where the alleged negligent act involves "an exercise of parental authority over the child"; and (2) where the alleged act involves "an exercise of ordinary parental discretion with respect to the provision of food, clothing, housing, medical and dental services, and other care."[445] Part two of this rule would probably shield a parent from his child's suit alleging failure to provide needed mental health services or the converse, forcibly providing unneeded or inappropriate services. At least four states have adopted the Wisconsin test or one quite similar.[446]

In 1971 the California Supreme Court in *Gibson v. Gibson*[447] purported to end parental immunity in that state. The court rejected the disruption-of-family-harmony rationale, partly because "virtually no suits are brought except where there is insurance. And where there is, none of the threats to the family exists at all."[448] The court rejected the collusion and fraud argument on the basis that the threat of fraud is "no greater when a minor child sues his parent than in actions between husbands and wives, brothers and sisters, or adult children and parents, all of which are permitted in California."[449] But to leave parents some degree of authority and control, the court stopped short of holding that tort law's reasonable *man*[450] rule governs a parent's conduct toward his child. Instead, it held the proper standard to be: what would a reasonable and prudent *parent* have done in similar circumstances?[451] In explanation, the court stated that a parent obviously may spank his child without being liable for battery or may order the child to remain in his room without being sued for false imprisonment.[452]

Although the new Wisconsin and California approaches claim to broaden children's rights to sue, they provide a considerable degree of latitude within which parents may still function with immunity (if not complete impunity). The Wisconsin test's "authority and discretion" exception would seem to encompass practically all situations related to mental health services. California's "reasonable and prudent parent" test might impose liability in similar cases, but this is far from certain. "Particularly when one considers the large number of jurors who are parents themselves and who will presumably empathize with the defendant, it may well be that it will require something equivalent to gross negligence to find a parent guilty of a tortious act toward his child."[453]

Moreover, it should be noted that in the ten years following establishment of the Wisconsin rule, "almost as many jurisdictions . . . upheld immunity as . . . abolished it. In recent years, for example, courts for the District of Columbia,[454] Iowa,[455] Maine,[456] Maryland,[457] Missouri,[458] New Mexico,[459] North Carolina,[460] Oklahoma,[461] and Tennessee[462] have all been presented the rationale of [the Wisconsin] or subsequent decisions, yet have concluded, at best, that if a change is desirable it is for the legislature to make. And many of the courts have concluded that the policy reasons for creating parental immunity initially still outweigh the arguments for abolishing it."[463]

In light of the avowed retention of parental tort immunity in many states, and the nature of the exceptions associated with its abrogation in others, it appears safe to conclude that unemancipated minors are still barred from bringing civil suit against their parents for torts of the types most likely to be committed (or charged) relevant to the provision of mental health services.

Notes

1. Agreement is not unanimous, however. *See generally* J. Holt, Escape from Childhood (1974).

2. *See* appendix A.

3. The Dialogues of Plato (4th ed. B. Jewett transl. 1953) as quoted in J. Conger, Adolescence and Youth: Psychological Development in a Changing World (1973) [hereinafter cited as Conger], at 4.

4. Conger, note 3 above, at 5 (citations omitted).

5. "[T]he notion [of adolescence] as it is commonly understood in contemporary thought did not prevail prior to the last two decades of the nineteenth century and was 'on the whole an American discovery.' " D. Bakan, *Adolescence in America: From Idea to Social Fact*, 100 Daedalus 979 (1971) [hereinafter cited as Bakan], quoting Demos and Demos, *Adolescence in Historical Perspective*, 31 J. Marr. & Fam. 632 (1969), at 632.

6. Bakan, note 5 above, at 979.

7. *Id.*

8. J. Tanner, *Sequence, Tempo, and Individual Variation in the Growth and Development of Boys and Girls Aged Twelve to Sixteen*, 100 Daedalus 907 (1971) [hereinafter cited as Tanner, *Sequence*].

9. "The term *puberty* derives from the Latin word *pubertas* (meaning 'age of manhood') and refers to the first phase of adolescence when sexual maturation becomes evident. Strictly speaking, in current scientific usage puberty begins with the gradual enlargement of ovaries (and such related organs

as the uterus) in females and the prostate gland and seminal vesicles in males."
Conger, note 3 above, at 94. "Puberty. The earliest age at which persons are
capable of begetting or bearing children . . . In the civil and common law, the age
at which one becomes capable of contracting marriage. It is in boys fourteen,
and in girls twelve years." Black's Law Dictionary 1392 (rev. 4th ed. 1968).

10. Tanner, *Sequence*, note 8 above, at 907.

11. Conger, note 3 above, at 95 (citations omitted).

12. J. Tanner, *Growing Up*, 229:3 Scient. Amer. 34, 36-37 (Sept. 1973).

13. Conger, note 3 above, at 95 (citations omitted).

14. Tanner, *Growing Up*, note 12 above, at 36-37.

15. *Id.*, at 36.

16. *Id.*, at 38; Conger, note 3 above, at 102-5.

17. Tanner, *Sequence*, note 8 above, at 908.

18. Tanner, *Growing Up*, note 12 above, at 42. "[F]airly reliable data
indicate that during periods of nutritional deprivation, such as that during World
War II in a number of European countries, age of menarche was significantly
retarded. Furthermore, within countries, there appear to be significant differences related to socioeconomic status." Conger, note 3 above, at 108 (citations
omitted).

19. Conger, note 3 above, at 101 (citation omitted).

20. Conger, note 3 above, at 127, quoting D. Elkind, Children and
Adolescents: Interpretive Essays on Jean Piaget (1970).

21. Conger, note 3 above, at 127.

22. H. Ginsburg & S. Opper, Piaget's Theory of Intellectual Development:
An Introduction 181 (1969) [hereinafter cited as Ginsburg & Opper]. "The
newer emphasis on stages of cognitive development owes more to the Swiss
psychologist Jean Piaget than to any other theorist or investigator. According to
Piaget, there are four major stages in cognitive development: the *sensorimotor
stage* (from birth to 18 months), the *preoperational stage* (18 months to 7
years), the stage of *concrete operations* (7 to 12 years), and the stage of *formal
operations* (from about age 12 onward)." Conger, note 3 above, at 155 (citations
omitted).

23. Ginsburg & Opper, note 22 above, at 203-4.

24. *Id.*, at 204-5.

25. The adolescent manipulates and transforms experimental conclusions
according to formal logical rules which Piaget designates the INRC group:
Identity, Negation, Reciprocity, and Correlativity. Ginsburg & Opper, note 22,
above, at 196.

26. N and R: Negation and Reciprocity.

27. Ginsburg & Opper, note 22 above, at 204-5.

28. Conger, note 3 above, at 162.

29. *Id.*, at 140.

30. Ginsburg & Opper, note 22 above, at 206.

31. Conger, note 3 above, at 160-61, quoting L. Yudin, *Formal Thought in Adolescence as a Function of Intelligence*, 37 Child Devel. 697 (1966). Conger notes that "[s]ome adolescents and adults never acquire true formal operational thought, because of either limited ability or cultural limitations." *Id.* (citations omitted).

32. Conger, note 3 above, at 20.

33. *Id.*, at 20-21, citing E. Erikson, Childhood and Society (1963) and E. Erikson, Identity: Youth and Crisis (1968).

34. A. Freud, *Adolescence as a Developmental Disturbance*, in Adolescence: Psychosocial Perspectives (G. Coplan and S. Lebovici ed. 1969); A. Freud, *Adolescence*, in Adolescence: Contemporary Studies (A. Winder and D. Angus ed. 1968); A. Freud, *Adolescence*, 13 Psychoanalyt. Study of Child 37 (1958).

35. K. Lewin, *Field Theory and Experiment in Social Psychology*, 44 Am. J. Sociol. 868 (1939).

36. Hall conceived of adolescence as a period of "storm and stress" (Sturm und Drang). G. Hall, Adolescence: Its Psychology and Its Relations to Physiology, Anthropology, Sociology, Sex, Crime, Religion, and Education (1904-5).

37. A. Gesell, F. Ilg & L. Ames, Youth: The Years from Ten to Sixteen (1956).

38. Blos has delineated five adolescent phases. P. Blos, *The Child Analyst Looks at the Young Adolescent*, 100 Daedalus 961 (1971).

39. "[T]he writings of Anna Freud, Geleerd, Spiegel, Harley, Eissler, and Fountain . . . illustrate the conviction of most psychoanalytic clinicians that the normal adolescent is at least transiently a disturbed, maladjusted person." Irving B. Weiner, Psychological Disturbance in Adolescence (1970).

40. *See generally* L. Kohlberg & C. Gilligan, *The Adolescent as a Philosopher: The Discovery of the Self in a Postconventional World*, 100 Daedalus 1051 (1971).

41. *Id.*, at 1066-67.

42. *Id.*, at 1067-68.

43. *Id.*, at 1068.

44. *Id.*, at 1072. In support of the theory that attainment of a particular cognitive stage is a necessary but not sufficient condition for attainment of a particular moral stage, Kuhn, Langer, and Kohlberg found that although 60 percent of persons over sixteen had attained formal-operational thinking, only 10 percent of those over sixteen showed Stage 5 and 6 moral thinking; but all of these 10 percent were capable of formal-operational logical thought. *Id.*, at 1071.

45. Now age eighteen in all but nine states and the District of Columbia. See appendix A.

46. We shall refrain from referring to adolescents by their other legal appellation, "infants," which though of ancient heritage and still in common use, may appear to many to demean today's youth.

47. *See generally* H. Rodham, *Children Under the Law*, 43 Harv. Ed. Rev. 487 (1973) [hereinafter cited as Rodham].

48. *See* discussions in this chapter at notes 163-197 and 257-274.

49. Prince v. Massachusetts, 321 U.S. 158, 170 (1944).

50. *See* note 437 in this chapter.

51. L. Arthur, *Should Children Be As Equal As People?* 45 N.D.L. Rev. (1968), at 221.

52. *See* discussion in this chapter at notes 198-214.

53. *See* discussion in this chapter at notes 163-182.

54. The United States Supreme Court recognized the fallacy of many of the "protection" justifications in the landmark case involving Gerald Gault. "If Gerald had been over 18, he would not have been subject to Juvenile Court proceedings. For the particular offense involved, the maximum punishment would have been a fine of $5 to $50, or imprisonment in jail for not more than two months. Instead, he was committed to custody for a maximum of six years." In re Gault, 387 U.S. 1, 29 (1967) (citation omitted), discussed in this chapter at note 215 *et seq.*

55. *See generally* Holt, note 1 above.

56. *See* Rodham, note 47 above, at 505 *et seq.*

57. Aristotle, Politics 32-33 (E. Barker transl. 1962), at 316, as quoted by A. Kleinfeld, *The Balance of Power Among Infants, Their Parents and The State, II. Parental Power*, 4 Fam. L.Q. 409 (1970), at 411 [hereinafter cited as Kleinfeld II].

58. Rodham, note 47 above, at 489, citing 1 W. Blackstone, Commentaries on the Laws of England (12th ed. 1700-1795).

59. Ex parte Crouse, 4 Whart. 9 (Sup. Ct. Pa. 1839), at 11.

60. J. Mill, On Liberty (Kirk ed. 1955), at 13.

61. Kleinfeld II, note 57 above, at 413.

62. *Id.*

63. *Id.*

64. Genesis 22: 1-13.

65. Kleinfeld II, note 57 above, at 412, citing F. Pollock & F. Maitland, The History of English Law 436-37 (2d ed. 1898).

66. 262 U.S. 390 (1923). Discussed in chapter 6, at note 10.

67. 268 U.S. 510 (1925). Discussed in chapter 6, at note 11.

68. "[T]o marry, establish a home and bring up children is one form of liberty protected by the due process clause." Meyer v. Nebraska, 262 U.S. 390, 399 (1923), as quoted in Note, *State Intrusion into Family Affairs: Justifications and Limitations*, 26 Stan. L. Rev. 1383 (1974), at 1384 [hereinafter cited as *State Intrusion*].

69. Pierce v. Society of Sisters, 268 U.S. 510, 535 (1925), as quoted in *State Intrusion*, note 68 above, at 1384.

70. 24 Eng. Rep. 659 (Ch. 1722).

71. A. Kleinfeld, *The Balance of Power Among Infants, Their Parents and*

the State: III. The Relation to The State, 5 Fam. L.Q. 63 (1971), at 66 [hereinafter cited as Kleinfeld III].

72. The General Laws and Liberties of Massachusetts Bay, Ch. XVIII, § 13 (1634).

73. See, e.g., Mass. Gen. Laws Ann. ch. 119, § 39E: "A parent or legal guardian . . . may apply for a petition . . . alleging that said child persistently runs away from the home of said parent or guardian or persistently refuses to obey the lawful and reasonable commands of said guardian resulting in said parent's or guardian's inability to adequately care for and protect said child."

74. See, e.g., Wis. Stats. § 118.15 (1969).

75. Wisconsin v. Yoder, 406 U.S. 205 (1972). Discussed in this chapter at note 152 et seq. and in chapter 6, at note 21.

76. "Against arguments that the compulsory school laws invaded 'the natural right of a man to govern and control his own children,' State v. Bailey held that the parent owed a duty to educate his child to the state as well as the child, and the state could properly regulate the discharge of this duty by making schooling compulsory." 157 Ind. 324, 61 N.E. 730 (1901), as cited by Kleinfeld II, note 57 above, at 414.

77. See, e.g., Mass. Gen. Laws Ann. ch. 149, § 86.

78. In Prince v. Massachusetts, 321 U.S. 158 (1944), the Supreme Court upheld the conviction of a Jehovah's Witness under a state child labor act for permitting her nine-year-old child to sell religious literature with her.

79. 4 Eng. Rep. 1078 (H.L. 1828).

80. "Mr. Wellesley, while living with a Mrs. Bligh in Paris, to which he had gone to escape his creditors, had sent letters to his son with such moral advice as 'study hard, but as soon as you have completed your tasks go out, in all weathers, and play hell and Tommy, etc., chase cats, dogs, and women, old and young, but spare my game.' " (citation omitted). Kleinfeld III, note 71 above, at 66.

81. Kleinfeld III, note 71 above, at 66 n.10.

82. U.S. Const. amend. IX.

83. Some amendments enacted shortly after the Civil War and in recent years are exceptions to this original purpose. One possible effect of the Fourteenth Amendment on parental power is discussed in chapter 6.

84. In an extreme example of obeisance to parental authority, the Washington Supreme Court once found that a fifteen-year-old girl could not sue her father for raping her because allowing recovery would open the door to suits for injuries to children resulting from parental negligence. The peace of the family would be marred if the conduct of a parent could be thus challenged in a civil suit. Roller v. Roller, 37 Wash. 242, 79 P. 788 (1905).

85. R. Pound, Individual Interests in the Domestic Relations, 14 Mich. L. Rev. 177, 186-87 (1916), as quoted in Kleinfeld II, note 57 above, at 434.

86. See P. Strauss, et al., The Relationship Between Promise and Perfor-

mance in State Intervention in Family Life, 9 Colum. J. of Law and Soc. Probs. 28 (1972); M. Wald, *State Intervention on Behalf of "Neglected" Children: A Search for Realistic Standards*, 27 Stan. L. Rev. 985 (1975).

87. In re Gault, 387 U.S. 1 (1966) at 16. *See also* R. Burt, *Developing Constitutional Rights Of, In, and For Children*, 39 Law and Contemp. Prob. 118 (1975).

88. With acknowledgment to Andrew Jay Kleinfeld's excellent three-part essay, *The Balance of Power Among Infants, Their Parents and the State.* Part I, discussing representation in court, is published at 4 Fam. L.Q. 319 (1970) [hereinafter cited as Kleinfeld I]. Parts II and III are cited above, notes 57 and 71 respectively.

89. *See* discussion on juvenile delinquency at notes 215-56 and education at notes 116-62 in this chapter.

90. "These cases, [*Meyer v. Nebraska*, note 68 above, and *Pierce v. Society of Sisters*, note 69 above] never mention rights or interests of the children involved. Since they rest instead entirely on a doctrine of parental right, the question of whether the parent may not be loyal to the interests of his child is not discussed." Kleinfeld II, note 57 above, at 418.

91. *See* discussion in this chapter at notes 244-47.

92. *See* Bartley v. Kremens, 402 F. Supp. 1039 (E.D. Pa. 1975), *remanded sub nom* Kremens v. Bartley, 97 S. Ct. 1709 (1977); discussed in chapter 6, at note 92.

93. *See* Planned Parenthood v. Danforth, 428 U.S. 52 (1976), mentioned in this chapter at note 195 and discussed more fully in chapter 6, at note 61 *et seq.*

94. T. James, *The Age of Majority*, 4 Amer. J. of Legal Hist. 22 (1960), at 24-25 [hereinafter cited as James].

95. *Id.*, at 25.

96. *Id.*, at 26 (citation omitted).

97. *Id.*, at 27.

98. "See, for example, Shakespeare, Henry VI, Part III, Act 2, Scene 2, where Henry VI knights his own Edward, Prince of Wales; St. Palaye, *Memoires sur L'Ancienne Chevalerie* (1975), trans. 1784, pp. 3-42." James, note 94 above, at 28.

99. James, note 94 above, at 28-29, quoting L'Ancienne Coutume de Normandie, (Wm. Lawrence de Gruchy ed. 1881) c. 33.

100. By 1966, only four states permitted persons under twenty-one to vote. Note, *Legislative History of Title III of the Voting Rights Act of 1970*, 8 Harv. J. Legis. 123 (1970) at 137 and 139 [hereinafter cited as Title III Note].

101. Title III Note, note 100 above, at 132-33.

102. *Id.*, at 133.

103. *Id.*, generally.

104. *Id.*, at 139.

105. *Id.*, at 145, quoting Senator Cook, 116 Cong. Rec. S3214 (daily ed. March 9, 1970).

106. Oregon v. Mitchell, 400 U.S. 112 (1970).

107. Meanwhile, several state legislatures were also adjusting the voting age downward by various degrees. At the time the suit was filed, only two states, "Georgia and Kentucky allowed 18-year-olds to vote, and only two other States, Hawaii and Alaska, set the voting age below 21. In subsequent referenda [held before the Court's decision], voters in 10 States declined to lower the voting age; five states lowered the voting age to 19 or 20; and Alaska lowered the age from 19 to 18." Oregon v. Mitchell, note 106 above, Harlan, *concurring in part*, at 213 n.90.

108. The amendment was proposed March 23, 1971; ratification was completed June 30, 1971.

109. "The right of citizens of the United States, who are 18 years of age or older, to vote shall not be denied or abridged by the United States or any state on account of age." U.S. Const. amend. XXVI.

110. Alabama, Colorado, District of Columbia, Mississippi, Missouri, Pennsylvania, and South Carolina set twenty-one as the age of majority; however, Colorado and Pennsylvania set eighteen as the contracting age. See appendix A.

111. Alaska, Nebraska, and Wyoming. *See* appendix A.

112. *See* appendix A. *See also* this chapter at notes 302-3.

113. U.S. Const. art. I, § 2.

114. *Id.*, at art. I, § 3.

115. *Id.*, at art. II, § 1. The belief that persons should not be entrusted with certain rights until ages above majority still exists. A committee of psychiatrists and lawyers charged with devising appropriate controls for the performance of psychosurgery recently recommended that "[n]one of the following persons shall have psychosurgery performed on them under any circumstances: (a) Patients who are adolescents or young adults where there is still the possibility of developmental maturation. We designate that age as 30." Mass. Dept. of Mental Health Task Force on Psychosurgery, Majority Report, ¶ 6 (1974).

116. Adolescents' rights in the other judicial-active context, juvenile justice, are discussed in this chapter at notes 198-256.

117. 1 W. Blackstone, *Commentaries* *453, as quoted by W. Buss, *Procedural Due Process for School Discipline: Probing the Constitutional Outline*, 119 U. Pa. L. Rev. 545 (1971), at 559 [hereinafter cited as Buss].

118. As of 1972, appparently all states except Mississippi had compulsory education laws. Wisconsin v. Yoder, 406 U.S. 205 (1972), at 226 n.15.

119. Buss, note 117 above, at 559 n.65, citing Goldstein, *The Scope and Sources of School Board Authority to Regulate Student Conduct and Status: A Nonconstitutional Analysis*, 117 U. Pa. L. Rev. 373, 384 and n.44 (1969); Sumpton, *Responsibility of Principal for Planning and Supervision in Connection with Field Trips and Errands*, in Law and the School Principal (R. Seitz ed. 1961).

120. Kleinfeld III, note 71 above, at 98, citing Leonard v. School Committee, 349 Mass. 704, 212 N.E.2d 468 (1965).

121. 294 F.2d 150 (5th Cir. 1961), *cert. denied*, 368 U.S. 930 (1961).

122. *Id.*, at 158.

123. *Id.*, quoting Seavey, *Dismissal of Students: "Due Process,"* 70 Harv. L. Rev. 1406 (1957), at 1407.

124. Wright, *The Constitution on the Campus*, 22 Vand. L. Rev. 1027 (1969), at 1032.

125. 363 F.2d 744 (1966).

126. 363 F.2d 749 (1966).

127. Kleinfeld III, note 71 above, at 97-98.

128. 393 U.S. 503 (1969).

129. *Id.*, at 508.

130. 393 U.S. 503, 506.

131. *See* Goss v. Lopez, 419 U.S. 565, at 576, n.8 (1975) and Wood v. Strickland, 420 U.S. 308, at 323 n.15 (1975).

132. 419 U.S. 565 (1975).

133. *Id.*, at 581.

134. 420 U.S. 308 (1975).

135. *Id.*, at 322.

136. 419 U.S. 565, at 583.

137. *Id.*

138. *School Suspensions: 1092 Minority, 550 White*, Boston Globe, Dec. 9, 1974, at 40. This trend has continued through 1975. "Between Sept. 8 and Oct. 31, [1975] 1122 students were suspended—710 blacks, 361 whites and 51 members of other racial-ethnic groups." Boston Globe, Dec. 9, 1975, at 5.

139. Thomas I. Atkins, NAACP, Boston branch; Mark Weddleton, Boston Human Rights office; and Joyce Miller, Massachusetts Advocacy Center, quoted in Boston Globe, note 138 above.

140. "The U.S. Dept. of Health Education and Welfare conducted a study of expulsion by race in 2831 of the nation's school districts in 1971. The analysis found that the expulsion rate for minority students was twice that for nonminority students, and the expulsion rate for black students was three times that of nonminority students." Boston Globe, note 138 above.

141. Boston Globe, note 138 above.

142. *See, e.g., Court Says R.I. Student Can Sit During Pledge, Anthem*, Boston Globe, Jul. 16, 1975, at 11.

143. 393 U.S. 503, at 509.

144. *See* Note, *Recent Cases: Constitutional Law—Schools and School Districts—Prohibition of Long Hair Absent Showing of Actual Disruption Violates High School Student's Constitutional Rights . . .*, 84 Harv. L. Rev. 1702 (1971) [hereinafter cited as *Long Hair Note*].

145. 426 F.2d 1154 (5th Cir. 1970), *cert. denied*, 400 U.S. 957 (1970).

146. 419 F.2d 1034 (7th Cir. 1969), *cert. denied*, 398 U.S. 937 (1970).

147. *Long Hair Note*, note 144 above, at 1704.

148. 395 F. Supp. 294 (M.D.N.C. 1975), *affirmed* 423 U.S. 907 (1975).

149. The court laid down four procedural steps which it held to be the minimum required to satisfy due process in such cases:

1. The use of corporal punishment must be approved in principle by the principal of a school before it may be used therein;
2. It may be used only after a warning has been given that specific behavior may occasion its use (except that conduct so antisocial or disruptive as to "shock the conscience" may not require such warning);
3. The punishment may only be administered in the presence of a second school official who has been informed beforehand of the reason for its use; and
4. Upon request, the child's parents must be provided by the teacher with a written explanation, and the name of the second school official.

395 F. Supp. 294, at 301.

150. *See* note 87 above.

151. Letter of Thomas Jefferson to Joseph Cabell, Sept. 9, 1817, in 17 Writings of Thomas Jefferson 417, 423-24 (Mem. ed. 1904) as cited in Wisconsin v. Yoder, 406 U.S. 205 (1972), at 226 n.14.

152. 402 U.S. 205 (1972).

153. *Id.*, at 207 n.1.

154. *Id.*, at 244-46 (citations omitted).

155. *Id.*, at 231.

156. Merriken v. Cressman, 364 F. Supp. 913 (E.D. Pa. 1973).

157. The questionnaire asked "such personal and private questions as the family religion, the race or skin color of the student . . . , the family composition, including the reason for the absence of one or both parents, and whether one or both parents 'hugged and kissed me good night when I was small', 'tell me how much they love me', 'enjoyed talking about current events with me', and 'make me feel unloved'." 364 F. Supp. 913, 916.

158. *Id.*, at 919.

159. Note 128 above.

160. 411 U.S. 1 (1973).

161. "Strict scrutiny" and other levels of judicial review are discussed in the "Equal Protection" section of chapter 6.

162. Confidentiality of student records is another frequently litigated issue in the education field, but this topic will be included in the section on confidentiality in chapter 8. On the other hand, racial segregation and desegregation, legal issues of overriding significance in many school systems, will not be directly discussed in this book. Although legislative and judicial approaches to

these issues are obviously of great importance, they are not specifically concerned with either mental health or with the capacities or rights of adolescents to act autonomously, and will therefore be omitted.

163. Corbin, Contracts § 227, at 318 (1 vol. ed. 1952).

164. According to the law of most states, if a minor reaped some gain from a contract, he must return any goods which he still has at the time of his disaffirmance, but if such goods are damaged or lost the minor is not generally required to make any restitution. *See* Mutual Life Insurance Co. v. Schiavone, 63 App. D.C. 257, 71 F.2d 980 (1934).

165. *See* Benson v. Tucker, 212 Mass. 60, 90 N.E. 589 (1912).

166. *See* Atwell v. Jenkins, 163 Mass. 362, 40 N.E. 178 (1895).

167. At least one commentator disagrees that the rule affords even a theoretical advantage to minors. John Holt argues that, ideally, young people should be able to choose to assume full legal and financial responsibility, including the right to make contracts, "at any age." Holt, note 1 above, at 236. *See also* Note, *Infant's Contractual Disabilities: Do Modern Sociological and Economic Trends Demand a Change in the Law?*, 41 Ind. L.J. 140 (1965-1966).

168. It is, however, common knowledge that very young minors regularly encounter merchants ready to sell them toys, bubble gum, comic books, and other such items. Although such sales technically constitute legal contracts which the minor might disaffirm to recover his purchase price, merchants apparently perceive the chance of such an eventuality to be exceedingly small (or, probably more commonly, are entirely ignorant of this possibility), and thus accept the risk.

169. The other two principal classes of exceptions to the disaffirmance rule are equitable estoppel from pleading the infancy defense and ratification. *See* 42 Am. Jur. *Infants* §§ 118-127, at 112-21 (1969).

170. *E.g.*, Valley National Bank v. Glover, 62 Ariz. 538, 159 P.2d 292 (1945); Borgnis v. Falk Co., 147 Wis. 327, 133 N.W. 209 (1911).

171. *See, e.g.*, Colo. Rev. Stat. § 13-22-103 (1974) (consent for medical and dental care); Ark. Stat. § 55-102 (marriage contracts: males, 17; females, 16); Colo. Rev. Stat. § 13-22-104(2) (consent for organ donation).

172. Mass. Gen. Laws Ann. ch. 175, § 128 (1970).

173. Colo. Rev. Stat. § 13-101 (1973).

174. *See* discussion in Edge, *Voidability of Minors' Contracts: A Feudal Doctrine in a Modern Economy*, 1 Ga. L. Rev. 205, 207 (1967).

175. Sternlieb v. Normandie National Securities Corp., 263 N.Y. 245, 188 N.E. 726 (1934).

176. Burnand v. Irigoyen, 30 Cal. 2d 861, 186 P.2d 417 (1947).

177. Gregory v. Lee, 64 Conn. 407, 30 A. 53 (1894).

178. White v. Sikes, 129 Ga. 508, 59 S.E. 228 (1907). *Contra* International Textbook Co. v. Connelly, 206 N.Y. 188, 99 N.E. 722 (1912).

179. *See, e.g.*, McAllister v. Saginaw Timber Co., 18 P.2d 41 (Wash. 1933). *See also* 71 ALR 227.

180. Moskow v. Marshall, 271 Mass. 302, 305, 171 N.E. 477, 479 (1930).

181. *See* Mitchell v. Cambell & Fetter Bank, 135 Ind. App. 523, 195 N.E.2d 489 (1964).

182. Stimpson v. Hunter, 234 Mass. 61, 125 N.E. 155 (1919).

183. *See* 70 C.J.S. *Physicians & Surgeons* § 48, at 968 (1951); Comment, *Informed Consent in Medical Malpractice*, 55 Cal. L. Rev. 1396 (1967).

184. Cobbs v. Grant, 8 Cal. 3d 229, 502 P.2d 1 (1972); Bonner v. Moran, 126 F.2d 121 (D.D.C. 1941).

185. W. Prosser, Handbook of the Law of Torts 104 (3d ed. 1964). *See also* Reddington v. Clayman, 134 N.E. 2d 920, 334 Mass. 244 (1956); Barfield v. South Highlands Infirmary, 191 Ala. 553, 68 So. 30 (1915).

186. Smith v. Seibly, 72 Wash. 2d 16, 431 P.2d 719 (1967).

187. For a discussion of the mature minor exception, *see* Bellotti v. Baird, 428 U.S. 132, 96 S. Ct. 2857 (1976).

188. *See, e.g.*, Hawaii Rev. Stat. § 577 A-4 (1975 Supp.).

189. *See, e.g.*, Mo. Stat. Ann. § 202.783 (1972); Mont. Rev. Code § 38-1303 (1975 Supp.).

190. *See, e.g.*, Idaho Code § 66-318 (1976 Supp.).

191. *See, e.g.*, Mich. Stat. Ann. § 14.800 (417) (1976); Iowa Code Ann. § 229.2 (1975 Supp.).

192. *See, e.g.*, Bartley v. Kremens, note 92 above.

193. *See, e.g.*, Colo. Rev. Stat. 1973, § 13-22-105 (1974).

194. *See* Planned Parenthood of Missouri v. Danforth, 428 U.S. 52 (1976), discussed in chapter 6 below, at note 61 *et seq.*

195. 428 U.S. 52 (1976).

196. Carey v. Population Services International, 97 S. Ct. 2010 (1977).

197. *See, e.g.*, Mass. Gen. Laws Ann. ch. 112 § 12F (1975 Supp.).

198. The President's Commission on Law Enforcement and Administration of Justice, Task Force Report: Juvenile Delinquency and Youth Crime 2 (1967) [hereinafter cited as Task Force Report].

199. *Id.*

200. L. Weinreb, Criminal Law: Cases, Comment, Questions (1969). *See also* S. Fox, The Law of Juvenile Courts in a Nutshell 14-25 (1971).

201. *See* Glueck and Glueck, One Thousand Juvenile Delinquents (1934); Lou, Juvenile Courts in the United States (1927).

202. Task Force Report, note 198 above, at 2, quoting Lou, note 201 above, at 7.

203. Tappan, Juvenile Delinquency 169 (1949), as quoted in Task Force Report, note 198 above, at 2.

204. U.S. DHEW, Standards for Specialized Courts Dealing with Children 55, Children's Bureau Pub. No. 346 (1954), as cited in Task Force Report, note 198 above, at 2.

205. Task Force Report, note 198 above, at 3.

206. *Id.*

207. *Id.*

208. Judge Julian Mack, as quoted in Task Force Report, note 198 above, at 3.

209. Task Force Report, note 198 above, at 3.

210. Title of article by Waite in 12 J. Crim. L. & Criminol. 339 (1922). "The court which must direct its procedure even apparently to do something *to* a child because of what he *has done*, is parted from the court which is avowedly concerned only with doing something *for* a child because of what he *is* and *needs*, by a gulf too wide to be bridged by any humanity which the judge may introduce into his hearings, or by the habitual use of corrective rather than punitive methods after conviction." *Id.*, at 340.

211. Foreword to Young, Social Treatment in Probation and Delinquency (1937), at xxvii, as quoted in In re Gault, 387 U.S. 1 (1967).

212. In re Gault, 387 U.S. 1, 18-19 (1967).

213. *Id.*, at 26, citing Wheeler & Cottrell, Juvenile Delinquency—Its Prevention and Control 33 (1966).

214. In re Gault, 387 U.S. 1, 27 (1967) (citations omitted).

215. In re Gault, 387 U.S. 1 (1967). The Court had, nineteen years previously, extended the Fourteenth Amendment protection against coerced confessions to a fifteen-year-old boy in a criminal trial (Haley v. Ohio, 332 U.S. 596 (1948)). However, this and other "[p]rior cases involving children were not addressed to the question of whether children in contradistinction to adults are entitled to the protections of the Bill of Rights." (L. Forer, *Rights of Children: The Legal Vacuum*, 55 A.B.A.J. 1151 (1969), at 1151 n.1). Kent v. U.S., 383 U.S. 541 (1966), did discuss children's constitutional rights *per se*. It held that the D.C. Juvenile Court Act, "read in the context of constitutional principles," required that a sixteen-year-old boy be afforded a hearing before being transferred from the juvenile justice system to an adult jail and the jurisdiction of adult criminal court. (*Id.*, at 554 and 557). *Kent* noted that "[t]here is evidence . . . that there may be grounds for concern that the child receives the worst of both worlds; that he gets neither the protections accorded to adults nor the solicitous care and regenerative treatment postulated for children." (*Id.*, at 556). It remained for *Gault*, the following year, to make explicit the procedural protections constitutionally required in the juvenile justice system.

216. *Id.*, at 7-8.

217. *Id.*, at 29.

218. *Id.*, at 27-28.

219. *Id.*, at 31-57.

220. In re Winship, 397 U.S. 357 (1970).

221. McKeiver v. Pennsylvania, 403 U.S. 528 (1971).

222. *See, e.g.*, Piland v. Clark County Juvenile Court, 85 Nev. 489, 457 P.2d 523 (1969) (right to a speedy trial); In re Carl T., 1 Cal. App. 3d 344, 81 Cal. Rptr. 655 (1969) (police lineups).

223. There is movement also in Canada away from the *parens patriae* philosophy and toward greater procedural protections and a more legalistic approach to juvenile justice. G. Cote-Harper, *Age, Delinquent Responsibility and Moral Judgment*, 11 Les Cahiers de Droit 489, 492 (1970).

224. Technically, "delinquent" or "not delinquent," rather than "guilty" or "not guilty," is the plea to be made in juvenile court; most juvenile hearings, however, are rife with the argot of the criminal court.

225. 393 U.S. 503 (1969).

226. *See, e.g.*, Minn. Rules for Juv. Proc., Rule 9.1 (1974).

227. *See* Stanley v. Illinois, 92 S. Ct. 1208 (1972).

228. 304 U.S. 458 (1938).

229. *Id.*, at 464.

230. *Id.* Citations and footnotes omitted.

231. Miranda v. Arizona, 384 U.S. 436, 475 (1966).

232. *Id.*, at 55.

233. Nat'l Juv. Law Center, *Children Are Easy Victims of the Law*, 7 Clearinghouse Rev. 597, 597 (Feb. 1974).

234. In re Dennis M., 70 Cal. 2d 444, 75 Cal. Rptr. 1, 450 P.2d 296 (1969); Behms v. State, 491 S.W.2d 740 (Tex. Civ. App. 1973); Mullen v. State, 505 P.2d 305 (Wyo. 1973).

235. Note 228 above.

236. *See, e.g.*, In re Lawrence S., 29 N.Y.2d 206, 325 N.Y.S.2d 921, 275 N.E.2d 577 (1971).

237. 332 U.S. 708 (1947).

238. *See, e.g.*, People v. Lara, 67 Cal. 2d 365, 62 Cal. Rptr. 586, 432 P.2d 200 (1967), *cert. denied*, 392 U.S. 945. Judge Peters, in his dissent to *Lara*, is particularly critical of the court's focus on voluntariness rather than on knowing waiver. In re Lawrence S., 29 N.Y.2d 206, 325 N.Y.S.2d 921, 275 N.E.2d 577 (1971) and United States v. Miller, 453 F.2d 634 (4th Cir. 1972) are two recent cases in which courts inquired whether the youths "really understood" the consequences of waiver.

239. A recent study showed that most adolescents do not understand the *Miranda* warnings, whether given in the standard form or in a simplified version. Ferguson & Douglas, *A Study of Juvenile Waiver*, 7 San Diego L. Rev. 39 (1970).

240. *See* Lewis v. State, 288 N.E.2d 138 (Ind. Sup. Ct. 1972); McMillian and Garabedian, *Attitudes of Probation Officers Towards Due Process for Juvenile Offenders*, in Becoming Delinquent 266 (P. Garabedian ed. 1970).

241. *See* discussion in this chapter at notes 163-97.

242. *See, e.g.*, Colo. Rev. Stat. § 22-2-2-(3)(c) (Supp. 1971); Lewis v. State, 288 N.E.2d 138 (Ind. Sup. Ct. 1972).

243. Lewis v. State, 288 N.E.2d 138 (Ind. Sup. Ct. 1972); In re K.W.B., 500 S.W.2d 275 (Mo. App. 1973); State v. White, 494 S.W.2d 687 (Mo. App. 1973).

244. Minn. Rules for Juv. Proc., Rule 2-1 (1974); N.M. Stats. Ann. 13-14-25 (E) (Supp. 1973).

245. The Supreme Court noted, in Powell v. Alabama, 287 U.S. 45 (1932), that "[a] n intelligent and educated layman has small and sometimes no skill in the science of law." *Id.*, at 69.

246. Lefstein, Stepleton & Teitelbaum, *In Search of Juvenile Justice: Gault and Its Implementation*, 3 Law & Soc'y Rev. 491 (1969); Note, *Recent Developments—Minor's Request to See Parents Made Before or During Custodial Interrogation Invokes Fifth Amendment Privilege*, 1972 U. Ill. L. Forum 625; Schlam, *Police Interrogation & "Self"-Incrimination of Children by Parents: A Problem Not Yet Solved*, 6 Clearinghouse Rev. 618 (1973).

247. 2 Cal. 3d 513, 86 Cal. Rptr. 76, 468 P.2d 204 (1970).

248. *See generally* Lefstein, note 245 above; Children's Bureau, Legislative Guide for Drafting Family and Juvenile Court Acts, § 26 (1969). The New Mexico legislature recently amended its Children's Code to require that a child must have an attorney's advice for a statement to be admissible at a later hearing. N.M. Stats. Ann. § 13-13-25(b) (Supp. 1973).

249. *See* Note, *Waiver of Constitutional Rights by Minors: A Question of Law or Fact?*, 19 Hastings L.J. 223 (1967); Note, *The Confessions of Juveniles*, 5 Willamette L.J. 66 (1968). For a somewhat different criticism of the efficacy of counsel in these contexts, see Note, *Some Questions About "Judicializing" the Juvenile Court Procedure*, 1965 Wis. L. Rev. 32 (Winter 1965).

250. *See* text in this chapter at note 72.

251. *See* Fox, note 200 above, at 38-41.

252. *See, e.g.*, S.C. Code §§ 15-971(c) & 15-975. In at least one state, there is not even a statutory requirement that a court pass on such commitments: "Kentucky has returned to the notion that children are the property of their parents by permitting the 'voluntary' commitment of a child under age eighteen to the Department of Child Welfare (which runs the training schools) on the 'consent' of his parents, without court action." J. Glen, *Developments in Juvenile and Family Court Law*, 15 Crime & Delinq. 295, 300 (1969). *See* Ky. Rev. Stat. § 199.375 (1974 Supp.).

253. In re Snyder, reported in 1 Fam. L. Rep. 2347 (Oregon 1975).

254. *Id.*, at 2348.

255. *See* Fox, note 200 above, at 42-46.

256. For a criticism of the practice of limiting use of the word "treatment" to the psychoanalytical model, *see* J. Polier, *Justice for Juveniles*, 52:1 Child Welfare 5, 11 (1973).

257. *See, e.g.*, Cal. Const. art. XX, § 22 (1975 Supp.); Cal. Bus. & Prof. Code §§ 25658-65 (1975 Supp.). *See also* this chapter at notes 302-3.

258. *See* Ginsberg v. N.Y., 390 U.S. 629 (1968); discussed in chapter 6, at note 36.

259. *See* Jacobellis v. State of Ohio, 378 U.S. 184 (1964). *But see* Interstate Circuit Inc. v. City of Dallas, 390 U.S. 676 (1968) (movie classification ordinance found unconstitutionally vague).

260. *See, e.g.*, Bykofsky v. Borough of Middletown, 401 F. Supp. 1242 (M.D. Pa. 1975).

261. *See, e.g.*, Cal. Vehicles Code § 12512 (West 1971).

262. *See, e.g.*, Cal. Labor Code §§ 1293.1-1294 (West 1976).

263. Mass. Gen. Laws Ann. ch. 138, § 34.

264. *See* Bykofsky v. Middletown, note 259 above.

265. Mass. Gen. Laws Ann. ch. 90, § 8.

266. Note 258 above.

267. *Id.*, at 639.

268. Text at notes 72 and 250 above.

269. Text at notes 251-53 above.

270. Text at note 194 above. Although the Missouri statute requiring parental consent to abortion was struck down, the question of constitutionality has not yet been settled for a similar Massachusetts statute which includes a provision for obtaining judicial consent if parental consent is denied. *See* Baird v. Bellotti, 393 F. Supp. 847 (D. Mass. 1975); *vacated and remanded sub nom* Bellotti v. Baird, 428 U.S. 132 (1976). *See* discussion in chapter 6.

271. Ginsberg v. N.Y., note 258 above, at 639. The court cites one commentator who takes the view that, "[w]hile many of the constitutional arguments against morals legislation apply equally to legislation protecting the morals of children, one can well distinguish laws which do not impose a morality on children, but which support the right of parents to deal with the morals of their children as they see fit." Henkin, *Morals and the Constitution: the Sin of Obscenity*, 63 Col. L. Rev. 391, 413 n.68 (1963), cited at 639-640 n.7.

272. Prince v. Massachusetts, 321 U.S. 158 (1944).

273. *See, e.g.*, Purdon's Pa. Stat. Ann., tit. 35 § 10001 (1976 Supp.). For results of a study of adolescent donors' motivations and reactions after the more serious act of donating (with parental consent) a kidney, see D. Bernstein & R. Simmons, *The Adolescent Kidney Donor: The Right To Give*, 131 Am. J. Psychiat. 1338 (1974). The authors found that adolescent donors are more likely than adult donors to experience a boost in self-esteem and feel rewarded by, rather than regretful of, their decision a year later.

274. *See, e.g.*, Mass. Gen. Laws Ann. ch. 210, § 2 (1973).

275. *E.g.*, "[The period of minority extends to age eighteen] but all minors attain their majority by marriage." Iowa Code § 599.1 (1973).

276. *See* chapter 4 at note 49.

277. *See* In re Hook, 95 Vt. 497, 115 Atl. 730 (1922); D.C. Code § 21-104 (1967).

278. Richardson v. Browning, 18 F.2d 1008, 1012 (D.C. Cir. 1927).

279. Iowa Asst. Atty. Genl. Opinion #74-10-4 (Oct. 3, 1974), at 3. *See also* In re Davidson's Will, 26 N.W.2d 223 (1947); Des Moines v. Reisman, 248 Iowa 821, 83 N.W.2d 197 (1957); and In re Lundy, 82 Wash. 148, 143 P. 885 (1914).

280. *See* C. Foote, R. Levy & F. Sander, Cases and Materials on Family Law (1966), at 222 *et seq., Checks against Immature and Hasty Marriages*.

281. A study based on data derived from 52,722 marriages and 8040 divorces of white couples in Iowa between 1945 and 1947 concluded that "divorced couples had married about one year earlier than all couples getting married for the first time" and that "the marriages of teenagers are of noticeably shorter duration than those where marriage occurred at an older age." *Id.*, at 227-29, citing Monahan, *Does Age at Marriage Matter in Divorce?*, 32 Soc. Forces 81 (1953). It remains to be seen how such 1953 conclusions would be affected by more recent sociological phenomena: "The Census Bureau reports an increase in both the U.S. divorce rate and the number of young people not getting married at all. Noting that the divorce rate in the last four years has surpassed that of the entire previous decade, the Bureau's report does not purport to provide an explanation for this recent increase. As to the increase in the number of youthful 'singles,' the report states that '[w]hether the tendency among the younger group to refrain from marrying represents merely a postponement of first marriage or a development of a tread [sic] toward lifelong singleness is not known.' " New Briefs, *Divorce Rate,* 1 Fam. L. Rep. 2070 (Nov. 26, 1974).

282. James, note 94 above, at 31.

283. *Id.*, at 32.

284. N.H. Rev. Stat. Ann., ch. 457:4 (1968) states that "[n]o male below the age of fourteen years and no female below the age of thirteen years shall be capable of contracting a valid marriage. . . ." Ch. 457:5 (1973 Supp.), however, sets eighteen as the age of consent to marriage for both males and females, and ch. 457:6 holds that a marriage between persons below that age may be contracted only with the consent of a judge of the superior or probate court and of the parent or guardian of the underage person (if available), and only if "special cause exists rendering desirable" such marriage. Periodic attempts are made to raise the ages. *E.g.*, N.H. House Bill 285, introduced in the 1975 session, would have increased the minimum ages from 14 to 16 for males and from 13 to 15 for females. 1 Fam. L. Rep. 2298 (March 11, 1975).

285. Mass. Gen. Laws Ann. ch. 207, § 7 (1973).

286. *E.g.*, Fla. Stat. Ann. § 741.06 (Supp. 1976) (no marriage license shall issue to any female under 16 or male under 18).

287. Stanton v. Stanton, 30 Utah 2d 315, 517 P.2d 1010 (1974), at 517 P.2d 1012, *reversed* 421 U.S. 7 (1975). The Utah court might have, but did not, cite the following authorities on the subject of male and female roles. Freud believed that woman's social and psychological needs were fulfilled by bearing and rearing children, that "women have but little sense of justice" and that "their social interests are weaker than those of men. . . ." S. Freud, *Totem and Taboo*, in Basic Writings of Sigmund Freud 818 (A. Brill ed. 1938) and S. Freud, New Introductory Lectures on Psychoanalysis 183 (W. Sprott transl. 1933), as quoted by R. Roth & J. Lerner, *Sex-Based Discrimination in the Mental Institutionalization of Women*, 62 Cal. L. Rev. 789, 793 n.14 (1974). "Carl Jung believed that woman's role was similarly limited and that a woman

who took up 'a masculine calling, studying, and working in a man's way . . . is doing something not wholly in agreement with, if not directly injurious to her feminine nature.' " *Id.*, at 793, citing C. Jung, Contributions to Analytical Psychology (1928). "Even Alfred Adler, a strong advocate of equality of the sexes, espoused a 'sensible' form of the traditional male-female 'division of labor,' in which 'woman has taken over a certain part of the world's work [which might otherwise occupy a man, too] in return for which man is in the position to use his powers to greater effect.' " *Id.*, citing A. Adler, Understanding Human Nature (W. Wolfe transl. 1927), at 22, 129-33.

288. 421 U.S. 7, 95 S. Ct. 1373 (1975).

289. *Id.* at 14 and at 95 S. Ct. 1378.

290. *Id.*

291. *See* K. Davidson, R. Ginsburg and H. Kay, Sex-Based Discrimination (1974), reviewed by N. Gertner in 54 Bost. Univ. L. Rev. 1016 (1974). *See also* L. Kanowitz, Sex Roles in Law and Society, reviewed by Brown in 53 Bost. Univ. L. Rev. 1170 (1973); and B. Babcock, A. Freedman, E. Norton & S. Ross, Sex Discrimination and the Law (1975).

292. Bradwell v. Illinois, 83 U.S. (16 Wall.) 130 (1873), Bradley *concurrence* at 140-42, as cited in D. Sassower, *Women and the Judiciary: Undoing "The Law of the Creator,"* 80 Case & Comment 30 (Jan.-Feb. 1975) (upholding Ill. court's denial to women of license to practice law).

293. 404 U.S. 71, 92 S. Ct. 251 (1971).

294. 421 U.S. 7, 14 (1975) and 404 U.S. 71, 76. *See also* Frontiero v. Richardson, 411 U.S. 677 (1973), holding that federal statutes concerning benefits for dependents of military service people unconstitutionally discriminated of against servicewomen, in which four of the nine justices concluded that "classifications based upon sex, like classifications based upon race, alienage, or national origin, are inherently suspect, and must therefore be subjected to strict judicial scrutiny. *Id.*, at 688. (*See* chapter 6's Equal Protection section for a discussion of the significance of the Court's labeling any classification "inherently suspect.")

295. However, Attorney Bryce E. Roe, arguing *Stanton* (note 287 above) before the U.S. Supreme Court, stated that "[t]he idea that girls mature earlier than boys is an 'old notion' that has no place in upholding a sex-based distinction. As to the argument that girls tend to marry earlier, Mr. Roe asked: 'Which is cause, and which is effect?' " Arguments Heard, Equal Protection—Age of Majority. Stanton v. Stanton, No. 73-1461, argued 2/19/75, 1 Fam. L. Rep. 2262 (Feb. 25, 1975).

296. Illinois Attorney General's Opinions S-490 (June 30, 1972) and S-491 (July 17, 1972). *See also* Note, *Effects of the Equal Rights Amendment on Minnesota Law*, 57 Minn. L. Rev. 771 (1973).

297. S-491, note 296 above, at 2.

298. Ill. Council of Youth and Ill. Commission on Children, Report of

Committee on the Age of Majority and Legal Rights and Responsibilities for Youth (Nov. 1971), at 33-34.

299. *See generally* Tanner, *Sequence*, note 8 above.

300. The Supreme Court has, of course, addressed adult sex discrimination in several cases in recent years. See *Reed* and *Frontiero* (note 294 above). *See also* Weinberger v. Wiesenfeld, 420 U.S. 636 (1975) (widowers entitled to same Social Security survivor's benefits as widows).

301. Text at note 287 above. *See also* note 295 above.

302. 97 S. Ct. 451 (1976).

303. *Id.*, at 460.

304. Lamb v. Brown, 456 F.2d 18 (10th Cir. 1972).

305. *Id.*, at 19.

306. *Id.*, at 20.

307. *See Lawmakers Say State Is "Dumping" Women Patients*, Boston Globe, Mar. 23, 1976, at 39.

308. *See* L. Shapiro, *Ladies Last*, The [Boston] Real Paper (June 9, 1976), at 8.

309. *Id.*

310. Brenden v. Independent School District, 477 F.2d 1292 (8th Cir. 1973).

311. *Id.*, at 1300.

312. Vorchheimer v. School Dist. of Philadelphia, 532 F.2d 880 (3rd Cir. 1976), *aff'd* 97 S. Ct. 1671 (1977).

313. A 1972 New York suit charged child neglect by the state Department of Mental Hygiene with respect to its mentally retarded wards residing in the Willowbrook School. The court, however, held that its jurisdiction did not extend to neglect allegedly committed by state institutions rather than natural persons. In re D., 335 N.Y.S.2d 638, 70 Misc. 2d 953 (Fam. Ct. 1972).

314. McAllen v. McAllen, 106 N.W. 100 (1906).

315. 67 C.J.S. *Parent and Child* § 9, at 818 (1950).

316. *Id.*

317. *Id.*

318. 59 Am. Jur. 2d *Parent and Child* § 55, at 145. *See* State v. Waller, 90 Kan. 829, 136 P. 215 (1913); Dyer v. State, 58 Okla. Crim. 317, 52 P.2d 1080 (1935).

319. Some state statutes distinguish between "neglect" and "dependency." In "dependency" cases, a parent, through no fault of his own, is unable to care for a child. "Neglect" generally involves "fault" on the part of the parent.

320. "The duty to support includes the duty to furnish necessary medical attention for a child." 67 C.J.S. *Parent and Child* § 15, at 687 (1950).

321. In re Carstairs, 115 N.Y.S.2d 314, 317 (1952).

322. "EVAN-G," the Committee to End Violence Against the Next Generation, gives its bimonthly newsletter the sardonic title "The Last? Resort."

323. 1 W. Blackstone, Commentaries *444 (1765); Stedman, *Right of Husband to Chastise Wife*, 3 Va. L. Reg., N.S., 241 (1917), cited by W. Prosser, The Law of Torts 139 (3d ed. 1964).

324. W. Prosser, The Law of Torts 139 (3d ed. 1964), citing Fulgham v. State, 46 Ala. 143 (1871) and Comm. v. McAfee, 108 Mass. 458 (1871).

325. Prosser, note 185 above, at 139.

326. See note 149 above for recent restrictions placed on corporal punishment in schools.

327. Prosser, note 185 above, at 139.

328. *Id.*

329. *Id. See also* Kleinfeld II, note 57 above, at 426.

330. Prosser, note 185 above, at 140.

331. B. Grumet, *The Plaintive Plaintiffs: Victims of the Battered Child Syndrome*, in The Youngest Minority: Lawyers in Defense of Children (S. Katz ed. 1974) [hereinafter cited as *The Youngest Minority*], at 151.

332. R. Light, *Abused and Neglected Children*, 43 Harv. Ed. Rev. 556, 559 (1973).

333. C. Kempe, Silverman, Steele, Droegemueller & Steele, *The Battered Child Syndrome*, 13 J.A.M.A. 105 (1962).

334. V. DeFrancis, Child Abuse—Preview of a Nationwide Survey 5-6 (1963), as cited by Grumet, note 331 above, at 152 n.5.

335. Gil, *Incidence of Child Abuse and Demographic Characteristics of Persons Involved*, in The Battered Child 19, 21 (Helfer and Kempe eds. 1968), as cited by Grumet, note 331 above, at 152.

336. *Hard Times for Kids Too*, Time Magazine, March 17, 1975, at 88.

337. *Child Abuse: A Growing National Tragedy*, Boston Globe (Mar. 31, 1976), at 1, 8.

338. *Id.*, at 8.

339. Note 336 above.

340. "All fifty states have passed laws either encouraging or requiring citizens to report incidents of child abuse. Hospitals, police and social agencies are also required to report." R. Light, *Abused and Neglected Children*, 43 Harv. Ed. Rev. 556, 559 (1973). *See also* R. Brown, *Controlling Child Abuse: Reporting Laws*, 80:1 Case & Comment 10 (Jan.-Feb. 1975); R. Hansen, *Child Abuse Legislation and the Interdisciplinary Approach*, 52 A.B.A.J. 734 (1966); and R. Mnookin, *Child-Custody Adjudication: Judicial Functions in the Face of Indeterminacy*, 39 Law and Contemp. Probs. 226 (1975) [hereinafter cited as Mnookin, *Child-Custody*], at 241 n.69.

341. Mnookin, *Child-Custody*, note 340 above, at 241.

342. *Id.*, at 241 n.69, citing J. Pers, Somebody Else's Children: A Report on the Foster Care System in California (Sept. 1, 1974) (unpublished manuscript on file at the Institute of Governmental Studies, U. Cal., Berkeley).

343. R. Mnookin, *Foster Care—In Whose Best Interest?*, 43 Harv. Ed. Rev.

599 (1973), at 601, citing California State Social Welfare Board, Report on Foster Care, Children Waiting (1972) 7 and S. Jenkins and M. Sauber, Paths to Child Placement, Family Situations Prior to Foster Care (1966) at 74.

344. Mnookin, *Child-Custody*, note 340 above, at 241 n.69.

345. Mass. Gen. Laws Ann. ch. 119, § 1 (1969).

346. Report of the [Mass.] Governor's Commission on Adoption and Foster Care (1973) [hereinafter cited as Gruber Report] at 72.

347. *See* Mnookin, *Child-Custody*, note 340 above, at 272. "Even when [preventive or protective services for children within the home] are available, neglect statutes and the best-interests standard do not [generally] require that before ordering removal, a court conduct an inquiry into whether the child can be protected if left in parental custody." *Id.* "Minnesota is an exception, for its statute provides that a child may be removed from the parents 'only when his welfare or safety and protection of the public cannot be adequately safeguarded without removal.' Minn. Stat. Ann., § 260.011 (1971)." *Id.*, at 272-73 n.206.

348. *See* Note, *A Fit Parent May be Deprived of Custody of His Child if the Best Interest and Welfare of the Child Would Be Served by Allowing Another Person to Raise Him*, 4 Houston L. Rev. 131 (1966).

349. Mnookin, *Child-Custody*, note 340 above, at 240. *See also* S. Katz, When Parents Fail: The Law's Response to Family Breakdown 83 *et seq.* (1971).

350. *See, e.g.*, Colo. Rev. Stat. Ann., § 19-1-103(20)(a) (1974).

351. According to Mnookin, every state, except perhaps Maine and West Virginia, includes in its jurisdictional statute at least one such vague and broad provision. Mnookin, *Child-Custody*, note 340 above, at 241 n.68.

352. *See, e.g.*, Wash. Rev. Code Ann., § 13.04.010(2) (1962).

353. *See, e.g.*, Fla. Stat. Ann. § 39.02(1) (1975).

354. Thirty-one states appear to have statutes that provide explicitly for the best-interest-of-the-child test in some form. For a listing of these statutes with notations regarding their differences, *see* R. Mnookin, *Child-Custody*, note 340 above, at 236 n.45. *See also* Note, *Domestic Relations—Custody of a Minor—Best-Interest-of-the-Child Rule*, 32 Tul. L. Rev. 499 (1958).

355. It has, however, been suggested that the standard might more properly be termed "the least detrimental alternative." J. Goldstein, A. Freud & A. Solnit, Beyond the Best Interests of the Child (1973), at 53.

356. *Id.*

357. *Id.*, at 31.

358. *Id.*, at 12.

359. *See generally* D. Katkin, B. Bullington & M. Levine, *Above and Beyond the Best Interests of the Child: An Inquiry into the Relationship Between Social Sciences and Social Action*, 8 Law & Soc'y Rev. 669 (1974).

360. "Although the best interest rule is generally discussed, and sometimes applied, the general rule is that the parent will prevail unless clearly shown to be unfit, and there is a presumption that he is fit." H. Simpson, *The Unfit Parent:*

Conditions Under Which a Child May be Adopted Without the Consent of his Parent, 39 U. Det. L.J. 347, 357 (1962). Mark Twain has satirized judicial obeisance to parents' custody rights. "When Huckleberry Finn acquired wealth, his drunken vagrant father returned to claim his 'rights.' Thereupon those who had been looking after the boy 'went to law to get the court to take me away from him and let one of them be my guardian; but it was a new judge that had just come, and he didn't know the old man; so he said courts mustn't interfere and separate families if they could help it; said he'd druther not take a child away from its father. So Judge Thatcher and the widow had to quit on the business.

" 'That pleased the old man till he couldn't rest. He said he'd cowhide me till I was black and blue if I didn't raise some money for him. I borrowed three dollars from Judge Thatcher, and pap took it and got drunk, and went a-blowing around and cussing and whooping and carrying on; and he kept it up all over town, with a tin pan, till most midnight; then they jailed him, and next day they had him before court, and jailed him again for a week. But he said he was satisfied: said he was boss of his son, and he'd make it warm for him.' " Adventures of Huckleberry Finn, Chap. 5, as quoted in R. Pound, *Individual Interests in the Domestic Relations*, 14 Mich. L. Rev. 177 (1916), at 187 n.37.

361. By, *e.g.*, Attorney Monroe Inker, in A Debate: The Best Interests of the Child: The Legal and Psychiatric Interface of Child Placement and Custody, sponsored by The Child Psychiatry Service of New England Medical Center Hospital and Tufts University School of Medicine, Boston (Feb. 13, 1975). [Hereinafter cited as Debate.] Professor Goldstein responded that, although it is no doubt fair for a society to assert that the child's interest is not paramount, if society wishes to do this, it should do so openly and not under the rubric of "best interests of the child." *See also* Comment, *Custody of Children: Best Interests of Child vs. Rights of Parents*, 33 Cal. L. Rev. 306 (1945).

362. R. Mnookin, *Child Custody*, note 340 above, at 254.

363. *See, e.g.*, M. Inker and C. Peretta, *A Child's Right to Counsel in Custody Cases*, in The Youngest Minority, note 331 above, at 32.

364. Goldstein *et al.*, note 355 above, at 65.

365. Michigan Stat. Ann. § 25.121 (1974).

366. Debate, note 361 above.

367. Debate, note 361 above.

368. This question is usually addressed in custody disputes between two parents, rather than between the state and the parents. *See, e.g.*, McGregor v. McGregor, 257 Ala. 232, 58 So. 2d 457 (1952). For children twelve years of age or over, the preference is sometimes made dispositive. *See* Ohio Rev. Code Ann., § 3109.04 (1975).

369. *See* Mnookin, *Child-Custody*, note 340 above, at 255; Kay and Segal, *The Role of the Attorney in Juvenile Court Proceedings: A Non-Polar Approach*, 61 Ga. L.J. 1401 (1973); Comment, *The Attorney-Parent Relationship in the Juvenile Court*, 12 St. Louis L.J. 603 (1968).

370. Mass. Bar Assoc. Committee on Ethics, Opinion No. 76-1 (Feb. 25, 1976), at 4-5 (emphasis added).

371. *See* Mnookin, *Child-Custody*, note 340 above, at 228.

372. *See, e.g.*, Goldstein *et al.*, note 355 above, at 49-52; President's Comm. on Law Enforcement and the Administration of Justice, Task Force Report on Juvenile Delinquency and Youth Crime 7 (1967); Kay, *A Family Court: the California Proposal*, 56 Cal. L. Rev. 1205, 1208 (1968).

373. *See, e.g.*, Foster and Freed, *Child Custody*, 39 N.Y.U. L. Rev. 423, 627 (1974).

374. Mnookin, *Child-Custody*, note 340 above, at 228 (some citations omitted).

375. *See, e.g.*, Utah Code Ann., § 55-10-87 (Supp. 1965).

376. *See, e.g.*, N.Y. Family Ct. Act § 322. See also Kleinfeld II, note 57 above, at 430. Paulsen, *The Legal Framework for Child Protection*, 66 Colum. L. Rev. 679 (1966), at 708 discusses some of the problems created by authorizing social workers to intrude into a family's privacy on slighter bases than would justify full court proceedings.

377. *See* The Community's Children: Long-Term Substitute Care: A Guide for the Intelligent Layman (J. Parfit ed. 1967); G. Trasler, In Place of Parents: A Study of Foster Care (1960); Eisenberg, *The Sins of the Fathers: Urban Decay and Social Pathology*, 32 Am. J. Orthopsychiat. 14 (1962); Maas, *Highlight of the Foster Care Project: Introduction,* 38 Child Welfare 5 (July, 1959).

378. *See* Mnookin, *Child-Custody*, note 340 above, at 270.

379. *Id.*, at 271-72 (citations omitted).

380. *Id.*, at 271 n.201.

381. "Despite the temporary purpose of foster care, it is more often than not a permanent status for the child." Gruber Report, note 346 above, at 72.

382. S. Katz, *Legal Aspects of Foster Care*, 5 Fam. L.Q. 283, 285 (1971).

383. Occasionally, however, the foster parents are permitted to adopt their foster child. *See* Simpson, note 360 above.

384. In re Jewish Child Care Ass'n, 5 N.Y.2d 222, 226, 156 N.E.2d 700, 702, 183 N.Y.S.2d 65, 68 (1959).

385. Mnookin, *Child-Custody*, note 340 above, at 271 n.201. The case is also discussed by Katz, note 382 above, at 290-96. For a similar case with the opposite outcome, *see* In re Alexander, No. 155-165C (Fla. Cir. Ct. March 24, 1967), also discussed by Katz, note 382 above, at 296-301. *See also* E. Weinstein, The Self-Image of the Foster Child (1960), at 47.

386. Smith v. Organization of Foster Families for Equality and Reform, 97 S. Ct. 2094 (1977).

387. *See, e.g.*, In the Matter of Lee and Wesley, Cir. Ct. of Cook County, Illinois, Juvenile Div. Nos. 68 J(D) 1362; 68 J(D) 6383, 68 J 15850, (March 5, 1975).

Twelve years after the state assumed responsibility for her case, the future of a 17-year-old East Boston girl is on the line today in Suffolk Superior Court.

Although doctors say Anna K. (not her real name) is not a mental patient, she has spent most of the last 14 months at the Lindemann Mental Health Center in Boston, living in a ward with 20 psychotic women, most of them middle-aged.

Anna has been a foster child of the Welfare Department since 1963, when the state determined that her mother and grandmother had too many problems to take care of her.

Now, she has sued the state and Welfare Comr. Jerald L. Stevens, charging the Welfare Department with "gross neglect" in its legal duties to her.

Boston Globe, June 6, 1975, at 3.

388. M. Wald, *State Intervention on Behalf of "Neglected" Children: A Search for Realistic Standards*, 27 Stan. L. Rev. 985, 1039 (1975).

389. R. Burt, *Forcing Protection on Children and their Parents: the Impact of Wyman v. James*, 69 Mich. L. Rev. 1259 (1971).

390. *Id. See also* Note, *State Intrusion into Family Affairs: Justifications and Limitations*, 26 Stan. L. Rev. 1383 (1974).

391. Black's Law Dictionary 834 (Rev. 4th ed. 1968).

392. Allen, Ferster, and Weihofen, Mental Impairment and Legal Incompetency 70 (1968).

393. Black's, note 391 above, at 834.

394. Allen *et al.*, note 392 above, at 95.

395. *See, e.g.*, Fratcher, *Toward Uniform Guardianship Legislation*, 64 Mich. L. Rev. 983 (1966).

396. Allen *et al.*, note 392 above, at ix.

397. Black's, note 391 above, at 834.

398. *See* Nothem v. Vonderharr, 189 Iowa 43, 175 N.W. 967 (1920); In re McNaughton's Will, 138 Wis. 179, 120 N.W. 288 (1909).

399. *See* Stewart v. Ferar, 163 F.2d 183 (10th Cir. 1947); Old Colony Trust v. Townsend, 324 Mass. 298 (1949).

400. Wis. Stat. Ann. § 48.25.

401. Wis. Stat. Ann. § 319.11.

402. Winter v. Director of Dept. of Public Welfare, 217 Md. 391, 143 A.2d 81, *cert. denied* 358 U.S. 912 (1958).

403. Lewis v. Children's Home, 218 S.W.2d 683 (Ky. 1949).

404. *See, e.g.*, United States v. Dupont, 13 F.R.D. 98 (U.S.D.C. Ill. 1952).

405. In re Rinck's Guardianship, 29 N.J. Sup. 579, 103 A.2d 49 (1954).

406. Saladiner v. Polanco, 160 S.W.2d 531 (Tex. 1942).

407. U.S. v. Noble, 269 F. Supp. 814 (E.D.N.Y. 1967).

408. *Id.*, at 816.

409. Note, *Guardian ad litem in Wisconsin*, 48 Marq. L. Rev. 445, 456 (1965).

410. Hazeltine v. Johnson, 92 F.2d 866 (9th Cir. 1937) (father appointed).

411. LaSalle Extension University v. Campbell, 36 A.2d 397, 398 (N.J. 1944).

412. Allen *et al.*, note 392 above, at 90-91.

413. *Id.*, at 86-87. *See also* Jones v. Henderson, 153 So. 214 (Ala. 1934).

414. 43 C.J.S. *Infants* § 107, at 275 (1950).

415. U.S. v. Dupont, note 404 above, at 104-5.

416. Parsons v. Balson, 129 Wis. 311, 109 N.W. 136 (1906).

417. *Morris v. Glazer*, 151 A. 766 (N.J. 1930); Leonard v. Chicago Title and Trust, 287 Ill. App. 397, 5 N.E.2d 282 (1936).

418. Will of Jaeger, 218 Wis. 1, 259 N.W. 842 (1935).

419. Bartonelli v. Galoni, 331 Pa. 73 (1938).

420. Miller v. Clark, 356 P.2d 965 (Colo. 1960).

421. Allen *et al.*, note 392 above, at 89.

422. Text at note 418.

423. *See generally* D. Hinkle, *Intrafamily Litigation—Parent and Child*, 542 Insurance L.J. 133 (March, 1968).

424. 68 Miss. 703, 9 So. 885 (1891).

425. *Id.*, at 9 So. 887.

426. Hinkle, note 423 above, at 133. *See also* Note, *The Vestiges of Child-Parent Tort Immunity*, 6 U. Cal. Davis L. Rev. 195, 196 (1973) [hereinafter cited as *Vestiges* Note].

427. Note 84 above.

428. This notion carries weight in quite disparate contexts. Rev. John J. McLaughlin, in rejecting suggestions that he sue to enjoin his Jesuit superior from interfering with his work as a deputy special assistant to President Nixon, was quoted as saying, "You don't bring lawyers into a family situation." Boston Globe, May 29, 1974, at 2.

429. "By far the majority of all the cases involving intrafamily lawsuits thus far on record [by 1968] involve the use of automobiles." Hinkle, note 423 above, at 146.

430. *Vestiges* Note, note 426 above, at 196.

431. Hinkle, note 426 above, at 134.

432. *See* Hinkle, note 426 above, at 135-45.

433. *See, e.g.*, Worrell v. Worrell, 4 S.E.2d 343 (Va. 1939) (child injured while riding in commercial bus owned and operated by her father).

434. *See, e.g.*, Harlan National Bank v. Gross, 346 S.W.2d 482 (Ky. 1961).

435. *See, e.g.*, Emery v. Emery, 45 Cal. 2d 421, 289 P.2d 218 (1955).

436. *See* text above at notes 186 and 197, and the parental consent section of chapter 4.

437. Hinkle, note 426 above, at 137. Because minors are not generally accorded "standing" to sue by most court systems, the manner in which a child sues a stranger is usually by having the action brought by a "next friend," who is frequently, though not necessarily, one of his parents. *See generally* Kleinfeld I, note 88 above.

438. *See* Hinkle, note 426 above, at 136 and cases cited in n.14.

439. *See, e.g.*, Trundell v. Leatherby, 212 Cal. 678, 300 P. 7 (1931).

440. *See, e.g.*, Foley v. Foley, 61 Ill. App. 577 (1895); Cook v. Cook, 232 Mo. App. 994, 124 S.W.2d (1939).

441. *See* McCurdy, *Torts Between Persons in Domestic Relation*, 43 Harv. L. Rev. 1030 (1930); Sanford, *Personal Torts Within the Family*, 9 Vand. L. Rev. 823 (1956); Prosser, note 185 above, at 879; Belzer, *Child v. Parent: Erosion of the Immunity Rule*, 19 Hast. L.J. 201 (1967); Pate, *Parent-Child Immunity: The Case for Abolition*, 6 San Diego L. Rev. 286 (1969). "A lengthy list of critical articles is included in the dissenting opinion in Hastings v. Hastings, 33 N.J. 247, 254-55, 163 A.2d 147, 151 (1960)." *Vestiges* Note, note 426 above, at 197 n.16.

442. R. Pound, *Individual Interests in the Domestic Relations*, 14 Mich. L. Rev. 177 (1916). *See also* text at note 85 above.

443. The rule has been eliminated in Hawaii, N.H., N.J., N.Y., N.D., La., Pa., and Vt. (*Vestiges* Note, note 426 above, at 198-99) and greatly restricted in Alas., Ariz., Cal., Ill., Ky., Mich., Minn., Va., Wis., and possibly Tex. (*Id.*).

444. *Id.*, at 195. For a listing of current state rulings on children's suits against parents for support, see 13 ALR2d 1142 (1950).

445. Goller v. White, 122 N.W.2d 193, 198 (1963), cited in *Vestiges* Note, note 426 above, at 198.

446. Ill., Ky., Mich., and Minn. *Vestiges* Note, note 426 above, at 198.

447. Gibson v. Gibson, 3 Cal. 3d 914, 479 P.2d 648, 92 Cal. Rptr. 288 (1971).

448. *Id.*, at 479 P.2d 653, quoting James, *Accident Liability Reconsidered: The Impact of Liability Insurance*, 57 Yale L.J. 549, 553 (1948). One year before *Gibson*, in ruling that "parent child negligence suits will be allowed in Hawaii regardless of the presence or absence of insurance coverage." (Petersen v. City and County of Honolulu, 462 P.2d 1007, 1008 (Hawaii 1970)), the Supreme Court of Hawaii reasoned that "when a wrong has been committed, the harm to the family relationship has already occurred; and to prohibit reparations can hardly aid in restoring harmony." *Id.*, at 1009.

449. 479 P.2d at 651.

450. The Reasonable Man is always thinking of others; prudence is his guide. . . . He is one who . . . even while he flogs his child is meditating only on the golden mean. Devoid . . . of any human weakness, . . . this excellent but odious character stands like a monument in our Courts of Justice, vainly appealing to his fellow-citizens to order their lives after his own example. . . .
[I]n all that mass of authorities which bears upon this branch of the law *there is no single mention of a reasonable woman*. A.P. Herbert, Uncommon Law (1935), at 2-5 (emphasis in original).

451. 479 P.2d at 653.

452. 479 P.2d at 652.

453. *Vestiges* Note, note 426 above, at 204.

454. Dennis v. Walker, 284 F. Supp. 413 (D.D.C. 1968). *Dicta* in Emmert v. U.S., 300 F. Supp. 45 (D.D.C. 1969) suggests, however, that parental immunity may no longer be the law in D.C.

455. Barlow v. Iblings, 156 N.W.2d 105 (Iowa 1968).

456. Downs v. Poulin, 216 A.2d 29 (Maine 1966).

457. Latz v. Latz, 10 Md. App. 720, 272 A.2d 435 (1971).

458. Bahr v. Bahr, 478 S.W.2d 400 (Mo. 1972).

459. Nahas v. Noble, 77 N.M. 139, 420 P.2d 127 (1966).

460. Skinner v. Whitley, 281 N.C. 476, 189 S.E.2d 230 (1972).

461. Workman v. Workman, 498 P.2d 1384 (Okla. 1972).

462. Campbell v. Gruttemeyer, 222 Tenn. 133, 432 S.W.2d 894 (1968).

463. *Vestiges* Note, note 426 above, at 204-5 (some citations omitted).

3 Psychological and Psychiatric Issues

In this chapter, we shall discuss briefly a number of issues in adolescent psychology, then explore in considerably greater depth several current issues in mental health science, and conclude with a detailed consideration of the issues of diagnosis, prognosis and treatment as they relate to adolescents. Before beginning, however, a few general words are in order. In terms of the depth of their understanding and the sophistication of their methods, the behavioral sciences are infant sciences. Further, there is good reason to believe that adolescent behavior is especially refractory to adequate study. One reviewer, commenting on a spate of recent books on adolescent psychopathology,[1] has offered the following observation:

One takes on the chore of reviewing four books on adolescent psychiatry in the hope of learning what new ideas, if any, have emerged from the close clinical study of the afflicted young. Four books: a text, a research study, and two collections (one psychoanalytic, one eclectic-psychiatric)—enough variety, surely, to obtain some sense of where the field is now and where it may be heading. Alas, if these books are a fair sampling, then both the present and the visible future are disappointing, if not altogether lugubrious. We find an absence of useful new ideas, a clinging to old ideas which have worn badly, a rather total innocence about developmental psychology, and in general little evidence of the quality of thought we take for granted in other areas of clinical psychology and psychiatry.

These remarks about adolescent psychology are unfortunately too true. Few questions can be answered definitively. In most cases, legal analysts must rely on weak and, too often, unreplicated research. All one can do is raise the appropriate questions.

Issues in Adolescent Psychology

This section will present an overview of some of the relevant issues in "normal" adolescent psychology. We shall deal with the definition of adolescence, the tasks of adolescence, cognitive development, the uniqueness of adolescence as a stage of life, and the conflict between generations.

This chapter was contributed by Stephen J. Morse, J.D., Ph.D., Associate Professor of Law and Psychiatry, University of Southern California Law Center.

81

Adolescence fascinates theoreticians and researchers. Numerous theories have been posited to account for the social, sexual, and cognitive development of the adolescent.[2] Many of these theories have not been subjected to rigorous analysis and empirical test. Cultural bias, personal preferences and values, and even pure romanticism have infected theorists' objectivity. Today, however, there is increasing emphasis on sophisticated empirical research rather than on theoretical speculation; theory still fuels research, but more as a guide and less as a final statement of empirical reality. Until these empirical techniques yield "answers" to long-standing questions about adolescent psychology, we must be humble about how much is really known.

The Definition of Adolescence

The adolescent literature contains many different definitions of adolescence which reflect the vantage point of the definer—psychological, physiological, legal, etc. All the definitions seem to reflect, however, the common-sense observation that in the preteen or early teen years children experience a leap in physical maturation, interrupting the generally orderly progression of the preceding years ("latency"). As discussed in chapter 2, sexual maturation is accompanied by what is usually referred to as a "growth spurt" in height and weight, with an accompanying increase in physical strength. There is great variability in the order of these developments in different individuals, but all aspects of the changes, from height spurt to fertility, occur somewhat earlier on the average for females than for males (although the curves do overlap).

Some writers define the onset of adolescence according to the appearance of certain physical indicators of these changes,[3] while others prefer a more psychological approach, emphasizing the ". . . youngster's initial psychological reaction to his pubescent physical changes."[4] A variable definition would be unworkable for legal purposes, and our selection of age twelve as the onset comports well with both physiological and psychological data.

If the onset of adolescence is hard to define, the definition of its termination is even more difficult. Physical changes are completed long before the end of psychosocial adolescence, which is quite variable. The nineteen-year-old college sophomore engaging in "streaking" is in a quite different psycho-social position from the nineteen-year-old worker who has been employed for three years and who is supporting a growing family with two children.

The termination criterion must be psychosocial, but finding a generally acceptable one is difficult. Most psychological or psychosocial definitions seem to focus on some variant of Erikson's notion of the resolution of the "identity crisis," an event which usually occurs somewhere between the late teens and the age of thirty in our culture. Recent studies on the psychology of adulthood, however, demonstrate that continuing identity crises and their "resolutions" may not be uncommon throughout adulthood.[5] Therefore, the termination of adolescence perhaps should be defined as the resolution of the "first identity crisis." In our society, considering all classes and subcultures of society, twenty-one is arguably the mean age at which the first identity crisis is resolved (it is probably somewhat earlier in the working classes, and somewhat later in those classes in which higher education is the norm). However, as discussed in chapter 2, eighteen is (for most purposes in most states) the age at which the legal encumbrances and benefits of childhood are removed.[6] For that reason, eighteen will be considered the end of adolescence.

The Psychological Tasks of Adolescence

The normal psychological tasks of adolescence are, as might be expected, defined variously by different authors, depending upon their theoretical preconceptions and notions of normality. Despite their divergences, most posit four essential types of developmental tasks undertaken by all adolescents. To avoid some of the question begging about what is a "successful" or "normal" resolution of adolescence, these shall be stated as processes rather than as outcomes. First, the adolescent attains some degree of independence from his family; he becomes "his or her own person." Second, the adolescent adopts a sexual orientation, including his final sexual identification and preferences. Third, the adolescent develops the interpersonal style (including intimacy levels) that he prefers. Fourth, the adolescent finds some type of work that he or she is willing to pursue.[7]

Identity seems to be a broad formulation of the resolutions of these four tasks, and since the publication of Erik Erikson's epochal work *Childhood and Society*,[8] the concept of identity has been crucial in theoretical and empirical discussions of the psychology of adolescence.[9] The stage of identity is the fifth in Erikson's theory, and it is mostly coterminous with adolescence. In 1968 he described the psychological tasks of the adolescent as follows:[10]

Thus in later school years young people, beset with the physiological revolution of their genital maturation and the uncertainty of adult roles ahead, seem much concerned with faddist attempts at establishing an adolescent subculture with what looks like a final rather than a transitory or, in fact, initial identity formulation. They are sometimes morbidly, often curiously, preoccupied with what they appear to be in the eyes of others as compared with what they feel they are, and with the question of how to connect the roles and skills cultivated earlier with the ideal prototypes of the day. In their search for a new sense of continuity and sameness, which must now include sexual maturity, some adolescents have to come to grips again with crises of earlier years before they can install lasting idols and ideals as guardians of a final identity. They need, above all, a moratorium for the integration of the identity elements ascribed ... to the childhood stages: only that now a larger unit, vague in its outline and yet immediate in its demand, replaces the childhood milieu—"society."

In an earlier work,[11] Erikson offered the following definition of identity resolution:

The integration now taking place in the form of ego identity is . . . more than the sum of the childhood identifications. It is the accrued experience of the ego's ability to integrate all identifications with the vicissitudes of the libido, with the aptitudes developed out of endowment, and with the opportunities offered in social roles. The sense of ego identity, then, is the accrued confidence that the inner sameness and continuity prepared in the past are matched by the sameness and continuity of one's meaning for others, as evidenced in the tangible promise of a "career."

According to Erikson, adolescence is a period of "psychosocial moratorium," a time of delay prior to the commitments and choices of adulthood. It is a time when ". . . the young adult through free role experimentation may find a niche in some section of his society, a niche which is firmly defined and yet seems to be uniquely made for him."[12] Put briefly, adolescence is the time when the young person finds out, "Who am I and where do I fit in?" These tasks of adolescent development are obviously broad, and a broad continuum of final results is clearly possible. Nevertheless, however defined, these tasks and their resolution are crucial to a person's life.

Cognitive Development in Adolescence

A discussion of the rights of adolescents should be based to some extent on the degree to which adolescents are capable of making decisions for themselves. Because most discussion of cognition is addressed to formal capacities and capabilities, at the outset it is important to distinguish between intelligence and the capacity for certain types of formal reasoning on the one hand, and wisdom on the other. There must be some relationship between the first two variables and wisdom, but the nature and strength of the relationship are unknown, and perhaps can never be defined. (What is wisdom? and who decides?) Despite these difficulties, we do believe that to make a minimally competent decision, one ought to be minimally capable of thinking reflectively, of being aware of and considering alternative courses of action. An assessment of the choice made may largely fall under the rubric of wisdom, but the minimal capacity to reason probably depends more on cognitive capacity and intelligence. At what age, then, do human beings become minimally capable of the kind of reflective reasoning and assessment described above?

As mentioned in chapter 2,[13] the research of Jean Piaget and his associates has demonstrated that at adolescence there is a major shift in cognitive capacity, leading to the ability to use hypothetico-deductive and reflective reasoning. That is, at adolescence the person becomes capable of the type of formal thinking and reasoning that supposedly marks adulthood.[14] Further, I.Q. at adolescence tends to remain stable and to predict very accurately adult I.Q. Bayley[15] found that the correlation between adolescent and adult I.Q.s was about +.80. Naturally there are individual differences in cognitive growth and in I.Q. development and consistency, but for purposes of law, which must focus on the average person, both "final" or adult cognitive capability and adult I.Q. are achieved in adolescence. Although data reported by Kohlberg and Gilligan[16] demonstrates "... that a large proportion of Americans never develop the capacity for abstract thought," they also note that, "Most who do, develop it in earlier adolescence...."[17] In sum, most persons who are capable of "higher" modes of thinking achieve this capability in early adolescence. Others do not achieve it in later adolescence or thereafter.

Is Adolescence a Unique Stage?

The study of adolescence has yielded conflicting views about whether it is a unique period in the life cycle or whether it represents an orderly transitional stage between childhood and adulthood.[18] Most theorists agree that adolescence is somewhat unique, but the conclusions drawn depend on how one views the data. Given the considerable disagreement on the particulars of adolescent development, a rehashing of various authors' theoretical views would not be useful.

Research evidence[19] demonstrates that although many childhood behavioral patterns are "moderately" good predictors of adult patterns (for example, dependence on family, social anxiety), many other childhood behavior patterns are not. There may be continuities and consistencies from childhood to adulthood, but adolescence does not necessarily proceed smoothly to a predictable result. Conger's assessment of the issue[20] is perhaps one of the most balanced:

... although most theorists do not deny the existence of significant continuities, they have been impressed with what they perceive as crucial changes during puberty and the years immediately thereafter. These changes can be viewed quantitatively in terms of an accelerated rate of change, and qualitatively in terms of personality organization and defense mechanisms; the emergence of new needs, motives, capabilities, and concerns; and new developmental tasks that must be confronted. For such theorists, the concept of adolescence as a stage of development is considered useful because it serves to focus attention on the importance of these perceived changes. The "nature" of the postulated stage, however, varies from one theorist to another, depending on what each considers to be the essential aspects of this developmental period.

As we have noted, the adolescent era is marked by rapid physiological and cognitive changes, accompanied by complex responses to these changes. Consideration of the importance of the tasks of adolescence and common-sense observation leads to the conclusion that adolescence is often marked by unique psychological dislocation or conflict that is both quantitatively and qualitatively different from adulthood and childhood.

The "Generation Gap"

The uniqueness of adolescence as a stage of life is characterized by, and contributes to, substantial conflict between adolescents and adults, especially the parental generation. Despite the alleged current quiescence of adolescents, it is still felt, as it has always been, that this conflict exists. Adults and adolescents supposedly do not understand one another.

Let us look at the empirical evidence concerning this phenomenon. According to recent national surveys and limited studies, one in four adolescents felt there was a large gap, and seven out of ten parents felt that there was a gap but that it was exaggerated.[21] Conger states that 57 percent of the adolescents surveyed said that they "got along fine" with parents, that one in three adolescents were fond of their parents but had communication difficulties, and that only 4 percent did not enjoy spending time with their parents.[22] Further, Conger reports that there is widespread intergenerational agreement on variables such as respect for traditional values. Most adolescents feel that their parents approve of their *own* adolescents' values and ideals, but not those of the adolescent generation.[23] From this and other evidence, Conger concludes that, ". . . there *is* a generation gap between the average parent of today and his adolescent young, but that it is neither as wide nor as totally new as we have been led to believe, nor is it qualitatively very similar to popular stereotypes."[24]

One may fairly interpret Conger's data differently, however. Given the immense number of adolescents today, the 25 percent who feel that there is a large gap comprise an extremely large number of persons, especially if one also considers the 33 percent with communication difficulties and the 43 percent who do not "get along fine" with parents (it is not clear to what extent the latter two groups overlap with the 25 percent). Depending on one's viewpoint, these figures could be seen as evidence of either a large or a small gap.

A more qualitative critique produces similar unease with Conger's conclusions. Because both generations agree on a majority of traditional values does not mean that intense conflict is nonexistent. Even if values are shared, there may be intense conflict as the adolescent strives to be autonomous, often by behaving in ways disapproved of by his or her parents. Parents may unconsciously feel highly ambivalent about the emerging autonomy and sexuality of their adolescent children.[25] Further, blaming the adolescent generation but not one's own adolescent seems open to the interpretation that parents defensively displace onto others their anger at *their own* adolescent. Finally, one wonders if survey data, aimed at a cognitive level of experience, is the best source of information concerning issues (parent-adolescent relations) which are so emotionally charged for both generations.

Conger admits that[26]

... there are important differences between generations in their attitudes toward sex, education, war, foreign policy, social justice, religion, the use of drugs, and social and political activism as well as in such obvious areas as personal tastes in dress, music, art and social customs.

Conger feels that these differences have been exaggerated. It is undeniable, however, that they encompass an extremely broad spectrum of very important issues.

Conger is right in noting that the generation gap is not new; it can be found in Plato, Augustine, Rousseau and writers throughout the ages. But this assertion cuts two ways. It certainly does argue for the uniqueness of the adolescent period, even as it undercuts claims that the current situation is unusual. Whether there is a generation gap is a matter of how one interprets the figures. But no matter how one interprets the evidence, a great deal of conflict, even if not a total gap, exists between adolescents and adults. Adolescence tends to be a trying time for adolescents and their families.

Current Issues in Mental Health Science[27]

The state of mental health science, including mental health services, has long been a matter of concern and has been disputed with heightened intensity during the past two decades.[28] The nature of the debate and its intensity are well-known to all mental health professionals and to experts on the mental health legal system. The debate need not be recreated and cannot be resolved here. We shall simply present the major conceptual issues involved and then turn to an analysis of the practical problems of providing mental health services and administering the mental health legal system.

Mental Disorder and Normality

The fundamental conceptual dispute in mental health science is whether and to what degree the concept of mental illness or mental disorder has theoretical or practical usefulness. Since the publication of Szasz's *The Myth of Mental Illness,*[29] this question has been constantly debated in the literature, and the debate shows no signs of abating. As evidence of the continuing vitality of the issue, one need only observe the furor created by Rosenhan's 1973 study, "Being Sane in Insane Places."[30]

Much of the debate has been obscured by imprecise definition of what is meant by the "mental illness" model. There are many definitions of an illness or medical model (including those which hold that the behavior of the person in question "authorizes" medical intervention), but most refer to the hypothesis that disordered behavior (the term "behavior," as used herein, includes thoughts and feelings as well as actions) is caused by an underlying physical abnormality or by an underlying psychological abnormality that is analogized to physical abnormality. This version of the illness model clearly provides the rationale for the special legal rules that apply to mentally disordered persons. It is argued that special rules should be applied to mentally disordered persons because their disordered behavior is the product of an underlying disease, and therefore, unlike normal persons, the "crazy"[31] actor cannot control his behavior (including his reason) and is not responsible for it.

At present, there is insufficient conclusive data to determine whether crazy behavior is caused by an "underlying" disorder of any type. All that experts can agree upon is that some people, by reasonable standards, behave crazily for some period of time and for inexplicable reasons. Researchers and clinicians have adopted many models with which to understand and study disordered behavior.[32] Biological, psychological, sociological and moral models all have adherents, but no adequate, scientifically conclusive explanation of crazy behavior can yet be given. Almost certainly, variables from all levels of explanation contribute to the causation of all behavior, crazy and sane alike. But we do not know why some persons behave inexplicably crazily, and we do not know whether or to what extent such persons are capable of controlling their behavior. Indeed, if there is a demonstrable physical pathology that seems to produce crazy behavior, the actor is rarely considered to be suffering from a mental disorder. Rather, the person is considered to be suffering primarily from a physical disorder with behavioral correlates.

Although many of the models are suggestive, there is little indication that any one model is the most useful for understanding crazy behavior. All that is known is that some people are so crazy that everyone, laypersons and experts alike, can identify such persons and agree that they are not "normal." Clearly crazy persons are often extremely disorganized, suffering terribly, and incapable of managing their lives with even minimal "success," and there does seem to be a small, readily identifiable class of such persons in all cultures.[33]

The number of persons who may be labeled mentally ill or mentally disordered according to current diagnostic categories is much larger than the number of persons who are clearly crazy. Because there is no underlying, independent criterion other than behavior with which to determine whether an actor is mentally disordered, it is extremely hard to answer the question, "What is normal behavior?" in those cases where everyone would *not* agree that the actor is crazy. Evaluation of behavior tends to be more relative and culture- and value-bound than evaluation of biological structures and processes. Further, biology is generally easier to measure reliably than behavior. Even when everyone agrees that an actor is crazy, the conclusion of craziness is to some extent a matter of our cultural values.

When the person in question is not *clearly* crazy, then the determination of abnormality becomes a matter not only of general cultural agreement, but also of the values, preferences and tolerances of the persons making the determination.[34] This is not surprising, because it is nearly impossible to assess behavior without having culture-bound ethical, political and social concerns influence the determination. Persons who may seem disordered to some observers but who are not clearly crazy may not, by some reasonable standards, be abnormally disorganized and suffering, and they may conduct their lives "successfully." Except in extreme cases, there is no agreed-upon culture- free and validated standard of normality with which particular behavior may be compared to determine if it is abnormal.

The most objective meaning of behavioral normality possible at present would be a statistical evaluation. Using operational standards, behavioral sci- entists could determine how frequently particular behaviors occur in society. In common-sense terms, less frequent behavior is more abnormal; but, for legal purposes, the point at which society draws the line of "normality" on the distribution curve would be a moral, political, and legal determination. For example, some abnormal behavior, such as extremely high intelligence, is positively valued in our society, whereas other abnormal behavior, such as extremely low intelligence, is negatively valued. Thus, even if a "scientific" standard of normality were used, the decision of where to draw the cutoff points would not be a value-free, empirically determined decision. It would, again, depend on the social values and preferences of those drawing the lines and, in a society as heterogeneous as ours, there is little likelihood of general agreement.

In sum, there is great uncertainty and confusion about the answers to the two related underlying conceptual questions in mental health science: "What is mental disorder?" and "What is normal behavior?" This uncertainty and confusion should not prevent us from trying to formulate policies for dealing with crazy behavior. It exists, and special rules to deal with it may be necessary. If we maintain such rules, however, we should be quite candid about the incertitude of their supporting rationales.

The Practical Skills of Mental Health Scientists and Clinicians

Even if a legislature or court were convinced that the conceptual underpinnings of mental health science are sound enough to authorize in the abstract special treatment of crazy persons, we must still ask whether and to what extent the practical skills of the scientists and clinicians make such treatment feasible. To explore this issue we must ask how expert are the experts in diagnosing, prognosing and treating mental disorder. More precisely, the questions are, first, to what extent can experts reliably identify crazy behavior? second, to what extent can experts reliably predict the legally relevant future behavior of persons identified as crazy? and third, how effectively can experts change crazy behavior (compared to a control condition of no treatment)? Because the mental health legal system relies so heavily on experts, we must also note the related question of whether experts are more skillful than laypersons in identifying, predicting and changing crazy behavior. The viability and procedures of the mental health legal system rest on the answers to all these questions.

Legal policy makers recognize that no scheme of rules and procedures is perfect, but they try to devise schemes that realize the fairest and most efficient balance of interests. Even if there are some mentally disordered persons for whom special legal treatment is warranted, unless the system devised to administer that treatment is capable of working fairly and effectively, the scheme should not be instituted. If mental health professionals cannot skillfully diagnose, prognose, and treat most mental disorders, then legal rules premised on the effective practice of those skills cannot be justified. Restrictive practices may be justified for truly crazy persons, but in these cases lay judgment is as accurate as a professional opinion to trigger legal action.

Diagnosis in General

If the just application of special legal rules depends on the reliable identification of a person as suffering from a particular mental disorder or class of disorders, then such rules are warranted only if such reliable identification is possible. Technically, the term "reliability" refers to "the consistency or stability that is possible in terms of observing a given fact. Reliability means that given the same circumstances the observer who perceives the fact will perceive it again, and given the same set of circumstances other observers will perceive the same fact."[35] Thus, a key test of the reliability of identification is "inter-rater reliability," the level of agreement on diagnosis achieved by two professional raters who independently diagnose a sample of prospective patients.

It is now considered crucial in studies of diagnostic reliability that the researcher control for the "base-rate" of diagnosis of specific diagnoses by the clinicians in question.[36] For instance, if two raters each independently diagnose schizophrenia in 80 percent of *any* population of prospective patients, then in a specific study these raters are likely to agree *by chance* on a diagnosis of schizophrenia in 64 percent of cases. Thus, the true level of reliability refers to how much better than chance their agreement is.

Let us review the evidence concerning diagnostic reliability, assuming at first that the clinical conditions or entities being diagnosed—the disorders—exist in empirical reality. Most studies of diagnostic reliability have examined inter-rater reliability. Unfortunately, many were methodologically unsound, and, until very recently, did not control for base rates of the raters. Recently, however, two experts on diagnosis have examined the leading reliability studies whose raw data is available and appropriate and have reanalyzed the data using a reliability formula (kappa) that controls for base rates.[37] Their findings, which agree substantially with those of other reviewers,[38] demonstrate that the diagnosis of those mental disorders or classes of disorder that account for most legally relevant behavior (that is, psychosis, psychotic affective disorders, and sociopathic personality disorder) at best achieve a reliability level of about 0.5. For the broadest category, psychosis, which should be the most reliably diagnosed, the reliability coefficient is only about 0.55.[39]

This is extremely low reliability for purposes of making social judgments with potentially serious consequences.

In contrast to the standards in basic research in many applied settings a reliability of .80 is not nearly high enough. In basic research, the concern is with the size of correlations and with the differences in means for different experimental treatments, for which purposes a reliability of .80 for the different measures involved is adequate. In many applied problems, a great deal hinges on the exact score made by a person on a test. If, for example, in a particular school system children with IQs below 70 are placed in special classes, it makes a great deal of difference whether the child has an IQ of 69 or 70 on a particular test. . . . Even with a reliability of .90, the standard error of measurement is almost one-third as large as the standard deviation of test scores. In those applied settings where important decisions are made with respect to specific test scores, a reliability of .90 is the minimum that should be tolerated, and a reliability of .95 should be considered the desirable standard.[40]

In sum, if special rules are to be applied to some crazy persons (mostly those persons diagnosed as psychotic), reliable identification of proper persons for such treatment is not possible in most cases. Although considerably higher reliability certainly will be achieved in cases of utterly clear craziness,[41] no expert is needed to make the determination in these cases; they are few in number, and they are rarely problematic for the mental health legal system.

Whether these figures are encouraging or discouraging depends upon one's scientific and social expectations and preferences, but many mental health experts concerned with diagnosis find these figures discouraging.[42] A number of reasons for the lack of higher reliability have been put forth, including differing orientation and training of professionals, differing contexts in which diagnosis occurs, class and culture backgrounds of professional and patient, personal bias of the professional and, most fundamentally, the ambiguity and inadequacies of present diagnostic systems and psychiatric data in general.[43] In short, human behavior is extremely ambiguous and value-laden, and thus very difficult to classify reliably.

At present, many experts are attempting to formulate diagnostic schemes and rating scales which use explicit observable variables and specific inclusion and exclusion criteria to classify behavior.[44] It is believed that the reliability of classification can be increased by using such observable, "operationalized" criteria and by basing classification on quantitative empirical studies as well as clinical qualitative studies. For instance, the American Psychiatric Association is currently testing a provisional draft for the *Diagnostic and Statistical Manual III* that is based on firmer scientific evidence than was *DSM-II*.[45] These efforts may soon provide a somewhat more reliable diagnostic system than the present one.[46]

We should not be surprised by the findings on diagnostic reliability, because there is substantial evidence that, contra to our earlier assumption for purposes of the discussion, evidence for the validity of the conditions or clusters of behavior (the disorders) being diagnosed is quite weak. Technically "validity" refers to the "relationship of one fact or variable to another. It is a term for determining what a fact means, what conclusions can be drawn from it. . . . It is entirely possible for there to be a perfectly reliable phenomenon which, however, is not related to anything else. It would, then, be reliable but would have no validity."[47]

In terms of our discussion, the lack of validity means that the objective existence of discrete, homogeneous and exclusive disorders is still unproven. Present diagnoses do not seem to describe clinical entities that exist in reality. Invalid diagnoses convey little information about the symptoms, etiology, prognosis or appropriate treatment of the alleged disorders. For instance, no present diagnosis tells us very specifically or accurately how the person is now behaving or how he will behave in the future.[48] Indeed, some writers claim that there is no valid measure of psychological disorder.[49] As diagnoses become more precise, however, there will certainly be an increase in some forms of validity.[50]

In addition to problems with the reliability and validity of psychiatric diagnosis, there is substantial evidence that diagnosis may have damaging iatrogenic effects.[51] Sociological "labeling" theory argues that deviant careers, including psychiatric patienthood, are often initiated and maintained by formal labeling of the actor. It holds, in other words, that deviance is in large part produced by societal reaction to the actor rather than by any quality inherent in him or her.[52] Expectancies and self-fulfilling prophecies combine to increase the probability that, once labeled, a person will have trouble shedding that label and role.[53] Although many researchers strongly dispute the conclusions of the labeling theorists,[54] there is sufficient, albeit inconclusive, evidence of the damaging effects of labeling to occasion caution before officially and authoritatively affixing a label of deviance to an individual.[55]

One concluding caveat is in order. Because the validity of studies of prognosis and treatment depends upon reliable diagnosis of the subjects, the conclusions to be drawn from prognosis and treatment studies must be evaluated in the light of the data on diagnostic reliability. When assessing prognosis and treatment, we shall not always reiterate this fundamental point, but it should be borne in mind in reading the following sections.

To summarize, we may note that there is some behavior that is clearly crazy, but there is substantial doubt about the validity of the disorders now defined by mental health professionals. Further, and most importantly for assessing the justice and efficiency of the mental health legal system, the most legally relevant diagnostic categories achieve very low diagnostic reliability coefficients. Finally, inaccurate diagnosis may have pernicious effects. How legal policy makers will choose to react to these findings is a matter of the balancing of various social, legal and moral interests. But the balancing should weigh the reliability and validity of diagnoses as they are, and not as we hope they might be.

Diagnosis and Psychopathology of Adolescents

As was noted in the general introduction of this chapter, adolescent mental health science suffers from all the difficulties of mental health science in general, as well as from some unique problems. For various reasons, less rigorous research is frequently done on child and adolescent psychopathology than on adults. Thus, less hard evidence is available to policy makers. Even more than adult mental health science, adolescent mental health science is more an art than a science.[56] Also, it should be remembered that all studies on the epidemiology, prognosis and treatment of adolescent psychopathology rely on diagnosis. Recall our caveat that, to the extent that diagnosis is unreliable, the validity of the results of those studies is in very considerable doubt.

Adolescent psychiatry, unlike adult psychiatry, has never accepted a common classification scheme.[57] In addition, current diagnostic practice is in flux because professionals are especially sensitive to labeling and expectancy effects when they deal with children and adolescents. As a result, it is believed that adolescent psychiatrists are more inclined to assign "benign" diagnostic labels, such as "situational disorder," when other diagnoses may be warranted.[58] Further, research has revealed only one modern study of the reliability of psychiatric diagnosis in adolescence,[59] and that study, although interesting, is flawed for so many reasons (for example, it relies on written case studies, not patients; it does not control for base-rates; it uses a system of diagnosis that is less complex than those used in actual practice) that few, if any, conclusions can be drawn from it.

Given the weaknesses of psychiatric diagnosis in general, coupled with the problems in adolescent diagnosis and adolescent psychiatry in general, it is fair to conclude that adolescent diagnosis is probably considerably less reliable than adult diagnosis. As we have seen, reliability coefficients for adult diagnoses rarely exceed 0.50; for adolescents, if proper studies are performed, we must expect considerably lower coefficients.

An important issue bearing on the reliability and validity of diagnoses of adolescent psychopathology is the degree to which "turmoil" is normative or normal in adolescence. Let us examine, therefore, the extent of such turmoil, whether it can be considered normal, and whether it can be distinguished from true pathology.

Many professionals associated mainly with the psychoanalytic school hold that the instinctual dislocations and the reawakened and exacerbated conflicts of puberty make adolescence such a stressful period that it is normatively and normally marked by psychopathological manifestations.[60] This view is usually held by clinicians. On the other hand, most social scientists who have studied large samples of adolescents, using interviews, questionnaires and, sometimes, psychological tests, have come to the opposite conclusion—that is, for the normative and normal adolescent the period is fairly smooth, except for some bickering with parents over minor matters in early adolescence.[61] Other researchers conclude that adolescent turmoil is not as universal as some hold, but that significant numbers of young adolescents do experience inner feelings of turmoil.[62] Muuss, a leading expert on adolescence, concludes that[63]

The hypothesis of a universal period of storm and stress is no longer tenable, and . . . one can no longer accept the storm-and-stress concept as applicable to even the majority of adolescents in our society.

Even if adolescent turmoil is not universal, however, a significant amount of it does exist. Just before reaching the conclusion noted above, Muuss notes that, "[t]he disposition to emotional and social difficulties during this period is substantially greater than during other developmental periods."[64] We have seen in our discussion of "normal" adolescence that it is, to some degree, a unique developmental stage during which there is a great deal of stress and conflict, and thus it follows that there is some evidence for significant turmoil in substantial numbers of adolescents.[65] But is all turmoil (or emotional and social difficulty), to the extent it exists, necessarily pathological? And, if all turmoil is not pathological, how can it be differentiated from pathology?[66]

Many writers claim that most serious turmoil is pathological and that normality (which includes minor, normal turmoil) can be distinguished from pathology by careful clinical investigation, even if differential diagnosis among related disorders in adolescence is difficult.[67] These claims are open to two serious objections, however. First, the writers beg the question of what is normal behavior. In the most recent and comprehensive study addressing this issue, Weiner and Del Gaudio seem to define "true" psychopathology (as opposed to "normal" behavior or "normal" turmoil) as any symptom greater than "fleeting episodes of anxiety or depression."[68] According to the leading epidemiological studies,[69] however, this threshold standard is so low that nearly everyone of any age would be diagnosed as suffering from a disorder. But Weiner and Del Gaudio claim that most adolescents do *not* suffer from psychiatric disorders. It appears, therefore, that either Weiner and Del Gaudio have chosen an inadequate threshold indicator of true psychopathology or their conclusion that most adolescents are not suffering from psychopathology is wrong, because many of the studies do show that most adolescents are "symptomatic."[70] If so, one is hard pressed to understand what normality is, or how "normal symptoms" (a contradiction in terms?) can be distinguished from "abnormal symptoms" (a redundancy?).

A second objection is that the claim that adolescent psychopathology can be distinguished from normal behavior and normal or minor turmoil is based upon studies which are exceedingly flawed. For example, those who claim that normal adolescent turmoil can be clearly distinguished from psychiatric disorder in adolescence universally cite a series of studies conducted in New York City by Masterson and his associates.[71] These studies suffer from methodological weaknesses in the criteria used for selection of subjects for the experimental and control groups, in the nonindependence of raters, in the use of differing assessment methods for experimental and control groups, in value-laden variables of assessment, and in the use of some functions as both independent and dependent variables. Further, the researchers recognized that it is possible to function well ". . . at the cost of, rather than through the expression of their [the adolescents'] inner emotional needs,"[72] so impairment was redefined in terms of *underlying* conflicts, which cannot be measured reliably, rather than in terms of observable behavior. There are other flaws in this well-meaning and interesting group of studies, but those mentioned are enough to demonstrate that almost no conclusions may be drawn from them.

Given the conceptual difficulties in defining normality and the weaknesses of psychiatric diagnosis in general and adolescent diagnosis in particular, it is fair to conclude that it has not been demonstrated that all turmoil is pathological and that normality can be reliably distinguished from true pathology in any except extreme, clear cases. Some serious turmoil is certainly pathological, but it is by no means clear that all is,[73] and it is not clear that experts can distinguish the truly pathological adolescents from those experiencing disturbing but benign turmoil. Finally, the claim that turmoil is not normal is based, in part, on the theory that adolescents who suffer from abnormal turmoil tend to be psychiatrically disabled as adults. We shall examine in detail this theory in our section on adolescent prognosis.

Turning now to prevalence studies of psychiatric disorders in adolescence, we find that few such studies exist.[74] Moreover, because of diagnostic reliability problems and because those studies use differing definitions of disorder and are carried out in different locations, the results vary widely, and it is very hard to reach any firm conclusions about either the prevalence or the forms of adolescent disorder.[75] Using conservative figures from various school surveys, the Joint Commission on the Mental Health of Children estimated in 1969 that among the 95 million persons under twenty-five years of age, (1) 0.6 percent are psychotic; (2) 2 to 3 percent suffer from severe mental disorders and need immediate psychiatric care; (3) an additional 8 to 10 percent are emotionally disturbed and require some form of intervention.[76] The overall rate, from 10 to 15 percent, agrees with figures from various other studies.[77] It is difficult to interpret these figures, but 10 percent is probably a fair estimate of the number of adolescents whose behavior raises threshold questions of mental disorder; the number whose behavior raises questions of true "craziness" is certainly smaller. But two conclusions do seem reasonable: adolescents suffer from more disorder than children and from less disorder than adults.[78]

Reliable figures on differential diagnosis are more difficult to obtain than figures on the extent of any form of disorder. A recent, comprehensive epidemiological study of Monroe County, New York, furnishes the best, albeit shaky, estimates.[79] A few of the more noteworthy findings of that study merit discussion here. One is that, of adolescent patients *who received psychiatric services,* the more benign diagnoses (personality disorder, situational disorder) account for approximately 58 percent of the cases, whereas the most malignant diagnoses (schizophrenia, suicide attempt, organic brain syndrome) account for approximately 14 percent. The percentage of the latter group that are "clearly crazy by any reasonable standard" would, of course, be much smaller than 14 percent. Serious affective disorder is largely absent.[80] A final observation is that, as with adults,[81] the most serious disorders may be considerably more prevalent in the lower socioeconomic classes.[82]

Let us now examine the degree to which various forms of adolescent "problem" behavior, such as delinquency, promiscuity, drug use and school problems, are related to psychopathology. These forms of behavior, often generically labeled "acting out," are nearly always considered symptoms of psychopathology or psychopathological per se when they are exhibited by adolescents. We shall refer generally to these types of behavior as *misbehavior.* Two questions must be distinguished, however: (1) are these behaviors pathological per se or (2) are they signs or symptoms of underlying psychopathology? Both of these questions are related to the primary conceptual issue of all mental health science, the difficulty in defining mental disorder and normal behavior. Because the adolescent behaviors under consideration are common and often raise questions of psychopathology, let us examine the above questions somewhat carefully.

To begin with, there is no scientific agreement concerning how much misbehavior must be demonstrated to raise the threshold question of psychopathology. Is minor shoplifting enough, or must the adolescent commit a more serious criminal offense? Is any premarital sexual activity enough, or must the adolescent engage in a constant series of encounters without personal commitment? Is experimenting with marijuana enough, or must the adolescent habitually use marijuana or more powerful and dangerous substances? Is occasional truancy or poor school performance enough, or must the adolescent be habitually truant or underperforming? Where does one draw the line of pathology on these continua? When is the behavior a "symptom"? There is no consistent "scientific" answer to these questions. Different parents and different mental health professionals will reach different conclusions, depending on their scientific, political, ethical and social preferences and values.[83]

The lack of agreement in the answers to the above questions points out the difficulty in labeling misbehavior "pathological." To state that all misbehavior is disease is philosophically untenable,[84] unless the disease analogy is simply another way of saying that these are deviant behaviors which ought to authorize some form of intervention. We might then choose to label these behaviors pathological so we can treat them medically or quasi-medically. Indeed, as many commentators have noted (foremost among them, Szasz[85]), our society has continuously expanded the definition of deviant behavior as pathological because of an ideological commitment to an illness-treatment model of such behavior.[86] (It should be noted, however, that the pendulum is swinging back towards a "moral model" for understanding and dealing with criminal and delinquent behavior.)[87] However, unless it can be demonstrated that the disease model is more appropriate because misbehavior is the product of some form of underlying physical or psychological abnormality, deviant behavior might be labeled "immoral" as easily as "pathological."

There is, of course, some correlational evidence linking biological factors to delinquent and criminal behavior, but there is no persuasive evidence that biological abnormality is a necessary and sufficient cause of most misbehavior.[88] In general, criminal behavior is not linked to psychiatric disorder (except certain character disorders: sociopathy, alcoholism and drug dependence),[89] and thus is not marked by craziness and arguably is not usefully conceptualized as illness. Some adolescents who misbehave show independent evidence of being inexplicably crazy, but these cases are few, and even more rarely is it obvious that the craziness is causally related to the misbehavior (for example, an adolescent who shoplifts because voices told him to do it). In sum, there is no scientific reason to believe that most misbehavior is related to psychopathology.

Labeling and expectancy effects are additional, important factors in assessing psychiatric diagnosis in adolescents. We have already seen that the literature on labeling is in conflict,[90] but there is sufficient evidence of the pernicious effects of labeling to encourage caution in applying labels. Although much of the labeling research has studied psychiatric labeling,[91] these studies do not focus on adolescence. Labeling literature which is concerned with adolescents, especially the fostering of delinquent careers,[92] presents results similar to those for adult mental patients.

It is reasonable to conclude that psychiatric labeling affects adolescents as much as adults. Indeed, we might hypothesize that adolescents are more severely affected than adults by labeling, because they have less power and fewer social resources with which to combat a label. And the mental illness label implies that the actor has little if any control over his deviant behavior. Labeling misbehavior as "bad" or "delinquent" connotes that the adolescent has done wrong but that he or she could have chosen to do right and may do so in the future. Labeling the misbehavior "illness" implies that the adolescent was not responsible and will not be responsible until he or she is "cured." We can only speculate about the differential effects of those opposite self-perceptions upon the future course of an individual's life.

Let us sum up the evidence on adolescent psychiatric diagnosis and pathology. First, diagnosis is likely to be highly unreliable. Second, there exists some degree of significant adolescent turmoil, although it is considerably less than was previously supposed. Third, some turmoil is normal and may, in some cases, confuse accurate diagnosis. Fourth, the ability of professionals to distinguish reliably nonpathological turmoil from pathological turmoil is not known, but general considerations of diagnostic reliability occasion caution. Fifth, epidemiological data is tentative. Sixth, there is considerable conceptual and empirical reason to question the utility of conceptualizing adolescent misbehavior as psychopathological, even though it may be cause for concern and intervention on other, for example, legal, grounds. Seventh, the labeling literature should caution professionals against the overuse of psychiatric diagnoses with adolescents.

Prognosis in General

Now let us turn to an assessment of mental health prognosis. The term is used in two ways: it can mean the general "natural history" or course of a "behavioral condition," or it can mean a prediction of specific future behavior. The two meanings are related, but for legal purposes, as opposed to clinical or research purposes, the second meaning is far more important.

There is much clinical wisdom about the course of various mental disorders, but little hard, reliable data. Some facts seem relatively well established. These include the observation that persons who are depressed, even severely, feel better after some time whether or not they are treated,[93] and that persons who seem chronically crazy throughout childhood and adolescence will tend to remain chronically crazy throughout life.[94] However, there are serious problems with most prognostic statements. To the extent that an original diagnosis is rather unreliable and invalid, we cannot be sure when we follow a case or group of cases that the behavior we observe is the natural history of the disorder originally diagnosed. Moreover, while there do seem to be some consistent temporal behavioral patterns for some of the behaviors labeled mental disorders, and there are suggestive predictive indicators,[95] prognoses are often very general, the supporting data for them is often soft, and seemingly good predictors are often invalid.[96]

Although general and soft prognostic data may be useful to clinicians, the mental health legal system should be concerned with how accurately professionals can predict specific legally relevant behavior, especially when services are to be provided involuntarily. The important prognosis for the legal system is whether legally relevant behavior (for example, dangerousness or inability to manage in the community) will occur or continue if there is no intervention. From an extremely simplistic but common-sense point of view, we may say that this legally relevant behavior is a function of personal and environmental variables. These variables make a prediction of future behavior overwhelmingly difficult, however, because even if there are good data on every relevant personal variable (a feat well beyond present, and perhaps future, expertise), mental health professionals will not know the future environmental factors that will powerfully influence behavior.[97]

Most studies that have assessed the accuracy of predictions about specific legally relevant behavior have focused on predictions of violence to others or to the self. All reviewers agree that, at best, such predictions are accurate about one-third of the time.[98] And even one-third accuracy can be obtained only under ideal conditions; in most studies the accuracy rates are consideraly lower. Moreover, because suicide, a common form of violence to self, is such an infrequent event and because of weak general predictive ability, predictions of suicide are even less accurate than predictions of violence to others.[99] At best, suicide prediction is unlikely to be more than 20 percent effective, and eliminating false negatives is a more practical means to increase efficiency than eliminating false positives.[100]

Another type of prediction of legally relevant behavior is whether persons can manage their lives or "get along" without professional intervention, especially hospitalization. In such cases, as with predictions of violence, mental health professionals tend to be quite inaccurate, usually predicting incorrectly as often or more often than correctly.[101] Nearly always, professionals err in the direction of *over-predicting* the occurrence of legally relevant behavior.[102]

We may conclude that, in general, mental health professionals are as likely or more likely to be wrong than right when they predict legally relevant behavior. For predictions of violence, dangerousness and suicide, they are far more likely to be wrong than right.[103] Of course the mental health legal system may choose to use these findings in many different ways when it balances various interests to develop standards and procedures. But to the extent those standards and procedures are based on the ability of professionals to predict legally relevant behavior, they should reflect the actual abilities of the professionals.

Prognosis for Adolescents

As we noted above, mental health professionals are poor predictors of those behaviors that are legally relevant for adults. For adolescents, however, different behavior may be legally relevant. For example, the "need-for-treatment" standard is in disfavor as an authorizing justification of involuntary services for adults, not only because of the recognized unreliability of diagnosis, but also because it seems to many to be unduly paternalistic.[104] For adolescents, on the other hand, similar paternalism may not appear unsuitable. Adolescents are generally not considered capable of fully independent life management, and many believe they can be saved from adult difficulty, because they are in a "developmental stage" and thus are especially amenable to treatment. Given the dangers of unnecessary intervention, however, the important practical questions for the mental health legal system appear to be the same for adolescents and adults—the degree of accuracy with which professionals can *predict* later serious pathology and the efficacy with which professionals can *prevent* later difficulty when it is predicted. We shall discuss the latter issue below in the section on treatment, but now let us consider the prediction of later difficulty.

Two separate but related questions must be addressed: first, do adolescents who display symptoms outgrow them; and second, are there indicators which predict with substantial accuracy which adolescents will suffer from psychiatric disorder as adults (whether or not they are seriously disabled as adolescents).

Definite answers to these questions cannot be found in the research literature. Longitudinal studies depend on diagnoses at differing times in the subjects' lives. To the extent that the diagnoses are unreliable, the validity of the studies is considerably weakened. Further, few prognostic studies have attempted to control for the effects of labeling and self-fulfilling prophecies. Where a subject has been diagnosed earlier, rates of later disorder may be artificially inflated because of labeling effects, rather than being accurate reflections of the course of the disorders per se.[105]

As we mentioned above in discussing the possible "normalness" of adolescent turmoil, controversy exists over whether adolescents who experience turmoil outgrow their difficulties. All experts agree that some adolescents are clearly chronically crazy and that these persons will probably experience continued difficulty. There is still considerable disagreement, however, concerning less clear cases.

Most experts who believe that the prognosis of turmoil is poor rely on the Masterson studies referred to above,[106] which are also used to demonstrate that pathological turmoil can be distinguished from minor upset or normal turmoil. We have already noted many of the conceptual flaws of these studies on turmoil, but now we must adduce others that bear on their conclusions about prognosis. On follow-up, the ratings of the subjects were done by only one rater, who was *not* blind to the original diagnosis. The criterion used on follow-up was "fuctional impairment," defined as ". . . the degree to which the patient's total capacity to function is impaired by psychiatric illness." The author comments on this broad, vague clinical criterion by stating, "[t]hough this is admittedly a gross judgment and open to a greater degree of individual bias, it still gives the greatest weight to all the variables operating at a given time and uses the most appropriate instrument for measurement—the psychiatrist's judgment."[107] Finally, a functional impairment is expressed in "percents of impairment." These flaws demonstrate that the Masterson studies are lacking in conditions that would promote reliability and validity, and, in the absence of reliability statistics, it is reasonable to conclude that the studies neither prove nor disprove that adolescents grow out of their symptoms. The studies of outgrowing turmoil are simply not sufficiently rigorous to allow firm conclusions to be drawn.

To see if newer research projects have clarified the matter, let us turn to the most recent, comprehensive study. Weiner and Del Gaudio[108] searched the Monroe County, New York, cumulative psychiatric case register for all adolescents who received services in 1961 and 1962. This search yielded a cohort of 1,334 adolescent patients. The register was then searched again for the ten-year period ending December 31, 1972, to determine how many of the original cohort had received further psychiatric service. Subsequent diagnoses were available for 723 patients (54.2%). No attempt was made to determine how many of the original cohort had left the area or received services elsewhere. The only initial diagnoses which showed any significant degree of stability over time were schizophrenia and alcoholism. The authors feel that adolescent schizophrenia may be underdiagnosed because clinicians are reluctant to diagnose incipient schizophrenia, but they admit there are insufficient data in the study to support this belief.

The authors conclude that significant numbers of adolescents do not outgrow their symptoms, because at least 54 percent of them returned for later care. Further, they note that a large portion of the adolescents were diagnosed as having a situational disorder (27%), whereas few adults are so diagnosed (6%). The authors doubt that the figures concerning situational disorder, a benign diagnosis with a good prognosis, may accurately reflect the true state of affairs; they believe that many of the adolescents so diagnosed actually suffered from more serious disorders.

The Weiner and Del Gaudio study is useful and suggestive, but it also suffers from serious methodological and conceptual difficulties. For one thing, there is no reliability data for the original or subsequent diagnoses. Because these diagnoses were made for purposes of clinical practice, we may safely assume that there were no independent ratings. Indeed, the authors' belief that professionals often diagnose situational disorder on the basis of factors other than the clinical picture casts further doubt on the objectivity of diagnosis in general. Furthermore, we do not know whether the subsequent diagnosticians were blind to either the occurrence of, or the nature of, the earlier diagnoses. Unless subsequent raters are blind to earlier ratings, the later rating may be an artifact of halo effects. Given this possibility, even the reasonable stability of the diagnoses of schizophrenia is highly suspect.

Moreover, in addition to the possibility that the *later diagnosis* was a function of earlier labeling, it is possible that the *later problem behavior* was fostered by earlier labeling rather than being an outcome of the natural history of the disorder per se. Also, the percentage of persons returning for subsequent help does not necessarily indicate the stability of disorder. Many if not most persons have problems in living which beset them with varying degrees of seriousness from time to time. Many such persons may consult mental health professionals for these problems, especially in areas such as Monroe County (Rochester, New York), which are well provided with psychiatric services. Although they are diagnosable, because of the vagaries of the diagnostic system and because it is the practice of clinicians to make a diagnosis, many of these persons did not have on original contact, and do not have on later contact, a condition that is so disabling that the disease analogy is compelling (such as chronic schizophrenia). Many mental health professionals now admit that the less severe disorders—many neuroses and personality disorders—are perhaps not best viewed as illnesses.[109]

Furthermore, we do not know to what extent other factors may influence such results. For example, adolescents identified as psychiatric cases may, upon reaching adulthood, be more willing than other persons to so identify themselves once again. Such persons, who are familiar with the mental health system, may be more inclined to turn to it than to a clergyman, friend, or no one, when confronted with serious but non-extraordinary problems in living.

We may draw the following conclusions from the studies of Masterson, Weiner and Del Gaudio, and others. Some small percentage of crazy adolescents continue to be crazy into adulthood. Many more adolescents, even many with severe symptoms,[110] probably either outgrow their symptoms or learn to manage their adult lives reasonably, even though they have problems in living for which others might seek help. (It may simply be harder to manage life difficulties when one is an adolescent, because one has fewer resources.) In addition, there is little evidence that most adolescents who experience difficulty become progressively worse in adulthood. (As a footnote to the Weiner and Del Gaudio study, we might point out that the adolescents who allegedly had difficulties later on, supposedly proving the stability of psychopathology, did so *despite* their psychiatric treatment in adolescence.)

Although the literature on whether adolescents outgrow their turmoil or pathology is not conclusive, some reasonable prognostic information is available. What we know of the course of early-onset severe disorder, for example, suggests that a chronically and severely disordered adolescent will probably have been disordered as a child[111] and will also be disordered as an adult. An adolescent who seems acutely and severely disordered as a result of stress is less likely to have a lifelong course of chronic disorder[112] (although such adolescents are more likely to be transiently or situationally incapacitated in the future than adolescents who have not had severe problems).[113]

Those who are chronically crazy are probably in a different class from those who are situationally and transiently crazy. A very high percentage of the former will probably experience serious difficulty no matter how life events turn out. On the other hand, a substantial portion of those who are severely disordered in childhood may make a "satisfactory" but vulnerable adult adjustment.[114] Persons who are situationally disordered will tend to have difficulty only under various kinds of severe stress. However, persons who clearly are chronically, inexplicably crazy probably account for no more than 1 to 5 percent of the adolescent *patient population*. As we know from reliability studies, most of these cases of severely crazy behavior can be reliably identified by lay observers and experts alike.

Further, there is evidence[115] that sociopathic or acting-out traits in children and adolescents are poor prognostic signs. Robins's study seemed to demonstrate that the presence of sociopathic symptoms in adolescents predicted continued sociopathy and other psychopathology in adulthood. However, the diagnosis of sociopathy is most unreliable.[116] Also, it is undecided whether misbehavior leading to a diagnosis of sociopathy should be conceptualized as an illness and whether children should be diagnosed sociopathic.[117]

Prognostic data are available, but the crucial question for legal policy makers must still be the *accuracy* with which professionals can predict later difficulty from adolescent behavior, whether such behavior is psychopathological or not. At present, longitudinal research, especially on high-risk children, is very popular,[118] but such research is extremely difficult. There is much suggestive evidence, and many studies do find significant prognostic indicators that differentiate psychopathological adults from nonpathological adults,[119] but the critical question is the accuracy of these indicators in specific cases. To put the question another way, if professionals predict adult difficulty using the indicators for which there is currently some evidence, what percentage of false positives and false negatives will result for adolescents in trying to predict future adult pathology?

It is hard to give a general figure in answer to this question. Data from various studies[120] tend to show that even 50 percent accuracy would be excellent. For instance, Robins found that sociopathic indicators in adolescence predicted adult difficulties with only 50 percent accuracy. Predictors of future schizophrenia were fewer and less accurate. In cases of chronic clear craziness the prediction accuracy would be higher, but in such cases there is no question about intervention under a "need-for-treatment" standard. Researchers who have tried to predict long-term outcome[121] are consistently disappointed by the inaccuracy of their predictions of later pathology. In conclusion, experts do not yet have the tools to predict substantially accurately the future psychopathology of specific adolescents.

Adolescents who behave crazily or in ways that are disturbing to adults (for example, misbehavior, severe turmoil) should perhaps receive services to change their behavior—but not because such intervention is necessary to prevent future pathology or because we can predict which adolescents will have trouble in the future if services are not provided now. As previously mentioned, we cannot predict future pathology very accurately, and, as we shall see, treatment of adolescents is probably less effective than treatment of adults. Further, even when it is effective, there is no guarantee that treatment will not be needed later in life or that future difficulties would have been more severe without earlier treatment.

Treatment in General

For the mental health legal system the important questions concerning mental health treatments are: (1) how effective are they? (2) what are their risks? and (3) how intrusive[122] are they? Our discussion will consider the four main treatment modalities—psychotherapy (including behavior therapy), hospitalization per se, chemotherapy, and convulsive therapy (especially electroconvulsive therapy).

Any discussion of the effectiveness of mental health treatments must begin with a general discussion of the methodology of all outcome studies. First, good outcome studies require reliable diagnoses of the subjects before and after treatment. To the extent that ratings are "global" and diagnostic reliability is not reported, the studies are suspect. Second, the outcome measures should be validated. Third, the post-treatment raters should be blind to the pre-treatment diagnosis, to avoid contaminating the later diagnosis with an expectancy or halo effect. Fourth, control groups should be used,[123] and the raters should be blind as to whether a subject is an experimental or control subject. Fifth, a long-term follow-up should be carried out to note the residual efficacy of the treatment.[124] Properly performed, a good outcome study should cast some light on how effective a treatment is compared to no treatment and to a placebo treatment. It is hard, if not impossible, to draw reasonable conclusions from studies that do not meet at least the first four criteria.

Only a small fraction of outcome studies meet these criteria. Older studies are especially flawed in this regard. Further, many of the reasonable studies are noncomparable because, for example, the outcome measures used are too dissimilar or because the demographic characteristics of the subjects are different. In sum, conclusions about treatment practices and efficacy should be greeted with caution.[125]

Psychotherapy

Psychotherapy outcome studies are rather primitive compared to drug studies,[126] but a substantial body of evidence has accumulated. It indicates that psychotherapy is generally somewhat more efficacious than no treatment at all for neuroses and personality disorders.[127] Approximately one-third of neurotics will spontaneously remit, whereas from 15 to 45 percent more will improve with psychotherapy.[128] Success rates seem to vary considerably, depending on whether the rating is being done by the therapist, the patient, or an objective judge,[129] but this is a problem in outcome studies of all treatments.

Other problems arise because diagnosis and choice of treatment are less closely associated than one might suppose.[130] Little is known about optimum matching of specific psychotherapies to specific disorders or specific patients.[131] It seems clear, however, that in some situations psychotherapy is not the best treatment; for example, although there is some evidence and strong argument to the contrary,[132] psychotherapy, *especially* psychotherapy alone, is probably not the treatment of choice for schizophrenia.[133] It may, however, be a somewhat useful adjunct to other forms of treatment.[134]

The psychonoxious effects of psychotherapy are little researched and little understood, but there can be no doubt that some small percentage of patients seem to deteriorate because of it.[135] Furthermore, it is fair to say that most forms of psychotherapy are relatively nonintrusive, although some forms of behavior therapy (such as aversive conditioning) may be highly intrusive.

Hospitalization

Let us now turn to a discussion of hospitalization. We should first recognize that involuntary hospitalization is clearly an intrusive treatment because it involves a significant deprivation of liberty. Even voluntary hospitalization is somewhat intrusive, because it removes the person from his or her usual environment. Long-term hospitalization is especially intrusive because of the deprivations and dislocations involved, and because its risks are very great compared to its benefits.

Granted, some persons clearly seem incapable of managing except in a hospital. These, however, are only a tiny fraction of those considered mentally disordered, and the hospital provides more a protective than a curative environment for such persons. Indeed, the best evidence indicates that hospitalization confers few benefits that could not be obtained with less restrictive alternatives[136] and that hospitalization entails major risks, such as institutionalism and stigma.[137] One of the factors in recent optimism about the prognosis of schizophrenia is that long-term hospitalization is less likely to be utilized.[138] Further, repeated studies have shown that the best predictor of decisions to hospitalize a patient is a history of past hospitalization,[139] even though admitting professionals will deny that this was a factor in their decision.[140]

Hospitalization still has advocates,[141] but many experts advocate the abolition of long-term hospitalization and the large state hospital. The majority of experts, in fact, appear to favor at most only short-term (especially community-based) hospitalization to deal with acute disorder, and then only in the absence of other alternatives.[142]

The population in mental hospitals (although not the number of admissions) has dropped steadily in the last fifteen years, for a number of reasons. Experts no longer widely believe in the therapeutic effectiveness of hospitalization, especially long-term hospitalization. Civil rights advocates consider hospitalization (especially long-term) an abuse and have been successful in convincing courts and legislators of this. Additionally, powerful psychotropic drugs reduce anxiety and help psychotic persons reconstitute, thus enabling many to manage their lives more effectively outside the hospital. Indeed, the best use of hospitalization today may be to start and stabilize patients on chemotherapy regimens. On the other hand, this function could be achieved without hospitalization in most cases, and there is considerable reason to believe that efficient drug treatment is not given in large hospitals.[143]

Chemotherapy

Psychotropic drugs have clearly revolutionized the symptomatic treatment of mental disorders. Enormous numbers of double-blind studies have examined their efficacy. A number of these studies, however, have utilized rating systems of questionable reliability and validity. The evidence is as follows: For controlling acute disorder and for relieving symptoms, psychotropic drugs are clearly more efficacious than placebos,[144] and they are almost certainly more effective than any other means of dealing with psychoses, especially schizophrenia.[145] It is difficult to determine how absolutely effective various psychotropic drugs are, but they are more effective than no treatment, even though they are not effective in all cases.[146] Psychotropic medications do not "cure" underlying diseases;[147] rather they ameliorate symptoms, which tend to return after drug treatment ends. But stability through drug treatment may enable the patient to profit from other forms of therapy which were not helpful when he or she was severely disabled.

For cases of neuroses and character disorders where significant anxiety is involved, the minor tranquilizers are prescribed.[148] Antidepressants, especially the tricyclics, are indicated for the depressive disorders. There are also drugs that combine anti-anxiety and antidepressant medication. For bipolar depressive disorder lithium may also be used, and for mania, lithium is the drug of choice. Chlorpromazine may also be useful in controlling acute mania. The "major tranquilizers," phenothiazines and related drugs, are the therapy administered for schizophrenia and disabling anxiety. Phenothiazines are considered most useful for patients who are acutely "crazy" or who have a good prognosis,[149] but the usefulness of these drugs for chronic schizophrenics is in considerable question.[150] Unfortunately, there is little information to help a clinician predict which specific drug, within the class indicated (such as phenothiazines or antidepressants), is likely to be most effective.[151] Successful drug therapy is most frequently a matter of trial and error.[152]

Although psychotropic drugs may be very helpful, they also entail serious social and medical dangers. We are already an overdrugged culture according to many commentators, and minor tranquilizers such as Valium are undoubtedly overprescribed as a panacea to deal with the anxieties of ordinary life.[153] The minor tranquilizers may be ineffective, addicting, and lethal, and the major tranquilizers can be abusively prescribed to control persons in closed institutions. There is some evidence that major tranquilizers can exacerbate psychotic behavior.[154] Further, the long-term use of such drugs can cause severe and sometimes irreversible side effects such as tardive dyskinesia.[155] There is evidence that patients are often given unnecessarily high dosages of these drugs;[156] this problem is probably especially acute in state hospitals, where inadequate staff-patient ratios may encourage the practice.

Scheff[157] has written that adequate cost-benefit analysis of the use of psychotropic medication is lacking. In his preliminary attempt at such analysis, he concludes that the drugs are less useful and more dangerous than is often supposed. Because of their ability to control a patient's behavior despite his resistance, and because of their potential for abuse and serious side effects, psychotropic medications, especially the more powerful ones, must be rated as potentially very intrusive.

Convulsive Therapy

Despite the strong claims of its adherents to the contrary, there is limited rigorous evidence on the efficacy of electroconvulsive therapy (ECT). A 1967 observer noted only a small number of reasonably controlled studies;[158] nine years later, a methodologically oriented reviewer found adequate controls in even fewer studies.[159] This 1976 review concluded that because so few hard data exist, ECT should be considered an experimental treatment. The primary condition for which evidence suggests it may be effective is endogenous, affective psychosis (depression), a condition whose diagnostic reliability coefficient is about .30.[160] If used with restraint and with modern safeguards, ECT is arguably safe. Some, however, contend that significant evidence shows ECT to be highly morbid,[161] causing brain damage, long-term memory loss, and other serious problems.[162] ECT is extremely terrifying to a very large number of patients. Given the limited amount of hard efficacy data, the controversy concerning morbidity, and the aversive nature of the treatment, ECT must be considered an extremely intrusive treatment.

As a final comment on the four treatment modalities discussed above, it is important to assess the success with which professionals can predict treatment outcome in a given case before beginning a course of therapy. In view of the soft reliability of diagnostic assessment, the lack of very high success rates for all treatments (albeit some are considerably more successful than others), and the inability of clinicians to know exactly which treatment within a class (or sometimes even which class) to choose for a specific patient, it is not surprising that the few studies on this question are not encouraging.[163] Professionals cannot yet generally and highly accurately predict therapeutic outcome for a given patient.

Treatment of Adolescents

Adolescents receive the total gamut of treatments, but they receive less of the highly intrusive, organic treatments than adults, probably because much adolescent difficulty is viewed as relatively benign. Outcome studies of treatment are as difficult, if not more difficult, for adolescents as for adults, because it is harder to get a clear picture of adolescent behavior.[164] Indeed, the adolescent outcome literature is, for a variety of reasons, even less rigorous than adult outcome literature.[165]

Various forms of psychotherapy, including family therapy, are usually considered the treatments of choice for adolescents. Unfortunately, most clinicians who practice psychotherapy with adolescents consider them the most difficult age group with which to work. All patients resist therapy and test their therapists, but adolescents do this more than adults or young children. It is, consequently, more difficult to form an effective working alliance with them.[166] As a result, psychotherapy with adolescents is probably somewhat less effective than psychotherapy with adults but more effective than no therapy whatsoever.[167] No study has been discovered that examines the psychonoxious effects of psychotherapy on adolescents specifically.[168]

In examining the legal rights of adolescents who receive mental health services, the most important treatment issues are the efficacy and negative effects of very intrusive treatments such as hospitalization, chemotherapy, and convulsive therapies (especially electroconvulsive therapy). We have already reviewed the general literature on these methods and shall now consider their use with adolescents.

There seems to be little doubt that hospitalization should be a treatment of last resort and that most of its benefits can be achieved using less intrusive alternatives.[169] As we have seen, little rigorous evidence supports the view that hospitalization is efficacious for any but the most seriously disabled persons who cannot function outside the hospital even with help. Surely some adolescents can be treated more effectively in a hospital even if they could "get along" without hospitalization. But we cannot accurately identify those adolescents in advance, and the possible negative effects of hospitalization for adolescents are enormous.[170]

The major issue in adolescent chemotherapy is the degree to which the "major tranquilizers" are efficacious and safe for use by psychotic or borderline adolescents. (The use of these powerful drugs for less serious conditions is clearly unjustified theoretically and empirically.) In contrast to the enormous numbers of studies using these drugs on adults, there is little systematic evidence concerning their use with young patients; few rigorous, controlled double-blind studies of their use have been carried out with adolescents.[171]

For adults, these drugs, especially in concert with psychotherapy, are probably the most efficacious treatment for ameliorating schizophrenic behavior, although we cannot predict very effectively which patients will react well to which particular drug. There seems little reason to believe that the average, physically mature adolescent will react to them much differently from the average adult. However, as we have seen, the drugs can have very serious side effects, especially if they are given for extended periods. There is some clinical evidence that the risk of side effects might be especially high for adolescents;[172] indeed, the potential risks are especially heightened because reliable diagnosis is so difficult in this age group.

Reactively psychotic adolescents will tend to remit without drug treatment, although drug treatment will often hasten considerably the reduction of psychotic behavior. Antipsychotic agents may be less useful for chronic schizophrenics,[173] whose prognosis is poor and who need the drugs long-term, increasing the risk of serious side effects. For chronically schizophrenic adolescents, as for chronic schizophrenics in general, there is no safe and efficacious treatment of any kind available at present.

Few adolescents are diagnosed as suffering from hyperkinesis or severe affective disorders and thus should not, and probably do not, often receive stimulant or antidepressant chemotherapy.[174] A recent reviewer reports almost no studies of this type of chemotherapy with adolescents.[175]

As noted above, there are few good studies of the efficacy of the convulsive therapies, and none of these focuses on adolescent patients. As we have seen, the most recent reviewer of the literature on electroconvulsive therapy concluded that there are so few reasonable studies of ECT efficacy that the treatment ought to be considered experimental.[176] ECT is indicated (if at all) only for severe affective disorders that cannot be treated successfully by other means. These are rare in adolescence.[177] Although some hospitals and clinicians regularly prescribe ECT for adolescents,[178] such a practice seems unjustified and abusive. Indeed, the evidence suggests that convulsive therapies should be prescribed for adolescents only in the rarest cases, if ever.

Can the outcome of adolescents' treatment be reliably foretold? As discussed above, there are few valid prognostic indicators of treatment outcome in general; adolescent treatment is no exception. A recent empirical investigation concludes that, "[p]revious empirical studies . . . have been too divergent in methods, samples, and coverage of variables, as well as too limited in numbers, to permit the identification of reliable predictors of the duration and outcome of child or adolescent therapy."[179] Furthermore, many studies, even quite modern ones, do not meet minimal criteria of rigor, such as the use of control groups.[180]

Using more operationalized criteria, several researchers recently found that they could differentiate those adolescents who would continue in treatment from those who would not, but they could *not* predict which cases would respond successfully to treatment.[181] In another review of the thirteen available studies of prognostic indicators of treatment outcome among hospitalized and mostly schizophrenic adolescents, four other investigators (J.T. Gossett *et al.*) found six variables seemingly related to long-term outcome following hospitalization.[182] These were: (1) severity of psychopathology, (2) process versus reactive nature of psychopathology, (3) intelligence, (4) a specialized adolescent treatment program, (5) completion of the recommended treatment, and (6) continuation of psychotherapy after hospitalization. However, not all these factors were found in all thirteen studies. These researchers commented as follows[183] on the studies reviewed:

Methodology varied.... Researchers in the field did not replicate previous studies and the thirteen are not strictly comparable. For example, the studies emanated from twelve different hospitals whose treatment programs dealt with selected patients with a variety of demographic and diagnostic differences. Also, the criteria for measurement of change varied from study to study.

From our knowledge of the general rigor of outcome studies, it is fair to conclude that many of these studies, especially the earlier ones, were methodologically inadequate. Gosset *et al.* concluded with a call for more research to refine the predictors and to develop multivariate prediction formulas that would use the factors in combination.[184] The six factors found by Gossett *et al.* may be considered suggestive as guides to future research on treatment outcome prediction. But by no means are there yet reliable indicators that predict the outcome of treatment of adolescents with substantial accuracy.

One final point needs to be made. It is often thought that, because adolescents are still in a "developmental" period, they are especially amenable (compared to adults) to amelioration of developmental difficulties through treatment. As we have seen, the evidence simply does not bear out this contention. Nothing indicates that adolescents are any more amenable to treatment than adults; they may, in fact, be less so.

Conclusions

Mental health science is an infant science. For a long time its methods, data base and wisdom were clinical. Clinical methods, data and wisdom may be suggestive, but they tend to be quite soft. It is not surprising, therefore, that much clinical wisdom has not been confirmed by methodologically rigorous research.

Now, however, a harder, "scientific" attitude has begun to gain ascendancy in the field. At the same time, more sophisticated clinical methods are being developed. As a result, future professionals may understand the nature and causes of craziness and may very well achieve considerably greater success in diagnosis, prognosis and treatment. Although the more rigorous intellectual attitude makes improvement more likely, it is also arguable that the conceptual underpinnings of mental health science are so fragile that future gains will be limited.

If society chooses to intervene (or to permit parents to authorize intrusive intervention) with adolescents when it would not do so with adults, it must be recognized candidly that such intervention does not rest on more effective diagnosis, prognosis, or treatment for adolescents. Further, the belief that the side effects of unnecessary intervention will be less serious for adolescents than for adults is not justified. Other rationales will have to be found and justified. Some adolescents are clearly crazy, and some adolescents behave very disturbingly. When devising rules and procedures for dealing with them, however, the legal system should recognize the serious limitations of existing mental health skills and practice.

Notes

1. J. Adelson, *A Disappointing Sample*, 21 Contemp. Psychol. 120 (1976).

2. *See, e.g.,* the expository compendium in R.E. Muuss, Theories of Adolescence (3d ed. 1975).

3. *See* chapter 2, at note 9 *et seq.*

4. I. Weiner, Psychological Disturbance in Adolescence (1970), at 7.

5. *See generally* G. Vaillant, Adaptation to Life (1977); G. Sheehy, Passages (1976).

6. *See* chapter 2 generally, and at note 110 *et seq.*

7. Considering the nature of many of the occupational roles available in our society, formulations about work tasks that describe occupational "interests," intellectual skills, etc. seem elitist and biased towards a very small stratum of our society. The alienating and mechanistic nature of many jobs is an accepted reality. *See generally* S. Terkel, Working (1974).

8. E. Erikson, Childhood and Society (1950) [hereinafter cited as Erikson, Childhood (1950)], (2d ed. published in 1963). *See also* E. Erikson, *The Problem of Ego Identity*, 4 J. Amer. Psychoanalyt. Assoc. 56 (1956); E. Erikson, Identity: Youth and Crisis (1968) [hereinafter cited as Erikson, Identity].

9. *See* Muuss, note 2 above, at 256-64.

10. Erikson, Identity, note 8 above, at 128.

11. Erikson, Childhood (1950), note 8 above, at 261-62.

12. Erikson, Identity, note 8 above, at 156.

13. Chapter 2 at note 20 *et seq.*

14. J. Piaget & B. Inhelder, The Psychology of the Child (1969). *See also*

generally, J.H. Flavell, The Developmental Psychology of Jean Piaget (1963); J. Kagan, *A Conception of Early Adolescence*, 100 Daedalus 997 (1971).

15. N. Bayley, *Behavioral Correlates of Mental Growth: Birth to Thirty-six Years*, 23 Amer. Psychologist 1 (1968).

16. L. Kohlberg & C. Gilligan, *The Adolescent As a Philosopher: The Discovery of the Self in a Post-Conventional World*, 100 Daedalus 1051 (1971).

17. *Id.*, at 1065.

18. The following sources are exemplary, however: S. Freud, *Three Essays on the Theory of Sexuality*, in 7 The Standard Edition of the Complete Psychological Works of Sigmund Freud 125 (1905/1955); H.S. Sullivan, The Interpersonal Theory of Psychiatry (1953); A. Gessell, F. Ilg & L. Ames, Youth: The Years from Ten to Sixteen (1956); P. Blos, On Adolescence (1962); Group for the Advancement of Psychiatry, Normal Adolescence (1968) [hereinafter cited as G.A.P., Adolescence] ; E.Z. Friedenberg, The Vanishing Adolescent (1959); J.S. Coleman *et al.*, Youth: Transition to Adulthood (1974); Erikson, Childhood, note 8 above; Piaget *et al.*, note 14 above; and Muuss, note 2 above. *See also* chapter 2 at notes 3-44.

19. J. Kagan & H.A. Moss, Birth to Maturity (1962).

20. J.J. Conger, Adolescence and Youth: Psychological Development in a Changing World (1973), at 20.

21. *Id.*, at 185.

22. *Id.*

23. *Id.*, at 185-88.

24. *Id.*, at 185. *See also* M. Rutter, P. Graham, D.F.C. Chadwick & W. Yule, *Adolescent Turmoil: Fact or Fiction?*, 17 J. of Child Psychol. & Psychiat. 35 (1976); A. Tolor, *The Generation Gap: Fact or Fiction?*, 94 Genetic Psychol. Monographs 35 (1976).

25. G.A.P., Adolescence, note 18 above.

26. Conger, note 20 above, at 186.

27. Many of the issues developed throughout the remainder of this chapter are derived from S. Morse, *Crazy Behavior, Morals, and Science: An Analysis of Mental Health Law* to be published in 51 S. Cal. L. Rev. ___ (1978).

28. The following sources are representative: D. Ausubel, *Personality Disorder Is Disease*, 16 Amer. Psychologist 69 (1961); B. Ennis & T. Litwack, *Psychiatry and the Presumption of Expertise: Flipping Coins in the Courtroom*, 62 Cal. L. Rev. 693 (1974); S. Kety, *From Rationalization to Reason*, 131 Amer. J. of Psychiat. 957 (1974); R. Leifer, In the Name of Mental Health (1969); M.S. Moore, *Some Myths about Mental Illness*, 32 Arch. of Gen. Psychiat. 1483 (1975); D. Rosenhan, *Being Sane in Insane Places*, 179 Science 250 (1973); R. Spitzer, *On Pseudoscience in Science, Logic in Remission, and Psychiatric Diagnosis: A Critique of D.L. Rosenhan's "On Being Sane in Insane Places,"* 84 J. of Abnorm. Psychol. 442 (1975); T. Szasz, The Myth of Mental Illness (rev. ed. 1974); E.F. Torrey, The Death of Psychiatry (1974).

29. Szasz, note 28 above.

30. *See, e.g.*, the recent collection of articles on Rosenhan in 84 J. of Abnorm. Psychol. 443-74, 589-620 (1975).

31. Hereinafter, "crazy" shall be used as a descriptive word of art to denote the type of behavior that is readily recognizable as a serious mental disorder or mental illness.

32. *See, e.g.*, A. Lazare, *Hidden Conceptual Model in Clinical Psychiatry*, 288 New Eng. J. of Med. 345 (1973); M. Siegler and H. Osmond, Models of Madness, Models of Medicine (1974).

33. *See* J.M. Murphy, *Psychiatric Labeling in Cross-Cultural Perspective*, 191 Science 1019 (1976).

34. *See, e.g.*, J. Schwartz & S. Abramowitz, *Value Related Effects on Psychiatric Judgment*, 32 Arch. of Gen. Psychiat. 1525 (1975). *But see* C.V. Abramowitz & P.R. Dokecki, *The Politics of Clinical Judgment: Early Empirical Returns*, 84 Psychol. Bull. 460 (1977).

35. J. Ziskin, Coping with Psychiatric and Psychological Testimony (2d ed. 1975), at 38.

36. R. Spitzer & J. Fleiss, *A Re-Analysis of the Reliability of Psychiatric Diagnosis*, 125 British J. of Psychiat. 341 (1974). *See also* D. Davis, *On Being Detectably Sane in Insane Places: Base Rates and Diagnosis*, 85 J. Abnorm. Psychol. 416 (1976). *See generally* J.E. Helzer *et al.*, *Reliability of Psychiatric Diagnosis. I. A Methodological Review*, 34 Arch. Gen. Psychiat. 129 (1977).

37. Spitzer & Fleiss, note 36 above.

38. J. Ziskin, note 35 above; Ennis & Litwack, note 28 above. *Compare* J.E. Helzer *et al.*, *Reliability of Psychiatric Diagnosis. II. The Test/Retest Reliability of Diagnostic Classification*, 34 Arch. Gen. Psychiat. 136 (1977) (somewhat higher reliability for most diagnoses; considerably higher for mania; considerably lower for organic brain syndrome; same for schizophrenia).

39. Although these reliability figures are low, generally they are statistically significant.

40. J. Nunnally, Psychometric Theory (1967) at 226.

41. A. Stone, Mental Health and the Law: A System in Transition, (1975).

42. Spitzer & Fleiss, note 36 above; R. Kendell, The Role of Diagnosis in Psychiatry (1975); R. Spitzer, J. Endicott & E. Robins, *Clinical Criteria for Psychiatric Diagnoses and DSM–III*, 132 Amer. J. Psychiat. 1187 (1975) [hereinafter cited as Spitzer *et al.*, *Clinical Criteria*].

43. Ennis & Litwack, note 28 above; Spitzer & Fleiss, note 36 above. *See generally* J. Kuriansky, W. Deming & B. Gurland, *On Trends in the Diagnosis of Schizophrenia*, 131 Amer. J. Psychiat. 402 (1974); J. Morrison, *Changes in Subtype Diagnosis of Schizophrenia: 1920-1966*, 131 Amer. J. Psychiat. 674 (1974); L. Piggot & C. Sampson, *Changing Diagnosis of Childhood Psychoses*, 5 J. Autism and Childhood Schiz. 239 (1975).

44. *See, e.g.*, J. Feighner *et al.*, *Diagnostic Criteria for Use in Psychiatric Research*, 26 Arch. Gen. Psychiat. 57 (1972); R. Woodruff, Jr., D. Goodwin & S.

Guze, Psychiatric Diagnosis (1974); Spitzer *et al., Clinical Criteria,* note 42 above; J. Endicott, R. Spitzer, J. Fleiss & J. Cohen, *The Global Assessment Scale,* 33 Arch. of Gen. Psychiat. 766 (1976).

45. *See Field Trials Begin on DSM Draft,* 12:6 Psychiatric News 1 (1977). It is hoped, despite much criticism, that the new scheme will be more reliable, valid and clinically useful. For an account of psychiatric criticism of the new draft and its rebuff, see *Assembly Rebuffs DSM-III Opposition,* 12:11 Psychiatric News 1 (1977).

46. However, the new systems may well not prove significantly better when applied generally. Preliminary data suggest that those who develop new systems can use them more reliably than older ones. On the other hand, others who have tried to use these new schemes have had less success. *See* M. Taylor & R. Abrams, *A Critique of the St. Louis Psychiatric Research Criteria for Schizophrenia,* 132 Amer. J. Psychiat. 1277 (1975).

47. "While reliability may exist without validity, it is unlikely for validity to be very high in the absence of high reliability." Ziskin, note 35 above, at 39. *See* Ziskin *(Id.)* and Ennis & Litwack, note 28 above, for a review of the literature on validity.

48. E. Zigler & L. Phillips, *Psychiatric Diagnosis and Symptomatology,* 63 J. Abnorm. & Soc. Psychol. 69 (1961). *See also* H. Lehmann, *Schizophrenia: Clinical Features,* 1 *Comprehensive Textbook of Psychiatry II,* 890 (A.M. Freedman *et al.* ed. 1975). "There are no objective criteria today for the diagnosis of schizophrenia. . . . [N]o characteristic morphological changes in the brains of schizophrenics have been demonstrated; no specific laboratory findings signal its presence; no consistent premorbid history, course, or outcome can be ascertained; and no single cause is known." *Id.,* at 890.

49. B.P. Dohrenwend & B.S. Dohrenwend, Social Status and Psychological Disorder: A Causal Inquiry (1969), at ch. 7.

50. For instance, operational, exclusive criteria will help ensure that a diagnosis will convey accurate information about symptoms; *see* R.E. Kendell, *The Role of Diagnosis in Psychiatry,* at 39-48 (1975); *see also,* G. Murphy, R. Woodruff, Jr., M. Herjanic & J. Fisher, *Validity of the Diagnosis of Primary Affective Disorder,* 30 Arch. of Gen. Psychiat. 751 (1974).

51. *See generally* T. Scheff, Labeling Madness (1975).

52. *Cf.* C. Werthman, *The Function of Social Definitions in the Development of Delinquent Careers,* in President's Commission on Law Enforcement and Administration of Justice, Task Force Report: Juvenile Delinquency and Youth Crime (1967), at 155-70; E. Goffman, Stigma: Notes on the Management of Spoiled Identity (1963); D. Rosenhan, note 28 above.

53. *See* T. Scheff, Being Mentally Ill (1966), at chs. 2 & 3, for a model of the effects of the labeling process. *See also* Goffman, note 52 above.

54. The Labeling of Deviance (W. Gove ed. 1975), at chs. 1-9.

55. T. Scheff, *Reply to Imersheim and Simons,* 41 Amer. Sociological Rev.

563 (1976); T. Scheff, *Reply to Chauncey and Gove*, 40 Amer. Sociological Rev. 252 (1975); T. Scheff, *The Labeling Theory of Mental Illness,* 39 Amer. Sociological Rev. 444 (1974); T. Scheff, Labeling Madness, note 51 above.

56. E. Anthony, *The State of the Art and Science in Child Psychiatry*, 29 Arch. of Gen. Psychiat. 299 (1973).

57. M. Freeman, *A Reliability Study of Psychiatric Diagnosis in Childhood and Adolescence*, 12 J. of Child Psychol. and Psychiat. 43 (1971). *See also* J. Ashburner, *Some Problems of Classification with Particular Reference to Child Psychiatry*, 2 Aust. & N. Z. J. Psychiat. 244 (1968); Piggot & Sampson, note 43 above.

58. I. Weiner & A. Del Gaudio, *Psychopathology in Adolescence*, 33 Arch. of Gen. Psychiat. 187 (1976).

59. Freeman, note 57 above.

60. *See, e.g.*, A. Freud, *Adolescence*, 13 Psychoanalyt. Study of Child 255 (1958); Blos, note 18 above.

61. *See, e.g.*, E. Douvan & J. Adelson, The Adolescent Experience (1966); D. Offer, The Psychological World of the Teen-Ager (1969).

62. *See, e.g.*, Rutter *et al.*, note 24 above.

63. Muuss, note 2 above, at 270.

64. *Id.*

65. A. Thomas & S. Chess, *Evolution of Behavior Disorders into Adolescence*, 133 Amer. J. Psychiat. 539 (1976).

66. *See, e.g.*, Rutter *et al.*, note 24 above. Whether or not turmoil is statistically normative, if there exists some serious turmoil which is not pathological, it may mask true pathology and confuse accurate diagnosis. Psychologists use the term "turmoil" as a term of art, giving it varying meanings. It refers to behavior ranging from minor troublesomeness to serious behavioral difficulties and has no agreed upon "scientific" meaning. What type and how much turmoil is indicative of pathology is disputed. We shall use the term turmoil in several different ways, trying to make the meaning clear in each case by context or appropriate modifiers.

67. *E.g.*, Weiner, note 4 above; Weiner & Del Gaudio, note 58 above.

68. Weiner & Del Gaudio, note 58 above, at 191.

69. Reviewed in Dohrenwend & Dohrenwend, note 49 above.

70. J. Masterson, *The Symptomatic Adolescent Five Years Later: He Didn't Grow Out of It*, 123 Amer. J. of Psychiat. 1338 (1967) [hereinafter cited as Masterson, *Five Years Later*].

71. J. Masterson, *The Psychiatric Significance of Adolescent Turmoil*, 124 Amer. J. Psychiat. 1549 (1968); J. Masterson, *Five Years Later*, note 70 above; J. Masterson & A. Washburne, *The Symptomatic Adolescent: Psychiatric Illness or Adolescent Turmoil*, 122 Amer. J. Psychiat. 1240 (1966).

72. Masterson, *Five Years Later*, note 70 above, at 1339.

73. Thomas & Chess, note 65 above.

74. Rutter *et al.*, note 24 above.

75. J. Thompson, *The Prevalence of Psychiatric Disorder in an Undergraduate Population*, 21 J. Amer. C. Health Assoc. 415 (1973).

76. Joint Commission on Mental Health of Children, Crisis in Child Mental Health: Challenge for the 1970's (1969), at 38.

77. D. Offer, note 61 above; Rutter *et al.*, note 24 above.

78. Dohrenwend & Dohrenwend, note 49 above; Rutter *et al.*, note 24 above.

79. Weiner & Del Gaudio, note 58 above.

80. *See also* Rutter *et al.*, note 24 above.

81. Dohrenwend & Dohrenwend, note 49 above.

82. T. Langner, J. Gersten, E. Greene, J. Eisenberg, J. Herson & E. McCarthy, *Treatment of Psychological Disorders Among Urban Children*, 42 J. Consulting and Clin. Psychol. 170 (1974). *Contra*, A. Conger & J. Coie, *Who's Crazy in Manhattan: A Re-examination of "Treatment of Psychological Disorders Among Children,"* 43 J. Consult. and Clin. Psychol. 179 (1975), who also claim on methodological grounds that true prevalence studies are generally meaningless.

83. *Compare* H. Steadman, *The Psychiatrist as a Conservative Agent of Social Control*, 20 Soc. Prob. 263 (1972).

84. A. Flew, Crime or Disease? (1973).

85. Note 28 above.

86. *Compare* M. Hakeem, *A Critique of the Psychiatric Approach to the Prevention of Juvenile Delinquency*, 5 Soc. Prob. 194 (1959).

87. *See generally* S. Morse, *The Twilight of Welfare Criminology: A Reply to Judge Bazelon*, 49 S. Cal. L. Rev. 1247 (1976); D. MacNamara, *The Medical Model in Corrections: Requiescat in Pace*, 14 Criminology 439 (1977).

88. S. Shah & L. Roth, *Biological and Psychophysiological Factors in Criminality*, in Handbook of Criminology (D. Glaser ed. 1974), at 101; A. Nassi & S. Abramowitz, *From Phrenology to Psychosurgery and Back Again: Biological Studies of Criminality*, 46 Amer. J. Orthopsychiat. 591 (1976).

89. S. Guze, Criminality and Psychiatric Disorders (1976).

90. *See, e.g.,* Gove, note 54 above.

91. *See generally* The Mental Patient: Studies in the Sociology of Deviance (S. Spitzer & N. Denzin ed. 1968).

92. C. Werthman, *The Function of Social Definitions in the Development of Delinquent Careers*, in President's Commission on Law Enforcement and Administration of Justice, Task Force Report: Juvenile Delinquency and Youth Crime (1967), at 155; E. Schur, Radical Non-Intervention (1973).

93. A. Beck, Depression (1967).

94. *But see* G. Serban & C. Gidynski, *Differentiating Criteria for Acute-Chronic Distinction in Schizophrenia*, 32 Arch. of Gen. Psychiat. 705 (1975).

95. *See, e.g.*, A. Pokorny, J. Thornby, H. Kaplan & D. Ball, *Prediction of Chronicity in Psychiatric Patients*, 33 Arch. of Gen. Psychiat. 932 (1976).

96. D. Trainor, *Follow-up Study Fails to Find Predictive Signs*, 11:19 Psychiatric News 38 (1976).

97. On the importance of environmental factors, *see generally* A. Bandura, Principles of Behavior Modification (1969); W. Mischel, Personality and Assessment (1968); B. Skinner, Science and Human Behavior (1953).

98. J. Monahan & L. Cummings, *Social Policy Implications of the Inability to Predict Violence*, 31 J. of Soc. Iss. 153 (1975); B. Diamond, *The Psychiatric Prediction of Dangerousness*, 123 Univ. of Pa. L. Rev. 439 (1974); Ennis & Litwack, note 28 above.

99. D. MacKinnon & N. Farberow, *An Assessment of the Utility of Suicide Prediction*, 6 Suicide & Life-threatening Behav. 86 (1976); D. Greenberg, *Involuntary Psychiatric Commitments to Prevent Suicide*, 49 N.Y.U. L. Rev. 227 (1974).

100. MacKinnon & Farberow, note 99 above.

101. Ennis & Litwack, note 28 above; N. Scheer & G. Barton, *A Comparison of Patients Discharged Against Medical Advice with a Matched Control Group*, 131 Amer. J. Psychiat. 1217 (1974). *See also* J. Barrett, J. Kuriansky & B. Gurland, *Community Tenure Following Emergency Discharge*, 128 Amer. J. Psychiat. 958 (1972).

102. Ennis & Litwack, note 28 above; Monahan & Cummings, note 98 above.

103. We shall defer until the section on treatment a discussion of the ability of professionals to predict the outcomes of specific treatments in specific cases.

104. *See generally* Note, *Developments in the Law—Civil Commitment of the Mentally Ill*, 87 Harv. L. Rev. 1190 (1974).

105. Conversely, any portion of behavioral consistency which is a function of intrapersonal variables such as "traits" will be cemented in the course of adolescence. If craziness or maladaptive coping is a trait, then it would be completely counterintuitive to expect that no adolescent disorder continues into adulthood. However, the notion that behavior is largely a function of such intrapersonal variables is contradicted by many researchers (*e.g.*, Mischel, note 94 above) who believe that "personality" is much more dependent on context and environmental stimuli.

106. Masterson, notes 70 and 71 above.

107. Masterson, *Five Years Later*, note 70 above, at 1339.

108. Weiner & Del Gaudio, note 58 above.

109. *E.g.*, Kety, note 28 above; R. Kendell, *The Concept of Disease and Its Implications for Psychiatry*, 127 Brit. J. Psychiat. 305 (1975).

110. *See, e.g.*, L. Bender, *The Life Course of Children with Schizophrenia*, 130 Amer. J. Psychiat. 783 (1973).

111. *See, e.g.*, Bender, *id.*; T. Aarkrog, *Psychotic and Borderline Psychotic Adolescents: Frequency of Psychiatric Illness and Treatment in Childhood in 100 Consecutive Cases*, 52 Acta Psychiatrica Scandinavia [Act. Psychiat. Scand.] 58 (1975).

112. *See, e.g.*, G. Vaillant, *Prospective Prediction of Schizophrenic Remission*, 11 Arch. of Gen. Psychiat. 509 (1964).

113. *But compare* G. Serban & C. Gidynski, *Differentiating Criteria for Acute-Chronic Distinction in Schizophrenia*, 32 Arch. of Gen. Psychiat. 705 (1975).

114. *See* Bender, note 110 above.

115. L. Robins, Deviant Children Grown Up (1966); N. Garmezy, *Children at Risk: The Search for the Antecedents of Schizophrenia, Part II: Ongoing Research Programs, Issues, and Intervention* 9 Schizophr. Bull. 55 (1974).

116. Spitzer & Fleiss, note 36 above.

117. D. Lewis & D. Bulla, *"Sociopathy" and its Synonyms: Inappropriate Diagnoses in Child Psychiatry*, 132 Amer. J. Psychiat. 721 (1975).

118. *See generally* Garmezy, note 115 above. *See also* Life History Research in Psychopathology (M. Roff & D. Ricks ed. 1971); 2 Life History Research in Psychopathology (M. Roff, L. Robins & M. Pollack ed. 1972) [hereinafter cited as Roff, Robins & Pollack].

119. *See, e.g.*, M. Woerner, M. Pollack, C. Rogalski, Y. Pollack & D. Klein, *A Comparison of the School Records of Personality Disorders, Schizophrenics, and their Sibs*, in Roff, Robins & Pollack, note 118 above, at 47; Robins, note 115 above.

120. *E.g.*, L. Robins, note 115 above; N. Watt & A. Lubensky, *Childhood Roots of Schizophrenia*, 44 J. Consult. and Clin. Psychol. 363 (1976); Weiner & Del Gaudio, note 58 above.

121. *E.g.*, M. Jones, N. Bayley, J. MacFarlane & M. Honzik, The Course of Human Development (1971).

122. M. Shapiro, *Legislating the Control of Behavior Control: Autonomy and the Coercive Use of Organic Therapies*, 47 S. Cal. L. Rev. 237 (1974).

123. Single-case methodology may also reasonably be used in some instances. These are few, however, and this methodology has various other requirements for rigor. *See* H. Leitenberg, *The Use of Single-Case Methodology in Psychotherapy Research*, 82 J. of Abnorm. Psychol. 87 (1973).

124. Outcome studies for particular treatments require further, specific methodological controls, but the five enumerated are crucial for all treatments.

125. Another point about effectiveness studies is that the success or failure of a particular treatment modality neither proves nor disproves the theoretical assumptions upon which the modality is based. J. Durell, *Introduction* in Biological Psychiatry (J. Mendels ed. 1973).

126. P. May, *Schizophrenia: Evaluation of Treatment Methods* [hereinafter cited as May, *Evaluation*], in 1 Comprehensive Textbook of Psychiatry (A. Freedman, H. Kaplan & B. Sadock ed. 1975), at 955.

127. A. Bergin, *The Evaluation of Therapeutic Outcomes* [hereinafter cited as Bergin, *Evaluation*], in Handbook of Psychotherapy and Behavior Change (A. Bergin & S. Garfield ed. 1971), at 217; L. Luborsky, B. Singer & L. Luborsky, *Comparative Studies of Psychotherapies*, 32 Arch. of Gen. Psychiat. 995 (1975).

128. Bergin, *Evaluation*, note 127 above; *see also*, M.L. Smith & G.V. Glass, Meta-Analysis of Psychotherapy Outcome Studies, 32 Amer. Psychol. 752 (1977).

129. *See, e.g.*, M. Harty & L. Horowitz, *Therapeutic Outcome as Rated by Patients, Therapists, and Judges*, 33 Arch. of Gen. Psychiat. 957 (1976).

130. D. Bannister, P. Salmon & D. Lieberman, *Diagnosis-Treatment Relationships in Psychiatry: A Statistical Analysis*, 110 Brit. J. Psychiat. 726 (1964).

131. Luborsky, *et al.*, note 127 above.

132. *See, e.g.*, J. Gunderson, *Controversies About the Psychotherapy of Schizophrenia*, 130 Amer. J. Psychiat. 677 (1973).

133. P. May, Treatment of Schizophrenia (1968) [hereinafter cited as May, Treatment] ; May, *Evaluation*, note 126 above; P. May, *Rational Treatment for an Irrational Disorder: What Does the Schizophrenic Patient Need*, 133 Amer. J. Psychiat. 1008 (1976). *But cf.* B. Karon & G. VanderBos, *Clinical Outcome and Treatment Costs of Psychotherapy Versus Medication for Schizophrenics*, 6 Prof. Psychol. 293 (1975); B.P. Karon, Psychotherapy Is Effective: Summary of Michigan State Psychotherapy Project (n.d.), (mimeo available from author).

134. May, Treatment, note 133 above; May, *Evaluation*, note 126 above. *But see* Group for the Advancement of Psychiatry, Pharmacotherapy and Psychotherapy: Paradoxes, Problems and Progress (1975).

135. Bergin, *Evaluation*, note 127 above.

136. *See, e.g.*, A. Davis, S. Dinitz & B. Pasaminick, *The Prevention of Hospitalization in Schizophrenia: Five Years After an Experimental Program*, 42 Amer. J. Orthopsychiat. 375 (1972); L. Mosher, A. Menn & S. Matthew, *Soteria: Evaluation of a Home-Based Treatment for Schizophrenia*, 45 Amer. J. Orthopsychiat. 455 (1975); L. Stein, M. Test & A. Marx, *Alternative to the Hospital: A Controlled Study*, 132 Amer. J. Psychiat. 517 (1975).

137. R. Stuart, Trick or Treatment (1970), at ch. 2.

138. R. Bland & J. Parker, *Prognosis in Schizophrenia: A Ten-Year Follow-Up of First Admissions*, 33 Arch. of Gen. Psychiat. 949 (1976).

139. A. Rosenblatt & J. Mayer, *The Recidivism of Mental Patients: A Review of Past Studies*, 44 Amer. J. Orthopsychiat. 697 (1974).

140. W. Mendel & S. Rapport, *Determinants of the Decision for Psychiatric Hospitalization*, 20 Arch. of Gen. Psychiat. 321 (1969).

141. *E.g.*, C. Rabiner & A. Lurie, *The Case for Psychiatric Hospitalization*, 131 Amer. J. Psychiat. 761 (1974); R. Rieder, *Hospitals, Patients and Politics*, 11 Schizophr. Bull. 9 (1974).

142. *See, e.g.*, M. Herz, J. Endicott, R. Spitzer, *et al.*, *Brief Hospitalization of Patients with Families*, 132 Amer. J. Psychiat. 413 (1975). *See also*, M. Herz *et al.*, *Brief Hospitalization: A Two-year Follow-up*, 134 Amer. J. Psychiat. 502 (1977); M. Linn *et al.*, *Hospital v. Community (Foster) Care for Psychiatric Patients*, 34 Arch. Gen. Psychiat. 78 (1977); M. Herz, J. Endicott & R. Spitzer, *Brief Versus Standard Hospitalization: The Families*, 133 Amer. J. Psychiat. 795

(1976). *But compare* W. Hargreaves *et al., Short vs. Long Hospitalization: A Prospective Controlled Study. VI. Two-year Follow-up Results for Schizophrenics*, 34 Arch. Gen. Psychiat. 305 (1977) (long-term results initially better but differences decreased two years after admission; long-term hospitalization defined as only 90-120 days).

143. T. Scheff, *Medical Dominance: Psychoactive Drugs and Mental Health Policy*, 19 Amer. Behav. Scient. 299 (1976) [hereinafter cited as Scheff, *Medical Dominance*].

144. J. Davis & J. Cole, *Antipsychotic Drugs*, in 2 Comprehensive Textbook of Psychiatry, note 126 above, at 1921. *But see*, E.Z. DuBose, Jr., *Of the Parens Patriae Commitment Power and Drug Treatment of Schizophrenia: Do the Benefits to the Patient Justify Involuntary Treatment?*, 60 Minn. L. Rev. 1149 (1976) (considerably more cautious evaluation of the efficacy of phenothiazines); D. Marholin & D. Phillips, *Methodological Issues in Psychopharmacological Research: Chlorpromazine–A Case in Point*, 46 Amer. J. of Orthopsychiat. 477 (1976) (extremely cautious evaluation of the efficacy of phenothiazines based on methodological analysis of outcome studies). For an exchange on the Marholin & Phillips article, *see* J.M. Davis & S.W. Hurt, *Letter to the Editor*, 47 Amer. J. of Orthopsychiat. 523 (1977); D. Marholin & D. Phillips, *Reply*, 47 Amer. J. of Orthopsychiat. 528 (1977).

145. P. May, *Evaluation*, note 126 above. *Contra*, Karon, Psychotherapy Is Effective, note 133 above. Karon claims, on the basis of a long-term research project, that psychotherapy is more effective in the long run with schizophrenics.

146. Scheff, *Medical Dominance*, note 143 above. For a representative table of findings from a major study, see G. Klerman, *Clinical Efficacy and Actions of Antipsychotics*, in *Clinical Handbook of Psychopharmacology* (A. Di Mascio & R. Shader ed. 1970), at 41, 50.

147. Scheff, *Medical Dominance*, note 143 above.

148. *But compare* Scheff, *Medical Dominance*, note 143 above, who notes that the minor tranquilizers may have little value.

149. May, *Evaluation*, note 126 above.

150. Scheff, *Medical Dominance*, note 143 above.

151. *See, e.g.*, P. May *et al., Predicting Individual Responses to Drug Treatment in Schizophrenia: A Test Dose Model*, 162 J. Nerv. & Mental Disease 177 (1976).

152. For an attempt to rationalize this process, *see* J. Overall & B. Henry, *Decisions About Drug Therapy: III. Selection of Treatment for Psychiatric Inpatients*, 28 Arch. of Gen. Psychiat. 81 (1973).

153. Scheff, *Medical Dominance*, note 143 above.

154. G. Simpson, E. Varga & E. Haher, *Psychotic Exacerbations Produced by Neuroleptics*, 37 Diseases of the Nervous System 367 (1976).

155. *See, e.g.*, Special Report, *Neurological Syndrome Associated with Antipsychotic Drug Use*, 28 Arch. of Gen. Psychiat. 463 (1973).

156. Scheff, *Medical Dominance*, note 143 above.

157. *Id.*

158. A. Beck, Depression (1967).

159. C. Costello, *Electroconvulsive Therapy: Is Further Investigation Necessary?*, 21 Canadian Psychiat. Assoc. J. 61 (1976). *Compare* I.S. Turek & T.E. Hanlon, *The Effectiveness and Safety of Electroconvulsive Therapy (ECT)*, 164 J. Nervous & Mental Disease 419 (1977) (more optimistic but still quite cautious evaluation of the efficacy of ECT).

160. R. Spitzer & J. Fleiss, note 36 above.

161. *E.g.*, J. Friedberg, *Shock Treatment Is Not Good for Your Brain* (1976).

162. *See generally* B. Roueche, *Annals of Medicine: As Empty as Eve*, The New Yorker (Sept. 9, 1974).

163. Ennis & Litwack, note 28 above.

164. *Compare* Weiner & Del Gaudio, note 58 above.

165. For a rather comprehensive review, *see* J. Snyder, Treatment Approaches to Adolescent Problems: How Effective Are They? A Literature Review (1974) (unpublished paper on file with the Center for Law and Health Sciences, Boston University School of Law).

166. J. Meeks, *Psychiatric Treatment of the Adolescent*, in 2 Comprehensive Textbook of Psychiatry, note 126 above, at 2262.

167. *Compare* Luborsky *et al.*, note 127 above; Bergin, *Evaluation*, note 127 above.

168. *But compare* Bergin, *Evaluation*, note 127 above.

169. Stuart, note 137 above; Amer. Orthopsychiat. Assoc. *et al.*, Amici Curiae Brief in Kremens v. Bartley, 97 S. Ct. 1709 (1977); Mosher *et al.*, note 136 above.

170. Amer. Orthopsychiat. Assoc. *et al.*, note 169 above.

171. *Campbell Says Drug Effects in Youth Poorly Understood*, 11:19 Psychiatric News 26 (1976) [hereinafter cited as *Campbell Says*]. For a bibliographic listing, see I. Berlin, *Bibliography of Child Psychiatry* (1976), at 246-49.

172. *Campbell Says*, note 171 above.

173. May, *Evaluation*, note 126 above.

174. *But see* D. Safer & R. Allen, *Stimulant Drug Treatment of Hyperactive Adolescents*, 36 Diseases of Nervous Sys. 454 (1975), who report that this view, with which they disagree, is dominant with regard to hyperactivity.

175. Berlin, note 171 above.

176. Costello, note 159 above.

177. Weiner & Del Gaudio, note 58 above.

178. G. Grosser, D. Pearsall, C. Fisher & L. Geremonte, *The Regulation of Electroconvulsive Treatment in Massachusetts: A Follow-Up*, 5 Mass. J. of Mental Health 12 (1975).

179. E. Lessing, M. Black, L. Barbera & F. Seibert, *Dimensions of Adolescent Psychopathology and Their Prognostic Significance for Treatment Outcome*, 93 Genet. Psychol. Monographs 155 (1976), at 162. *See also* J. Gossett, S. Lewis, J.

Lewis & V. Phillips, *Follow-Up of Adolescents Treated in a Psychiatric Hospital: 1. A Review of Studies*, 43 Amer. J. of Orthopsychiat. 602 (1973).

180. *See, e.g.*, E. Herrerra, B. Lifson, E. Hartman & M. Solomon, *A 10-Year Follow-Up of 55 Hospitalized Adolescents*, 131 Amer. J. Psychiat. 769 (1974).

181. Lessing *et al.*, note 179 above.

182. Gossett *et al.*, note 179 above.

183. *Id.*, at 603.

184. For an example of further empirical research that attempts to refine prediction, *see* J. Gossett, J. Meeks, F. Barnhart & V. Phillips, *Follow-Up of Adolescents Treated in a Psychiatric Hospital: Onset of Symptomatology Scale*, 11 Adolescence 195 (1976).

4

Impediments to Adolescents' Access to Treatment

An adolescent seeking services on his or her own initiative confronts a number of legal and economic impediments. According to a general rule of law, minors do not have unrestricted access to medical care. They are barred from obtaining treatment by two major legal impediments: (1) the requirement that parents must consent to medical treatment performed on their children, and (2) the inability of minors to enter into the binding contractual relationship which is usually the basis of the physician-patient relationship. We have touched on these legal rules generally in chapter 2; we shall now consider them in detail with respect to an adolescent's access to general medical care and to various types of mental health services.

Parental Consent Requirement

A minor is, in general, not capable of giving a valid consent to medical treatment. Several rationales are cited to support this rule. In one sense it is a means of societal protection for minors who, as a group, are considered immature and unable to make wise decisions.[1] This view underlies the supposition that a minor cannot understand the nature or consequences of medical procedures.[2] The parental consent requirement, furthermore, protects children from adult providers who might otherwise take advantage of their immaturity.[3] The requirement also provides financial protection to parents who, because they will be liable for medical costs, are given authority to control the decision to obtain care.[4] Moreover, because parents are legally responsible for support and maintenance of their children and legally entitled to their children's services, it is argued that they should be able to control those factors which may deprive them of such services for short or extended periods, or which may otherwise increase the cost of child rearing.[5]

The requirement that parents must consent to medical treatments performed on their children stems from the rule that no physician may treat a patient without first obtaining a valid consent from the patient or a person able to consent for the patient.[6] The premise underlying the consent rule is that "every human being of adult years and sound mind has the right to determine what shall be done with his own body."[7] The term consent has been defined as "voluntary agreement by a person in possession and exercise of sufficient mentality to make an intelligent choice to do something proposed by another."[8]

123

Consent has been characterized as "active acquiescence," as distinguished from assent, which implies "silent acquiescence."[9] A physician who fails to procure a patient's consent faces liability for battery,[10] and the general rule in most jurisdictions is that a physician providing medical care to a minor without first obtaining parental consent may be civilly liable for committing the same tort.[11]

A developing aspect of the doctrine of consent is the requirement that it be based on knowledge and information about the proposed therapy.[12] As articulated by several courts, physicians have a duty to inform a patient of possible serious collateral risks and hazards which may be associated with a proposed medical treatment.[13] Some courts have held that patients are entitled to a full explanation of the proposed treatment, its risks, chances for favorable and unfavorable results, alternative methods of treatment, and the risks of receiving no treatment.[14]

The informed consent doctrine recognizes that it is important that a patient understand the medical treatment proposed. It is thus evident that the assumption that minors cannot comprehend all the relevant information may further hinder them from winning the right to consent to treatment. However, although the parental consent requirement is rationalized in part as a means of protecting minors, in certain circumstances it may bar a child from receiving necessary medical care—either because the parents refuse to consent or because the child is deterred from seeking treatment.

This bar may present particularly acute problems with respect to access to mental health treatment.[15] Parents may be unwilling to consent to mental health treatment for their children for a number of reasons. They may feel that society attaches a stigma to individuals who require mental health treatment, and may believe that the entire family will suffer social disapproval.[16] They may also feel that they are responsible for the child's illness and may fear that acknowledging the illness will be an admission of their failure as parents.[17] They may feel a sense of guilt.[18] Parents may also fear that, during the course of therapy, the child will reveal family secrets and that as a result the physician will blame them for the child's illness.[19] Alternatively, a child who wants treatment may not want to admit this to his or her parents. The child may believe (accurately or not) that many of his or her emotional problems stem from the familial setting and that calling attention to them will merely exacerbate problems in the home.

The reluctance of children to discuss health-related concerns with parents extends beyond mental health to other types of medical problems.[20] Similarly, the reluctance of parents to consent to certain treatments is not limited to mental health. In recognition of these problems, some states have enacted statutes eliminating the need for parental consent in certain instances. These laws were touched upon in chapter 2. They will be discussed at greater length in the following section.

Statutory and Judicial Exceptions to
Parental Consent Requirement

Although the parental consent rule is generally recognized, it contains both statutory and judicial exceptions which permit minors to gain access to treatment without the consent of others. These exceptions in part reflect a recognition that the rule may have a harsh effect of minors who need certain types of care; they relate both to the abilities and status of the particular child and to the nature of the services being sought.

The emergency exception, which is applicable to both adults and minors, provides that no consent is required to perform a medical procedure on an incompetent, unconscious, delirious, or otherwise irresponsible patient if there is imminent danger to life and limb or if waiting to obtain consent would result in death or injury.[21] Originally a common law exception, it has now been incorporated into statute in many states.[22] Only a few of these statutes, however, refer specifically to emergencies relating to mental health.[23] Nevertheless, in certain situations it is arguable that the need for mental health treatment is so critical that it constitutes a life or death situation.[24]

Two other judicially articulated exceptions apply to adolescents who meet certain criteria relating to the minor's independence from his or her parents or demonstrated emotional and/or mental maturity. One exception permits so-called emancipated minors to consent to medical treatment, provided they understand its nature and consequences.[25] The concept of emancipation (which applies also in other areas of the parent-child relationship)[26] refers to the termination of all or certain parental rights and obligations stemming from the parent-child relationship during the child's minority.[27]

Emancipation may be expressed or implied from the total factual pattern of a particular case.[28] Factors relevant to a court's consideration include whether the minor is married, enlisted in the armed forces, living alone or self-supporting.[29] Some courts hold that emancipation must be achieved by the act or statement of a parent, not by that of the child.[30] For example, parental neglect, or the failure of parents to meet their legal responsibilities, may result in the emancipation of a child.[31]

Whether a court finds that a minor is emancipated may depend upon the purpose for which that status is claimed.[32] A court may be more willing to find that a minor is emancipated only for certain purposes, that is, is partially emancipated, than rule in favor of complete emancipation.[33] In *Bach v. Long Island Jewish Hospital,*[34] for example, the court held that the consent of a nineteen-year-old married woman to a nonemergency surgical procedure was valid. After reviewing the state law concerning the ability of minors to consent in many areas of the law, and recognizing a distinction between personal rights and property rights, the court held that although not emancipated with respect to property rights, the minor was emancipated with respect to personal rights, including consent to the particular medical procedure.[35] This approach is consistent with the general presumption against emancipation[36] and indicates the restrained manner with which courts approach this issue.

Although developed by the courts, several states have codified the emancipation doctrine in their statutes as it relates to medical treatment.[37] Some statutes merely state that emancipated minors may consent to treatment; others define the term.[38] In some instances the statutory definition seems to broaden the court-made common law rule by providing that the minor need only be living away from home and managing his or her own financial affairs, regardless of the source of income.[39]

A more recent, judicially created exception to the common law has been termed the mature minor rule.[40] Under this doctrine, an unemancipated minor may consent to medical care if he or she has sufficient intelligence to understand the nature and consequences of the treatment.[41] In addition, the recommended therapy must be for the minor's benefit.[42] The development of this exception may have been influenced by the informed consent doctrine, with its focus on the patient's understanding of proposed medical treatment.[43] The rule has been legislatively enacted in Mississippi[44] in a statute which provides that "any unemancipated minor of sufficient intelligence to understand and appreciate the consequences of the proposed surgical or medical treatment or procedure" may consent for him or herself.[45]

In general, evolution of exceptions to the parental consent requirement reflects an increasing sensitivity to the child as a person; the focus of the exceptions has shifted from emphasis on bodily integrity (emergency) to judicial recognition of de facto majority (emancipation), to concern over characteristics and mental capabilities of the minor (maturity).[46]

Legislatures have also adopted provisions allowing minors to consent to treatment for specific types of medical problems. Such statutory exceptions to the parental consent rule include provisions relating to birth control and pregnancy-related problems, venereal disease, and drug addiction. A common concern in these areas appears to be the seriousness of the problem to the individual and to society, coupled with its sensitive nature, which may make an adolescent hesitant to discuss the need for treatment with his or her parents.[47]

Minors have been granted increasing rights to consent to treatment relating to contraception, pregnancy, and abortion. Legislative changes in these areas have been defended on the grounds that these procedures and services are important to the child and the community. Frequently mentioned, for example, are the debilitating effects of a teenage pregnancy on the adolescent mother, who may be forced to terminate her education or agree to a marriage neither she nor the father wants. Alternatively, she may attempt a self-induced abortion that would endanger her health.[48] Because the interests of parent and child may conflict in these situations, a minor may be deterred by a parental consent requirement from seeking necessary information or treatment.

In the last few years, many states enacted legislation specifically authorizing physicians to provide birth control services without parental consent.[49] The statutes vary; some permit physicians to treat all minors,[50] while others specify that only those above a certain age may be treated.[51] Some statutes authorizing the provision of information about contraception specifically permit minors to consent to treatment related to pregnancy.[52] Legislation in other states is restricted solely to medical and surgical treatment arising from pregnancy,[53] and does not by its terms permit minors to obtain birth control information.

Two actions by the United States Supreme Court have recently clarified adolescents' rights in this area. In May 1976, the Court summarily affirmed the ruling of a three-judge federal court in Utah that states may not require that minors have parental consent to obtain contraceptive information through welfare or Medicaid programs.[54] Because the Supreme Court wrote no opinion, the precise rationale for its decision is unknown. However, in June 1977, in *Carey v. Population Services International,*[55] the Court held unconstitutional a New York statute which made it a crime to sell contraceptives to minors under sixteen, insofar as it applied to nonprescription contraceptives. In light of these decisions, the constitutionality of any statute which attempts to deny contraceptives to adolescents must be considered extremely doubtful.[56]

After the 1973 decision *Roe v. Wade*[57]—the case in which the Supreme Court held that the constitutionally protected right of privacy prevented states from regulating abortions except in limited circumstances[58]—many states rewrote their abortion laws to comply with the standards announced in *Roe*. Many of the new statutes permitted minors to seek abortions only with parental consent. A rapid state of court challenges to the parental consent requirements resulted in the striking down of almost all such provisions.[59] A pair of these decisions, contrastingly decided, found their way to the United States Supreme Court. In the summer of 1976, the Court held, in *Planned Parenthood of Central Missouri v. Danforth,*[60] that it is unconstitutional for parents to possess absolute veto power over their minor daughter's abortion decision. However, in *Bellotti v. Baird*[61] it indicated that minors' privacy rights in this area are not as highly protected as those of an adult. These cases, discussed at greater length in chapter 6,[62] represent the evolving state of the law in this unsettled area.

The most widely adopted exception to the parental consent requirement appears to be the one permitting minors to consent to treatment for venereal disease. Almost all states have passed statutes to this effect;[63] more than half of these have been enacted since 1968.[64] The broad acceptance of this exception reflects concern about the grave threat to public health posed by the spread of venereal disease, coupled with the minor's anticipated reluctance to approach his or her parents about the problem.[65] Some statutes, however, contain a clause permitting physicians to inform parents that their children are being treated for venereal disease[66] —a requirement that obviously may discourage minors from seeking therapy.[67]

Treatment of minors without parental consent for medical problems related to drug addiction and abuse is permitted in a growing number of states.[68] Like venereal disease, drug-related problems pose serious health and social problems,[69] and the need for parental consent may significantly deter minors from seeking medical assistance.[70] However, although statutes removing the parental consent requirement make treatment more accessible to minors, several contain provisions granting the physician discretion to inform parents that their child is receiving treatment for drug abuse.[71] As in the case of venereal disease, these provisions have been criticized as undercutting the impact and utility of the elimination of parental consent requirements.[72] They are defended, however, by arguments that a lasting "cure" can frequently be achieved only by involving the parents and other family members in the therapy.

Several states also have enacted legislation explicitly excepting mental health treatment from the parental consent requirement for certain minors.[73] Maryland permits minors sixteen or older who profess to have mental or emotional disorders to consent to treatment provided by a private physician or an agency physician.[74] In Colorado, minors fifteen years of age or older may consent to receive mental health services from a hospital or person licensed by the state to practice medicine.[75] One criticism applicable to both statutory provisions is that only medical providers are protected from liability. Nonphysician counselors, who provide a wide range of services, are excluded from coverage.[76] In addition, the Maryland statute has been criticized for granting the doctor discretion to inform parents that he is rendering services.[77]

Adolescents who desire inpatient treatment in mental health facilities generally may seek such treatment only through parental application.[78] Even though this form of hospitalization is characterized as a "voluntary admission" in most states, the parent or guardian is legally empowered to act on behalf of the minor child and may "voluntarily" admit the child regardless of the desires of the minor.[79] This practice may therefore lead to situations in which parents seek to hospitalize an unwilling child;[80] in addition, it may work to prevent a minor who desires inpatient treatment from receiving it. The constitutionality of these practices is discussed in chapter 6,[81] and model procedures for hospital admissions are presented in chapter 9.

In the last decade, many states have encouraged voluntary admission to mental hospitals.[82] Advocates of the concept of voluntary admission[83] —admission to a mental hospital initiated by the patient or someone empowered to act for the patient[84] —cite several reasons to support the procedure. First, voluntary admissions may reduce the harmful experiences frequently associated with compulsory hospitalization.[85] Second, voluntary hospitalization may encourage the mentally ill and their families to obtain care early in an illness, when the chances for recovery are greatest.[86] Third, the effectiveness of treatment may be increased when the patient, who has recognized a need for it, cooperates with his physicians.[87]

For these reasons, some commentators have argued that older adolescents, at least, should be able to hospitalize themselves voluntarily and without parental consent. For example, the 1952 NIMH Draft Act Governing Hospitalization of the Mentally Ill provided that any person over sixteen years of age could apply for inpatient treatment of mental illness.[88] In commentary accompanying the model act, the drafters explained that, although the choice of age sixteen was basically arbitrary, the idea of lowering the age for admission without parental consent was based on nonarbitrary rationales. According to the drafters, individuals in their mid- to late teens bear responsibilities similar to those assumed by adults.[89] NIMH also indicated that minors fifteen years or older are probably sufficiently mature to understand the nature of treatment and therefore should not be denied the opportunity to apply for hospital care on the basis of age.[90]

Several states have enacted legislation which reflects the approach suggested in the Draft Act.[91] A few go beyond the Act and permit individuals under sixteen to apply for their own admissions.[92] Some others are silent[93] or confusing[94] on the question. The majority of states, however, appear to confer upon parents the power to compel or prevent the "voluntary admission" of their children up to age eighteen. Appendix B summarizes these laws for all states and the District of Columbia.

Although several states have adopted only some of the statutory exceptions relating to the provision of medical treatment to minors, others have enacted more comprehensive statutory schemes.[95] Generally, these schemes lower the age of consent to all types of medical care and incorporate other exceptions which apply to all or most minors. Alabama, for example, permits any minor who is fourteen or older to give effective consent to medical, dental or mental health services; in addition, minors of any age may consent to treatment relating to pregnancy, venereal disease, drug dependency and alcohol toxicity.[96] Finally, no parental consent is needed in Alabama when, in the physician's judgment, the effort to secure consent would delay treatment and increase the risk to the minor's life, health or mental health.[97]

Liability of Providers for Treating Minors Without Parental Consent

What, if any, is the liability of a mental health provider who provides services to an adolescent without parental consent in circumstances not covered by the exceptions discussed above? Civil liability may be imposed under any of several theories. Before considering those theories, however, it should be noted that several factors complicate a discussion of potential liabilities. First, a wide range of people—from physicians to trained social workers to volunteer telephone hotline operators—are encompassed by the term "mental health provider" (as used in this study), and each group may require different consideration. Case law concerning medical doctors, for example, may apply to psychiatrists,[98] but it may not be applicable to nonmedical personnel. Second, no case law directly addresses the potential liability of many of the providers included in the study, possibly because the number of youth counseling centers, crisis drop-in centers, and telephone hotlines has mushroomed only in recent years. It also may reflect the fact that, until recently, very few children were seeking these services on their own.

Even though judicial law is lacking, many agencies and providers are concerned about the possibility of being sued. This concern is illustrated in two books prepared to assist crisis centers. In one, the authors advise the staff of an emergency agency not to be deterred by the possibility of a lawsuit from offering assistance to any person, including a minor, who seeks counseling.[99] They argue that even if a decision were favorable to the parents in a suit for treatment without consent, the damages "would in all likelihood be nominal, if assessed at all."[100] The authors of the other book, however, suggest that "when the client requesting assistance or advice is a minor, the best legal advice to the crisis center is hands off."[101] Because fear of lawsuits may cause agencies to reduce or limit services available to adolescents, it is important to consider whether certain providers should be protected and, if so, in what manner.

Several theories of liability have been advanced for possible use against a person who provides services to an adolescent without parental consent. These theories include battery, failure to obtain informed consent, intentional and negligent infliction of emotional harm, child enticement, and contributing to the ungovernability of a child. Liability for a provider's possible negligence in treatment, diagnosis, or choice of treatment[102] will not be addressed directly here.

Liability for Battery

One of the first questions involved in considering lack of parental consent is whether, in treating a minor, a provider has committed a battery for which he may be held civilly liable. The law defines battery as an unpermitted contact,[103] and this concept is applicable to physicians in their treatment of patients. Thus, if a doctor fails to obtain consent prior to treating an individual, the doctor has committed a battery for which he or she is liable.[104] According to a number of reported cases, it is also a battery when physicians treat minors without parental consent.[105]

Whether battery would be an appropriate action against more mental health providers who have treated minors without parental consent is questionable.

Treatments such as electroshock therapy, drug therapy, and other techniques involving physical contact or bodily invasion fit most clearly under the "battery" rubric.[106] However, many forms of counseling, particularly those offered by nonmedical counselors, consist only of verbal communication, not physical contact. Thus it is important to determine whether verbal therapy can constitute a battery and whether consent to such therapy by the minor or the minor's parents is necessary. There is, unfortunately, no case law resolving those issues. At least two commentators have suggested that since no physical contact is involved, no consent is required;[107] one of those authors suggests, however, that to be safe, a counselor should secure consent.[108] In the opinion of a third writer, the principle that an unauthorized invasion of one's person violates one's rights is not limited to physical invasions but applies also to "unorthodox methods of psychotherapy."[109] However, this author did not explain to which therapies he was referring or why the concept is not limited to physical invasion. It is therefore not clear whether parents may successfully maintain battery actions against individuals who counsel children without parental consent.

Liability for Failure to Obtain Informed Consent

Another doctrine relating to consent—the requirement that it be informed—also may not be broadly applicable to mental health counseling of adolescents. This doctrine generally requires a physician to inform a patient of the risks and hazards associated with a particular medical procedure;[110] failure to do so may constitute negligence on the part of the physician.[111] It has been held that the doctrine requires psychiatrists to inform patients of the risks associated with convulsive therapy,[112] but whether psychiatrists must inform patients of risks stemming from verbal psychotherapy appears never to have been addressed in the case law. However, because there may be adverse reactions from some forms of counseling,[113] it is not unreasonable to argue that, as with other medical treatments, an informed consent should be required.[114] But even if the doctrine applies to verbal therapy provided by a psychiatrist, it is questionable whether it applies to nonmedical counselors. Perhaps it should, if it can be shown that their counseling sometimes produces serious adverse effects; it is arguable, moreover, that the doctrine should apply with even greater force to less-trained practitioners, as a restraint on poorly administered or ill-conceived modes of therapy.

If a counselor obtains consent only from the minor patient, and either fails to inform the parents or fails to explain to the parents the nature or risks of counseling, an informed consent theory might permit recovery for injury to the child. However, it seems clear that negligence actions of this sort, which allege failure to obtain an informed consent, are not currently a serious threat to the mental health provider.[115]

Liability for Intentional and Negligent
Infliction of Emotional Harm

Although parents may experience mental distress as a result of the provision of mental health services to their child, it is doubtful that they could successfully sue solely on a theory of infliction of emotional distress. Traditionally, courts have been willing to permit damages in this kind of case only when the distress can be linked to an accompanying physical injury[116] caused by negligence or to an independent tort such as assault, battery, or false imprisonment.[117] However, as the law in this area has developed, some courts have been willing to allow recovery for emotional distress which is inflicted intentionally.[118] In certain circumstances, for example, courts have permitted plaintiffs to recover for emotional injury caused by insults and extreme and outrageous conduct.[119]

Psychological counseling, however, would not appear to cause the kind of emotional injury for which courts have permitted recovery. It is usually not extreme or outrageous,[120] and therefore, even if harm results, it would not be classified as an intentional infliction of emotional distress. It appears that a successful suit could be brought only if it could be shown that a counselor, by treating a child without parental consent, was negligent toward the parent and that both mental disturbance and physical harm resulted.

Liability for Child Enticement

Although a mother or father probably could not establish an independent claim sufficient to permit recovery for mental distress, they might be able to recover for such damages as part of an action for child enticement. This sort of action is viewed as a protection of the parents' interests in the custody, companionship, services and affection of their child.[121] At common law, a person who abducted a child, that is, enticed a child away from home or harbored a child who had left home, was held liable to the parent.[122] The interference had to be deliberate, but it need not have been motivated by ill will or by anything more sinister than kindness or affection toward the child.[123] Traditionally, the parents had to establish a loss of the child's services as the foundation of such an action.[124] Once established, the parents could then recover for deprivation of the child's society, the money expended to recover the child, and injury to the parents' own feelings.[125] Some courts, adopting a "modern view," no longer require a showing of loss of services.[126]

Under certain, not improbable circumstances, the enticement doctrine could be found to apply to individuals who counsel adolescents.[127] A counselor may, to varying degrees, influence a minor to disobey a parental directive. In a particular situation, for example, a counselor may advise a minor to move out of a home situation which the counselor perceives as intolerable. If the counselor further aids the child in finding a place to live and refuses to tell the parents of the child's whereabouts, a strong case might be built against the advisor.[128] The more a counselor's advice interferes with and disrupts the parent-child relationship, the greater the likelihood that a court will find the counselor liable.[129]

Liability for Contributing to the Delinquency of a Child

It is even possible that criminal charges may be brought against a counselor for treating an adolescent without parental consent. Most state juvenile codes contain a section similar to this Massachusetts provision:[130]

Any person who shall be found to have caused, induced, abetted, or encouraged or contributed, toward the waywardness or delinquency of a child, or to have acted in any way tending to cause or induce such waywardness or delinquency, may be punished by a fine of not more than five hundred dollars or by imprisonment of not more than one year, or both.

Certainly some types of counseling, concerning, for example, sexual activities or living arrangements,[131] might well be viewed by some parents—and, more importantly, by some judges—as contributing to the waywardness or delinquency of adolescent children.

A counselor accused of such a crime might claim that he lacked a *"mens rea,"* a guilty mind or criminal intent, and that even if substantial harm resulted, the most serious charge possible would be that of civil negligence. It is questionable whether such a defense would succeed, as the counselor undoubtedly would intend the counsel given, if not the harmful consequences. Further, even if he were only negligent, his actions or statements could be considered criminal negligence. Liability for negligence, even for rather great negligence, is not characteristic of the criminal law, but it is not entirely lacking. When the negligence is "gross and culpable" and serious harm has resulted, courts have been willing to convict persons who lack a specific intent to do harm.[132] Case law on the criminal liability of counselors is, however, exceedingly rare.

As is evident from the preceding discussions, the liability of providers for treating adolescents without parental consent is not very clearly defined or settled in either civil or criminal law. This is because the issue has only rarely been litigated. But if this in turn indicates that the legal risk associated with such practices is not great, why is it important that such liabilities be more clearly defined?

One reason is that, although the risks to providers may not be great, they are not entirely absent, and providers have the right to know precisely what they are. An even better reason, however, is that the present situation probably results in the denial of needed services to a not insignificant number of adolescents. Statutes clarifying this confused and undefined area of law should be enacted without delay, both to ensure that needed services are not withheld because of providers' fears (whether justified or groundless) of suit, and to protect minors from potentially harmful treatments. These statutes should define which providers may treat adolescents, the types of services they may provide, the circumstances of treatment, and which minors may be treated without parental consent.

Economic Impediments

Aside from the legal impediments associated with incapacity to give valid consent or enter into binding contracts, adolescents seeking mental health services may be unable to pay for treatment. Many mental health services rank high among the more expensive products in the American market place. In 1969 the average cost of a private psychiatric session (usually fifty minutes) had already reached $35.[133] By now it is undoubtedly significantly higher. In 1974 a rate of $15 per one-half hour was set for diagnostic and therapy sessions at Massachusetts mental health clinics.[134] In December 1976, daily rates for inpatient care ranged up to $169 for adults and older adolescents and $218 for children and very young adolescents at the more prestigious private mental hospitals.[135] Even some public facility inpatient rates now approximate $50 per day for patients with the means to pay.[136] How many adolescents can afford such services?

Private Health Insurance

Since its genesis in the Baylor University Hospital plan of the 1920s, private health insurance has grown to be the principal mechanism relied upon by middle- and upper-income American families for coping with high medical costs.[137] For many years, however, mental health care was generally not included among the "named perils" covered by such insurance. This was apparently because, for most of this period, chemotherapy and other organic treatment modalities were largely unknown; few general hospitals had any psychiatric beds, much less psychiatric wards; and mentally ill persons, if not confined to a back room, were generally banished to a state institution. As for mental health benefits, the early insurers "must have thought (if they thought of [such] benefits at all) in terms of treatment as it then existed. That was reason enough for not including benefits, since no private insurer viewed its proper function as subsidizing the state mental hospital."[138] Private mental hospitals at the time served only the wealthy, who raised no serious outcry to this lack of insurance coverage.

The introduction by commercial insurers in the early 1950s of "major medical" protection in place of the "named perils" approach brought mental health services within the coverage of the typical policy for the first time. This original, practically unlimited coverage was short-lived, however. Some "disastrous early loss experiences" attributable to claims for long-term, expensive, and somewhat faddish psychoanalysis quickly caused insurers to write in limits on outpatient psychiatric services. Many of these limitations, involving mostly coinsurance requirements or maximum dollar or time limits, still exist.[139] Although the bulk of the restrictions apply to outpatient services,[140] most current Blue Cross contracts also have special limitations on hospitalization[141] for mental conditions. The result is that subscribers enjoy substantially less inpatient protection for mental illness than for other conditions.[142]

In this decade, however, there has developed a legislative movement to increase insurance protection for mental illness. In 1971 Connecticut passed law providing that no medical or hospital insurance plan may be sold unless it provides for coverage of mental health expenses.[143] In 1973 Massachusetts followed suit.[144] The Massachusetts statute provides that all insurance carriers, including Blue Cross, have to *offer* mental illness coverage beginning in 1974, and it *mandates* such coverage in all health insurance contracts after January 1, 1976. Benefits must include at least sixty days inpatient care in a mental hospital, care in a general hospital equal to the benefits paid for any other illness in such hospital, and outpatient treatment of at least $500 per year.

By 1972, approximately 67 percent of the United States population had some insurance coverage for inpatient mental health services, and 43 percent had insurance for outpatient services.[145] The percentage of these policies held by unmarried adolescents was miniscule, however, as minors are generally dependent upon their parents' policies for coverage. In a typical Blue Shield family contract, the unmarried children of the policyholder under nineteen years of age are covered whether or not they live with (or even in the same state as) their parents.[146]

"Except in rare instances, Blue Shield makes its payments directly to the physician who renders and reports his services and the subscriber is so notified."[147] It would therefore appear that if an adolescent can furnish his parents' Blue Shield policy number, the provider can receive payment from the family policy for any covered services provided to the minor, even though no parental consent is obtained. However, an adolescent attempting to use this method of paying for mental health services may encounter several difficulties. Note that Blue Shield's subscriber notification procedure means that the minor cannot prevent his parents from learning of his treatment. Also, only certain kinds of mental health treatment are reimbursable by third party insurers, and the rather narrow coverage provided by some policies appears, on occasion, to have been narrowed still further by court decisions. For instance, the Oaks Residential Treatment Center of Austin, Texas, a private psychiatric hospital specializing in the diagnosis and treatment of emotionally disturbed children and adolescents, was found not to be a "hospital," as that term was used in a group hospitalization policy. It failed to qualify because, since there were no surgical facilities at the center, it did not primarily engage in providing "diagnostic and therapeutic facilities for surgical and medical diagnosis and treatment and care of sick individuals by or under the supervision of a doctor."[148] The facts that there was little or no need for surgical facilities at the Center and that arrangements had been made with another institution for any required surgery were deemed irrelevant.[149]

The National Association for Mental Health has taken the position that, under the current health delivery system in this country, services rendered by independent, nonphysician mental health practitioners and agencies should be included only if they are relevant to the adolescent's problem as defined by a screening physician.[150] An adolescent acting without parental backing may be reluctant to seek services which entail formal screening procedures. Some third-party payers have recently extended coverage to services rendered by licensed psychologists,[151] but few, if any, go beyond that to include psychiatric social workers or other unlicensed counselors. Yet the latter category are most likely to be approached by adolescents acting on their own initiative.

Public Funds

Private health insurance is not, of course, the only potential source of funds to pay for adolescent mental health services. Public funds, both federal and state, may also be available to certain adolescents for certain services. It is well known that governments pay for some health care, but the huge growth of such payments in recent years has not generally been recognized. "By 1973, federal and state governments were meeting the costs of 38 cents of every dollar spent on health care."[152] In cities the governmental share is even larger, and it is growing rapidly. In 1960, for example, public expenditures accounted for 50.5 percent of the care rendered in New York City hospitals and nursing homes. By 1971, this figure had risen to 72 percent![153] During this period, the federal government's share of this public payment increased from 18 percent to 43 percent.[154] Government funds were paid out under various programs, most of which do not apply to adolescent mental health services.[155] Two of the more important and relevant of these programs will be discussed briefly below.

Medicaid

A major source of medical assistance for low-income people is the Medicaid program.[156] This program is cooperatively financed by the federal and state governments, with the federal government paying at least 50 percent of the cost. Unlike some other federal programs, each state designs and administers its own Medicaid plan.[157] A determination of Medicaid's applicability to an adolescent's mental health needs requires an examination of two topics: eligibility and services covered.

Eligibility. Under the federal statute, the various states administering Medicaid programs may elect to include very wide or very narrow classes of persons. For certain groups, however, coverage is mandatory. The two of them most relevant to this discussion are families receiving AFDC benefits[158] and persons under twenty-one who would be excluded from AFDC eligibility solely because of the age or school attendance requirements of AFDC.[159] An adolescent in either of these groups thus meets the eligibility requirements in any state.

One of the "optional categorically needy" groups which states may or may not choose to make eligible for Medicaid consists of persons under twenty-one who qualify for AFDC on the basis of financial eligibility but not as dependent children under the state's AFDC plan.[160] Adolescents in this category thus satisfy Medicaid eligibility requirements in states, such as Massachusetts,[161] which have elected to extend eligibility to this group, but not in other states which have not.

Services Covered. If an adolescent qualifies for Medicaid, there is a question whether the treatment he or she is seeking will be covered by that program. Clearly, when such treatment is not covered, the likelihood of the adolescent not seeking the treatment at all increases. Medicaid covers two categories of medical services. The first consists of five services which must be available to persons for whom Medicaid is mandated. These are inpatient hospital services (in other than a tuberculosis institution or, except for persons under twenty-one, a psychiatric facility),[162] outpatient hospital services, laboratory and X-ray services, physician services, and skilled nursing home services for persons over twenty-one (and some health services for persons who previously were in nursing homes).[163] The federal law also requires that participating states provide comprehensive diagnostic services—termed Early and Periodic Screening, Diagnosis and Treatment (EPSDT)[164]—to persons under twenty-one who are eligible for Medicaid.

The second major category of services includes those additional services that *may* be made available to mandatory enrollees, as well as optional enrollees, at the states' election. These consist of eleven specified types of services, as well as a blanket provision for "any other medical care."[165] Among the specified services are inpatient psychiatric services for individuals under twenty-one,[166] which was added by the Social Security Amendments of 1972.[167] Federal regulations promulgated for these services in 1976 are designed to eliminate or reduce problems of "institutionalization" by sanctioning admission only when "available alternative local community resources for ambulatory care[168] do not meet the treatment needs of the individual,"[169] and by requiring, after admission, "active" treatment, "reasonably expected to improve the individual's condition . . . to achieve the individual's discharge from inpatient status at the earliest possible time."[170] The regulations also include salutary requirements for use of an "individualized plan of care," formulated and reviewed every thirty days by an "interdisciplinary team."[171]

Although this program is specifically tailored to provide mental health services to adolescents and younger children,[172] its usefulness is substantially limited by several factors: it applies only to inpatient services rendered in an institution accredited as a psychiatric facility by the Joint Commission on Accreditation of Hospitals (JCAH);[173] federal financial participation is limited by formula;[174] and, perhaps most importantly, the services are available only in those states which choose to participate.

In summary, the Medicaid program provides, at best, only partial coverage for mental health services to adolescents. Even when an adolescent qualifies for medical benefits thereunder, the benefits covered will generally not include the type of mental health services which he or she most needs or desires.

Health Maintenance Organizations

Health Maintenance Organizations (HMOs) represent a federal effort to improve the health care delivery system throughout the country. Essentially, an HMO is a community-based plan for prepaid medical care, funded to a great extent by federal money.[175] Members of an HMO are usually employees of a participating institution and their families, membership being an incidence of the employment relationship (in lieu of an alternative health insurance program for employees).[176] The federal statute creating and defining HMOs lists among the "basic health services" to be provided to members "short-term (not to exceed twenty visits), outpatient evaluative and crisis intervention mental health services"[177] as well as "inpatient and outpatient hospital services."[178] Thus, an adolescent member of a family belonging to an HMO may be able to utilize these mental health treatment opportunities and facilities. Such treatment, however, may only be acquired at the HMO facility, from members of the HMO staff, and the adolescent's parents are likely to be informed. Nevertheless, although a number of problems have been encountered by many HMOs during their start-up phase,[179] and HMO membership is thus far extremely limited, the program does possess the long-range potential for making needed mental health services readily accessible to adolescents.

Notes

1. Bonner v. Moran, 126 F.2d 121, 122 (D.C. Cir. 1941):

In deference to common experience, there is a general recognition of the fact that many persons by reason of their youth are incapable of intelligent decision, as the result of which public policy demands legal protection of their personal as well as their property rights.

See generally Note, *Counseling the Counselors: Legal Implications of Counseling Minors without Parental Consent*, 31 Md. L. Rev. 332, 335 (1971) [hereinafter cited as *Counseling the Counselors*].

2. *See* H. Pilpel, *Minors' Rights to Medical Care*, 36 Albany L. Rev. 462 (1972), at 463.

3. Bonner v. Moran, note 1 above.

4. *See* Lacey v. Laird, 166 Ohio St. 12, 19 (1956):

The (general) rule . . . is based upon the right of parents whose liability for support and maintenance of their child may be greatly increased by an unfavorable result from the operational procedures upon the part of a surgeon. (concurring opinion).

5. *Id. See* L. Glantz, Legal Problems of Providing Medical Care to Minors (1972) (unpublished paper prepared for Center for Law and Health Sciences, on file at the center).

6. Pratt v. Davis, 118 Ill. App. 161, 166 (1905); Mohr v. Williams, 95 Minn. 261, 104 N.W. 12, 14 (1905); Schloendorff v. Society of New York Hospital, 211 N.Y. 125, 129-30, 105 N.E. 92, 93 (1914); Gray v. Grunnagle, 423 Pa. 144, 155, 223 A.2d 663 (1966); Grannum v. Berard, 70 Wash. 304, 306, 422 P.2d 812 (1967); J. Waltz & T. Scheuneman, *Informed Consent to Therapy*, 64 Nw. U.L. Rev. 628, 629 (1970); Note, *Informed Consent in Medical Malpractice*, 55 Calif. L. Rev. 1396 (1967).

7. Schloendorff v. Society of New York Hospital, 211 N.Y. 125, 129, 105 N.E. 92, 93 (1914).

8. Gray v. Grunnagle, 423 Pa. 144, 155, 223 A.2d 663 (1966).

9. *Id.*, at 156, 223 A.2d at 669, *quoting* People v. Lowe, 209 App. Div. 498, 205 N.Y.S. 77, 78 (1924).

10. Canterbury v. Spence, 464 F.2d 772, 783 (D.C. Cir. 1972); Schloendorff v. Society of N.Y. Hosps., 211 N.Y. 125, 129-30, 105 N.E. 92 (1914).

11. Bonner v. Moran, note 1 above; Tabor v. Scobee, 254 S.W.2d 474, 475-76 (Ct. App., Ky. 1951); Zoski v. Gaines, 271 Mich. 1, 260 N.W. 99, 102 (1935); Gulf & S.I.R. Co. v. Sullivan, 155 Miss. 1, 119 So. 501, 502 (1928);

Lacey v. Laird, 166 Ohio St. 12, 19, 139 N.E.2d 25 (1956) (dicta); Rogers v. Sells, 178 Okla. 103, 61 P.2d 1018 (1936) (syllabus); Moss v. Rishworth, 22 S.W. 225, 226-27 (Comm. App. Tex. 1920). *Gulf* and *Lacey* state the general rule but find that in circumstances of the respective cases exceptions to the rule are applicable. *See* Luka v. Lowrie, 171 Mich. 122, 134-35 (1912); H. Pilpel, note 2 above; Note, *Parental Consent Requirements and Privacy Rights of Minors: The Contraceptive Controversy*, 88 Harv. L. Rev. 1001 (1975) [hereinafter cited as *Contraceptive Controversy*].

12. *See* Canterbury v. Spence, 464 F.2d 772 (D.C. Cir. 1972); Natanson v. Kline, 186 Kan. 393, 350 P.2d 1093 (1960) *clarified* 187 Kan. 186 (1960). The *Canterbury* court stated that the disclosure requirement reflected more a change in doctrinal emphasis than a substantive addition to malpractice law. *Id.*, at 782. *See generally* Waltz & Scheuneman, *Informed Consent to Therapy*, note 6 above; Note, *Informed Consent in Medical Malpractice*, note 6 above; Note, *Advise and Consent in Medicine: A Look at the Doctrine of Informed Consent*, 16 N.Y.L. Forum 863 (1970); Note, *Informed Consent—A Proposed Standard for Medical Disclosure*, 48 N.Y.U. L. Rev. 548 (1973); Comment, *A New Standard for Informed Consent in Medical Malpractice Cases—The Role of the Expert Witness*, 18 St. Louis L. Rev. 256 (1973); Note, *Informed Consent as a Theory of Medical Liability*, 1970 Wis. L. Rev. 879 (1970); Note, *Restructuring Informed Consent: Legal Therapy for the Doctor-Patient Relationship*, 79 Yale L.J. 1533 (1970) [hereinafter cited as *Informed Consent Note*].

13. *See* Cobbs v. Grant, 502 P.2d 1 (Cal. 1972); Wilkinson v. Vesey, 295 A.2d 676 (R.I. 1972).

14. In addition to reinforcing the protection of bodily integrity, it has been suggested that the informed consent doctrine could counteract the effect of the depersonalized, authoritarian patient-physician relationship characteristic of modern medical practice. Because doctors have little sustained personal contact with patients, they cannot judge a patient's need or capacity to understand and evaluate a proposed treatment. Thus, the patient should be given the information on which to base his or her decision. *Informed Consent Note*, note 12 above, at 1541, 1559.

15. *See* J. Ellis, *Volunteering Children: Parental Commitment of Minors to Mental Institutions*, 62 Calif. L. Rev. 840, 859-62 (1974). *See generally* C. Vincent, *Mental Health and the Family*, J. Marr. & Fam. 18, 22-24 (Feb. 1967). The author discusses the significance of the family in the prevention, cause and treatment of a family member's mental illness. The author notes an increasing emphasis on the therapeutic function of the family in treating a mentally ill patient. This emphasis may underscore the need for involvement of the parents in their child's mental health treatment. However, as noted by another commentator, "parental involvement can—and should—be obtained by means short of giving the parent absolute discretion." Ellis, above, at 862.

16. *See* Ministering to Families of the Mentally Ill, prepared by the

National Association for Mental Health (NAMH Pamphlet No. 142-1-72-5M, 1972).

17. *Compare* L. Deasy & O. Quinn, *The Wife of the Mental Patient and the Hospital Psychiatrist*, 11:4 J. Soc. Iss. 49 (1955).

18. *See* Schuham *et al.*, note 17 above, at 440. That psychological study attempted to evaluate the role of parental guilt feelings over the child's mental illness in the parents' decision to place their child in a residential treatment institution. Although stating that the precise role of parental guilt feelings in the placement process remained unclear, the researchers suggested that guilt might be either a motivational factor or a resistance factor. Guilt feelings may motivate the parents to seek institutionalization as an outlet for their anxiety. Parents may feel some relief at taking some positive action. However, parental guilt may increase resistance to institutionalization because of the parents' perception of the nature of the treatment to be administered. *Id.*, at 448-49.

19. *Id.*, at 449.

20. *See The Implications of Minor's Consent Legislation for Adolescent Health Care: A Commentary*, 45 Pediatrics 481, 482 (Oct. 1974).

21. Pratt v. Davis, 224 Ill. 300, 309-10 (1906); Jackovach v. Yocom, 212 Iowa 914, 237 N.W. 444, 449 (1941); Luka v. Lowrie, 171 Mich. 122, 136 N.W. 1106 (1912); Sullivan v. Montgomery, 155 Misc. 448, 449, 279 N.Y.S. 75 (City Ct. of N.Y., Bronx County 1935).

22. *E.g.*, Mass Gen. Laws Ann. ch. 112, § 12F (1975) (physician will not be liable if he fails to obtain parental consent when "delay in the treatment will endanger the life, limb or mental well being of the patient . . . "); Minn. Stat. Ann., ch. 144, § 144.344 (Cum. Supp. 1975-76) (no parental consent required when, in professional's judgment, the risk to the minor's life or health is such that treatment should be given without delay); Md. Code Ann., § 135 (a)(4) (Supp. 1974).

23. *E.g.*, Mass. Gen. Laws Ann. ch. 112, § 12F (1975), quoted in note 22 above; Minn. Stat. Ann. § 144.246 (Cum. Supp. 1975-76).

24. *Compare* J. Stern, *Medical Treatment and the Teenager: The Need for Parental Consent*, 7 Clearinghouse Rev. 1, 2.

25. Bach v. Long Island Jewish Hosp., 49 Misc. 2d 207, 267 N.Y.S.2d 289 (Sup. Ct. Nassau County 1966); Smith v. Seibly, 72 Wash. 2d 16, 21, 431 P.2d 719 (1967); Pilpel, note 2 above, at 465; *Contraceptive Controversy*, note 11 above, at 1002.

26. *See* S. Katz, Schroeder & L. Sidman, *Emancipating Our Children—Coming of Legal Age in America*, 7 Fam. L. Q. 211, 219-32 (1973). The authors discuss how courts have utilized the emancipation doctrine to overcome the intrafamily tort immunity doctrine, and to decide questions in connection with actions to recover a minor's wages or damages for loss of a minor's services.

27. Katz *et al.*, note 26 above, at 214. Parents generally are held responsible

for providing financial support, health care and educational opportunities for their children. To facilitate their performing these obligations, parents are vested with custody and control of their child. They also are entitled to the child's services and any money earned by the minor child. When the child is judged to be emancipated, the reciprocal rights and responsibilities are no longer legally enforceable. *Id.*, at 214-15. However, emancipation does not necessarily remove all the legal disabilities of childhood (such as the child's inability to enter into binding contracts or to own property). *See Id.* at 229-30; *Summary and Analysis of State Laws Relating to Contraceptive Services to Minors*, from Dep't. of Health, Education and Welfare, *Family Planning—An Analysis of Laws and Policies in the U.S.* (1971) [hereinafter cited as DHEW, *Summary and Analysis*], at 70-71.

28. Emancipation may result from an express agreement between parents and child in which the parents relinquish their rights of control and the child agrees to relieve them of their financial obligations. Implied emancipation occurs when a court finds that the conduct of the parties is inconsistent with the minor's occupying a subordinate status in the family. *See* Katz *et al.*, note 26 above, at 215-16.

29. *See* Katz *et al.*, note 26 above, at 217-18; *Contraceptive Controversy*, note 11 above, at 1002; DHEW, *Summary and Analysis*, note 27 above, at 72. In one article several commentators stated that marriage and enlistment are generally deemed sufficient in themselves to create emancipation. Katz *et al.*, note 26 above, at 217. However, marriage or enlistment may result in partial emancipation only. *See, e.g.,* Bach v. Long Island Hosp., 49 Misc. 2d 207, 267, N.Y.S.2d 289 (Sup. Ct. Nassau County 1966) (married minor emancipated for purposes of consenting to alteration of personal rights but not property rights).

30. Wurth v. Wurth, 322 S.W.2d 745, 746 (Sup. Ct. of Missouri 1959); Bates v. Bates, 62 Misc. 2d 498, 502, 310 N.Y.S.2d 26 (Fam. Ct. Westchester County 1970). *See* Katz *et al.*, note 26 above, at 217. However, the parents' conduct may imply the intent to emancipate the child. Bates v. Bates, above, at 502.

31. Spurgeon v. Mission St. Bank, 151 F.2d 702 (8th Cir. 1945) (law implies emancipation when father neglects or refuses to support child, so that child must be self-supporting); Town of Plainville v. Town of Milford, 177 A. 138 (Conn. 1935).

32. DHEW, *Summary and Analysis*, note 27 above, at 72. *See also* Katz *et al.*, note 26 above, at 219. The authors argue that where the legal claim differs, a court faced with nearly identical factual patterns may reach different results. According to the authors, such differences reflect a court's attitude toward the child's place in the family. *Id.*

33. *See* Katz *et al.*, note 26 above, at 216.

34. 49 Misc. 2d 207, 267 N.Y.S.2d 289 (Sup. Ct. Nassau County 1966).

35. *Id.*, at 208-9; 267 N.Y.S.2d at 291.

36. Bates v. Bates, 62 Misc. 2d 498, 503, 310 N.Y.S.2d 26 (Fam. Ct. Westchester County 1970). *See* Katz *et al.*, note 26 above, at 216-17.

37. *E.g.*, Cal. Civ. Code § 25.6 (West Supp. 1971) (married minors are emancipated); § 25.7 (minors on active duty in the armed services); and § 34.6 (minor fifteen or over and living separate and apart from parents or legal guardian, whether with or without consent of parent or guardian and regardless of duration of such separate residence, and who is managing own financial affairs, regardless of source of income); Minn. Stat. Ann., § 144.341 (living apart from parents and managing financial affairs) and § 144.342 (married or has child). At least twenty-one states have statutes declaring that a minor who is emancipated or married or both can give effective consent to his or her own medical care. DHEW, *Summary and Analysis*, note 27 above, at 71.

38. DHEW, *Summary and Analysis*, note 27 above, at 72. For example, under the California statute, a minor may be emancipated if he or she is living apart from the parents (whether with their consent or not and regardless of the duration of separation) and who is managing his or her own financial affairs (regardless of source of income). Cal. Civ. Code § 34.6.

39. See DHEW, *Summary and Analysis*, note 27 above, at 72. Although broader than the common law definition and therefore permitting more extensive coverage, the California definition has been criticized for failing to define clearly which minors are covered. One commentator has questioned how providers of services are to determine whether a minor is living apart from his or her parents or whether the minor manages his or her own financial affairs. *See* 10 Santa Clara Law 334, 336-37 (1970). The author also notes that the section requires a physician to make a subjective determination about the minor's status. *Id.*, at 338.

40. *See, e.g.,* Younts v. St. Francis, 205 Kan. 292, 301, 469 P.2d 330 (1970). Other cases cited as representing this doctrine include Lacey v. Laird, 166 Ohio St. 12, 139 N.E.2d 25 (1956); Gulf & S.I.R. Co. v. Sullivan, 119 So. 501 (Miss. 1928).

41. *See Contraceptive Controversy*, note 11 above, at 1003; DHEW, *Summary and Analysis*, note 27 above, at 72.

42. *Contraceptive Controversy*, note 11 above, at 1003; DHEW, *Summary and Analysis*, note 27 above, at 72. This requirement thus would exclude all experimentation which is not therapeutic. One commentator has suggested that a third factor upon which courts rely is the complexity of the procedure. For the exception to apply, the treatment must be minor, not major. *See Contraceptive Controversy*, note 11 above, at 1003, citing Wadlington, *Minors and Health Care: The Age of Consent*, 11 Osgood Hall L.J. 115, 119 (1973).

43. *See Contraceptive Controversy*, note 11 above, at 1003.

44. Miss. Code Ann. § 41-41-3(h) (1972).

45. *Id.*

46. *Contraceptive Controversy*, note 11 above, at 1003-4.

47. *See* Pilpel, note 2 above, at 462-63, 467-68; R. Zuckerman, ACLU Reports: Abortion and the Constitutional Rights of Minors, 15-16 (1973). The author notes that the existence of statutes permitting minors to consent to treatment for venereal disease and contraceptive services indicates state awareness of both the sexual activity of many unmarried minors and the health needs of minors, which should be served irrespective of parental wishes.

48. *See* Pilpel, note 2 above, at 462.

49. *E.g.*, Colo. Rev. Stat. § 13-22-105 (1973) (birth control supplies may be furnished to any minor who is pregnant, married, a parent or who has been referred for such services); Md. Code Ann. § 135(a)(3) (1974 Supp.) (right to consent to contraception not amounting to sterilization); Oregon Rev. Stat. § 109.640 (1971) (any physician may provide birth control information without regard to age).

50. *E.g.*, Oregon Rev. Stat. § 109.640 (1971); Tenn. Code Ann. § 53-4604 (Cum. Supp. 1974).

51. *E.g.*, Colo. Rev. Stat. § 13-22-105 (birth control information to any minor who is pregnant, a parent, married or has been referred by clergyman or family planning clinic).

52. *See, e.g.*, Ga. Code Ann. ch. 88-2904 (Supp. 1974); Ky. Rev. Stat. § 214, 185(1) (Supp. 1974). Some statutes explicitly exclude abortion or sterilization from the kinds of treatment to which minors may consent. Ga. Code Ann. S88-2904. Ky. Rev. Stat. S214.185. At least one state specifically authorizes minors to consent to abortion. Del. Code § 708.

One court has held that abortion falls within provisions of the state statute permitting minors to consent to medical and surgical care related to pregnancy. Ballard v. Anderson, 95 Cal. Rptr. 1, 484 P.2d 1345 (1971). The court stated that "there was no basis for discriminatorily singling out therapeutic abortion as the only type of pregnancy related surgical care which requires parental consent." *Id.*, at 1352.

53. *E.g.*, Minn. Stats. Ann. § 144.343 (1975 Supp.); Ala. Code tit. 22 § 104(17) (1972) (any minor may consent to any legally authorized services to treat pregnancy; statute does not mention consent to contraception services).

54. Jones v. T.H., 423 U.S. 1030 (1975). See *Minor's Rights*, Health Law Newsletter, no. 62 (June 1976), at 2. *Compare* Doe v. Planned Parenthood Association of Utah, 29 Utah 2d 356, 510 P.2d 75 (1973).

55. Carey v. Population Services International, 97 S. Ct. 2010 (1977).

56. For arguments, written before these decisions, against the constitutionality of such laws, *see generally, Contraceptive Controversy*, note 11 above.

57. 410 U.S. 113 (1973).

58. *Roe* was a class action suit brought by a pregnant single woman challenging the constitutionality of the Texas criminal abortion laws. Those laws prohibited abortion except to save the life of the mother. The Supreme Court held that the right of privacy, embodied in the Fourteenth Amendment's

concept of personal liberty, encompassed a woman's decision whether to terminate a pregnancy. The Court held, however, that this right was not absolute and could be restricted under certain circumstances. Because a fundamental right—the right to privacy—is involved, the state could justify limiting it only by asserting compelling state interests and only by drawing the limitation narrowly to further those interests. *Id.*, at 155. The Court held that the state's interest in protecting the health of the mother became compelling at approximately the end of the first trimester of pregnancy. Thus, at that point the state "may regulate the abortion procedure to the extent that the regulation reasonably relates to the preservation and protection of maternal health." *Id.*, at 163. With respect to the state's interest in potential life, the Court held that the "compelling" point is when the fetus is viable (defined by the Court as potentially able to live outside the mother with artificial aid. *Id.* at 160) or approximately at the end of the second trimester. *Id.* at 163.

59. *E.g.*, Foe v. Vanderhoof, 389 F. Supp. 947 (D. Col. 1975); Baird v. Bellotti, 393 F. Supp. 847 (D. Mass. 1975) *vacated and remanded sub nom.* Bellotti v. Baird, 428 U.S. 132 (1976); Coe v. Gerstein, 376 F. Supp. 695 (S.D. Fla. 1973), *appeal dismissed for want of jurisdiction*, 417 U.S. 279 (1974); State v. Koome, 84 Wash. 2d 901, 530 P.2d 260 (1975); In the Matter of P.J., No. 922975 (Super. Ct. of D.C., Family Div. March 21, 1973). *See also* Note, *The Right of a Husband or a Minor's Parent to Participate in the Abortion Decision*, 28 U. of Miami L. Rev. 251 (1973).

61. 428 U.S. 132 (1976).

62. Chapter 6, at note 61 *et seq.*

63. According to the Department of Health, Education and Welfare, at least 47 states and the District of Columbia have enacted statutes providing that minors can consent to treatment of venereal disease (all states except South Carolina, Wisconsin, and Wyoming). In addition, South Carolina has enacted a general statute providing for the treatment of venereal disease, which the state attorney general has ruled permits minors to be treated without parental consent. DHEW, *Summary and Analysis*, note 27 above, at 75.

64. *Id.*

65. In the preamble to the New Jersey statute permitting minors to consent to treatment for venereal disease, the legislature stated:

... Since contraction of a venereal disease is subject to serious reproach within the family circle, the necessary parental consent to treatment may not be sought by the minor because of fear of embarrassment.... The threat to public health from venereal disease is of such gravity that the infected person should be treated as soon as diagnosed to protect his health and prevent the spread of the disease to others. In view of the danger posed and the increasing numbers of minors infected, it is essential that this highly vulnerable segment of our population be accorded greater freedom in securing prompt medical treatment.

N.J. Stat. Ann. § 9.17A-4 (1971 Cum. Supp.) quoted in DHEW, *Summary and Analysis*, note 27 above, at 75.

66. Ill. Ann. Stat. c. 91 § 18.5 (Supp. 1974-75) (provider of venereal disease health care to a minor may inform his or her parents).

67. Katz *et al.*, note 26 above, at 239.

68. *E.g.*, Colo. Rev. Stat. Ann. tit. 13, art. 22-102 (1973); Fla. Stat. Ann. tit. 27, ch. 397.099 (West 1973); Ill. Ann. Stat. ch. 91, §§ 18.4, 18.5 (Smith-Hurd 1975 Cum. Supp.).

69. *See* W. Whitford, *The Physician, the Law and the Drug Abuser*, 119 U.Pa. L. Rev. 933, 935 (1971); Stern, note 24 above, at 4.

70. Stern, note 24 above, at 4.

71. *E.g.*, Ill. Ann. Stat. ch. 91, § 81.5 (Smith-Hurd 1975 Cum. Supp.) (physician may, but shall not be obligated to, inform parents of any such minor as to treatment given or needed); Md. Code Ann. art. 43 § 135 (174 Cum. Supp.) (doctor may inform parents without consent of minor patient and over the express refusal of the minor patient).

72. *See* Whitford, note 69 above, at 968.

73. Colo. Rev. Stat. § 27-10-103 (1973); Md. Ann. Code § 135A (1971 and 1971 Supp.). In those states which do specifically include mental health treatment, but have enacted statutes lowering the age of consent for general medical treatment, it seems that minors may give effective consent to mental health treatment. However, because many of these statutes provide that minors may consent to treatment from a licensed physician, the minor's consent may be valid only to the extent the treatment is provided by a physician.

74. Md. Code Ann. § 135A (1971 and 1971 Supp.).

75. Colo. Rev. Stat. § 27-10-103 (1973).

76. *See Counseling the Counselors,* note 1 above, at 346-47.

77. *Id.*, at 346.

78. *See* Ellis, note 15 above, at 847.

79. The Mentally Disabled and the Law (rev. ed. S. Brakel & R. Rock 1971), at 19.

80. In most states, parents may admit their children to mental institutions without a hearing or any other form of judicial review. If the hospital agrees to accept the child, no legal authority will respond to the protests of the child or determine whether the child is in need of treatment. Ellis, note 15 above, at 840.

81. *See* chapter 6, text at note 64 *et seq.*

82. B. Ennis & L. Siegel, The Rights of Mental Patients (1973), at 36.

83. *See* W. Curran, *Hospitalization of the Mentally Ill*, 31 N.C.L. Rev. 274 (1953).

84. S. Brakel & R. Rock, note 79 above, at 18. Voluntary admission may be contrasted with involuntary hospitalization or commitment. Involuntary hospitalization "describes the removal of a person judged to be mentally ill from his normal surroundings to a hospital authorized to detain him." The criteria for involuntary hospitalization are specified by statute and vary from state to state. The determination whether to hospitalize an individual is usually made by a court, an administrative panel or a specified number of physicians. *Id.*, at 35.

85. A Draft Act Governing Hospitalization of the Mentally Ill, Public Health Service Publication No. 51 (rev. Sept. 1952) [hereinafter cited as Draft Act], commentary to Part II, reprinted in Brakel and Rock, note 79 above, Appendix A. One author notes that another reason for the medical profession's support of voluntary admission is that it necessitates only minimal court involvement. Curran, note 83 above, at 277. It is also argued that voluntary admissions carry less stigma than involuntary commitments.

86. Draft Act, note 85 above, in commentary to Part II.

87. Brakel & Rock, note 79 above, at 17.

88. Draft Act, note 85 above, at 457.

89. *Id.*, at 463. The drafters cited as an example that individuals in their later teens carry the same responsibilities for infractions of the law as do adults.

90. *Id.*, at 463-64.

91. *See, e.g.*, Mass. Gen. Laws Ann. ch. 123 § 10 (Cum. Supp. 1974-75).

92. *See, e.g.*, Colo. Rev. Stat. 1973, §§ 27-20-103(2), (3) (1974) (age 15 or older).

93. *See, e.g.*, La. Rev. Stat. Ann. § 28:51 (1975 Supp.).

94. *See, e.g.*, Idaho Code §§ 66-318, 66-320(a)(2) (1976 Supp.).

95. At least eleven states have statutes which may be considered comprehensive, according to an HEW publication. DHEW, *Summary and Analysis,* note 27 above, at 74.

96. Code of Ala., tit. 22 §§ 105(15)-(18) (1973 Supp.).

97. *Id.*

98. Note, *Injuries Precipitated by Psychotherapy: Liability Without Fault as a Basis for Recovery*, 20 South Dakota L. Rev. 401 (1975).

99. Brockopp & Oughterson, *Legal and Procedural Aspects of Telephone Emergency Services*, in D. Lester & G. Brockopp, Crisis Intervention and Counseling by Telephone 125 (1973). The authors note that it would be absurd to obtain proof of age in a telephone conversation before providing assistance.

100. *Id.*

101. P. Tate & C. Greenfield, *Legal Considerations in Crisis Center Operation*, in U. Delworth, E. Rudow & J. Taub, Crisis Center/Hotline, A Guidebook to Beginning and Operating (1972), at 59-60.

102. It is important to distinguish between liability for treating without parental consent and liability for other reasons. A statute permitting certain minors to consent to their own mental health treatment would not relieve a provider from liability caused by negligence relating to the treatment. *Compare* Committee on Legislation Concerning Adolescents' Medical Care, Society for Adolescent Medicine, *A Model Bill for Minors' Consent to Health Services*, 52 Pediatrics 750 (1973) (Section 12).

103. *See* W. Prosser, The Law of Torts (4th ed. 1971), at 34-37.

104. Schloendorff v. Society of New York Hospital, 211 N.Y. 125, 129, 105 N.E. 92, 93 (1914).

105. *E.g.*, Bonner v. Moran, 126 F.2d 121 (D.C. Cir. 1941); Lacey v. Laird, 166 Ohio St. 12, 139 N.E.2d 25 (1956).

106. Stowers v. Ardmore Acres Hosp., 172 N.W.2d 497 (Ct. App. Mich. 1969) (consent of psychiatric patient required before injection of drugs); *Wilson v. Lehman*, 379 S.W. 2d 478 (Ct. of App. Ky. 1964) (consent required prior to administration of electroshock therapy).

107. R. Gosse, *Consent to Medical Treatment: A Minor Digression*, 9 U.B.C.L. Rev. 56, 59 (1974); *Counseling the Counselors*, note 1 above, at 347.

108. Gosse, note 107 above, at 59-60.

109. H. Weihofen, Legal Services and Community Mental Health Centers 15 (1969).

110. Canterbury v. Spence, 464 F.2d 772 (D.C. Cir. 1972); Natanson v. Kline, 186 Kan. 393, 350 P.2d 1093 (1960) *clarified* 187 Kan. 186. *See generally* Waltz & Scheuneman, *Informed Consent to Therapy*, note 6 above, and other articles cited in note 12 above.

111. Canterbury v. Spence, 464 F.2d 772, 793 (D.C. Cir. 1972); Natanson v. Kline, 186 Kan. 393, 350 P.2d 1093 (1960) *clarified* 187 Kan. 186, 354 P.2d 670; Mitchell v. Robinson, 334 S.W.2d 11 (S. Ct. of Mo. 1960).

112. In Mitchell v. Robinson, 334 S.W.2d 11 (S. Ct. of Mo. 1960) plaintiff sustained convulsive fractures while undergoing insulin therapy for treatment of emotional illness. He sued the treating psychiatrists, alleging that they failed to inform him that the fracture of bones was a hazard of the treatment and that, had he known, he would not have consented to the procedure. The court held that "considering the nature of the plaintiff's illness and this rather new and radical procedure with its high incidence of serious and permanent injuries . . . , the doctors owed their patient . . . the duty to inform him generally of the possible serious collateral hazards." *Id.*, at 19. *See also* Lester v. Aetna Casualty & Surety Co., 240 F.2d 676 (5th Cir. 1957) (informed consent of wife sufficient when in physician's judgment it would be unsafe to require patient to undergo the strain and shock of discussing and considering the possible hazards involved with electroshock treatment). *See generally* H. Morse, *The Tort Liability of the Psychiatrist*, 16 Buff. L. Rev. 649, 655 (1967); H. Rothblatt & D. Leroy, *Avoiding Psychiatric Malpractice*, 9 Cal. W. L. Rev. 260, 268 (1973); Note, *Psychiatric Negligence*, 23 Drake L. Rev. 640, 644 (1974).

113. *See Injuries Precipitated by Psychotherapy: Liability Without Fault as a Basis for Recovery*, 20 South Dakota L. Rev. 401 (1975). In this article the author considers possible legal remedies against psychotherapists for patients who suffer iatrogenic injury. The article defines iatrogenic injury as "injury induced in a patient by a therapist's words or actions." *Id.*, at 402. Although noting that practitioners disagree over whether psychotherapy can cause iatrogenic injuries, the author concludes that "there is strong evidence that psychotherapy can effect [*sic*] the patient in an injurious manner . . . " *Id.*, at 403.

114. *See* Note, *The Liability of Psychiatrists for Malpractice*, 36 U. Pitt. L. Rev. 108, 119 (1974) [hereinafter cited as *Liability of Psychiatrists*], ("Although there have been no cases involving informed consent with regard to

analysis or psychotherapy, the same principles of informed consent should be applicable.")

115. It is interesting to note that in the case of minors, one traditional defense may be foreclosed to therapists. Mental health providers have sometimes successfully maintained that full disclosure of risk was not required because, given the patient's poor mental and emotional condition, such disclosure might result in even greater risk and would adversely affect treatment. (*See Liability of Psychiatrists*, note 114 above, at 119.) This argument loses its force when disclosure must legally be made to parents rather than the patient.

116. Prosser, note 103 above, at 52.

117. *Id.*, at 330.

118. *Id.*, at 49-50.

119. *Id.*, at 52-60.

120. There may be exceptions, however. The license of Hyde Park House, which was established to treat delinquent children, was revoked by the Massachusetts Office for Children because of allegations that the youths there were subjected to physical and verbal abuse. News item, *Hyde Park Home for Delinquents Loses License*, Boston Globe (March 25, 1977) at 6. Only seriously troubled children were placed in this facility, however, and the Chairman of the Board of Directors, James J. Dunlop, stated that intense confrontation was necessary to make these children accept responsibility for their behavior and was justified by the majority's subsequent law-abiding conduct. Letter to the Editor, *Hyde Park House Last Chance for Many*, Boston Globe (March 7, 1977) at 13.

121. See Stewart v. Gold Medal Shows, 14 So. 2d 549 (S. Ct. Ala. 1943); Prosser, note 103 above, at 883.

122. H. Clark, Law of Domestic Relations (1968), at 269, § 10.4.

123. Prosser, note 103 above, at 883.

124. *See* Magnuson v. O'Dea, 75 Wash. 574, 135 P. 640, 642 (1913).

125. *Id.*

126. Pickle v. Page, 252 N.Y. 474, 169 N.E. 650 (1930); Stewart v. Gold Medal Shows, 14 So. 2d 549 (S. Ct. Ala. 1943).

127. *See Counseling the Counselors*, note 1 above, at 340-42.

128. *Counseling the Counselors, id.*, posits several other hypothetical situations in which a counselor may be liable to some degree: (1) the counselor may advise a 16-year old to continue dating a 22-year old man whom her parents have forbidden her to see. (2) The counselor, in defiance of the parents, sends a 15-year old, who has had problems resulting from experimentation with hallucinogenic drugs, to a psychiatrist. *Id.*, at 340-41.

129. *Id.*, at 353.

130. Mass. Gen. Laws Ann. ch. 119, § 63 (1976 Supp.). *See also, e.g.*, Md. Ann. Code art. 26 § 70-2(7) (1973). Md. Ann. Code art. 26 § 70-1(i) (1973); N.Y. Family Court Act § 712 (McKinney 1963).

131. *See* note 128 above and accompanying text.

132. *See* Bell v. Commonwealth, 170 Va. 597, 195 S.E. 675 (1938). "In

the federal courts it has been established that ordinary negligence suffices for criminal liability under 18 U.S.C. § 1115, which makes it a felony for a ship's officers to cause a death by misconduct or neglect. *E.g.,* United States v. Abbot, 89 F.2d 166 (2d Cir. 1937)." L. Weinreb, Criminal Law: Cases, Comment, Questions (1969), at 152 n.64.

133. The Nation's Psychiatrists, Public Health Service Publication No. 1885 (1969). Even in 1969, senior psychiatrists in some metropolitan areas were receiving $50 an hour or more, but this was offset by lower fees charged by young psychiatrists.

134. Mass. Ass'n for Mental Health Newsletter (April, 1974), at 2.

135. *E.g.,* McLean Hospital, Belmont, Massachusetts. The rates drop about $20 per day after the first thirty days of treatment.

136. *E.g.,* $50.20 per day at Metropolitan State Hospital, Waltham, Massachusetts.

137. *See* C. Hall, *Financing Mental Health Services Through Insurance,* 131 Am. J. Psychiat. 1079 (1974).

138. *Id.,* at 1080.

139. *See* L. Clasquin, Mental Health, Dental Services and other Coverage in the Health Insurance Study 12 (1973).

140. *See* Herold v. Group Health Incorporated, 362 N.Y.S.2d 782 (Civil Ct. of N.Y.C. Dec. 24, 1974).

141. One interesting view of such limitations was provided in 1974 by Mr. Gilbert Marley, then Director of The Place, a multiservice center in Concord, Massachusetts. Mr. Marley felt that adolescents, because they are so impressionable, are too readily "institutionalized," that is, dispossessed of the desire to leave an institution. However, The Place counselors had found that they could refer an adolescent to a particular private mental health inpatient facility, which they perceived as "an excellent diagnostic facility," secure in the knowledge that there was very little danger of the child remaining there more than ninety days—the limitation on inpatient care paid by his or her parents' health insurance policy. Thus, Mr. Marley viewed the ninety-day limitation as a positive feature of such policies.

142. *Id.* For results of a 1965 national survey of insurance coverage for both inpatient and outpatient psychiatric care, see P. Scheidemandel, C. Kanno & R. Glasscote, *Health Insurance for Mental Illness* (1968).

143. Conn. Gen. Stat. Ann. sec. 38-174d (1976 Supp.).

144. Mass. Gen. Laws Ann. ch. 175, sec. 47B and ch. 176A, sec. 8A (Supp. 1975).

145. National Ass'n for Mental Health, *Facts About Mental Illness* (1972).

146. Letter from Mr. John Larkin Thompson, President, Massachusetts Blue Shield, Inc. to Henry A. Beyer (December 21, 1973) (on file at Center for Law and Health Sciences), at 1-2.

147. *Id.,* at 2.

148. Mertes v. California-Western States Life Insurance Co., 511 S.W.2d 609, 610 (Tex. Ct. Civ. App. 1974).

149. *See also* Herold v. Group Health Incorp., 362 N.Y.S.2d 782 (Civ. Ct. N.Y.C., 1974). On the other hand, at least one court has rejected the argument that, to be covered, psychiatric services must be rendered personally by a physician, registered psychologist, or psychiatric social worker under the supervision of a physician or registered psychologist. Malican v. Blue Shield of Western N.Y., Inc., 364 N.Y.S.2d 691 (City Ct. of Buffalo, 1975).

150. National Association for Mental Health, Position Statement on Standards for Third Party Payments for Therapists (adopted Nov. 17, 1970).

151. *E.g.*, on January 1, 1976 Massachusetts Blue Shield instituted a $500 limit on coverage for "psychiatric services" rendered by a state-licensed psychologist.

152. K. Davis, *What Price Children?: Budget Priorities, Children, and Health Care*, in Proceedings of Children's Advocacy Conference, Durham, N.H., sponsored by the New England Children's Task Force (Jan. 24-25, 1975), at 59, citing B. Cooper & P. Piro, *Age Differences in Medical Care Spending, Fiscal Year 1973*, 37:5 Soc. Sec. Bull. 3 (May 1974).

153. *Socialized Medicine*, 230:2 Scient. Amer. 45 (Feb. 1974), citing N. Piore, *Metropolitan Medical Economics*, Scient. Amer. (Jan. 1965) and a current study by N. Piore and P. Lieberman of the Columbia School of Public Health and the Center for Community Health Systems.

154. *Id.*

155. Some observers argue that health services for adolescents (and children generally) should receive a greater share of these public funds.

An objective appraisal of the returns to society of greater investment in children . . . indicates that children should receive much greater priority. Unlike adults who could take responsibility for deciding whether additional . . . medical care . . . would be of substantial personal benefit, children have neither the resources nor the mature judgment required for these choices. Parents' inability or unwillingness to invest in child development, therefore, unfairly penalizes their children. (Davis, note 152 above, at 63)

Ms. Davis also makes some cost estimates for expanding child mental health services:

Total cost for the care of mental illness in children averages about $2 billion annually. . . . Some experts estimate that 7 to 10 percent of all children could benefit from some mental health services. Yet, even with adequate financing of mental health care and health service delivery programs to overcome any other major obstacles to care, it is unlikely that all of these children would be identified and brought within the mental health system. A generous estimate of the initial impact of improved financing—for example, through national health insurance—accompanied by health delivery programs would be a doubling of children receiving mental health attention. Those children brought in by new programs could also be expected to have less severe mental health problems than those currently treated, and would make greater use of outpatient services rather than inpatient services. Costs of mental health services for children, therefore, are unlikely to exceed $3 billion in initial years of operation. (*Id.*, at 72)

156. Title XIX of the Social Security Act, 42 U.S.C. § 1396 *et seq.* (1974). *See* 45 C.F.R. § 200 *et seq.*

157. G. Annas, The Rights of Hospital Patients (1975), at 187.

158. 42 U.S.C. § 601 *et seq.* (1974).

159. 42 U.S.C. § 1396a (b)(2) (1974); 45 C.F.R. § 248.10(b)(*1*)(ii).

160. 42 U.S.C. § 1396d (a)(i) (1974); 45 C.F.R. § 248.10(b)(iv).

161. *See* Mass. Public Assistance Policy Manual, ch. I, § F.

162. *See* discussion below, at note 166 *et seq.*

163. 42 U.S.C. §§ 1396a (a)(13)(c) and 1396d (a) (1974); 45 C.F.R. § 249.10(a) and (b)(*1*)-(5). Additionally, all states participating in Medicaid are required to establish a program to meet the cost of "family planning services and supplies furnished to individuals of childbearing age (including sexually active minors) who are eligible" for Medicaid and desire such services. 42 U.S.C. §§ 602(a)(14)-(15) and 606(d) (1974).

164. 42 U.S.C. § 1396d (a)(4)(B) (1974). Such services "could mean a significant improvement in the health care provided to poor children throughout the country." Annas, note 158 above, at 189. Unfortunately many states have thus far failed to comply with this federal requirement.

165. 42 U.S.C. §§ 1396d (a)(6)-(17) (1974).

166. 42 U.S.C. § 1396d (a)(16) (1974).

167. P.L. 92-603, § 299B.

168. Among the community resources which may be available are Community Mental Health Centers. These facilities, established by the Community Mental Health Centers Act of 1963 (42 U.S.C. § 2681 *et seq.*), have considerable potential for providing access to treatment to adolescents within their own communities. The Act emphasized the provision of comprehensive mental health services through federal allocation of funds, following the pattern of the Hill-Burton Act, to assist in the construction of community centers providing a wide range of services to the mentally ill. The centers must provide five types of services to qualify for federal funds: inpatient, outpatient, partial hospitalization, emergency, and consultation and educational services. (*See* S. Rep. No. 294, 90th Cong., 1st Sess. (1967); H.R. Rep. No. 212, 90th Cong., 1st Sess. (1967), *reprinted in* [1967] U.S. Code Cong. & Admin. News 1252, 1255-56; also, [1963] U.S. Code Cong. & Admin. News 1054.) Of particular relevance here are the amendments of 1970 allocating funds specifically for the construction, operation, staffing, and maintenance of facilities for the mental health of children. (42 U.S.C. § 2588u (1974); *see* [1970] U.S. Code Cong. & Admin. News 2514).

169. 45 C.F.R. § 249.10(b)(16)(iii), 41 Fed. Reg. 2198, 2199 (Jan. 14, 1976).

170. *Id.*, at § 249.10(b)(16)(iv)(a).

171. The team is to be composed of (1) (a) a Board eligible or Board certified psychiatrist or (b) a clinical psychologist holding a doctoral degree and a licensed physician or (c) a licensed physician with special training in the treatment of mental diseases and a state- or association-certified psychologist holding a master's degree in clinical psychology and (2) (a) a psychiatric social worker or (b) a registered nurse or occupational therapist with training or experience in treating the mentally ill or (c) a certified psychologist with a master's degree in clinical psychology. *Id.*, at § 249.10(b)(16)(v).

172. The constitutionality of this preferential treatment of persons under 21 has been upheld by both the District and Circuit Courts of the District of Columbia as a rational step toward broadening the class of persons receiving federal benefits. Kantrowitz v. Weinberger, 388 F. Supp. 1127, *aff'd* 530 F.2d 1034 (D.C. Cir. 1976).

173. 45 C.F.R. § 249.10(b)(16)(ii), 41 Fed. Reg. 2198, 2199 (Jan. 14, 1976). This requirement distinguishes this program from other federally funded programs such as the Defense Department's Civilian Health and Medical Program (CHAMPUS), which paid for extremely controversial "treatment" at non-JCAH-accredited centers such as the Green Valley School near Orange City, Fla. *See* Sen. H.M. Jackson, *Vital Signs in Finding the Right Treatment Center, The New Mandate*, 2 Pa. Ment. Retard. & Ment. Hlth. Newsletter, No. 6 (Apr. 1975).

174. 45 C.F.R. § 249.10(c), 41 Fed. Reg. 2198, 2199-2200 (Jan. 14, 1976).

175. 42 U.S.C. § 301e *et seq.* (1974).

176. Some older private organizations providing health services to similar groups (such as company employees or labor union members) have, in the last few years, taken steps to become HMOs. *See, e.g.*, the 1973 Annual Report of the St. Louis Labor Health Institute (June 30, 1973), at 1. For this institute's approach to mental health care, *see* L. Tureen & M. Wortman, *A Program, Sponsored by a Labor Union, for Treatment and Prevention of Psychiatric Conditions*, 35 Am. J. Orthopsychiat. 594 (1965); L. Tureen, *The Role of the Psychiatrist in a Prepaid Group Medical Program*, 49 Am. J. Pub. Health 1373 (1959).

177. 42 U.S.C. § 300e-1 (1)(D) (1974).

178. 42 U.S.C. § 300e-1 (1)(B) (1974).

179. *See* the Wall Street Journal, Feb. 12, 1975, at 1.

5 Special Education

"School age children generally make contact with the mental health system through the one system, outside of the family, that has contact with every child—schools."[1] "[F]rom ten to fifteen per cent of school children are estimated to be emotionally disturbed to the point where they present special problems to teachers, classmates, and school authorities."[2] If such estimates are anywhere near accurate, the importance of linkages between schools and the mental health system is apparent. Since school is the primary activity of children (including adolescents) outside the home, it is the place where children's emotional and behavioral problems tend to manifest themselves. In many instances emotional problems can prevent children from benefiting from the regular education program. Thus school-age children with emotional disturbances present two types of needs—the need for special educational programs from which they can benefit and the need for treatment of their emotional disturbances. Ideally, the special education system can coordinate the delivery of these two types of services in a comprehensive, integrated fashion.

Because of the key role that special education can play in children's access to mental health services, this chapter will explore recent educational and legal trends in this field and will examine some of the issues and problems incident to the operation of a particular special education law, Massachusetts Chapter 766.

The New Educational Philosophy

New Trends in Special Education

The field of special education is currently in great flux because of a new philosophy which holds that there is a *right* to education or, at least, to equal educational opportunity. In response to the mandate of new laws which declare education the right of every child, educators are indeed developing teaching techniques which demonstrate that so-called ineducable children can be educated.[3] Although the process of securing an education for all and of developing the necessary quantity and quality of special education services is very far from complete, dramatic changes have taken place in recent years. In the past, parents of handicapped children were fortunate if they were able to obtain decent custodial care for their children, let alone educational services. The "warehousing" of mentally retarded and emotionally disturbed children in state

155

institutions is not yet behind us. But at least a new day appears to have dawned. Just as courts and legislatures are recognizing the right of institutionalized people not only to decent living conditions but also to individualized treatment, so too the right of every child to an education suitable to his or her needs is being acknowledged.

The recent increase in special education services for handicapped children is illustrated in the national figures collected by the United States Office of Education. Studies by that office indicate that in 1948 12 percent of the country's handicapped children were receiving some special education. In 1963, 21 percent were being served; in 1967 the figure had grown to 33 percent; and by 1972 about 40 percent were receiving some special education services.[4] However, the quality and scope of many of these services is still far from adequate.

State Education Laws

Lawsuits in various states have accomplished a great deal in opening the door to public education for handicapped children who had previously been denied it.[5] But because the major legal basis of authority for education has developed as a power of the states,[6] it is only through major revisions of state education statutes that sweeping changes in the extent and quality of educational services for handicapped children will ultimately take place. States have traditionally classified handicapped children in terms of their particular disability. Children have been labeled "educable mentally retarded," "trainable mentally retarded," "emotionally disturbed," and so on. Through these labels, states have excluded certain children or "excused" them from the public schools. Past special education programs were monolithic in nature and designed to fit the supposed educational needs of entire categories of handicapped children. Those with different degrees of a handicap condition and those with multiple handicaps were poorly served, because no single educational program was completely suited to their needs.

Many state laws still do not make special education mandatory, and some of those that do require that there be a certain number of exceptional children in a district before particular services are provided. Some require that parents of a specified number of children with the same handicap(s) petition the school district for services to be made available.

New state special education statutes have broken with these traditional approaches in five major areas: mandate to local school districts, individualization, mainstreaming, due process, and single agency responsibility. Each is described briefly below.[7]

1. Because education is acknowledged as a right of all children, these laws make special education services a mandatory obligation of local school districts.

2. Special education services must be individualized. Each handicapped child has the right to an educational program suitable to his or her needs. Because each handicapped child presents a unique combination of needs, the educational program must be designed to fit the child, not vice versa as was frequently done in the past.

3. The handicapped child should be "mainstreamed" as much as possible. Previous special education programs were largely segregated from the regular public schools and conducted in separate classes and schools. The right-to-education philosophy addresses not only the exceptional child's right to an education in as normal a setting as possible, but also implicitly recognizes the value for other children in sharing their educational experience with a handicapped child.

4. In the past, children were too often identified as exceptional and assigned to special education programs by arbitrary or discriminatory methods of classification and assessment. Frequently, parents had little or no say about the way these decisions were made and little recourse from them. The new educational philosophy requires due process in identifying a child in need of special education, to guard against inappropriate classification and excessive labeling, which often result in stigmatizing the child. Classification as a result of a single test, a major practice of the past, is prohibited. Most of all, classification decisions must identify the handicapped child's special educational needs, not merely label the child's handicap. Some programs abandon the use of specific disability labels altogether in assigning children to special-education programs and adopt a more general and innocuous term, such as "exceptional" or "special needs" child.[8] The right to an evaluation by a variety of qualified professionals, the right of parents to an independent evaluation of their child, the right to periodic re-evaluation, and the right to appeal are some of the other crucial elements of due process incorporated into the new statutes.

5. A final basic principle of the new special education philosophy is that responsibility for special education services be vested in a single, accessible agency or authority. In the past, parents trying to obtain educational services for their children frequently had to contend with a bureaucratic labyrinth of state agencies; the local school systems had not generally accepted the responsibility for educating these children. In addition, mental health officials rather than educational personnel were typically responsible for the education of mentally retarded and emotionally disturbed children institutionalized in state schools and hospitals. The new approach to special education vests primary responsibility for handicapped children's education in the same authority that is primarily responsible for nonhandicapped children's education—the local school district.

Nevertheless, the state government must finance special education services for a handicapped child beyond the average per capita cost of educating a nonhandicapped child in a given school district. Putting the entire financial burden on local school districts for costly special education services would lead to resentment of the special needs child by local taxpayers and ultimately to inadequate services. However, to uphold the principle of basic local responsibility for the education of all children, the new philosophy requires that the local school system pay, for each handicapped child in its district, at least the average per capita educational expenditure which it makes available for each nonhandicapped child.

The Interface Between Mental Health and Education Systems

Historically, emotionally disturbed children constituted one of the groups of handicapped children most ignored by the educational system. Extremely low percentages of these children received regular educations or special education services.[9] Within public school systems many children with emotional disturbances were perfunctorily labeled "mentally retarded" and placed in special classes for mentally retarded children.[10] In these classes the emotionally disturbed children's need for treatment was largely ignored, and the educational program was ill suited to their intellectual abilities.[11]

Many school systems simply provided no special education services for emotionally disturbed children, especially for the mildly disturbed. The more seriously disturbed children were frequently institutionalized for psychiatric treatment. Within these institutions the lack of adequate educational services was a substantial problem. Data collected for 1969-70 by the National Institute of Mental Health indicates that of 261 residential treatment centers for children, 70 percent were providing special education services. However, the standard age limit for such services was from six to eighteen; very few centers offered any educational programs for those over eighteen.[12]

NIMH figures on educational services to children in hospital inpatient treatment units indicate that by 1971-72, 165 of 172 reporting units (96 percent) had formal educational programs. To a large extent, however, these gross figures present a distorted picture of how the educational needs of these emotionally disturbed children were being met. Many of these institutional education programs involved only a few hours of learning per day. For example, the NIMH 1971-72 survey of hospital inpatient treatment units found that 76.9 percent of the children had less than six hours of learning per day, the average length of a regular school day. Nearly half had less than five hours of instruction daily. In addition, very few children in these units attended regular schools in the community. With such a lack of educational services, institutionalized, emotionally disturbed children are effectively hindered from keeping up with their counterparts in the regular classrooms and are thus frequently prevented from eventually rejoining them. Parents whose children need intensified psychiatric treatment must therefore sacrifice their children's educational opportunities to meet their mental health needs.

Diagnosis of the emotionally disturbed child is a particularly complex problem. Traditional medical diagnoses of behavioral disorders are of questionable relevance in dealing with children's mental health[13] and are even less helpful in designing appropriate educational programs for them. A major problem has been the tendency of psychiatrists and psychologists to identify children's emotional problems in terms of adult pathologies. Phillips, Draguns and Bartlett[14] stress the importance, when dealing with behavioral disorders in children, of distinguishing between actual disorders and developmental lags. From an educational standpoint it is now generally considered most efficacious to approach a child's problem in developmental terms. The school's responsibility is to help maximize the child's educational potential without attaching a potentially stigmatizing psychiatric label which may have an ominous, often self-fulfilling prognosis for the child's future mental health. Also to be avoided is the use of labels of psychopathology with children whose behavior is merely socially unacceptable. "To an even greater extent than with adults, classification of psychopathology in children is based on externally judged social transgressions or deficiencies in intellectual or social performance."[15]

The educational system must guard against the ever-present danger of labeling a "disturbing" child "disturbed" just to get him out of the classroom.[16] It is frequently difficult for a school administrator to distinguish between a classroom teacher who is simply unwilling to cope with a disturbing child and a teacher who is trying desperately to handle a situation but cannot do better without outside assistance. Because a teacher may be biased, school systems have a serious obligation to provide a child with a professionally sound and impartial assessment of his condition before removing him from the classroom. The assessment must, as with other special needs children, be prescriptive rather than judgmental. It should cover the child's particular areas of educational strength and weakness, and it should be aimed at helping the child improve his educational abilities while simultaneously assisting him in overcoming his emotional or behavioral problems. In many cases the mildly disturbed child's needs may best be met through special assistance provided in the same classroom, or special help outside the class for only part of the school day, rather than by removing the child to a totally segregated environment. Although educators frequently object to mainstreaming a child with emotional problems, the new education philosophy holds that the school is nonetheless under an obligation to provide an education to each child in the least restrictive, most normal setting possible. When adequate auxiliary services are available, regular classroom teachers are much more willing to have mildly disturbed children remain in their classrooms for all or part of the school day. Unfortunately, there is a severe lack of trained personnel and funds to provide such services.[17]

What is generally needed for school-age children with mental health problems is a wider range of services, both educational and psychological. Increased guidance and counseling services and alternative school programs are two ways in which some schools are meeting this need. These programs may be initiated as special education programs for only a few special needs students, but they can soon form a fulcrum for more basic change in the overall curriculum of the school system. New educational techniques have proven that so-called ineducable children are capable of learning, and these may become valuable instructional tools for the regular classroom teacher. In this way the advancement of special education services can help make the school system more responsive to the needs of all its students.

In the past, special education meant a largely separate education for certain clearly defined categories of handicapped children. The routes into and out of the special education system often contained many barriers. The new programs promise not only that previously excluded handicapped children will gain access to educational services, but that all children may obtain some of the special qualities of a more individualized educational program.

Legal Basis for the New Educational Philosophy

As previously mentioned, the most significant forces underlying the new educational philosophy and shaping new special education programs have been, until recently, judicial decisions and state legislation. In this section we shall review the legal issues raised in some of the more important court cases; in a later section[18] we shall discuss some of the more significant state legislation, with emphasis on Massachusetts Chapter 766 and the recent federal special education act.

Judicial Decisions

Two major issues being litigated in courts today concern the right to equal educational opportunity for handicapped children and the right to procedural due process before being placed in special education programs. Both are significant for the adolescent with emotional difficulties.

The Right to Equal Educational Opportunity. Almost a quarter of a century ago, the landmark case of *Brown v. Board of Education*[19] established the constitutional principle of equal educational opportunity. The United States Supreme Court stated:[20]

Today education is perhaps the most important function of state and local governments. Compulsory school attendance laws and the great expenditures for education both demonstrate our recognition of the importance of education to our democratic society. It is required in the armed forces. It is the very foundation of good citizenship. Today it is a principal instrument in awakening the child to cultural values, in preparing him for later professional training, and in helping him to adjust normally to his environment. In these days, it is doubtful any child may reasonably be expected to succeed in life if he is denied the opportunity of an education. Such an opportunity, where the State has undertaken to provide it, is a right which must be made available to all on equal terms.

For the handicapped child, denial of equal educational opportunity may be manifested in two principal ways: first, the child may be excluded altogether from public education; and second, the child may receive an inferior education by being placed in a special classroom. Any claim of denial of equal educational opportunity is tested against the equal protection clause of the Fourteenth Amendment. In excluding some children from school altogether or in placing some children in special programs, a classification is obviously being made. The legal question thus becomes whether such classifictions are constitutional, as, clearly, not all classifications are contrary to the Fourteenth Amendment.[21]

In chapter 6[22] we point out that there are two or perhaps three standards for determining the constitutionality of legislation under the equal protection clause. Under the traditional method of analysis, courts will uphold a legislative classification which "bears some rational relationship to a legitimate state end."[23] A classification will not be set aside "if any state of facts reasonably may be conceived to justify it."[24] However, in the 1960s, a stricter standard of review under the equal protection clause emerged in those cases in which a "fundamental interest"[25] or "suspect classification" was involved.[26] Courts began to subject the statutes in these cases to "strict scrutiny," requiring that the state show that its interests in the classification are "compelling" and that no less discriminatory alternatives are available to meet the state's objectives.[27] A third, intermediate test appears to be emerging, which involves genuine judicial inquiry into the legitimacy of the classification.[28]

In this framework one can evaluate the constitutionality of excluding children from public education altogether because of emotional, mental or physical handicaps. Before the 1973 decision of the Supreme Court in *San Antonio Independent School District v. Rodriguez*,[29] many courts and commentators[30] held that education was the type of right that was "fundamental," deserving "strict scrutiny" in equal protection analysis. However, in *Rodriguez*, while recognizing the great significance of public education to the individual and to our society, the Supreme Court held that education is not a fundamental right. Finding that the right to education is not explicitly or implicitly guaranteed by the Constitution,[31] the Court applied the traditional equal protection test and refused to hold unconstitutional a system which permits wealth-based disparities in the financing of public education in different school districts.

Before *Rodriguez*, two courts had held (by consent decree in one instance and by court order in the other) that exclusion of children from public schools because of mental retardation was illegal. In 1971, in *Pennsylvania Association of Retarded Children v. Commonwealth of Pennsylvania,*[32] a federal district court stated[33] that because the commonwealth had undertaken to provide free public education to all children between the age of six and twenty-one, including exceptional children, the state could not deny any mentally retarded child access to a free public program of education and training.[34]

The following year, in *Mills v. Board of Education of District of Columbia,*[35] another federal district court held that insufficient financial resources would not justify exclusion of handicapped children from school. Although the court might have rested its decision on a District of Columbia statute which requires the education of all children, the court found it necessary to turn to constitutional grounds to provide adequate affirmative relief. The equal protection analysis used by the court appears to be closer to the new intermediate test than to either the lenient rational-basis standard or the strict scrutiny test. The court balanced the interests of the individual plaintiffs, the class of persons excluded, and the state.[36] The only defense raised by the state for excluding children was a lack of finances to provide education for the class affected. The court found this insufficient to outweigh the serious deprivations experienced by children excluded from public education.

The precedent established by *PARC* and *Mills* was not overturned by *Rodriguez.* In neither of those opinions did the courts rely on education as a fundamental right to make their determinations. Moreover, the opinion in *Rodriguez* focuses on differences in the quality of education and not its complete denial to certain classes of children. The *Rodriguez* opinion does not hold that a total denial of public education is not a violation of the equal protection clause.[37]

It would seem that challenges to policies of total exclusion of certain children from public education will generally prove successful, although lower courts may strain to base their decisions on statutory rather than constitutional grounds.[38] The more difficult issue is whether placing students in special classes denies equal protection of the laws. Given the holding of *Rodriguez,* which approves discrepancies in the quality of education on constitutional grounds, it has become quite difficult to challenge this practice under the equal protection clause. One legal scholar in the area of special education has suggested the following approach to determine the validity of special education placement for the mildly handicapped:[39]

These demonstrable harms—stigmatization, diluted educational offerings, and reduced life chances—suggest that special education placement for the mildly handicapped denies those individuals equal educational opportunity. For that reason, in a suit challenging special class placement, it seems appropriate to shift the burden of proof from parents and children to school officials. Once evidence of harm has been introduced, school officials should be required to show that the special education program accomplishes what it is supposed to do: that it sufficiently benefits students to justify the inevitable stigma that attaches to such placement. If benefit cannot be demonstrated, either for particular students or for all those placed in classes for the mildly retarded or handicapped, it makes constitutional (and pedagogical) sense to reassign those students to regular classes providing them with supplementary instruction to help recapture lost educational ground.[40]

This analysis recognizes that special classes are justified for the mildly handicapped in some instances and are often necessary for the more severely handicapped. An acknowledgment that such special treatment is sometimes required raises the second important constitutional issue: what procedures are required to assure due process of law to those considered for placement in special classes?

Due Process of Law. The United States Constitution's Fourteenth Amendment prohibits a state from depriving any person of life, liberty, or property without due process of law. It is clear that children as well as adults are protected by constitutional safeguards.[41] Moreover, young people do not "shed their constitutional rights" at the schoolhouse door.[42] A determination of the specific procedures required to meet due process standards in special education placements requires a two-part analysis. First, to determine whether the due process clause is even applicable, it must be established that placement in a special program is, in fact, a deprivation of life, liberty, or property. Then, if due process protections apply, a determination must be made of the process that is due, that is, the necessary safeguards that must be followed.

The United States Supreme Court, in the 1975 case *Goss v. Lopez,*[43] found that "[a]mong other things, the State is constrained to recognize a student's legitimate entitlement to a public education as a property interest which is protected by the due process clause."[44] As we mentioned in chapter 2,[45] the Court held that minimal procedures of notice and an informal hearing are required before a student can be suspended from public school for a period of up to ten days.

The due process clause has also been held applicable to actions likely to stigmatize. "Where a person's good name, reputation, honor, or integrity is at stake because of what the government is doing to him," the requirements of the clause must be met.[46] In *Goss v. Lopez,* the Court found that due process protections were required in part because charges of misconduct leading to suspensions of up to ten days could "seriously damage the students' standing with their fellow pupils and their teachers as well as interfere with later opportunities for higher education and employment."[47] In *Wisconsin v. Constantineau,*[48] the Court held that posting of a notice in all retail liquor establishments forbidding sales to Mrs. Constantineau because of her "excessive drinking" created such a stigma or badge of disgrace that due process required notice and a hearing prior to any such posting.

Applying the reasoning of these cases to the situation of a child singled out for special treatment—whether that treatment is supplementary help in the regular classroom, placement in a special education class, or placement in an institution—it is clear that a significant stigma may attach to that child. Such a stigma has many possible aspects.[49] The special education child is often isolated from normal school experiences and rejected by peers and even by many school personnel. The child is expected to conform to his or her label, and as a result the label may become a self-fulfilling prophecy. Moreover, his or her educational experiences, particularly when the child is placed outside the regular classroom, are often inferior to those of his or her peers. The child may thus fall farther and farther behind and never be able to return to his or her regular class. There is also a strong chance that the label will affect the student's life after leaving school. It may foreclose the opportunity to attend college, to prepare for many vocations, and to have a range of employment possibilities.

Even if the labeling or exclusion from regular education does not subject the student to a serious deprivation resulting from stigmatization, the due process clause will still be applicable. The Supreme Court, in *Goss v. Lopez,* held that "[a]s long as a property deprivation is not *de minimis,* its gravity is irrelevant to the question whether account must be taken of the Due Process Clause."[50] The gravity of the deprivation is taken into account in determining the extent of procedures required by the clause, but not the applicability of the clause. The difficult question, therefore, is not whether due process is applicable, but rather what specific procedures are required.

The courts use a balancing test to determine the extent of procedural formalities necessary to insure due process in any given situation.[51] In the area of special education, all parties are (or should be) primarily interested in providing the child with the proper educational curriculum and environment. Beyond this, however, each party has special personal interests. The child and the parents have the strongest interest in avoiding deleterious or incorrect labeling. (The parents' interests in this regard, however, are certainly not identical to the child's and must be considered separately.) The school is interested in avoiding time-consuming and costly procedures which might also create an adversarial and hostile educational climate.

In balancing these interests, the courts have set requirements of notice and a hearing as the minimum due process protections required.[52] The *Mills* court specifically and explicitly required:[53]

1. Notice to parents or guardian of the proposed placement and the reasons for it; of the right to a hearing if they oppose such placement,[54] with legal representation.
2. Right to waive the hearing by parent or child.
3. Right of the child to a representative of his own choosing, including legal counsel.

4. Right of the parent or guardian or his counsel to have access to all pertinent school records.
5. Right to confront any public school officials or other public employees with knowledge of the action and right to cross-examine witnesses.
6. Right of appeal from a decision of a Hearing Officer to a special committee of the Board of Education which may review the Hearing Officer's findings.

The opinion in *Mills* shows that the court was concerned with protecting the separate interests of the child; but the court did not go as far as it might have in requiring due process procedures for the student and his or her parents. For instance, the notice required before placement in a special education program need be sent only to the parents or guardian, not to the child. By contrast, when disciplinary action is proposed, both child and parents must be given notice.[55] Likewise, the parents or guardian, but not the child, may elect to have an open hearing concerning placement; however, under the disciplinary section, the child as well as his or her parents or guardian may choose an open hearing. Similarly, the child has a right to legal counsel of his or her own choice; if, however, the child cannot afford legal counsel, the school is to notify the child's *parents,* not the child, of the availability of volunteer legal services.

One may infer from the opinion that the court doubted whether children considered for special education would be capable of making meaningful decisions about their problems and placement. This would explain the court's greater recognition of the child's right to participate in proceedings leading to disciplinary action. If this was the court's reasoning, one can certainly argue that it was in error. Many emotionally disturbed adolescents are clearly capable of participating and should be allowed to participate in the decision-making process concerning their need for special education.

The requirements set forth in the *Mills* decision are more legalistic and extensive than many commentators believe is necessary. Kirp, for instance, points out that legal counsel may not be the most helpful representative for a child, because a lawyer may use familiar courtroom tactics of confrontation without sufficient understanding of their educational and psychological consequences. This may increase tension and fear, thereby preventing meaningful dialogue. Kirp feels that help from other experts may be more useful in analyzing school records and in understanding and interpreting for parents the basis of a school's action.[56] Other critics argue that an impartial hearing, adequate notice, the right to examine all school records, and the right to have present at the hearing a lay advocate representing the child are sufficient to meet due process requirements. They see no need for legal counsel to cross-examine witnesses.[57]

The *Mills* decision went a considerable way toward recognizing the due process rights of children in the area of special education. Perhaps the most important advance still required, from the perspective of the adolescent, is explicit recognition of his or her right to participate personally in all aspects of the decision-making process to the full extent that he or she is capable.[58] Such participation should be separate and apart from that of the adolescent's parents. Participation in the process by the adolescent will not only help to protect his or her rights, but may also prove to be an effective diagnostic and therapeutic tool.

Special Education Statutes

In November 1975, the United States Congress responded to the plight of "special needs" children by enacting the Education for All Handicapped Children Act.[59] The Act recognizes that more than half of the nation's estimated eight million handicapped children are denied equal educational opportunities, with one million excluded from public education systems altogether. To remedy this situation, Congress authorized an appropriation of over $300 million in the first two years, primarily to support local educational programs for the handicapped.[60] The long-range goals of the Act are to make "free, appropriate public education" available to all handicapped persons between the ages of three and eighteen by 1978, and to those up to age twenty-one by 1980.[61]

The new federal law is based on the Massachusetts special education statute.[62] The Massachusetts law, generally referred to as Chapter 766,[63] was enacted by the state legislature in 1972 and became effective on September 1, 1974. It is probably the most sweeping overhaul of any state special education law in the country, incorporating most of the educational rights and new concepts of special education discussed above. Because it is a model not only for the federal law, but also for a number of other state statutes, the policies and provisions of Chapter 766 will be discussed in some detail.

How Chapter 766 Transforms Special Education

Flexibility and Variety

The basic educational philosophy of Chapter 766 is that special education should have flexibility and variety. First of all, Chapter 766 has eliminated the wording typically used in so many special education laws, which excludes many handicapped children altogether from any public educational opportunity. Nor do children qualify for special education services by being identified with any of the traditional categories used to describe handicapped children. Instead, Chapter 766 explicitly affirms the right to education of any "school age child with special needs." A special-needs child is defined generally and flexibly as any school age child who "because of temporary or more permanent adjustment difficulties or attributes arising from intellectual, sensory, emotional or physical factors, cerebral dysfunctions, perceptual factors, or other specific learning disabilities or any combination thereof, is unable to progress effectively in a regular school program and requires special classes, instruction periods, or other special education services in order to successfully develop his individual educational potential. . . ."[64] The law specifically describes special education as educational services and programs designed to help each special-needs child develop his individual educational potential.[65] Children are not to be placed into categories and program slots. Rather the law recognizes that "such children have a variety of characteristics and needs" and require special education programs tailored to these individual characteristics and needs.[66] The law delegates the task of further specifying a definition of special needs to the state's education department, recognizing that definitions and standards written into administrative regulations can be changed and improved more readily than those congealed in legislation.

Secondly, the statute calls for the state to provide "the opportunity for a full range of special education programs."[67] Ten basic types of programs are described. These educational "prototypes" range from auxiliary services or instruction for special-needs children within the regular classroom, to special classes within the public school, to full-time separate day and residential programs.[68] The statute also permits total flexibility in program design by explicitly allowing each child's special education program to be any "combination or modification" of the basic prototypes.[69] In recognition of an acute need of many handicapped children that has been largely unmet in the past, the statute includes as one of its program prototypes "occupational and preoccupational training in conjunction with a regular occupational training program in a public school."[70]

Another way in which the law attempts to achieve flexibility is through its liberal age limits. A special-needs child can be anyone between the ages of three and twenty-one who has not yet received a high-school diploma.[71] Provisions for the screening and identification of preschool special-needs children are also included.

The statute's fourth method of achieving flexibility is a specific endorsement of collaborative arrangements among school districts to provide educational services to their special-needs students.[72] The law recognizes that joint agreements may be the most sensible and efficient way to provide services when only a few children in a school district require the same types of special facilities and services. School systems may also enter into contractual relationships with private and public schools, agencies, and institutions to obtain necessary services.[73]

A final noteworthy mechanism for achieving flexibility and variety is the evaluation process. No child may be assigned to a special education program without a prior evaluation of his or her needs. The Chapter 766 evaluation process usually includes assessments by the classroom teacher, a physician, a psychologist, a social worker, and various specialists as needed. The rationale is that no single professional can adequately assess the capabilities of a given child, evaluate the child's special needs, and devise an appropriate educational program. The statute specifically prohibits the exclusive use of "standardized or local tests of ability, aptitude, attitude, affect, achievement, or aspiration . . . in the selection of children for referral, diagnosis or evaluation."[74] Another significant aspect of the evaluation process is that it includes the child's parents. The parents can even obtain an independent evaluation of their child if they are not satisfied with the initial evaluation.[75] The law also stipulates that "the written record and clinical history from both the evaluation provided by the school committee and any independent evaluation, shall be made available to the parents, guardians, or persons with custody of the child."[76]

Consumer Involvement

Another basic philosophy of Chapter 766 is consumer involvement. In addition to the active role of parents in the evaluation procedures of their children, the law calls for the significant involvement of parents and consumer organizations in its overall implementation. Each of the six education regions of the state is to have a special education Regional Advisory Council (RAC) composed of sixteen members, at least eight of whom must be parents of children enrolled in special education programs.[77] According to the powers and duties described in the law, the RACs are to advise the regional office of the Department of Education "regarding all aspects of special education programs in the region."[78] Each year the RACs are to prepare a written report on the "quality and adequacy" of these programs. The RACs are also available to receive complaints and suggestions regarding special education programs in their regions.

In addition to the RACs, the law calls for the establishment of a State Advisory Commission (SAC). In addition to representatives of various state departments such as mental health, public health, and public welfare, the SAC must include two members of each RAC, one of whom must be the parent or guardian of a child receiving special education. The SAC's duties and powers include receiving the reports of the individual RACs on the quality and adequacy of special education services, and preparing an annual statewide report on special education services for submission to the Department of Education, including specific recommendations for improvement.

Although the SAC is an advisory body, its powers are not negligible. The Department of Education is under statutory obligation to "implement the recommendations of the commission . . ." or to "state in a written reply . . . the reasons why such recommendations cannot or should not be implemented."[79] Any disputes between the Department of Education and the advisory commission should be resolved informally if possible, but if a disagreement is not resolved, final power to decide the issue rests with the state Board of Education.

The potential for consumer involvement in the implementation of Chapter 766 is very great. The RACs and SAC have considerable consumer representation; by forming a structure parallel to the regional and state offices of the Department of Education, they are designed to prevent the educational system from growing apart from consumer interests at any level.

Due Process

Another major objective of Massachusetts's new special education law is to safeguard the legal rights of parents and children coming into contact with the special education system. Several provisions of the law are tailored to meet this objective.

First, recognizing that special education classification procedures have at times been used to discriminate against racial and linguistic minorities, the statute specifically prohibits various forms of discrimination. "Within any school district if in any special education program there is a pattern of assignment throughout the district on the basis of sex, national origin, economic status, race or religion of the students which is substantially disproportionate from the distribution [of these qualities generally within the district], the department [of education] shall notify such school district of its prima facie denial of equal educational opportunities."[80] The law requires that the local school district show a "compelling education interest" why such a disproportion of a certain group of students should exist in special education. If there is discrimination and it is not remedied, the Department of Education may turn to a superior court for injunctive and other relief.[81]

Similarly, the statute guards against the use of biased tests. All tests to be used for referral, diagnosis and evaluation of special-needs children must be approved by the Department of Education as being "as free as possible from cultural and linguistic bias or, wherever necessary, separately evaluated with reference to the linguistic and cultural groups to which the child belongs."[82] The regulation requires that notice to parents of a child's referral for a 766 evaluation be in the language of the home.

Procedures governing evaluation incorporate further due process safeguards. The initial referral of a child for special education may come from various sources, including "a school official, parent or guardian, judicial officer, social worker, family physician, or person having custody of the child for purposes of determining whether such child requires special education."[83] Regardless of who makes the referral, written notice of the upcoming evaluation must be sent to the parent within five days, and the evaluation must be provided within thirty days after that. The written notice must inform the parents of their right to an independent evaluation of their child. The evaluation must include an assessment of the child's educational status, a medical assessment, a psychological assessment and an assessment of the general home situation.[84] Finally, the burden of proof is on the evaluating personnel to show that the child is one "with special needs." "Until proven otherwise every child shall be presumed not to be a school age child with special needs or a school age child requiring special education."[85]

The law does not explicitly require parental consent for the initial core evaluation. During the statute's first year of life, school officials were often hesitant to proceed with this evaluation when parental consent could not be obtained, in some cases because the parent was simply not physically available. To clarify this situation, the associate commissioner of special education took the position that Chapter 766 clearly requires the core evaluation team to go forward without parental consent upon the proper referral of a child. He noted in a memorandum[86] that no Massachusetts statute or case expressly requires parental consent to any of the assessments which are part of the core evaluation, but he also recognized that a

legal issue is raised by the fact that there are sufficient references to consent (or lack of consent) in other situations to indicate that there is a possibility, albeit remote, of liability if a physical or psychological examination is given without parental consent.

The memorandum primarily addresses the practical problems caused by the lack of parental consent:[87]

There are two *practical* problems. The first is that, regardless of the remote likelihood of liability, school systems are very reluctant to administer physical or psychological assessments without parental consent. The second is that, where a parent objects to the core evaluation itself, it seems self-defeating and a bad policy to try to insist that the core evaluation go forward given the vital role of the parent in that process. Obviously, a resistant parent can make the core evaluation almost impossible to administer.

In our opinion, the reason why Chapter 766 does not require parental consent for the core evaluation is that it is attempting to deal with the situation where the interests of the parent and the child are adverse and where the child's best interests are served by overruling the parents. We believe that these cases represent a small minority of all cases and that they should be dealt with through referrals to social service agencies such as Children's Protective Services.

It might seem extremely difficult for a court of law to determine whether overruling the parents serves the child's best interests, but at least one commentator has suggested a workable standard. The parent should be overruled only when a "competent" child prefers the state policy and expert testimony shows that the child's interest would be "severely and irreversibly" damaged by the parents' choice.[88]

If, in the core evaluation, the child *is* found to be a special-needs child, the parent may appeal the decision. The statute and regulations provide that, pending appeal, the child is to remain in the regular education program unless the local school committee can show that placement of the child in the regular program "would seriously endanger the health and safety of the child or substantially disrupt the program for other children."[89] The appeals process starts with the regional office of the Bureau of Child Advocacy[90] of the Division of Special Education of the state's Department of Education and moves from there to the state office of the bureau. The bureau's final decision can later be appealed to the State Advisory Commission (SAC).[91] Ultimately, after all administrative appeals have been exhausted, the parents may appeal a decision to a state superior court.

As this appeals process illustrates, those who drafted Chapter 766 were sensitive to the legal rights of parents to accept, reject, or help to plan their child's special education program. Although the regulations emphasize the desirability of adjusting differences informally whenever possible,[92] the parent retains the full right to reject flatly a given plan and to appeal all the way to superior court. Interestingly, the local school committee does *not* have the same option to appeal as the parents. Still more notable is the absence in the regulations of any provision allowing the child to participate in the evaluation and placement process, other than those provisions which give the special-needs child who is over eighteen the same rights as his parents.[93] The legal age of majority in Massachusetts is now eighteen, however, so the provisions regarding students eighteen and over now appear superfluous.

The statute and regulations do not recognize that many older special-needs students are capable of participating in planning their own special education programs. Their views ought to be considered in requesting evaluation and in accepting or rejecting a proffered plan, as their perceptions of their special education needs do not always coincide with those of their parents. Ironically, a form letter designed by the state Department of Education to notify a child over sixteen that he or she has been referred for an evaluation includes a bold-face statement that the child may refuse to be evaluated altogether because he or she is over the compulsory education age. The form also notifies the child over sixteen that he or she has the general right to bring someone of his or her own choosing to any meetings or conferences. The child is also implicitly given the rights to accept or reject a proposed educational plan and to request an independent evaluation. However, these rights are not written into the regulations; only the form letter makes reference to them.

The failure to allow children explicitly to have a *decisive* role in the evaluation process raises some difficult issues about those students whose special needs are in the mental health category. Minor behavioral problems in school, especially among adolescents, are often related to conflicts between the child and his or her parents. The student might be aware that he or she needs a special educational program, but under Chapter 766 the student cannot refer himself or herself for an evaluation.[94] Furthermore, if a special education plan is devised for the child (for example, after referral by a teacher), the parents retain the right to accept or reject such plan, and to gain access to the records and reports in the evaluation. As it stands, the law is probably not well equipped to deal with situations where the child's and his or her parents' interests diverge. Because such circumstances are increasingly prevalent with adolescents, consideration should be given to revising the regulations in this area.[95]

Confidentiality

Confidentiality of school records is necessary to protect a student with special needs against the stigma which may accompany the term "mental illness" and the possible discrimination against one who has been so labeled. Chapter 766 clearly requires that a child's special education records be kept confidential.[96]

The written record and clinical history from both the evaluation provided by the school committee and any independent evaluation, shall be made available to the parents, guardians, or persons with custody of the child. Separate instructions, limited to the information required for adequate care of the child, shall be distributed only to those persons directly connected with the care of the child. Otherwise said records shall be confidential.

Although regulations for the implementation of Chapter 766 do not specifically address the issue of confidentiality, in January 1975 the Department of Education issued comprehensive regulations pertaining to student records, including records relating to special education. These regulations were promulgated "to insure parents' and students' rights of confidentiality, inspection, amendment, and destruction of student records and to assist local school systems in adhering to the law."[97]

The regulations require that the contents of student records be limited to information relevant to the educational needs of the student.[98] Any report filed must include the name, signature, and position of the person who filed it. Both of these provisions help to prevent the inclusion of anonymous comments which might damage a student's reputation. The regulations also prohibit the inclusion of teachers' memory aids (grading books) in the files.

The regulations distinguish between the transcript of a student (including grades and courses) and a more personal, temporary record containing all the information not properly a part of the transcript. The school must maintain the transcript, but the personal record is to be destroyed five years after the student graduates.[99] Thus the young person will have to bear the burden of an unflattering personal school record for no longer than five years after he or she leaves the school.

The student and his parents are allowed access to the records, as are authorized school personnel.[100] Aside from this, with the exception of a few explicitly described unusual situations (such as a court subpoena), third parties do not have access to the files.[101] A student is also given an opportunity to amend information in his record which he feels is erroneous,[102] and the parent or student can further request that certain information be deleted.[103] Information inserted in the student's files by the 766 Core Evaluation Team (CET) is not subject to such a request until after the acceptance of the CET Educational plan, or, if the plan is rejected, after the completion of the special education appeal process.[104] If the parents or student feel that adding information is not sufficient to explain, clarify, or correct objectionable material in the student's record, the regulations set forth procedures for appeal to the school principal,[105] the superintendent of schools,[106] and ultimately the school committee.[107] This final appeal includes the right to a hearing before the school committee, at which the parent or student is entitled to an advocate of his or her choosing.[108]

These regulations appear to safeguard students' confidentiality rights as thoroughly as any in the nation. In conjunction with Chapter 766, they should serve well to protect the privacy of the special-needs child.

Reorganization of Responsibilities

Another important feature of Chapter 766 is the way in which it reorganizes the state educational bureaucracy and reallocates responsibility for special education services at the local, regional and state levels.

State Responsibilities. The statute prescribes certain duties and functions for the Division of Special Education within the state Department of Education. In addition to regulating and assisting in the identification, classification, referral and placement of special-needs children in special education programs, the division compiles and analyzes data on special education programs, develops public education and parent counseling programs, develops certification standards for special education personnel, works with academic institutions to develop appropriate training programs for these personnel, handles complaints regarding special education services and possible cases of discrimination, receives and allocates federal and state funds, and conducts or contracts for research and development projects. The law requires that the Division of Special Education have a "sufficient number of Bureaus" to carry out all of these functions.[109] One of these bureaus (now called the Bureau of Child Advocacy) is specifically constituted to hold hearings and conduct investigations on the development of special education training programs in academic institutions, the acquisition and maintenance of special equipment for use outside the regular classroom, and the evaluation and placement of children in special education programs.[110]

Regional Responsibilities. In addition to the state Division of Special Education, the new law mandates the establishment of regional offices, which form an important link between local school districts and the state. Along with regulating and assisting local school committees in identifying, diagnosing, and evaluating special-needs children, the regional branches possess the specific power and duty to approve all special education placements by local school committees.[111] A regional office must also facilitate collaborative agreements among local school districts for the provision of special education, investigate and evaluate any program if requested by the Department of Education or on its own initiative, and provide local school committees with lists of professionals qualified to evaluate children for special education.[112]

The Commonwealth of Massachusetts is divided into six educational regions, each of which has a regional office of the Division of Special Education. This regionalization makes the division more accessible to the needs and interests of consumers than a centralized bureaucracy could possibly be. Complaints and suggestions can be processed more efficiently at the regional level. Further, the Regional Advisory Councils (RAC) parallel the regional offices of the division and constitute a formal apparatus for consumer involvement, as discussed above.[113]

Local Responsibilities. A no less important feature of Chapter 766 is the way in which it emphasizes the concept of local responsibility. Although several important duties, especially a significant portion of the financial burden, still rest with the state, Chapter 766 places initial and primary responsibility for meeting children's special education needs squarely on the shoulders of the local school committee. In the past many handicapped children have been totally ignored by their local school systems. Now local school committees must take affirmative action to identify all special-needs children in their districts and to spend for each child at least the system's average per pupil expenditure.[114] For some communities which have habitually failed to meet the needs of handicapped children, serving these children properly may increase their educational budgets dramatically.

Under the statute the local school committee is generally required to "identify the school age children residing therein who have special needs, diagnose and evaluate the needs of such children, propose a special education program to meet those needs, provide or arrange for the provision of such special education program, maintain a record of such identification, diagnosis, proposal and program actually provided and make such reports as the department [of education] may require."[115] The state Department of Education, in conjunction with the state Departments of Mental Health and Public Health, is empowered to issue specific regulations, guidelines and other directives to local school committees on how to perform their duties.[116]

Under the regulations promulgated by the Massachusetts Department of

Education, each school committee is required to appoint an administrator of special education, whose major duty is "exercising general supervision over the identification, referral, evaluation and program planning for all school age children with special needs."[117] The local school committee must also submit a plan to its regional Special Education Office, stipulating how it intends to meet the educational needs of special-needs children.[118] As stated earlier, the school committee is allowed to provide the special education services directly, to join in a collaborative agreement with one or more other school systems, or to contract for services with any public or private school, agency or institution.[119]

The school committee is responsible for the education of all children residing with their parents "in the city, town or school district over which the school committee has jurisdiction."[120] But institutionalized children have not been forgotten. The committee is also responsible for the education of a child who lives in a state institution of the Department of Mental Health, Public Health or Youth Services, but whose parent, "with whom such child lives when at home," lives in the school district.[121]

Chapter 766 regulations have also delineated specific responsibilities of local school committees in identifying potential special-needs children. They include screening of all kindergarten children and children aged three and four whose parents believe they have substantial disabilities, free orientation workshops for such parents, public communication about the screening and orientation workshops, and notifying parents of the special education programs available in the community.[122] Each year the local school committee must submit a census of all school-age children with special needs within its jurisdiction.[123] The local school committee is prohibited from "revealing the identity of individual children or their parents." The committee must also submit a yearly case-finding plan specifying how it will "make a continuous and systematic effort to identify potential cases of school age children with special needs."[124]

The local school committee must provide for the evaluation of all children referred as potential cases for special education services.[125] The administrator of special education is responsible for designating a chairperson for each core evaluation team (CET) and assisting in the organization of CETs.[126] The local school committee *must* provide a child with any of the program prototypes recommended by a CET. The prototypes include: a regular education program with modifications, a regular education program with no more than 25 percent time out of the regular classroom, a regular education program with no more than 60 percent time out of the classroom, a substantially separate program, a day school program, a residential school program, a home or hospital program, parent-child instruction, and a diagnostic program.[127] In addition, if the CET recommends either social or psychological services for the child, his parents, or both, the local school committee must provide them.[128]

The regulations specifically recommend that, whenever possible, day schools and residential programs *within* the school district should be used for placement.

"Only if there is no suitable program within such city, town or school district shall such child be placed in a program outside of such city, town or school district."[129] Furthermore, the regulations which govern the placement of a child in a program outside the district are designed so that a school system may not rely on such programs indefinitely rather than develop programs of its own. If a suitable residential or day school program cannot be found—despite the assistance of the Division of Special Education in locating a program or in obtaining money to establish such a program—the local school committee must, "with or without financial assistance, establish such a program itself or through a collaborative."[130] As is apparent, the principle of local responsibility is a cornerstone of Chapter 766 and its regulations.

Parental Responsibility. Chapter 766 has also redefined the role of parents. In the past, parents of handicapped children have frequently been the only advocates for these children, lobbying local school systems and state bureaucracies to obtain educational services. Under Chapter 766 the right of all handicapped children to an education has now been unequivocally acknowledged, and the rights of parents in shaping their child's educational plan have clearly been emphasized throughout the statute and its regulations. The counterpart to such rights, of course, is parental responsibility. Chapter 766's screening and evaluation system is designed to function best when the parent takes a *positive, active* role. The regulations require that the parent take affirmative steps—whether to accept or reject a plan, whether to have an independent evaluation—at several important junctures during the evaluation process. Indeed, it is questionable whether the elaborate process established by the statute can function effectively to provide a child needed services without parental involvement.[131]

Educational Issues

For the most part, Chapter 766 regulations prescribe how the statute is to be implemented in a relatively legalistic sense. In the final analysis much of the success or failure of this legislation will spring not from following the "letter of the law" but from the particular ways in which local school systems adhere to its spirit. The following discussion deals with some of the major educational issues and problems which are likely to spell success or failure for special education programs.

Core Evaluation Concept

To assist teachers and local school officials in understanding the purposes of evaluation under Chapter 766, the Massachusetts Department of Education has developed an extensive core evaluation manual. Included in this manual is a short essay summarizing the basic concepts which ought to be incorporated in the evaluation process. As this essay states, "Core evaluation is the critical element in the educational reform mandated by Chapter 766. The core evaluation establishes the foundation for an information design which allows for systematic planning for individual students as well as entire school populations."[132]

In the past, children have been evaluated largely by testing procedures which measure their abilities against "normal" behavior. In dealing with handicapped children, the educational system has been preoccupied with their deviance from the norm. But as the Department of Education states in the core evaluation manual, "Chapter 766 promotes the premise that (a) all children are normal, (b) all children are different, and (c) the differences in children are normal."[133] The emphasis should be not upon a student's performance relative to his or her peers, but rather upon what the child can do now, and that assessment should be compared with what he or she has been able to do in the past. This approach entails evaluating a child in terms of a series of performance statements and setting realistic goals for the child's improvement by building upon his or her present skills. Only in this way can an *individualized* educational plan be devised.

Chapter 766 is also committed to the conference approach for determining a child's educational needs. In a full core evaluation, the core evaluation team (CET) must include a CET chairperson designated by the school system's administrator of special education; a registered nurse, social worker or guidance counselor; a psychologist; a physician or his or her designee; a teacher with previous or current contact with the child; an administrative representative of the local school department; the child's parents; the teacher with primary responsibility for teaching the child and any person who will be assisting the teacher with the child; any outside professional requested by the parent and who is currently working with the child; and, if the child is over sixteen, a vocational counselor.[134] The child's assessment includes a report on the child's educational status by the school department's representative, an assessment of the child's educational and behavioral capabilities by his or her teacher, a full health assessment, a psychological assessment, an assessment of pertinent family history and the home, and assessments by other specialists as needed. Each assessment must culminate in a written report describing the child's special needs "in educationally relevant and common terms"[135] and detailing the means for meeting those needs. To guarantee that the evaluation is multidimensional, the regulations specifically prohibit any one person from performing more than one of the professional assessment functions.[136] (The regulations also allow for a somewhat less elaborate, intermediate core evaluation in certain cases where every assessment described above is not needed.)[137]

After all initial assessments, the child's educational plan is devised by a conference composed of the individuals who have made assessments, the various other individuals required to be in the CET, and the child's parents.

The law and regulations require that the evaluation take place within thirty days after the parents are notified of the child's referral. Reports on the first year of implementation (1974-75), however, indicate that this time requirement was frequently not met. Some communities were simply slow in designating core evaluation chairpersons and in organizing the core evaluation teams; others were apparently deluged by far more referrals than expected. The problem in conducting timely evaluations has probably been exacerbated because not only did all new referrals for special education services have to be evaluated, but all of the children already in special education programs also had to be reevaluated.[138]

Referral

The types of children who potentially qualify as "school age children with special needs" under Chapter 766 are more varied and more numerous than the categories of children covered by more traditional special education laws. Therefore, classroom teachers may not be adequately versed in who can or who ought to be referred for special education under the new law. In anticipation of this problem, the Massachusetts Teachers Association prepared several short brochures and informational booklets to help teachers understand the major objectives of the law and to simplify some of its administrative complexities for them. These materials have been widely disseminated to school systems throughout the state, and if utilized, will be extremely useful tools for teachers and school administrators.[139] In addition, the core evaluation manual prepared by the state Department of Education's Division of Special Education contains, in much more detailed form, instructions on the evaluation process, performance statements for making educationally relevant assessments, and specific role descriptions for members of the CET.[140]

Mainstreaming

"Mainstreaming" the special-needs child is a difficult issue for many regular school teachers.[141] But to a certain extent, it is a bogus issue, since the purpose of Chapter 766 is not—as many teachers seem to feel—to place severely handicapped children in the regular classroom. On the other hand, the law mandates that each child be educated in the least restrictive setting possible—and this is "regular education program with modifications."[142] To be educated in the least restrictive setting is considered every child's right, and this right cannot be abridged "unless such placement endangers the health or safety of the child or substantially disrupts such education program for other children."[143] Clearly, mildly handicapped children previously placed in separate programs are more likely to be returned to the regular classroom under Chapter 766. However, the number of special-needs children to be placed in any one regular classroom is limited to four, unless a special exemption is obtained by the local school committee.[144]

When the educational plan of a special-needs child is "regular education program with modifications," the modifications are the responsibility of "the teacher who conducts the child's regular education program."[145] However, the CET can specify support services to help the regular teacher make these modifications. Knowing when such assistance will be necessary and commanding the resources to provide it is a crucial role of the CET, if mainstreaming is to be a successful policy. Otherwise, the new law runs the risk of alienating regular school teachers against special-needs students who are returned to their classrooms when their teachers feel poorly equipped to teach them.

Requirements and Incentives for Services

A careful adherence to referral and evaluation procedures for special-needs children is valueless unless the necessary services can be obtained. The most severe problems in the implementation of Chapter 766 have probably occurred in the area of service delivery. In many instances the services that core evaluation teams recommend are in inadequate supply or do not exist at all. When programs do exist, they are often prohibitively expensive, and occasionally unnecessarily so. Unfortunately, less costly, more efficient programs are sometimes the most scarce, such as programs for certain emotionally disturbed children. For many of these children the *only* available placements have been out-of-state residential treatment centers. Comparable residential centers or less costly nonresidential services in sufficient quantities have not been available within the state itself. Moreover, for several years prior to Chapter 766, the educational and treatment costs of these children were largely paid by the state.[146] Services for these children are now to be provided under a "grandfather" clause in Chapter 766,[147] but for each child local communities will receive only up to 110 percent of the average statewide cost of educating these children in institutions less the state average expenditure per public school pupil. If the state allowances do not keep up with the rising costs of services from private out-of-state providers, local school committees will still be obligated to obtain and finance the necessary services.

There is also the hidden danger that a core evaluation team will fail to recommend the appropriate services for a given child because it knows that a particular type of program is not available or because a less appropriate but less expensive program is available. The parent has the right to appeal such a decision,[148] but few parents are adequately equipped to refute the judgment of a group of professionals.

Protections against arbitrary or discriminatory actions on the part of educators and school administrators cannot by themselves ensure that children evaluated for special education services will actually receive the services most appropriate for them. As Kirp, Buss and Kuriloff explain, "if . . . the trouble lies . . . in the lack of resources or of viable programs from which to choose, public confidence in the results of classification decisions will not be restored by introducing due process procedures."[149] To have a full spectrum of appropriate services, specific requirements will have to be placed on local school committees to provide certain services, and incentives for developing new and better services must be devised. Such advances are not likely to occur in these times of government economic crises without the extensive and concerted efforts of consumer and advocacy organizations representing children and handicapped persons.

The responsibilities of local school committees to provide, within a reasonable time, all of the necessary services for their special-needs children—either within their own districts or through collaborative agreements and contracts—are indeed extensive. The state, however, has formidable power, including the power of the purse, to compel school committees' compliance with the regulations. Time schedules for the establishment of facilities and programs must be stipulated in written reports to the Division of Special Education by the local school committees. These provisions will create a strong incentive for the gradual development of the full range of necessary special education services at the local level. However, the initiative of local school committees themselves and the vigilance of the state and regional bureaucracies in detecting the delinquency of school districts and exercising their powers to force compliance are equally critical in meeting this goal.

Funding Issues and Problems

Funding Special Education

The best-planned programs achieve little or nothing unless they have adequate funding. Massachusetts's Chapter 766 is considered by many observers to be a radical breakthrough, not only in its approach to special education but in its overall educational philosophy; the funding mechanism must be equally innovative if the educational goals of the new law are to be reached.

Special education is, without question, usually more costly than a regular education program. Weintraub, Abeson, and Braddock quote a study by Rossmiller of twenty-four school districts in five states, which found that "the cost of special programs for handicapped children ranges from 1.18 times the cost of educating a normal child for educating a speech handicapped child to 3.64 for educating a physically handicapped child."[150] As they explain, the additional costs of special education derive primarily from the need for special personnel and equipment, lower pupil-teacher ratios, and transportation costs. This greater expense is the reason why states have traditionally shared the financial burden with local school districts. Some states, in fact, have borne the entire cost of certain types of programs.

Several funding mechanisms utilized by states determine the extent and nature of their financial support for special education. A typical method is *unit reimbursement,* a funding approach currently employed by twenty states.[151] Under this scheme the state reimburses the local community for each special class. The class must usually be designated for a certain disability group; thus the unit reimbursement system is not suitable for a special education program which emphasizes the mainstreaming of special-needs children and the elimination of rigid categorization of handicaps. In addition, the unit reimbursement system gives nearly complete fiscal power to the state, because the state determines which units it will fund.

Another common method of reimbursement for special education is the *percentage reimbursement* formula. Under this system local communities usually decide, within certain limitations, which services they will offer, and the state reimburses the local school districts for a certain percentage of their total expenditures. A 1974 study found that eight states then employed this method of reimbursement.[152]

A third funding mechanism has the state government reimburse local school districts directly for special education personnel. The state may choose to reimburse communities only according to disability groupings. Three states use this system.[153]

These three funding systems are similar in that the state reimburses the community directly for special education services and personnel. All tend to distort the provision of services at the local level. With the unit reimbursement scheme, if the state pays for only a specified number of special classes, local school districts have a financial incentive to squeeze excessive numbers of children into such classes. Under a percentage reimbursement formula, communities may tend to classify more children as special if the percentage of state reimbursement for special education exceeds that for regular education. This may also result when the state pays directly for special educators.

An alternative method of state funding for special education is *per pupil reimbursement.* The state may give a certain sum to the local school district for each special education pupil (straight sum reimbursement) or give reimbursements that are *weighted* according to the ratio of the cost of educating a handicapped child with particular handicap(s) to the average statewide cost of educating a nonhandicapped child. A danger of the per pupil reimbursement approach is that it may encourage more severe labeling to increase the amounts reimbursed; it may also encourage larger classes.[154]

A third variation of the per pupil method of reimbursement is the *excess cost* formula. Under an excess cost formula, the state reimburses the local district only for the expense of educating the handicapped child which is over and above the regular, "normal" per pupil expenditure. At least one study has found that "[t]he excess cost formula seems to have the best potential for success; since the state bears *all* [and *only*] the excess cost of educating exceptional children, there is no pressure on local educational administrators to categorize or label a child inappropriately."[155]

The Funding of Chapter 766

The excess cost method of reimbursement is probably also the most suitable for a program which seeks to foster the development of adequate and varied special education services by local communities. Under the excess cost principle, local communities cannot avoid the responsibility of paying at least the average per pupil expenditure for each handicapped child. Prior to Chapter 766, Massachusetts reimbursed local school committees for special education on a straight percentage basis; specifically, the state assumed 50 percent of total costs. Chapter 766's funding mechanism is a combination of a weighted formula and an excess cost formula. Under the statute, the local school committee is initially obliged to pay for "special education personnel, materials and equipment, tuition, room and board, transportation, rent and consultant services" for all of the school-age children with special needs residing in the district.[156] The state must then reimburse the local school district for any costs of the above services that exceed "the average per pupil expenditure of the city, town or school district for the education of children of comparable age."[157] However, the amount of such reimbursement for each special education pupil shall not exceed "one hundred and ten per cent of the applicable state average expenditure for each special education pupil minus the state average expenditure per public school pupil."[158]

Taken alone, the excess cost-weighted formula of Chapter 766 is both sensible and fairly equitable.[159] The formula fortifies the concept of local responsibility for special-needs children but does not require local communities to pay all special education costs.[160]

The Chapter 766 funding formula does not operate in a vacuum, however. Because state aid for special education must be allocated first from the regular state education assistance monies made available to local communities, several problems have arisen. First, the state failed to appropriate any money specifically for the additional costs of educating children under Chapter 766. Consequently, reimbursements for special education costs meant a comparable reduction in the state aid for regular education. Second, the failure of the state to fund Chapter 766 only helped to perpetuate the traditional rivalry between regular and special education. Although one purpose of Chapter 766 is to soften the line of demarcation between the regular and special education systems, the funding dilemma appears to have worked in the opposite direction. Many local school officials have complained bitterly about the lack of funding.[161] On the other hand, one of the major principles of the *Mills* case—that if the educational system will not increase its overall budget to pay for the education of its handicapped children, then existing funds must be allocated differently to give the handicapped children an equal educational opportunity—is central to Chapter 766, and is, at least in part, effected by the excess cost-weighted formula, even without additional funding.

Notes

1. D. Cohen, R. Granger, S. Provence & A. Solnit, *Mental Health Services,* in Issues in the Classification of Children (Nicholas Hobbs ed. 1975), at 103.

2. C. Schottland, *Introduction* to H. Hoffman, Take a Giant Step (September 1969).

3. "The exclusion of handicapped children has grown out of the view that they are ineducable. When diagnostic and remedial methods were primitive, the vast majority of children with special needs were lumped together under broad, undifferentiated labels and were presumed not to function or to grow cognitively. No purpose, therefore, was seen in providing schooling for them. More recent research has shown, however, that there are real differences among children with special needs, and that with appropriate instruction all such children can improve the extent to which they are independent." Children's Defense Fund of the Washington Research Project, Children Out of School in America (October 1974), at 94.

4. F. Weintraub, A. Abeson & D. Braddock, State Law and Education of Handicapped Children—Issues and Recommendations (1972), at 14.

5. *See, e.g.,* Pa. Association for Retarded Children v. Comm. of Pa., 334 F. Supp. 1257 (E.D. Pa. 1971); Mills v. Bd. of Ed. of D.C., 384 F. Supp. 866 (D.D.C. 1972), discussed below at note 32 *et seq.*

6. Weintraub, *et al.,* note 4 above, at 4.

7. For a more detailed list of the principles which should be incorporated into special education laws, see Council for Exceptional Children Policies Commission, *Basic Commitments and Responsibilities to Exceptional Children,* in Exceptional Children (October 1971), at 181-87. *See also* The Council for Exceptional Children in Canada, A Matter of Principle: Principles Governing Legislation for Services for Children with Special Needs, (1974).

8. A recent survey of state directors of special education found a "modest positive reaction to the potential use of the term *children with special problems* or *special needs* as a substitute for current practices; 65 percent of the respondents said that the adoption of this term would have either a positive

effect or no effect." J. Gallagher, P. Forsythe, D. Ringelheim & F. Weintraub, *Funding Patterns and Labelling,* in 2 Issues in the Classification of Children 432 (1975), at 458.

9. *See* Children Out of School in America, note 3 above, at 98-99.

10. As reported in Children Out of School in America, note 3 above, at 107: "In Somerville [Massachusetts] a principal said: 'Many people have been placed in EMR [educable mentally retarded] classes because they were a problem.' A special education official remarked: 'In the past, many kids were placed in EMR classes who didn't belong there, particularly emotionally disturbed children.' "

11. Nor have programs necessarily been appropriate for mentally retarded children. In many classes for "educable mentally retarded" children, the children are taught only to perform repetitious, monotonous exercises, and their intellectual capacities are not fully developed.

12. National Clearinghouse for Mental Health Information, Residential Treatment Centers for Emotionally Disturbed Children, 1969-70, DHEW Pub. No. (HSN) 73-9057, at 7.

13. *See* chapter 3 above.

14. L. Phillips, J. Draguns & D. Bartlett, *Classification of Behavioral Disorders,* in Issues in the Classification of Children, note 1 above, at 26-55.

15. *Id.,* at 41.

16. *See* the discussion of subjective evaluation of children by teachers in Children Out of School in America, note 3 above, at 106-7.

17. Children Out of School in America, note 3 above, at 100. *See also* Weintraub, *et al.,* State Law and Education of Handicapped Children, note 4 above, at 101.

18. Text below, at note 59 *et seq.*

19. 347 U.S. 483 (1954).

20. *Id.,* at 493.

21. In a classic analysis of the equal protection clause, the authors stated: "The equal protection of the laws is a 'pledge of the protection of equal laws.' But laws may classify. And 'the very idea of classification is that of inequality.' In tackling this paradox the Court has neither abandoned the demand for equality nor denied the legislative right to classify. It has taken the middle course. It has resolved the contradictory demands of legislative specialization and constitutional generality by a doctrine of reasonable classification." Tussman & tenBroeck, *The Equal Protection of the Laws,* 37 Calif. L. Rev. 341 (1949) [footnotes omitted].

22. *See* chapter 6, text at note 116 *et seq.*

23. McDonald v. Board of Election Commissioners, 394 U.S. 802, 809 (1969). *See Developments in the Law—Equal Protection,* 82 Harv. L. Rev. 1976 (1969).

24. McGowan v. Maryland, 366 U.S. 420, 426 (1961). The Supreme Court

has also stated that the legislature may attack one evil at a time, remedying the acute aspect of a problem before other aspects. Williamson v. Lee Optical Co., 348 U.S. 483 (1955).

25. Harper v. Va. Bd. of Elections, 388 U.S. 663 (1966) (voting); Shapiro v. Thompson, 394 U.S. 618 (1969) (interstate travel).

26. McLaughlin v. Florida, 379 U.S. 184 (1964) (race); Harper v. Virginia Bd. of Elections, 388 U.S. 663 (1966) (wealth or race).

27. *See* cases in notes 25 and 26 above and *Developments in the Law— Equal Protection,* note 23 above.

28. *See* G. Gunther, *The Supreme Court, 1971 Term Foreword—In Search of Evolving Doctrine on a Changing Court: A Model for a Newer Equal Protection,* 86 Harv. L. Rev. 1 (1972).

29. San Antonio Independent School District v. Rodriguez, 411 U.S. 1 (1973).

30. Serrano v. Priest, 96 Cal. Rptr. 601, 487 P.2d 1241 (1971); Van Dusartz v. Hatfield, 334 F. Supp. 870, 874-75 (D. Minn. 1971); Hoosier v. Evans, 314 F. Supp. 316 (D.V.I. 1970); Ordway v. Hargroves, C.A. No. 71-540C (D. Mass. 1971); Murdock, *Civil Rights of the Mentally Retarded, Some Critical Issues,* 48 Notre Dame Law. 133, 167-68 (1972).

31. It was argued that the right to education was implicitly guaranteed by the Constitution because it bears a very close relationship to the First Amendment right of free speech and to the right to vote. The Supreme Court rejected these arguments, stating that courts are not compelled to guarantee the most effective or informed speech or vote. 411 U.S. at 36.

32. Note 5 above.

33. The court's statement was made as part of its "Order, Injunction and Consent Agreement" and did not reach the substantive equal protection issues. The plaintiffs had argued that exclusion of some retarded children constituted a denial of equal protection. See Plaintiffs' Memorandum in Support of Their Motion to Convene a Three Judge Court, *reprinted in* Harvard Univ. Center for Law & Education, Classification Materials 44, 55 (1972) [hereinafter cited as "Classification Materials"].

34. 334 F. Supp. at 1259. The Court recognized that all mentally retarded persons, no matter how retarded, are capable of benefiting from a program of education and training.

35. Note 5 above.

36. For a critical evaluation of the analysis used by the Court in *Mills, see Significant Developments—Failure to Provide Education to Physically or Emotionally Handicapped Children,* 52 B.U.L. Rev. 884 (1972).

37. Fialkowski v. Shapp, 405 F. Supp. 946 (E.D. Pa. 1975).

38. *See* Frederick L. and Delaware Valley Association for Children with Learning Disabilities v. Thomas, No. 74-52 (E.D. Pa., Aug. 2, 1976), *reported at* 1 Ment. Disabil. L. Rptr. 125 (1976).

39. D. Kirp, *Student Classification, Public Policy and the Courts*, 44 Harv. Ed. Rev. 7 (1974) [hereinafter cited as *Student Classification*]. (This article is reprinted in edited form from D. Kirp, *Schools as Sorters: the Constitutional Policy Implications of Student Classification*, 121 U. Pa. L. Rev. 705 (1973).

40. *Id.,* at 29-30. The burden of proof should also shift to the state to justify its special education programs when a disproportionate number of minority students are placed in special classes. *See* Larry P. v. Riles, 343 F. Supp. 1306 (N.D. Cal. 1972), Stewart v. Phillips, C.A. No. 70-1199-F (D. Mass. 1970), *parts reprinted in* "Classification Materials," note 33 above, at 234; *compare* Hobson v. Hansen, 267 F. Supp. 401 (D.D.C. 1967).

41. In re Gault, 367 U.S. 1 (1967). *See also,* generally, chapter 2 above.

42. Tinker v. Des Moines Community School District, 393 U.S. 503, 506 (1969). *Accord,* Goss v. Lopez, 419 U.S. 565 (1975).

43. 419 U.S. 565 (1975).

44. *Id.,* at 574.

45. Chapter 2, text at note 133.

46. Wisconsin v. Constantineau, 400 U.S. 433, 437 (1971); Board of Regents v. Roth, 408 U.S. 564, 573 (1972); Goss v. Lopez, 419 U.S. 565, 574 (1975).

47. 419 U.S. at 575 [footnote omitted].

48. 400 U.S. 433 (1971).

49. *See* Kirp, *Student Classification,* note 39 above, at 22-23, F. Weintraub & A. Abeson, *Appropriate Education for All Handicapped Children: A Growing Issue,* 23 Syracuse L. Rev. 1037 (1972); Note, *Due Process in Placement Hearings for the Mentally Retarded,* 41 Geo. Wash. L. Rev. 1033 (1973) [hereinafter cited as *Placement Hearings Note*]; State Law & Education of Handicapped Children: Issues and Recommendations (The Council for Exceptional Children ed. 1971).

50. 419 U.S. at 576.

51. Goldberg v. Kelley, 397 U.S. 254 (1970); Goss v. Lopez, note 42 above; Dixon v. Alabama State Board of Education, 294 F.2d 150 (5th Cir. 1960), *cert. denied,* 368 U.S. 930 (1961). *See generally Placement Hearings Note,* note 49 above, at n.32; Kirp, *Student Classification,* note 39 above.

52. In P.A.R.C. v. Commonwealth of Pennsylvania, note 5 above, the court held that notice and a hearing must be given to a mentally retarded child recommended for any fundamental change in educational status.

53. 348 F. Supp. 866, at 880-83.

54. *Id.* at 880-81.

Such notice to the parents shall

(a) describe the proposed action in detail;

(b) clearly state the specific and complete reasons for the proposed action, including the specification of any tests or reports upon which such action is proposed;

(c) describe any alternative educational opportunities available on a permanent or temporary basis;

(d) inform the parent or guardian of the right to object to the proposed action at a hearing before the Hearing Officer;

(e) inform the parent or guardian that the child is eligible to receive, at no charge, the services of a federally or locally funded diagnostic center for independent, medical, psychological and educational evaluation and shall specify the name, address, and telephone number of an appropriate local diagnostic center;

(f) inform the parent or guardian of the right to be represented at the hearing by legal counsel; to examine the child's school records before the hearing, including any tests or reports upon which the proposed action may be based, to present evidence, including expert medical, psychological and educational testimony; and to confront and cross-examine any school official, employee, or agent of the school district or public department who may have evidence upon which the proposed action is based.

55. *Id.,* at 882.

56. Kirp, *Student Classification,* note 39 above, at 48-49.

57. *Placement Hearings Note,* note 49 above.

58. It has been suggested that the decision of whether or not to allow a student to participate should be determined by balancing the advantages and disadvantages. One should ask:

1. Will the child understand what is happening?
2. Will the child make any contribution to the decision?
3. Will it be beneficial or harmful to the child?

D. Kirp, W. Buss & P. Kuriloff, *Legal Reform of Special Education: Empirical Studies and Procedural Proposals,* 62 Calif. L. Rev. 40 (1974). It seems likely that for an adolescent, questions 1 and 2, at least, would most often be answered in the affirmative.

59. P.L. 94-142, 20 U.S.C. §§ 1401 *et seq.*

60. *Education for Handicapped Bill Signed by President,* 47:2 N.Y. Ment. Hyg. News 3 (Jan. 30, 1976).

61. *Id.* Like much federal social welfare legislation (*see, e.g.,* chapter 8, at note 124), this act effects compliance by threatening to withhold federal funds if certain state performance milestones are not met. States must demonstrate that they can provide "a free, appropriate public education to all their handicapped children, aged 3 to 18, by Sept. 1, 1978; to age 21, by 1980." P.L. 94-142, 20 U.S.C. § 1412.

62. D. Milofsky, *Schooling the Kids No One Wants,* N.Y. Times, Jan. 2, 1977 (Magazine), at 24.

63. Acts and Resolves of 1972, Chapter 766, "An Act Further Regulating Programs for Childen Requiring Special Education and Providing Reimbursement Therefor," Mass. Gen. Laws Ann. ch. 71B.

64. Mass. Gen. Laws Ann. ch. 71B, § 1.

65. *Id.*

66. Mass. Acts of 1972, ch. 766, § 1.

67. *Id.*

68. Mass. Gen. Laws Ann. ch. 71B, § 2.

69. *Id.*

70. *Id.*

71. Though the law appears quite flexible in its age limits, there have been complaints that there should be no age limit at all. The upper age limit of 21, in particular, has been criticized as being too restrictive, especially since special-needs students are automatically disqualified for special education services once they receive a high-school diploma.

72. Mass. Gen. Laws Ann. ch. 71B, § 4.

73. *Id.*

74. *Id.,* at § 7.

75. *Id.,* at § 3.

76. *Id.*

77. Mass. Gen. Laws Ann. ch. 15, § 1P.

78. *Id.*

79. *Id.,* at § 1Q.

80. Mass. Gen. Laws Ann. ch. 71B, § 6.

81. *Id.*

82. *Id.,* at § 7.

83. *Id.,* at § 3.

84. *Id.*

85. *Id.*

86. Parental Consent to Core Evaluations, Memorandum from Robert Audette, Massachusetts Assoc. Comm. for Special Education, May 19, 1975.

87. *Id.*

88. S. Baskin, *State Intrusion into Family Affairs,* 26 Stan. L. Rev. 1383 (1974).

89. *Id.*; Mass. Bd. of Ed., Regs. for Ch. 766, § 327.0.

90. Described below at note 110.

91. Mass. Gen. Laws Ann. ch. 71B, § 3.

92. Mass. Bd. of Ed., Regs. for Ch. 766, § 326.5.

93. "A school age child of ages eighteen through twenty-one shall be entitled to all of the rights given to school age children by these regulations and all of the rights given adults by applicable laws." *Id.,* at § 206.0.

94. Under the regulations (*id.,* at § 316.7), a school-age child may request any individual authorized to make an evaluation referral to do so on his behalf; however, the person receiving such a request is not obliged to make the referral.

95. October 1975 amendments to the Chapter 766 regulations recognized certain rights of the child under eighteen. These amendments permit any child

between the ages of 14 and 21 to be present at his core evaluation upon his request. They also allow for the presence of a child under 14, "if the CET decides that such presence is necessary or desirable." (Reg. 311.12). Similarly, the amendments added a requirement that the written notice which is made to parents when a child is referred for an evaluation must include a statement that their child can "be present and participate" at the meetings of the CET to decide his educational plan. (Reg. 317.5).

96. Mass. Gen. Laws Ann. ch. 71B, § 3.

97. Student Record Regulations, Mass. Dep't. of Ed. (Jan. 14, 1975).

98. *Id.*, § 3.0, at 4.

99. *Id.*, § 6.3, at 5.

100. *Id.*, § 7.1, at 5.

101. *Id.*, § 7.3, at 6.

102. *Id.*, § 8.2, at 8.

103. *Id.*

104. *Id.*

105. *Id.*, § 8.2.1, at 9.

106. *Id.*, § 9.1, at 9.

107. *Id.*, § 9.3, at 9.

108. *Id.*, § 9.4.2, at 9.

109. Mass. Gen. Laws Ann. ch. 15, §§ 1M and 1N.

110. Mass. Gen. Laws Ann. ch. 15, §§ 1M and 1N; ch. 71B, § 3.

111. Mass. Gen. Laws Ann. ch. 15, § 10(3).

112. *Id.*, at §§ 10(4), (5), and (6).

113. *See* text above, at note 77 *et seq.*

114. *See* text above, between notes 8 and 9.

115. Mass. Gen. Laws Ann. ch. 71B, § 3.

116. *Id.*, § 2.

117. Mass. Dep't. of Ed. Regs., § 310.1.

118. *Id.*, at § 201.2.

119. *Id.*, at § 201.1(a), (b), (c).

120. *Id.*, at § 202.1(a).

121. *Id.*, at § 202.1(c).

122. *Id.*, at § 304.0.

123. *Id.*, at § 301.0.

124. *Id.*, at § 303.0.

125. *Id.*, at § 309.1.

126. More specific requirements regarding evaluation are discussed below at note 132 *et seq.*

127. Mass. Dep't. of Ed. Regs., §§ 502.1-502.9.

128. *Id.*, at § 502.10(b).

129. *Id.*, at § 504.1.

130. *Id.*, at § 504.3(a)(ii).

131. Some critics argue that Chapter 766 is a law biased in favor of the middle class; its evaluation and appeals procedures are so multifaceted and complex that unsophisticated parents may find them too confusing for effective use.

132. Mass. Dep't. of Ed., Div. Of Special Ed., *Core Evaluation/Educational Plan Concept,* Core Evaluation Manual—Chapter 766 (1974), at 1.

133. *Id.,* at 2.

134. Mass. Dep't. of Ed. Regs., § 311.0.

135. *Id.,* at § 320.7.

136. *Id.,* at § 311.0.

137. *Id.,* at § 319.0.

138. *Id.,* at § 336.2.

139. Among the materials produced by the Massachusetts Teachers Association are: What Everyone Should Know About Chapter 766, and Puzzled About 766? Identification and Assessment.

140. Knowing whom to refer for a 766 evaluation and how to conduct an evaluation are not the only problems facing regular school teachers. Many regular teachers have voiced sharp complaints about what they consider the excessive paperwork required by the law. Whether this criticism will persist as teachers become familiar with the law and its various legal forms remains to be seen.

141. Under Chapter 766, not only is mainstreaming the preferred educational philosophy, but being educated in the least restrictive setting is considered a child's legally enforceable right.

142. Mass. Dep't. of Ed. Regs., § 502.1.

143. Mass. Gen. Laws Ann. ch. 71B, § 4.

144. Mass. Dep't. of Ed. Regs., § 502.10(a).

145. *Id.,* at § 502.1(b)(i).

146. *See* 1955 Mass. Acts ch. 626, § 2; 1956 Mass. Acts ch. 535, §§ 2 and 3; 1956 Mass. Acts ch. 570, § 4; 1960 Mass. Acts ch. 628; 1962 Mass. Acts ch. 708; 1966 Mass. Acts ch. 14, §§ 56 and 57; 1966 Mass. Acts ch. 647, § 1; 1968 Mass. Acts ch. 695.

147. Mass. Gen. Laws Ann. ch. 71B, § 18.

148. Mass. Dep't. of Ed. Regs., § 403.5.

149. Kirp *et al.,* note 58 above, at 122.

150. Weintraub *et al.,* note 4 above, at 56.

151. Gallagher *et al.,* note 8 above, at 442 *et seq.*

152. *Id.*

153. *Id.*

154. *Id.,* at 444.

155. *Id.*

156. Mass. Gen. Laws Ann. ch. 71B, § 5.

157. *Id.,* at § 13.

158. *Id.* "In determining the applicable state average expenditure for each special education pupil for the purposes of this section the department [of education] shall differentiate between types of programs on the basis of the amount of time a child requires special programs outside of the regular classroom to meet his particular needs and the ratio of personnel to pupils required for such programs." *Id.*

159. Problems can arise, of course, whenever a school district's excess expenditures in a particular type of program exceed the state's reimbursement for that type of program. This situation has apparently occurred with emotionally disturbed children placed in out-of-state schools. The total of tuition charges at such schools exceeded the state's maximum payment level in 1975-76. *See* M. Cohen, J. Worsham, P. Coons & V. Osgood, *Chapter 766: The Price Is the Problem,* Boston Sunday Globe, June 15, 1975.

160. "In 1974, the Commonwealth 'advanced' $25 m[illion] to cities and towns as 'start-up' monies to help initiate the program. Total reimbursements for the 74/75 school year amounted to approximately $82.7 m (in the FY 76 budget). It is estimated that the Commonwealth will provide approximately $92 m in the FY 77 budget for reimbursements for the 75/76 school year." Mass. Office of Federal/State Resources, Encyclopedia of Selected Federal and State Authorizations for Services and Benefits (1976), at 272.

161. One special education administrator in an affluent suburban community which has made notable progress in identifying, evaluating and servicing its special-needs students commented on the growing feeling of uneasiness between the regular and special education components of the school system. In this particular community, overall school enrollment happens to be decreasing, so that lay-offs among regular teaching staff are virtually inevitable. However, when several lay-offs of regular teachers coincided with the hiring of several new special education personnel to meet the demands of Chapter 766, the regular teachers' animosity became all the more intense.

6 The Rights of Adolescents to Refuse Mental Health Services

In chapters 4 and 5 we considered the rights of adolescents in seeking and gaining access to mental health services. We shall now take up an equally important and complex, related issue—the rights adolescents have, or should have, in refusing mental health services which others wish to impose upon them. Because in most cases parents or guardians are among such "others," we shall begin by examining in some depth the legal relationship between parents and their children.

The Parent-Child Legal Relationship[1]

Constitutional doctrine respecting the intertwining rights and duties of parents, children and the state is uncertain and in flux. To a degree this is because so few cases on the subject have reached the United States Supreme Court; as a result, the scope of these rights and duties remains poorly defined. The limited number of cases is in turn probably the result of longstanding, unchallenged assumptions about the primacy of parents and integrity of the family unit—assumptions which are now being reconsidered as the central role of the family is, for many, giving way to different social relationships.

To compound the uncertainty, in the few parents' rights cases which have been decided, the Court has been principally concerned with weighing parental interests against a general state interest. In defining parental rights, the Court has not often had to decide whether a different constitutional standard would apply if a state were upholding the rights of parents in a conflict with their children.[2] Similarly, in most children's rights cases, the child's personal interest has been weighed against the state rather than against some aspect of parental authority.[3] It appears, however, that the Court is willing to recognize parents' rights to control their children's activities in circumstances (such as the abridgment of free speech) in which it would not permit such limitation by the state acting alone.[4] The general question of interest here, and toward which this discussion will progress, is whether parents' authority includes the right to impose mental health services upon their unconsenting children. A more narrow inquiry within the general question is whether children, and especially adolescents, have any constitutional right to refuse to enter into a mental health facility to which their parents wish to admit them.

193

Parental Rights Under the Constitution

The small number of Supreme Court decisions which have considered the constitutionality of statutes affecting parental control over children have clearly demonstrated a special solicitude for parental interests: "It is plain that the interest of a parent in the companionship, care, custody and management of his or her children comes to this Court with a momentum for respect lacking when appeal is made to liberties which derive merely from shifting economic arrangements."[5] Unfortunately, the Court has not established any discernible standard by which to measure this "momentum for respect." Parental rights appear to be based upon a conception that parenthood is a form of constitutional "liberty" protected by the Fourteenth Amendment.[6] Thus the Court says: "It is cardinal with us that the custody, care and nurture of the child reside first in the parents, whose primary function and freedom include preparation for obligations the state can neither supply nor hinder. . . . And it is in recognition of this that these decisions have respected the private realm of family life which the state cannot enter."[7]

Early parental rights cases were based on a natural rights philosophy which postulates that parents should be free of state interference in making decisions affecting the upbringing of children. This point of view is not surprising. At least since Aristotle, western societies have reposed the burden of child raising in the family and have accorded broad latitude to parental authority in the achievement of this task.[8] The family is the primary socializing and educational unit in American society. It usually functions through strong feelings of mutual psychological attachment and trust among its members. These feelings uniquely equip parents for their child-rearing role. Moreover, the family is particularly significant in a diverse society. Americans' pluralistic beliefs concerning religion, education and cultural values militate against the establishment of comprehensive, state-defined standards for child raising; indeed, to permit undue state intrusion into family affairs might destroy the pluralistic character of American society.[9]

Deference to parental rights is clearly displayed in cases involving the education of children. Thus, in *Meyer v. Nebraska,*[10] the Court upheld the right of parents to teach their children foreign languages, striking down a statute which prohibited the teaching of modern foreign languages in any school before the ninth grade. Again, in *Pierce v. Society of Sisters,*[11] an Oregon statute prohibiting children from attending private schools between the ages of eight and sixteen was declared unconstitutional. The challenged law was held to violate "the fundamental theory of liberty upon which all governments in this union repose."[12]

These decisions, now many years old, are based upon a doctrine entitled "substantive due process." This doctrine, which will be discussed later in greater detail,[13] emanates from the due process clauses of the Fifth and Fourteenth

Amendments. It is not concerned directly with issues of procedure (which issues are considered under the rubric, "procedural due process"), but rather with questions essentially respecting the "reasonableness" of state legislation which affects certain rights. Substantive due process was most extensively applied in the first third of this century, when the Court, acting in the eyes of many as a super-legislature, employed it to find state economic and social welfare legislation unconstitutional. ·

A strong reaction against the use of this doctrine as a judicial tool, based upon a concern that it permitted judges to decide cases on the basis of their subjective political beliefs, led to its curtailment and near demise.[14] As stated in chapter 5,[15] the Court restricted the scope of its review, refusing to consider the constitutionality of state legislation if a minimally rational supporting justification could be found.[16] However, where "fundamental rights"[17] are involved, most notably the privacy right, elements of substantive due process have survived. The Court subjects state legislation infringing a "fundamental right" to strict scrutiny, requiring the state to advance a "compelling," not merely "rational," justification for its infringement of the right.[18] This mode of analysis, as we shall see, is also used to test the constitutionality of statutes under the equal protection clause.

Meyer and *Pierce* were substantive due process cases decided before the fundamental right—compelling interest standard was devised, but their continued viability suggests that they are grounded upon a notion of fundamental right. Two recent opinions by the Burger Court upholding parental rights appear to adopt this approach. In *Stanley v. Illinois*,[19] the Court struck down a law denying unwed fathers the opportunity to gain custody of their natural children without a hearing upon the death of their mother. Although the decision considered equal protection and procedural, rather than substantive, due process issues, it is clear that it rested heavily upon the significance of a father's custody rights to his children. In the words of the opinion: "The private interest here, that of a man in the children he has sired and raised, undeniably warrants deference and, absent a powerful countervailing interest, protection."[20] *Meyer v. Nebraska* was cited by the Court to support the constitutional significance of this interest.

that every child attend school until the age of sixteen; they argued that the law infringed the free exercise of their religious freedom protected by the First Amendment. The parents claimed that they had the right to withdraw their children from the Wisconsin public schools at the age of fourteen to inculcate them into the Amish way of life and protect them from the worldly education of the public high schools. Writing for the majority, Chief Justice Burger employed language reminiscent of *Meyer* and *Pierce* in asserting that the Amish parents' rights outweighed the state's interest:[22]

This case involves the fundamental interest of parents, as contrasted with that of the State, to guide the religious future and education of their children. The history and culture of Western civilization reflect a strong tradition of parental concern for the nurture and upbringing of their children. This primary role of the parents in the upbringing of their children is now established beyond debate as an enduring American tradition.

The rights of parents might also find constitutional protection within the expanding contours of the right to privacy. For example, in *Griswold v. Connecticut*,[23] a case testing the constitutionality of a Connecticut statute prohibiting the use of contraceptives, Justice Douglas cited prior parental rights cases, including *Meyer* and *Pierce,* as evidence of the Court's historical respect for the privacy of the home. Other fundamental rights cases, such as *Loving v. Virginia*,[24] (where a statute prohibiting interracial marriages was struck down) and *Skinner v. Oklahoma*[25] (where the Court recognized the importance of the right to procreation) evidence a judicial concern to preserve the freedom to make important decisions affecting marriage and parenthood. A plausible argument can be made that certain familial decisions about the raising and nurture of children involve privacy-type interests of parents and fall logically within the ambit of these opinions. Recently, in *Runyon v. McCrary*,[26] the Court acknowledged the similarity between parental rights and the privacy right: "The *Meyer-Pierce-Yoder* 'parental' right and the privacy right, while dealt with separately in this opinion, may be no more than verbal variations of a single constitutional right."[27]

Nevertheless, the *Stanley* and *Yoder* opinions suggest that the Court has preferred to base its analysis upon the broader concept of parental rights rather than the more narrow scope of the privacy right. The Court's approach in these cases seems similar to the fundamental right—compelling interest approach. In *Stanley* it held that the state must demonstrate "a powerful countervailing interest"[28] to deprive a father of custody. In *Yoder* the Court referred to the parents' "fundamental" interest . . . to guide the religious future and education of their children."[29]

Minors' Rights Under the Constitution

In recent years there has been a distinct trend toward expanding the constitutional right of minors. To a large extent, however, the expansion of minors' rights has occurred in cases where the Court has been called upon to weigh the interests of the minor against the asserted interests of the state. And in the weighing process, even though the Court has recognized minors' rights, it has consistently imposed a narrower, more limited scope to these rights than it would have in the case of adults.[30]

Thus, in *In re Gault*,[31] a case involving the procedural rights of minors in juvenile delinquency proceedings (to be described later in greater detail),[32] the

Court found a constitutional mandate for many of the protections afforded adult criminals, announcing that "[n]either the Fourteenth Amendment nor the Bill of Rights is for adults alone."[33] Yet four years later, in denying the right to a jury trial in these same proceedings, the Court cautioned that it had avoided "taking the easy way with a flat holding that all the rights constitutionally assured for the adult accused . . ." must be extended to minors.[34]

Similarly, in considering a minor's First Amendment rights, the Court has held that children are "persons" under the Constitution and are entitled to exercise free speech. In *Tinker v. Des Moines Independent School District*,[35] the Court upheld the right of children to wear black armbands in school to protest United States involvement in the Vietnam War. In *Ginsberg v. New York*,[36] however, the Court frankly applied a double standard in considering minors' First Amendment rights, holding that " 'material which is protected for distribution to adults is not necessarily constitutionally protected from restriction upon its dissemination to children.' "[37] Said Mr. Justice Stewart in a concurring opinion[38] in that case:

I think a State may permissibly determine that, at least in some precisely delineated areas, a child is not possessed of that full capacity for individual choice which is the presupposition of First Amendment guarantees. It is only upon such a premise, I should suppose, that a State may deprive children of other rights—the right to marry, for example, or the right to vote—deprivations that would be constitutionally intolerable for adults.

The distinctions drawn by the Court suggest that it perceives not only that the state has a greater, more justified caretaking role toward minors than toward adults, but also that a difference exists between those constitutional rights which are conditional upon the capacity to make relatively mature choices and those which attach regardless of the age or competence of the individual.[39] Examples of the former include the right to vote, the freedom to marry, and the right to exercise the full complement of First Amendment freedoms. Examples of the latter include the right to be free of cruel and unusual punishment and the right not to be imprisoned without due process of law. In those areas where the exercise of a right appears to require a measure of adult maturity, the Supreme Court has been willing to limit the scope of minors' rights.[40]

The Decision-Making Competence of the Adolescent

Are adolescents, in fact, less competent to make decisions about their own lives than adults with similar intelligence and psychological characteristics? Of course, adolescents have fewer years of experience than adults and, in most cases, less life experience of the sort that allegedly produces wisdom or judgment.

A full-scale analysis of competence standards is far beyond the scope of this work;[41] for our purposes it is sufficient to note a number of considerations. First, for persons of any age, a diagnosis of mental disorder is not a necessary or sufficient condition for a finding that a person is legally incompetent to make his own decisions about particular matters, such as whether to accept a preferred treatment. Second, it is doubtful whether experts are needed to help make such determinations.[42] Third, competency standards are often vague, and are rarely stated in useful, operational terms. Fourth, competency standards are often too general, applying to an unjustifiably wide range of activities. A person may be competent to engage in many activities even though he or she is incompetent to engage in others. For example, a person may be able to make a highly rational and informed decision about whether to accept treatment, although he or she may be unable to manage personal financial affairs.[43]

As we have seen in our discussions of adolescent psychology,[44] people who achieve the capacity for reflective thinking (and most do not) tend to achieve it in early to middle adolescence. As I.Q. remains relatively constant, it therefore appears that most adolescents can think in formal, structural terms as sophisticatedly as adults. The question, however, is whether adolescents are as wise as adults or whether their judgment is as good. Of course, the answer to this question cannot be "scientific," but is rather a matter of social values.

It is the strongest sort of fireside induction[45] that adolescents are less competent than adults, largely because they seem impulsive and lacking in the judgment and wisdom that supposedly are gained through experience. Indeed, this intuition is clearly part of the rationale for the plenary legal power given to parents to control the upbringing of their [adolescent] children and for the state's greater power to regulate the lives of children than adults (for example, compulsory schooling). On the other hand, many groups which were formerly denied various rights because it was strongly felt that they were incapable or unworthy of competently exercising those rights (for example, the vote for women) have now been given these rights, because the rationales underlying denial have been exposed as incorrect, albeit strongly felt and believed. Similarly, many thinkers, some of them quite extreme in their views, are now questioning the strong intuitions about the competence of adolescents and the consequent power of others to make decisions for them.[46]

At present we have little data besides our knowledge of the adolescent's capacity for formal reasoning[47] and an intuitive sense that adolescents are not as competent as adults. It would be possible to test the question empirically in various ways, but this has not yet been done. We do know, however, that many adults demonstrate very little wisdom and informed judgment, even (or perhaps especially) in those matters most crucial to their lives. We also know that many adolescents can make wise judgments and demonstrate very informed and rational decision making.[48] Therefore, in evaluating societal policies and legal rules which presume adolescent incompetence in decision making, we should always keep in mind the questionable bases on which they rest.

Constitutional Rights in the Parent-Child Relationship

As preceding sections indicate,[49] the few judicial opinions relevant to the parent-child relationship have been principally concerned with weighing the rights of parents or children against state interests. When balancing the rights of parents and children, the courts generally appear to adhere to a presumption that parent-child interests are in harmony,[50] so the case law provides very little guidance as to the relative importance of a minor's interests in the event of a conflict.

Great weight is attached to parental interests. As mentioned in chapter 2,[51] parents can substantially abridge the constitutional freedoms of their children in ways which would be impermissible to the state. Parents, for example, can legitimately control their children's freedom of speech within the home, limit their freedom of choice in a host of contexts, restrict their freedom of movement, prohibit them from marrying, and even subject them to reasonable, if arbitrary, discipline without due process safeguards such as notice and a hearing. In *Ginsberg v. New York*,[52] the Court recognized that the state's interest acquired greater significance because the statute was designed to reinforce parental authority:[53]

First of all, constitutional interpretation has consistently recognized that the parents' claim to authority in their own household to direct the rearing of their children is basic in the structure of our society.... The legislature could properly conclude that parents and others, teachers for example, who have this primary responsibility for children's well-being are entitled to the support of laws designed to aid in the discharge of that responsibility.

Nevertheless, despite its solicitude for parental authority, the Court has clearly begun to recognize that in certain contexts the rights of children must be distinguished and set apart from those of their parents. Turning again to *Wisconsin v. Yoder*,[54] we see intimations of this trend. The Court recognized that, in upholding the right of Amish parents to raise their children in the Amish way of life by withdrawing them from school at age fourteen, the children would be deprived of a public school education which would equip them better for life in society at large. Perceiving that, had the children challenged their parents' decision to withdraw them from public schools, a more complex issue would have been presented, the Court stated:[55]

Our holding in no way determines the proper resolution of possible competing interests of parents, children and the state in an appropriate State court proceeding in which the power of the State is asserted on the theory that Amish parents are preventing their minor children from attending high school despite their expressed desires to the contrary. Recognition of the claim of the State in such a proceeding would of course call into question traditional concepts of parental control over the religious upbringing and education of their minor children recognized in this Court's past decisions ... [s]uch an intrusion by a state into family decisions in the area of religious training would give rise to grave questions of religious freedom. ... On the record we neither reach nor decide those issues.

In a bitter dissenting opinion, Mr. Justice Douglas criticized this narrow approach, emphasizing that children's, not parents', rights are critically important in this context.[56] However, as there was no evidence that Amish children sought to continue their education, the *Yoder* majority may have been correct in denying the state's claim that it was seeking to protect them. In part this may be because there is no fundamental right to education,[57] whereas parents apparently possess significant constitutional rights in certain aspects of child rearing. Had competing fundamental rights been involved, a collision would have been unavoidable and a legally satisfactory resolution of the problem much more elusive.

Precisely this type of issue has been raised in subsequent cases involving a minor's right to abortion. In *Roe v. Wade*[58] the Supreme Court declared that women have a fundamental right, as part of their right to privacy, to terminate pregnancies. The Court, however, explicitly declined to decide whether that right extended to unmarried, pregnant minors, for whom written parental consent to abortion was statutorily required in some states.[59] In the wake of *Roe* a number of additional states, in amending their statutes, incorporated such a parental consent requirement.[60]

A Missouri statute of this sort, requiring parental consent whenever an unmarried minor sought an abortion, was challenged in the case of *Planned Parenthood of Missouri v. Danforth.*[61] Although the state asserted that the consent requirement was designed to preserve the privacy of the family and protect parental rights, the Court, on the basis of *Roe v. Wade,* held that it was unconstitutional for parents to possess an absolute veto over their daughter's abortion decision. It appeared, therefore, that in a collision of parent-child interests in the context of abortion, the rights of the minor would prevail. However, in *Bellotti v. Baird,*[62] a companion case challenging a somewhat similar Massachusetts statute, the Court indicated that it is constitutionally permissible for a state to place far greater constraints on a minor's exercise of her privacy right than would be tolerable for an adult. The Massachusetts statute requires parental consent unless (1) the minor is competent to provide informed consent under the emancipated minors doctrine or (2) the minor can persuade a court that an abortion is in her best interest. Unanimously, the Supreme Court held that the lower court should have abstained from passing on the statute's constitutionality, because these exceptions may make it susceptible to a favorable constitutional interpretation.

These two cases, taken together, reveal an attempt by the Court to strike a delicate balance between the rights of parent and child. Though parents may not possess an absolute veto in every case over their daughter's fundamental right to abortion, it is constitutionally permissible for them to be involved in the decision-making process when their child is not mature enough to consent to the procedure or when her best interest does not dictate an abortion. Decisions based upon the best interest of the child are not new; this concept is embodied in neglect and child abuse statutes.[63] But the respect paid to the maturation of a minor's rights is a seminal concept. The Court appears to be saying that although parents still possess substantial control over their children, the importance of parental rights decreases as their child's capacity to make mature decisions increases. As a minor female matures, so does her right to seek an abortion independently; and the right of parents to participate in the decision-making process, absolute for a young girl unless her best interest requires otherwise, is first modified and then must give way as their daughter grows in maturity.

The Maturation Principle and Voluntary Admissions

The principle at work in *Danforth* and *Bellotti* has equal if not greater applicability in the context of mental health services—especially in consent to admission into a mental institution. In most states parents can now admit their children into such institutions virtually without impediment, if they obtain the concurrence of the hospital authorities.[64] Yet several rights of the child protected by the Constitution may be affected. If admitted, not only will the child lose his or her liberty, an interest of transcending important, but also related rights to free association, to travel, and, possibly, to freedom of speech.

These deprivations may be particularly unjustified for maturing adolescents, who have a growing capacity to make choices affecting their fundamental interests. Of course the exercise of rights may be modified even for adolescents when it is in their best interest. But there is no more inherent justification for absolute parental power and control here than in the case of abortion. Indeed, to the extent that placement in some mental institutions is equivalent to imprisonment and, in some egregious circumstances, to cruel and unusual punishment,[65] an argument can be advanced that children should possess a right to resist admission regardless of age. Even where an institution is benign and genuinely committed to decent therapy, a mature adolescent should have the power to resist admission by presenting his views to an impartial fact finder, in view of the important rights which are jeopardized by hospitalization. Here, as in the case of abortion: "Constitutional rights do not mature and come into being magically only when one attains the state-defined age of majority."[66]

There are other, practical reasons for requiring an impartial fact finder for situations involving mental health services where a potential exists for parent-child conflict. Parents currently have nearly unchecked discretion to obtain medical treatment for their children, be it for physical or mental illnesses or defects. But this exercise of discretion exists without a clear awareness of the differences involved in parental decisions about these different treatments. A number of factors common in physical illness are frequently absent when parents confront an emotionally disturbed child: the diagnosis is likely to be unambiguous; treatment modalities or their lack are more likely to be well-known and understood; treatment is not likely to involve lengthy hospitalization; no stigma attaches to child or parents on account of the injury or disease; and parents and child are likely to agree on the desirability of treatment and cure.

A very different picture is frequently present in the case of the mentally ill child. As discussed in chapter 3,[6 7] mental health diagnosis and treatment are much more subjective, and, due to different approaches to understanding mental illness, there are sharp disputes between mental health professionals regarding the validity of diagnoses[6 8] and the efficacy of various modes of treatment. As a result, many fear that unexplainable deviant behavior may be labeled "mental illness," simply to impose some sort of social control on a problem of adjustment. Such control may be exercised by removing the child from his environment and treating him in an institution, whereas the "real" solution may require a change in the environment, perhaps in parental or family attitudes and practices. Parents may wish to excuse their inability to cope by calling a problem "sickness." It has been suggested that in an age when juvenile crime has increased alarmingly, and juvenile justice procedural protections have also grown, the apparent increase in adolescent mental illness is merely the result of an increased use of "sickness" labels for various misbehaviors to aid parental control.[6 9]

This situation highlights the basic distinction between physically ill and mentally ill children. Many times the presence of emotional disturbance generates (or exacerbates) serious conflicts among family members. There is likely to be at least a partial breakdown in the identity of interest assumed between parents and their child. The psychiatric disorder or problem of adjustment may be due to the faulty interaction of family members; on the other hand, it may cause faulty interaction. Latent or overt hostility may be present. Such hostility may generate an inadequate search for appropriate treatment or a search for punitive modes of treatment.

Even without hostility, parents may infuse their treatment decisions with other motives at variance with the best interests of the child. The stigma attached to mental illness may prompt concealment or the selection of a diagnosis and treatment which unduly support a favorable parental self-image at the expense of the child. The fear of mental illness and ignorance of its etiology may warp judgments about the need for treatment and the best treatment alternatives. These same factors, even more than in the case of the physically ill child, may cause undue deference to professional opinion.

In addition to the compromised identity of interest between parent and child, the assault on a child's self-image is likely to be greater for mental illness than for physical illness. The length of stay in a psychiatric hospital is often weeks or months. The reason for admission is "craziness," with all the stigma accompanying that label. Physically ill children may fear treatment, but they rarely oppose it in basic principle. Adolescent mental patients, on the other hand, frequently oppose admission violently.[70] Moreover, the adolescent may perceive his or her admission as the result of specific, incriminating behaviors, and not as a result of something that has happened to him or her. When one adds forced association with other disturbed people and the deplorable condition of some mental health institutions,[71] it is little wonder that, at least for some adolescents, hospitalization may be viewed as a form of captivity.

All of these factors—the growing maturity of the adolescent, the important rights jeopardized by hospitalization, the inexactitude of diagnosis, prognosis and treatment, and the conflicts which may be present in a parental decision to seek admission—argue for the establishment of procedures which enable a minor to resist hospitalization. Because of the important interests involved, protections should be afforded minors of any age, and certainly mature minors. Hospitalization in some cases is unfortunately analogous to incarceration, and it imposes a substantial deprivation on a patient. The argument that mature minors should have this right has particular force under the maturation principle, because the maturing minor has the cognitive capacity to exercise at least a limited version of adult rights, including the right to assert an interest in his or her own liberty.

Current Trends in the Law

In view of the circumstances described above, adolescents should be entitled to a variety of procedural safeguards in the voluntary admission process. In fashioning these safeguards, *Danforth*[72] and *Bellotti*[73] suggest that a delicate balance be struck which protects the interests of both children and parents. We now turn, therefore, to an examination of the ways this may have been done in recent statutory enactments and judicial decrees.

Where state power is directly applied, as in civil commitment proceedings, the trend in recent years has been strongly toward infusing the process with formality. Testimony before the Subcommittee on Constitutional Rights of the Senate Committee on the Judiciary, in hearings spanning nearly a decade, has strongly condemned the lack of safeguards in commitment and the loss of civil rights following commitment.[74] New statutory enactments, still few in number, have attempted to delineate the category of mentally ill persons subject to civil commitment with greater precision, have limited the grounds for commitment, and have provided a variety of new procedural protections in the civil commitment process.[75] Recent judicial opinions echo the same theme,[76] and in cases involving involuntary commitments of children, there has been an expansion of procedural protections similar to the new protections increasingly afforded adults. For example, in 1968 a federal appeals court upheld a minor's right to counsel at every step of an involuntary commitment proceeding.[77] And in 1974 a California court held that juvenile courts may not involuntarily commit a child without complying with all of the procedural safeguards of the state's adult civil commitment act.[78]

In the area of voluntary admissions by parents, however, there have been far fewer changes or attempts to safeguard the rights of children. As mentioned above,[79] a 1952 NIMH model statute proposes lowering the age at which a person may apply for voluntary admission to a mental hospital without parental consent to sixteen. States have varied widely in the degrees to which they have adopted the proposal.[80] In West Virginia, for example, the personal consent of persons over twelve is required by statute for voluntary admission by parents,[81] and minors twelve or over can refuse to be released upon parental application.[82] The Massachusetts statute allows persons sixteen or over to apply for voluntary admission, but parents or guardians may also voluntarily admit a child or ward under eighteen.[83] By regulation, release may be obtained on request of a voluntary patient, if sixteen or over.[84]

Michigan's Mental Health Code contains special provisions for adolescents.[85] Persons under eighteen may be admitted by their parents or guardians, but a patient over thirteen may object to a court in writing within thirty days of admission and every three months thereafter. The hospital must assist any patient in filing the objection, and an objection results in a court hearing within seven days. The patient is entitled to counsel, independent medical examination, and other statutory, procedural protections "which the court deems necessary to ensure that all pertinent information is brought to its attention."[86] It does not appear that the court must find the minor dangerous to continue hospitalization, but if less restrictive alternatives are available, they must be employed.[87] Lack of cooperation by parent or guardian is not grounds for continued hospitalization and may trigger a neglect proceeding.[88]

The procedural rights of minors subject to voluntary admission have also been considered in a few recent cases. These opinions hint that more widespread changes may be forthcoming. In Connecticut, for example, a fifteen year old boy, admitted by his parents to the Yale Psychiatric Institute, was granted a right to obtain release at his own request at age seventeen.[89] According to the court, the Connecticut statute which provides a right to admit oneself at age sixteen implies a corresponding right to demand release from a voluntary admission at the same age despite parental objection.

In Nashville, Tennessee, the federal district court, on due process grounds, ordered a number of procedural protections for minors under age sixteen whose voluntary admission to a mental retardation facility, the Clover Bottom Development Center, is requested by their parents or guardians.[90] An independent, three-member admission board, composed of people with expertise in the field of mental retardation, was established by order of the court. All admissions to the institution must now be approved by this board after hearings; the court further mandated representation by independent counsel, notice and an opportunity to be heard, and the right to judicial review of the action of the Admissions Review Board in the state courts.

Still another approach was adopted in 1972 in Cook County, Illinois. There, a state circuit court, in considering petitions for declaratory and injunctive relief on behalf of adolescents placed in mental institutions by their guardians, concluded that the adolescents had a right to request discharge.[91] After five days, their hospitalization could be continued only if a hearing for involuntary civil commitment had been requested by the confining institution. At this hearing the minor was entitled to assistance of counsel and other due process protections.

In July 1974 a far-reaching opinion[92] (subsequently remanded by the United States Supreme Court for the exclusion of moot claims and reconsideration of the class definition[93]) was rendered by a three-judge federal district court with respect to the Pennsylvania Mental Health and Mental Retardation Act. The lower court held certain provisions of the statute unconstitutional on due process grounds as they apply to all persons eighteen years of age or younger who have been or may be admitted or committed to mental health facilities in Pennsylvania. The court held that the plaintiffs were entitled to:[94]

1. a probable cause hearing within seventy-two hours from the date of initial detention, but not to a precommitment hearing;
2. a post-commitment hearing within two weeks of the date of initial detention;
3. written notice, including the date, time, and place of the hearing, and a statement of the grounds for the proposed commitment;
4. counsel at all significant stages of the commitment process and, if indigent, the right to appointment of free counsel;
5. the right to be present at all hearings;
6. a standard of clear and convincing proof (". . . a preponderance standard creates too great a risk of erroneous commitment, wrongfully depriving a child of his interest in liberty, an interest of 'transcending value,' and, given the subjectivity and 'relatively undeveloped state of psychiatry as a predictive science,' requiring proof beyond a reasonable doubt creates too great a risk of erroneously releasing children in need of institutionalization.")[95]

Significantly, while cognizant of the interests of parents, guardians and those standing *in loco parentis,* the district court recognized that at times such persons may act against the interests of their children. It thus denied parents the authority to waive their children's constitutional rights.[96] The court held, however, that the above procedural rights (which apply against the state), except the rights to notice and counsel, ". . . may be waived by the child and the unbiased tribunal may accept such a waiver upon approval by the child's counsel and upon a finding that the child understands his rights and is competent to waive them. Because there may be situations where the child either does not understand his rights or is not competent to waive them, any or all of these rights may also be waived by the child's attorney, and the unbiased tribunal may accept the waiver upon a finding that the waiver is appropriate."[97] In this way, presumably, the lower court attempted to deal with the situation where the child's illness is undisputed or where, despite the absence of competent consent by the child, all objective facts indicate that admission or commitment is warranted, even to the representative of the child. Although the Supreme Court reversed and remanded *Bartley* for reconsideration in view of a new Pennsylvania admission statute, the basic issues raised by the case are before the high Court once again in *Parham v. J.L. and J.R.,*[98] a suit appealed from a Georgia federal court.

Ways to Effect Change

The above statutes and cases suggest that changes in the procedures governing the voluntary admission of adolescents are forthcoming; their small numbers also demonstrate that thus far neither legislatures, courts, nor legal commentators have devoted great attention to the problem. It appears from recent developments that the means chosen to restrain parental discretion will assume different forms in different jurisdictions. These means will probably include an alternative decision maker, who will share authority with parents, and a variety of procedural safeguards designed to maximize the fairness, impartiality, and efficiency of admission proceedings. The right of parents to waive these safeguards will be eliminated.

The modes of restraining power may vary widely. Mental health facilities could promulgate internal rules and regulations which would provide minor patients with protections similar to those of adults in some jurisdictions. This type of change, however, would be sporadic and uneven in application. An appropriate government agency, most likely a state department of public or mental health, could issue regulations, but these would have to be consistent with existing statutes. More sweeping changes could occur if a state legislature, on the basis of *parens patriae* or the best interest of the child doctrines, enacted legislation with appropriate procedural protections. Such an approach would provide uniform standards and procedures throughout a state mental health system, and would further the development and funding of a coordinated program. Congress could also enact new legislation, at least for federal facilities, and perhaps with wider application under Section Five of the Fourteenth Amendment or the Commerce Clause.[99]

In the absence of new legislation, the principal means to effect change will be litigation in the courts. Court decisions may be based on "common law," statutes, or provisions of the federal or state constitutions. Common law is the body of rules developed by judges and enunciated in judicial opinions. For example, the concept that parents must act in the best interest of their child finds most frequent expression in the judicial process. In many areas, however, common law has been superseded by statutes. This is generally true of mental health admissions. To change such rules or procedures which have been promulgated by a legislature, judges may resort either to statutory interpretation or to holding a statute unconstitutional.

Statutory interpretation involves defining and applying the language and intent of a statute to achieve a result which the judge maintains that the legislature desired. There is, however, little room for judicial inventiveness in interpretation when the language of a statute is either terse or very precise, such as is frequently the case in statutes giving parents power to consent to psychiatric treatment of their minor children. A court would be more likely to change admissions procedures in such cases by finding an admission procedure unconstitutional, and it is this approach which has been followed most frequently in recent cases. The probable grounds for suit would be either the due process or equal protection clause of the Fourteenth Amendment, although a state constitution having similar provisions might also serve as a basis. The suit would probably be grounded on a violation of an adolescent's rights under these constitutional provisions with respect to the application to that adolescent of procedures required or permitted by state statute, regulation, or practice.[100]

Persuasive but somewhat complex arguments support the proposition that an adolescent's equal protection and due process rights are violated under most existing statutes on voluntary admission of minors.[101] The various components of the constitutional analysis, therefore, are considered separately below.

State Action

If a constitutional challenge to the right of parents and guardians to admit an adolescent into a mental institution is based upon the Fourteenth Amendment, it will be necessary to demonstrate at least minimal state action in the admissions process, because the amendment is directed at state, not private, action.[102] This task may be much more difficult than it first appears. In an age when state regulation of private life is pervasive and when state assistance is frequently provided to otherwise private entities,[103] the line separating government from private entities is frequently blurred. Case law on the subject is therefore confusing; courts have decided controversies involving similar fact situations in different ways, sometimes appearing to use state action analysis as an alternative to deciding difficult cases on their merits.

In analyzing whether the admission of an adolescent constitutes state action, however, there seems little room for serious argument when an adolescent is admitted to a public institution supported entirely from the public treasury and staffed entirely by state employees.[104] Similarly, if a minor may only be admitted to a public or private mental health facility after detailed procedures required by state legislation, it seems that the state has substantially infused itself into the admissions process.

Difficulties in proving state action arise in the admission of an adolescent to a privately owned and operated facility when the statutory authorization appears to do no more than codify, in minimal language, the right of parents to admit their child, and no further provisions of the statute or regulations spell out the admissions procedures. Lastly, if there is no legislative authorization whatsoever in a particular jurisdiction, an argument for the presence of state action in an admission to a privately operated facility may be tenuous indeed.

Even in such circumstances, however, an absence of state action may not be conclusively presumed. A legal analysis of the possibility should begin by asking whether any factors so color the actions of the private facility that it may legitimately be regarded as an instrumentality of the state for purposes of constitutional litigation. The reported cases suggest two major lines of inquiry.

First, to use the terminology of appellate opinions, we may ask whether there is a sufficient "nexus" between the state and the challenged action of a regulated, private entity so that the action may be fairly treated as that of the state.[105] Unfortunately, in itself this formulation provides little assistance in deciding when the nexus is sufficiently close. In deciding the question, therefore, courts have inquired into the degree to which the state is identified with the action of the entity, the extent to which the entity benefits from state regulations or economic assistance, and the intrusiveness of the state's regulations into the business of the entity.

Applying these criteria to private mental institutions, one may surmise that the state licenses their operation, possibly regulates some of the treatments which are administered—for example, by limiting electroconvulsive therapy or requiring prescriptions for drugs—and may provide either direct financial benefits or preferential tax treatment. Nevertheless, as long as these indicia of state presence do not bear directly upon the act of admission, it may be difficult to argue successfully that the admissions process is the result of state action. In *Moose Lodge No. 17 v. Irvis,*[106] for example, the Supreme Court held that, despite the possession of a liquor license from the state, the refusal of the Lodge to serve a Negro guest did not constitute state action sufficient to invoke the protection of the Fourteenth Amendment against this type of discriminatory treatment. In a similar vein, two lower courts declined to find state action in situations where hospitals had received Hill-Burton funds and were subject to extensive federal and state regulation, but the action complained of related to granting or withholding staff privileges.[107] Both courts refused to subject the hospitals' operations in toto to the Fourteenth Amendment when there was no direct connection between the regulatory scheme and the actions in question.

The second major line of inquiry in assessing the presence of state action appears at first glance to be both more coherent and simpler to apply than an approach based upon a finding of nexus. The formulation is as follows: if the state gives private parties powers or functions which are governmental, then those private parties will be treated as instrumentalities of the state, subject to the same constitutional limitations as the state.[108] A governmental function or power is in turn defined as one which is traditionally reserved exclusively to the state, such as eminent domain.[109]

The defect of this rationale, however, is that it is at war with the role of constitutional law in a changing society. Standing alone, a historical test is insufficient. Governments develop and exercise new powers to meet the demands of changed circumstances, and any formulation designed to demonstrate when private persons are exercising governmental powers must be capable of growth and change. In addition, the "governmental function" test contains inherent ambiguities: how exclusive must governmental control have been, and after how much time does its exercise become traditional? Just as in the nexus cases, courts have split in their interpretation of "governmental function" even though confronted by seemingly similar fact situations.

As a case in point, the application of this approach to the treatment of mentally ill adolescents produces confusing and unsatisfactory results. Historically, most adolescents with serious mental disorders were "treated" at home because there were no appropriate public or private facilities for them. Concomitantly, state governments have clearly been involved in the hospitalization of the insane for well over a century, and today this task is predominantly a function of state government, even though treatment in private facilities is increasing.[110] Yet despite massive government intrusion into the field, a test requiring a "traditional" exercise of "exclusive" power by the state might find an absence of state action.

This conclusion is not compelled, however. In both approaches to determining state action, the responses of the judiciary appear to be based frequently upon a weighing of the interests involved rather than a close application of either test. In one line of governmental function cases,[111] for example, courts have acted to preserve freedom of speech in areas generally open to the public and functionally appropriate for expressive conduct even though privately owned. Other cases, involving both "governmental function" and "nexus" considerations, have found state actions where racial discrimination was present, even though the cases otherwise presented facts arguing against state action.

One of these[112] is nearly indistinguishable, save for the facts, from opinions holding the other way. In this case a hospital received Hill-Burton funds and was subject to substantial state and federal regulation. In similar cases involving disputes concerning staff privileges, no state action was found. In this case, however, the hospital in question practiced racial segregation. The hospital had stated on the government's funding application form that it was segregated and would remain so, and thus the government was aware of the hospital's practices at the time it granted its funds. These facts were sufficient for the court to characterize the hospital's discriminatory acts as actions by the state.

It appears, therefore, that even if a private mental health facility is not engaged in state action under a strict application of either a "nexus" or "governmental function" test when it voluntarily admits an adolescent, the opposite conclusion could be reached if the interests of a nonconsenting juvenile were found to have special constitutional significance. In such a case a court might subject the practice to strict scrutiny and accept lesser manifestations of state presence, such as financing or regulation, as sufficient.

However, it is not at all clear that the interests of an adolescent, even a purportedly mentally ill adolescent, have special constitutional significance. In the current language of the law, race is a suspect classification, and a state must meet a nearly unattainable standard—must demonstrate a compelling interest— before racial discrimination will be tolerated. The next section, on equal protection, discusses these constitutional standards in greater detail. That section makes clear that, although an argument can be made that mental disability is a suspect classification, that position is unlikely to prevail in the near future.[113] Thus it would appear that the status of mentally ill adolescents will not in itself be sufficient to tip the scales toward a finding of state action by a private entity, if other indicia are absent.

In the absence of statutes governing admission, it may be difficult to demonstrate state action on the part of a private mental health facility for purposes of constitutional litigation. Before abandoning the attempt, however, one other fairly novel and perhaps persuasive approach to this issue should be considered. It requires a shift in the focus of analysis from the actions of private institutions to the actions of parents. One responsible commentator has written that ". . . children are a subject population, no matter who exercises authority over them, and all such authority—whether school teachers, juvenile court judges, or parents—is supported by state sanction, by legal artifact."[114] It is not clear, however, that the state so much authorizes parental authority as recognizes it. In many cases parental rights are cast in a "fundamental" mold, and their fusion with state power may only be apparent in limited, serious circumstances, such as when "stubborn child" or runaway proceedings are invoked. If the fusion is complete at all times, it encounters the analytical problems of *Shelly v. Kramer*,[115] where state action appears to become omnipresent. The reasoning of that 1948 case, carried to its ultimate—and surely unintended—extension, would find the state always inculpated in all societal transactions, leaving no realm of private behavior whatsoever. This would occur because in all cases the state is willing either to enforce a private choice or to refuse a remedy to a party complaining of a private choice. It is not surprising that very few succeeding opinions have placed reliance upon *Shelley*.

Nevertheless, an argument to demonstrate state action in the exercise of parental authority may be based upon the maturation principle. To say that the power to exercise a constitutional right ripens over time is not to say that the process of maturation either commences or concludes at a definite point. But in the early teens this process for most minors is sufficiently advanced to give them a limited degree of independence. At this point absolute parental rights begin to wane. Concomitantly, the source of parental authority may also begin to shift. If formerly a fundamental, innate right, this authority increasingly assumes the form of a duty delegated by the state. As such, when exercised it may constitute state, not private, action, and a challenge to it may involve a dispute with the state acting through an agent rather than a collision with fundamental parental interests.

Equal Protection

The Fourteenth Amendment states the proposition that "[n]o state shall . . . deny to any person within its jurisdiction the equal protection of the laws."[116] A key purpose of this constitutional provision is to ensure that legislatures do not enact statutes which abuse a minority. Legislative enactments should apply equally to classes of people similarly situated. As stated by Mr. Justice Jackson:[117]

[T]here is no more effective practical guaranty against arbitrary and unreasonable government than to require that the principles of law which officials would impose on a minority must be imposed generally. Conversely, nothing opens the door to arbitrary action so effectively as to allow those officials to pick and choose only a few to whom they will apply legislation and thus to escape the political retribution that might be visited upon them if larger numbers were affected. Courts can take no better measure to assure that laws will be just than to require that laws be equal in operation.

It is not permissible, however, to infer from Justice Jackson's statement the simple proposition that all laws must apply equally to all persons. As we have seen in comparing the rights of minors and adults, there are often legitimate distinctions between comparable groups of people in comparable situations. To use a homely example, different laws may regulate the different business activities of butchers, bakers and candlestick makers, even though all are tradespeople engaged in earning a living.

Pursuant to the Fourteenth Amendment or similar state constitutional provision, courts are often called upon to determine whether the state may treat one group of people differently from another in some contexts. In performing this task, they must review statutes passed by state legislatures and consider to what extent their determinations should take precedence over laws formulated as a result of a complex political process. Before adjudicating questions regarding equality of treatment, therefore, courts must first define the circumstances in which such adjudication is permissible.

The scope of judicial review has not been static over time. Early in this century, in the heyday of "substantive due process," courts frequently overrode economic legislation such as wage and hour laws as having "no reasonable foundation."[118] This intervention was subsequently discredited as an unwarranted extension of judicial authority[119]—an attempt by an aged, conservative majority of the Supreme Court to thwart new social legislation. As we pointed out previously,[120] the Court subsequently redefined and limited its role, refusing to invoke review except in narrowly defined circumstances. "For protection against abuses by legislatures the people must resort to the polls, not to the courts."[121]

This attitude may be explained as a recognition by the Supreme Court of its own institutional limitations and a corresponding desire to leave governmental policy decisions to the legislature. One rationale for this arrangement is that a legislature has more time and resources to make factual determinations supporting legislative judgments than does a court. A more persuasive rationale is that, in a majoritarian system, the most representative institution should decide general policy and implementation, and any mistakes should be corrected not by an autonomous, authoritarian judiciary, but through the political process.

As previously stated, with the ascendancy of this attitude, the use of "substantive due process" to strike down state laws greatly declined.[122] A similar deference to the judgment of legislatures and the intricacies of the political process has been shown in applying equal protection doctrine.[123] Standards have been developed to assist courts in deciding when judicial intervention is necessary. As a result, a two-tiered approach is generally applied.[124] Most legislation is on the first tier, where courts employ a "minimum rationality" standard, that is, as long as a separate classification bears a rational relationship to a legitimate governmental objective, and there is some minimum justification for it, the courts will not review its constitutionality. Moreover, a state need show only a conceivable, not an actual, set of facts which would support a constitutionally acceptable purpose and which would make the challenged classification appropriate for achieving that purpose.[125]

On the second tier, however, states must demonstrate convincingly in certain situations that separate treatment serves a legitimate and sometimes substantial governmental objective. The formula for judicial intervention in these cases has been phrased in the words of Mr. Justice Harlan:[126]

Statutory classifications which either are based upon certain "suspect" criteria or affect "fundamental rights" will be held to deny equal protection unless justified by a "compelling" governmental interest.

Courts will subject such statutes to strict scrutiny, and, with very few exceptions, an announcement that a strict scrutiny standard is applicable ultimately results in a declaration that the legislative scheme in question is unconstitutional.[127]

It might be claimed that minors admitted to mental institutions by their parents or guardians are denied equal protection as compared with other adolescents civilly committed to mental institutions or with minors incarcerated through the juvenile justice system. As we have seen, the trend is toward granting many more procedural protections to persons facing civil commitment. The procedural rights of minors in the juvenile justice system were extensively enlarged by *In re Gault*,[128] an opinion discussed in considerable detail elsewhere in this volume.[129]

Nonetheless, applying a minimum rationality standard, a state could easily justify the distinction. One rationale might be that, with all its inadequacies, the present system of parental or guardian authority and responsibility for child rearing has proven efficient and successful in providing for the broad range of a growing child's needs; a necessary corollary to this authority is a substantial degree of discretion, including the discretion to provide mental health care when prescribed by an admitting physician. A minimally rational distinction between the "voluntarily" admitted child and persons involved in civil commitment or juvenile delinquency proceedings, then, is the presence of a "benevolent" parent or guardian in the former situation and the direct presence of the state as a party in the latter two situations. In "voluntary" admission, it is assumed that the child lacks the maturity to exercise independent, informed judgment but that his best interests are being weighed properly by others who have an intimate concern for his welfare. On the other hand, in civil commitment or juvenile delinquency proceedings, it is the more remote and impersonal state which seeks detention. In theory, therefore, the procedures for civil commitment and adjudication of delinquency should be more rigorous. In addition, delinquency proceedings may be seen as quasi-criminal in nature, whereas voluntary admissions are for mental health treatment.

A state could argue that these distinctions are consistent with its statutory purpose of minimizing unnecessary impediments to mental health treatment for juveniles. But countervailing arguments might be advanced. For example, many minors who are "voluntarily" admitted to mental institutions experience the same sense of coerced confinement as those placed in the same or similar institutions following an involuntary civil commitment proceeding or an adjudication of delinquency. In all three situations the adolescent's status is maintained through the power of the state; if a voluntarily admitted minor "elopes" from an institution, the police may be notified to apprehend and return him or her. Under the circumstances, it seems irrational to contend that procedures to test the validity of confinement must be followed in cases of civil commitment or detention for delinquency, but that similar, albeit arguably less stringent, procedures need not be adopted for voluntary admissions. In the last case the burden imposed on parents and guardians appears trivial in comparison to the prolonged loss of liberty which may occur and the harm that may be caused if the decision to admit is based on erroneous grounds.

The difficulty of drawing a viable distinction is increased when one considers that the reasons for confinement, based upon an adolescent's behavior, may be identical in all cases. In the admission of mentally retarded minors to an institution in Pennsylvania, for example, the reasons given were: "running away, robbing a gas station, stealing in general, chasing and striking a girl, arson, delinquent behavior in general, [and] truancy . . ."[130] These same kinds of behaviors could be a basis for involuntary civil commitment. They could also result in apprehension by a police officer and an eventual adjudication of delinquency by a juvenile court. In a delinquency proceeding, and in a civil commitment proceeding in many states, a minor would be entitled to a panoply of procedural protections, including representation by counsel, a hearing, proof beyond a reasonable doubt or by clear and convincing evidence, and a right of appeal. By contrast, a child may be admitted voluntarily to a mental institution at the unmonitored discretion of a parent and admitting psychiatrist.

Moreover, this disparity cannot be justified by an assertion that the underlying rationale for confinement in each case is significantly different. Except possibly in a case where an extremely disturbed child is civilly committed because of potential danger to others, placement in a mental institution or in a state school for delinquent children is always premised upon the objectives of "treatment" and eventual rehabilitation. To be sure, the conditions in many institutions of both types inhibit the achievement of this goal,[131] but this fact has simply buttressed the argument that greater procedural protections should be made available in commitment and delinquency proceedings. Because children subjected to voluntary admission are placed in the same kinds of institutions, it makes little sense to ignore their need for similar protection.

Nevertheless, despite these cogent arguments, it is highly doubtful that a court would find a denial of equal protection under the minimum rationality standard. A state need only show a conceivable set of facts supporting a legislative judgment, and courts will defer to that judgment. Here the parent-child relationship is a plausible rationale for disparate treatment. The result might be different, however, if a court could apply a strict scrutiny standard of review and require a compelling state interest. To do so, a court would have to find that mentally ill minors who are voluntarily admitted to state mental institutions are a suspect classification or that their fundamental rights are violated by present procedures. In pursuing this approach, therefore, it is necessary to consider the content and applicability of the terms "suspect classification" and "fundamental right."

Suspect Classification. A suspect classification has been defined as a group ". . . saddled with such disabilities or subjected to such a history of purposeful unequal treatment or relegated to such a position of political powerlessness as to command extraordinary protection from the majoritarian political process."[132]

Suspect classifications include race,[133] national ancestry,[134] and alienage.[135] The inclusion of sex is uncertain.[136] It has been suggested that poverty is a suspect classification,[137] but the principal cases may be read as based on other grounds.[138] Mental illness has never been suspect, although an interesting article in the Yale Law Journal has suggested that it should be.[139] This position is not likely to be adopted soon by the courts.

Although the criteria for deciding that a classification is "suspect" are unclear, much analysis seems to be concerned with the political powerlessness of the group in question and is based upon Justice Stone's suggestion that special judicial scrutiny is appropriate when legislation singles out "discrete and insular minorities."[140] Such a criterion would be consistent with judicial resolve to intervene in legislative determinations only when the political process seems most prone to majority abuse. However, it is difficult even to recognize a "discrete and insular minority,"[141] and discrete groups need not be numerical minorities to suffer a lack of political power. (Consider, for example, women, especially before passage of the Nineteenth Amendment.)

Another suggested measure of suspect classification is the immutability of the shared characteristics of the class.[142] Yet another suggestion depends on the number of members of affected classes in the legislative body.[143] The latter analysis would not scrutinize distinctions between groups whose members are not frequently legislators ("they-they" generalizations) but would consider suspect a distinction which benefited a group whose members are often legislators ("we-they" generalizations). This analysis, however, appears to overlook the dynamics of diverse political pressures and requires unseemly judicial scrutiny of the makeup of each legislative body.

When these various definitions are applied to the mentally ill adolescent voluntarily admitted to a mental institution, many of them seem apposite. The mentally ill and retarded—adults and children—have suffered a long history of purposeful unequal treatment when compared to the physically ill, and this treatment has often been shockingly cruel.[144] They have frequently been denied the right to vote, a right which is denied to children in any event. Thus the mentally ill—and particularly mentally ill children—may merit special protection as a politically powerless minority, unable to defend themselves in the majoritarian political process.

Nevertheless, it seems unlikely that mentally ill minors will, in the near future, be regarded as a suspect classification by the Supreme Court. Without political power themselves, they are represented by others in governmental processes. And the characteristics of the class are not immutable; mental illness is often cured or ameliorated, or it abates spontaneously. Furthermore, youth is a transient period (which may account for the fact that legislators often seem more concerned about old age, a status they expect to acquire, than youth, a status they have forever left behind).[145] Most important, the Court is very hesitant to extend the list of suspect classifications, and neither minority nor mental illness meets the test of having no relationship to any acceptable state purpose. There are many circumstances which reasonably require the law to treat children and the mentally ill differently from others for their own protection.

Fundamental Rights. A different situation may present itself in considering the "fundamental rights" of mentally ill children. A fundamental right is a right explicitly protected by the Constitution or, within carefully construed limits, one which the Supreme Court finds to be implicit in the language of the Constitution. In the latter category, however, objective standards to determine when the label should be applied may be even less possible than for suspect classifications. The Supreme Court seems to have decided that such rights include privacy,[146] voting,[147] interstate travel,[148] free association,[149] procreation,[150] and apparently hearings for criminal defendants.[151] A fundamental "right to be free" has been suggested, a right which undergirds all others, but it has not yet been recognized by the courts.[152] Education was also urged as a right but was finally rejected explicitly by the Supreme Court.[153]

Because of the difficulty in discerning a common source for these rights, some have seen this branch of equal protection analysis as a return to unfettered judicial subjectivity and usurpation of legislative prerogatives characteristic of substantive due process analysis earlier in this century.[154] But the equal protection clause does not leave courts the open-ended discretion that substantive due process might.[155] Equal protection demands only that the legislature protect a fundamental right of the affected group to the same extent that it protects that right for a similarly situated group.[156] As one commentator would have it:[157]

[T]he function of the equal protection clause is in large measure to protect against substantive outrages by requiring that those who would harm others must at the same time harm themselves—or at least widespread elements of the constituency on which they depend for reelection.

An argument can be made that some fundamental rights—the rights to privacy, to associate freely, and to travel—are clearly involved in each admission of a minor to a mental institution. Adults, of course, have a greater entitlement to these rights than children, i.e., they may enjoy them with fewer limitations. As stated previously, parents and guardians have broad discretionary authority; they may choose a child's form of religious worship, select a child's playmates, examine a child's possessions in a way which would violate the privacy rights of an adult, subject a child to reasonable confinement, and choose even the location in which the growing child obtains his or her formative life experiences.

This authority, however, is not limitless.[158] In all cases a parent or guardian is required to act in the best interest of the child. Failure to do so may result in a charge of neglect or child abuse. Thus a parent may confine a child to his or her room, but the child cannot be imprisoned there; moderate chastisement is permissible, severe and injurious beatings are not; selection of worthy companions is laudable, but exposing a child to the compansionship of the depraved is not. As *Danforth*[159] and *Bellotti*[160] make clear, minors' rights may be limited aspects of adult rights, but they are nonetheless real. Their abridgment should trigger the same constitutional analysis which is invoked when the fundamental rights of adults are abridged.

These rights appear to be placed in jeopardy in both civil commitment and delinquency proceedings, but in these situations minors may call upon a range of procedural protections to help them contest their possible confinement. The same rights also appear to be placed in jeopardy when a child is voluntarily admitted to an institution. Deference to parental authority may be a compelling reason for the distinction, but it does not seem sufficient to justify the child's near total lack of protection in the last case and not the first two.

However, any assertion that the rights of children are fundamental or that, if fundamental, they are involved in voluntary admissions must be advanced tentatively. Courts will naturally fear that an extension of previously recognized fundamental rights to this context will invite challenges by children to every denial of adult procedural protections in other contexts. Tentativeness is required for another reason as well. The primary difficulty with the two-tiered system of analyzing equal protection requirements is in discerning which rights are "fundamental" and which classifications are "suspect" in different situations. The courts have failed to describe "a rational standard, or even points of reference, by which to judge what differentiations are permitted and when equality is required."[161]

The perhaps predictable result, not acknowledged in opinions, is the occasional abandonment of the rigid two-tiered system.[162] There are intimations that the Supreme Court may be edging toward a new, more flexible standard (sometimes called intensified rationality scrutiny) somewhere between the two tiers which have become a familiar part of equal protection analysis. Most of the two-tiered approach was developed by the Warren Court, and there has been a discernible shift by the Burger Court.[163] In *James v. Strange*[164] and *Eisenstadt v. Baird,*[165] for example, the Supreme Court was less willing than in previous cases to strain for some minimum justification of a statute, yet it found the legislative enactments unreasonable and unconstitutional in each case without invoking strict scrutiny. The Supreme Court's 1971 opinion in *Reed v. Reed*[166] provides another good example. Without even mentioning strict scrutiny or finding that sex is a suspect classification, Chief Justice Burger nevertheless found invalid an Idaho statute which gave males preference as administrators of estates. Under ordinary minimum rationality analysis, the asserted purpose of administrative convenience would have been sufficient. Rather than condemning or accepting statutes according to their category for purposes of judicial review, cases such as *Reed v. Reed* seem to be merely narrowing the means which a legislature may use in certain situations to achieve acceptable statutory purposes.

A leading commentator admits that "Court adherence to the model of intensified rationality scrutiny is inchoate and fragmentary at present."[167] But this middle standard seems to have been used in adult commitment cases. Chief Justice Warren used the equal protection clause to extend to prisoners about to finish prison terms the same statutory rights afforded nonprisoners facing commitment to a maximum security mental institution.[168] That opinion does not mention fundamental rights or suspect classifications. At least one commentator has made a convincing argument that the case should be read narrowly as an avoidance of the then-confused procedural due process area.[169] (The doctrinal blockage of procedural due process seems to have been broken the following year in *In re Gault,*[170] with its extensive analysis of required procedures for juvenile delinquency hearings, and in *Specht v. Patterson,*[171] which used a due process analysis to require procedural protections in commitment of sex offenders.) However, the equal protection rationale of *Baxtrom* was picked up again in *Humphrey v. Cady*[172] and *Jackson v. Indiana,*[173] two Burger Court decisions regarding commitment of criminal defendants. Neither opinion demands proof of a compelling state interest or engages in a strict scrutiny analysis. Both seem appropriate examples of some middle standard of review, forgoing a minimum rationality standard yet avoiding the delineation of new "fundamental rights" which require strict scrutiny by courts and further limit legislative discretion.

Significantly, *Humphrey* and *Jackson* use both equal protection and due process arguments. A constitutional attack on existing procedural rights of adolescents in the mental health process will also likely be based on both grounds. The potential success of traditional equal protection arguments, standing alone, is difficult to gauge. Even a "middle ground" position may not succeed, although it probably stands the greatest chance of being adopted, at least *sub silentio,* by the courts. Unfortunately, like the two-tiered analysis, it lacks precision in terms of predicting when it will be applied and the results of its application. It is akin in this sense to Justice Thurgood Marshall's solitary "sliding scale" approach, not embraced by the Court, which allows varying degrees of protection depending on the "constitutional and societal importance of the interest adversely affected" and the "recognized invidiousness of the basis upon which the classification is drawn."[174] These terms are no more susceptible to precise interpretation than those of the two-tiered approach.

Thus, even employing a "middle ground" equal protection analysis, it cannot be asserted confidently that increased judicial flexibility will result in granting minors subject to voluntary admission procedural protections comparable to those afforded persons in civil commitment and juvenile delinquency processes. Without a strict scrutiny analysis the Supreme Court may refuse to demand equality in situations where there is a colorable assertion of benevolent protection by parents or guardians.

Due Process

A constitutional attack on the lack of procedural safeguards in the voluntary admission process may stand a better chance of success under the due process clause of the Fourteenth Amendment, which states sparingly that no State shall "...deprive any person of life, liberty, or property, without due process of law;..."[175] The issue would probably be framed in terms of a denial of an adolescent's "liberty or property" interest through state enforcement of a parental right to admit children voluntarily without procedural restraints. Although courts have not made the constitutional basis of their decisions entirely clear, the few cases which have considered the subject appear to have been based on the above approach.

The courts rely upon due process because "[i]t is the basic and essential term in the social compact which defines the rights of the individual and delimits the powers which the state may exercise."[176] Unfortunately, the term is not self-defining. Its scope is a subject of great complexity but consists essentially of two major branches. One of these, "substantive due process," has been described previously[177] and is not of immediate concern to us here. The other is "procedural due process," the essential elements of which are notice and an opportunity to be heard and to defend oneself in an orderly proceeding adapted to the nature of the case. These and other procedural protections are designed to limit the ill effects of a decision maker's incompetence, malice or other shortcomings by providing an effective forum for evidence and different viewpoints and by providing standards for effective review of decisions.

As long as the deprivation is not *de minimus*,[178] due process applies to minors as well as adults. In *Goss v. Lopez*,[179] a case discussed earlier[180] which involves the due process rights of nine high school students temporarily suspended from their high schools without a hearing, the Supreme Court held that the students must be given "oral or written notice of the charges" against them and, if they deny the charges, "an explanation of the evidence the authorities have and an opportunity to present [their] side of the story."[181] At a minimum, said the Court, the "abstract words of the Due Process Clause . . . require that deprivation of life, liberty or property by adjudication be preceded by notice and opportunity for hearing appropriate to the nature of the case."[182] But the Court stopped short of requiring other procedural protections, such as right to counsel or to confront and cross-examine witnesses, stating that "the timing and context of the notice and the nature of the hearing will depend on appropriate accommodation of the competing interests involved."[183]

In the adjudication of delinquency, the same balancing is present, although in less extreme form. In the 1967 opinion, *In re Gault*,[184] the United States Supreme Court seemed to promise juveniles the same protections afforded adult defendants. In condemning the lack of procedural safeguards in Gerald Gault's and other juvenile court proceedings of the time, the Court observed that "history has again demonstrated that unbridled discretion, however benevolently motivated, is frequently a poor substitute for principle and procedure."[185] The Court found that the alleged benefit of secret proceedings, "to hide youthful errors from the full gaze of the public, . . . is more rhetoric than reality,"[186] because records are generally available to government agencies and sometimes to private employers. Writing for the majority, Mr. Justice Fortas also thought the supposed therapeutic benefit of an informal, paternalistic proceeding based upon the doctrine of *parens patriae* would be better achieved through an atmosphere of fairness, impartiality, and orderliness, in a more structured hearing with counsel for the defendant.[187] He further maintained that it is of no constitutional consequence what an institution is called:[188]

The fact of the matter is that, however euphemistic the title, a receiving home or an industrial school for juveniles is an institution of confinement in which a child is incarcerated for a greater or lesser time. His world becomes "a building with whitewashed walls, regimented routine and institutional hours . . ." Instead of mother and father and sisters and brothers and friends and classmates, his world is people by guards, custodians, state employees, and "delinquents" confined with him for anything from waywardness to rape and homicide.

In light of these circumstances, Mr. Justice Fortas concluded that "it would be extraordinary if our Constitution did not require the procedural regularity and the exercise of care implied in the phrase 'due process.' "[189] Specifically, the Court held that six procedural requirements were essential in an adjudication of juvenile delinquency: (1) notice of charges, (2) right to counsel, (3) right to confrontation and cross-examination of witnesses, (4) privilege against self-incrimination, (5) right to a transcript of the proceedings, and (6) right to appellate review. In *In re Winship*,[190] the Court extended the reasoning of *Gault* and held that the quantum of proof necessary for a finding of delinquency must be beyond a reasonable doubt, the same standard required for an adult criminal conviction. As mentioned in chapter 2,[191] however, shortly thereafter it drew the line, holding in *McKeiver v. Pennsylvania*[192] that the due process clause does not compel a right to trial by jury in juvenile delinquency proceedings.

Gault is cited extensively in those few opinions which have dealt explicitly with the rights of minors "voluntarily" admitted to mental institutions by parents or guardians. *Goss* might also be cited, for it recognizes that a student's interest in his reputation and opportunity for higher education is a sufficient liberty interest to trigger due process requirements,[193] and surely an adolescent's interest in freedom itself should be accorded equal if not greater weight.

As the Supreme Court has stated, however, "[o]nce it is determined that due process applies, the question remains what process is due."[194] Results of tremendous consequence, such as the placement of a juvenile in a mental institution for a possibly extended period of time, should not be reached without ceremony,[195] but it does not follow that the procedures applicable in a delinquency adjudication would be the most appropriate in other, even analogous, situations such as voluntary admissions. Although some procedural protections are explicitly required by the Constitution for criminal trials (for example, the Sixth Amendment rights to counsel and to confront witnesses, and the Fifth Amendment privilege against self-incrimination), these protections do not necessarily apply in all cases.

Interpretation and application of the Due Process Clause are intensely practical matters and . . . the very nature of due process negates any concept of inflexible procedures universally applicable to every imaginable situation.[196]

Judicial inventiveness has developed a wide range of procedural schemes consistent with the issues and circumstances involved in particular classes of cases. Because of the loss of liberty and stigma of criminal conviction, criminal defendants have generally been afforded the most stringent safeguards. In the juvenile justice system the Supreme Court has allowed all but the full panoply of protections afforded adult criminals.[197] Lower courts have begun to afford similar due process rights in civil commitments.[198] In prison transfer situations, when the complaining party has already lost almost all of his freedom of movement and many of his civil rights, courts have insisted on limited procedural regularity, in particular protections such as notice and the right to a hearing and a reasonably objective fact finder.[199] When less serious deprivations are involved, such as garnishment of wages[200] or suspension of a driver's license and automobile registration,[201] hearings have been required. As we have seen, when a student is suspended from school, the Supreme Court has similarly required an "opportunity to be heard," but a range of other procedural protections were rejected as inappropriate in that context.[202] And with respect to Social Security Administration termination procedures for recipients of disability benefits, the Supreme Court found that in light of the evidence to be considered, written consideration prior to termination and an evidentiary hearing only afterwards was sufficient to satisfy due process requirements.[203]

Thus the unique aspects of the voluntary admission of an adolescent to a mental institution must be considered in fashioning appropriate procedural safeguards under the due process clause. Practical considerations to be weighed are the magnitude of the deprivation, the necessity of speed, the state's interest, the rights and interests of other parties, and the nature of the determination to be made. For example, in voluntary admissions, as contrasted to criminal proceedings, a parent and not the state is often the proponent, and the purpose of the admission is purportedly therapeutic rather than punitive. In addition:

"The opportunity to be heard must be tailored to the capacities and circumstances of those who are to be heard."[204] Yet another consideration involves the nature of the evidence to be considered and the appropriateness of particular proceedings for this purpose.

There can be no doubt that an adolescent's liberty interests are significantly—even grievously—affected by voluntary admission. His or her stay in an institution may range from a matter of hours to months or even years. But neither can there be doubt that the circumstances of admission may vary substantially from case to case. In some instances the adolescent will be a co-seeker of treatment, or at least be nonprotesting; in other instances, he or she may resist violently. The party seeking admission may be a loving parent, perhaps desperately seeking treatment for an emotionally ill child; or it may be an indifferent state agency, acting as guardian and arranging placement of a state ward whose only "illness" is the manifestation of aggressive, acting-out behavior. The treatment sought may be day or evening care at a local, up-to-date mental health facility; by contrast, it may be effective incarceration in a large, remote, understaffed, and antiquated institution.

These varying situations point up the need for flexible procedures which can be adapted to the facts of individual cases. Care must be taken to disrupt the parent-child relationship as little as possible while simultaneously protecting the rights of the child. Where concerned parents are doing their best to aid their nonprotesting, emotionally disturbed child, it would ill behoove the state to compel an adversary proceeding where their motives could be challenged and impugned, possibly in the presence of the child. Conversely, there may be other occasions when the proposed admission results not from mental illness in the adolescent, but from a total breakdown of the parent-child relationship.

In view of this situation, due process seems to demand procedures which can be invoked by interested parties but which for the most part are not automatically applied in every admission. Where no one, including the child, objects to the arrangements being made, there seems no reason to disrupt the parent-child relationship beyond a review of the good faith and informed consent of all competent parties involved and periodic review of the need for hospitalization and treatment. On the other hand, in view of the possible abuses of the voluntary admission process and the growing independence and maturity of a juvenile child, procedures should be available to test the need for admission whenever that child or another interested party raises an objection.

One method of accomplishing this delicate task would be to inject an independent third party into the situation—an advisor and advocate for the child whose presence and assistance could not be waived by the parents. This person would counsel the child, and if the child then objected to admission or was incompetent to consent to admission, would represent him or her in a hearing, probably before a multidisciplinary review board. Ultimate appeal to a court would be possible. The review board would be responsible for either authorizing or denying admission once an objection was raised. Thus in contested cases this board would effectively perform the decision-making function now performed, in most states, solely by parents and an admitting physician. The right to a hearing would thus balance the possibly competing interests of parent and child by providing an appropriate forum in which both could present arguments for or against admission. The rights of both would be recognized and afforded an opportunity for expression.

These changes, if adopted, would substantially protect a minor's due process rights in voluntary admission. Strict, carefully drafted standards for admission would seem to be a necessary additional safeguard, as current standards are often either vague or unarticulated; and the weights attached to them are unknown, vary from case to case, and are thus not amenable to careful review. On the other hand, due process does not appear to require adherence to strict rules of evidence in hearings before a review board, but adequate provision should be made for periodic review of the need for treatment and admission. An informal hearing, while safeguarding important rights, will not unduly disrupt the parent-child relationship and will probably further the provision of therapy to the child.

Notes

1. The parent-child legal relationship was also considered, but in considerably less detail, in chapter 2, at note 57 *et seq.*

2. *See* Wisconsin v. Yoder, 406 U.S. 205, 231 (1972).

3. *But see* Planned Parenthood of Missouri v. Danforth, 428 U.S. 52 (1976), discussed in chapter 4, at note 60, and below, at note 61 *et seq.*

4. Ginsberg v. New York, 390 U.S. 629 (1968). *See also* chapter 2, at note 62.

5. Stanley v. Illinois, 405 U.S. 645, 651 (1972), *quoting* Kovacs v. Cooper, 336 U.S. 77, 95 (1949) (Frankfurter, J., *concurring*).

6. Meyer v. Nebraska, 262 U.S. 390, 399 (1923). *See also* chapter 2, at note 68.

7. Prince v. Massachusetts, 321 U.S. 158, 166 (1944).

8. Aristotle, Politics 32-36, 316 (E. Barker transl. 1962).

9. *See* Note, *State Intrusion into Family Affairs: Justification and Limitations,* 26 Stan. L. Rev. 1383 (1974).

10. 262 U.S. 390 (1923).

11. 268 U.S. 510 (1925).

12. *Id.*, at 535.

13. Below, at notes 118-23.

14. Nebbia v. New York, 291 U.S. 502 (1934).

15. *See* chapter 5, text at notes 22-28.

16. Williamson v. Lee Optical, 348 U.S. 483 (1955).

17. For a discussion of "fundamental" constitutional rights, *see* text below at notes 146 *et seq.*

18. *See, e.g.,* Roe v. Wade, 410 U.S. 113 (1973).

19. 405 U.S. 645 (1972).

20. *Id.,* at 651.

21. 406 U.S. 205 (1972). *See also* discussion of this opinion in chapter 2, at note 152 *et seq.*

22. *Id.,* at 232.

23. 381 U.S. 479 (1965).

24. 388 U.S. 1 (1967).

25. 316 U.S. 535 (1942).

26. 427 U.S. 160 (1976).

27. 427 U.S. 160, at 178 n.15.

28. 405 U.S., at 651.

29. 406 U.S., at 232.

30. Ginsberg v. New York, 390 U.S. 629 (1968), McKeiver v. Pennsylvania, 403 U.S. 528 (1971), Bellotti v. Baird, 428 U.S. 132 (1976).

31. 387 U.S. 1 (1967).

32. Below, at note 184. *See also* chapter 2 at note 215 *et seq.*

33. 387 U.S. 1, at 13.

34. McKeiver v. Pennsylvania, note 30 above, at 545.

35. 393 U.S. 503 (1969) (described in chapter 2, at note 128).

36. 390 U.S. 629 (1968).

37. *Id.,* at 636. (Brennan, J., *quoting* Bookcase, Inc. v. Broderick, 18 N.Y.2d 71, 75, 271 N.Y.S.2d 947, 952, 218 N.E.2d 668, 671 (1966)).

38. *Id.,* at 649-50. (Stewart, J., *concurring*) (footnotes omitted).

39. *See* A. Kleinfeld, *The Balance of Power Among Infants, their Parents and the State, Part I,* 4 Fam. L. Q. 320, at 321-22 (1970).

40. *See* Ginsberg v. New York, note 30 above.

41. For a more thorough review of competence standards, *see* F. Allen, E. Ferster & H. Weihofen, Mental Impairment and Legal Incompetency (1968). *See also* G. Alexander & T. Lewin, The Aged and the Need for Surrogate Management (1972); P. Horstman, *Protective Services for the Elderly: The Limits of Parens Patriae,* 40 Mo. L. Rev. 215 (1975).

42. R. Leifer, In the Name of Mental Health (1969).

43. *Compare* Winters v. Miller, 446 F.2d 65 (2d Cir. 1971), *cert. denied* 404 U.S. 985 (1971).

44. *See* chapter 2, at note 19 *et seq.*; chapter 3, at note 13 *et seq.*

45. P. Meehl, *Law and the Fireside Inductions: Reflections of a Clinical Psychologist,* 27 J. Soc. Iss. 65 (1971).

46. *See generally* Symposium Issue, *Children and the Law,* 39:3 Law & Contemp. Prob. (Summer 1975); J. Holt, Escape from Childhood (1974); Wisconsin v. Yoder, note 21 above, Douglas, J., *dissenting,* at 241.

47. *See* chapter 2, at note 19 *et seq.*; chapter 3, at note 13 *et seq.*

48. *Compare* D. Bernstein & R. Simmons, *The Adolescent Kidney Donor: The Right to Give,* 131 Amer. J. Psychiat. 1338 (1974).

49. *See* text above, at note 2 *et seq.*

50. *See* Wisconsin v. Yoder, 405 U.S. 205 (1971).

51. Chapter 2 above, at note 61 *et seq.*

52. 390 U.S. 629 (1968).

53. *Id.*, at 639.

54. Note 21 above.

55. 406 U.S. 205, at 231 (1972) (footnote omitted).

56. *Id.*, at 243.

57. San Antonio Independent School District v. Rodriguez, chapter 5 note 10.

58. 410 U.S. 113 (1973).

59. *Id.*, at 165 n.67.

60. *See, e.g.*, Mass. Gen. Laws Ann. ch. 112, § 12p.

61. Note 3 above.

62. Note 30 above.

63. *See* chapter 2, at note 354 *et seq.*

64. *See* Ellis, *Volunteering Children: Parental Commitment of Minors to Mental Institutions,* 62 Cal. L. Rev. 840 (1974).

65. Inmates of Boys' Training School v. Affleck, 346 F. Supp. 1354 (D.R.I. 1972); Wheeler v. Glass, 473 F.2d 983 (7th Cir. 1973).

66. Planned Parenthood of Missouri v. Danforth, note 3 above, at 74.

67. Chapter 3, at note 35 *et seq.*

68. *See* Ellis, note 64 above, at 864-65.

69. *See id.*, at 851-52.

70. Interview with Dr. Alan Katz, Boston, Mass., July 23, 1975.

71. *See, e.g.*, Wyatt v. Aderholt, 503 F.2d 1305 (5th Cir. 1974).

72. Discussed above, at note 61.

73. Discussed above, at note 62.

74. Constitutional Rights of the Mentally Ill: Hearings before the Subcomm. on Constitutional Rights of the Senate Committee on the Judiciary, 87th Cong., 1st sess.; 88th Cong., 1st sess.; 91st Cong., 1st & 2nd sess. (1961, 1963, 1969 and 1970).

75. Calif. Welf. & Inst. Code §§ 5000-401; Mass. Gen. Laws Ann. ch. 123 §§ 1-37; N.C. Gen. Stat. §§ 122-58.1 to 122-58.8.

76. Lessard v. Schmidt, 349 F. Supp. 1078 (E.D. Wis. 1972), *vacated sub nom* Schmidt v. Lessard, 414 U.S. 473 (1974), *reheard* 379 F. Supp. 1376 (E.D. Wis. 1974), *again vacated* 421 U.S. 957 (1975), *prior judgment reinstated* 413 F. Supp. 1318 (E.D. Wis. 1976); Hawks v. Lazaro, 202 S.E.2d 109 (W.V. 1974); Bartley v. Kremens, 402 F. Supp. 1039 (E.D. Pa. 1975), *remanded sub nom* Kremens v. Bartley, 97 S. Ct. 1709 (1977) (discussed below at note 92 *et seq.*).

77. Heryford v. Parker, 396 F.2d 393 (10th Cir. 1968).

78. In re L.L., 39 Cal. App. 3d 205, 114 Cal. Rptr. 11 (1974). *See also* In re Michael E., 123 Cal. Rptr. 103, 538 P.2d 231 (1975).

79. Chapter 4, text at note 88.

80. *See* table 4-1.

81. W. Va. Code § 27-1-1 (1976 Supp.).

82. W. Va. Code § 24-4-3 (1976 Supp.).

83. Mass. Gen. Laws Ann. ch. 123, § 10 (1976 Supp.).

84. Mass. Dept. of Mental Health Regs., § 225.05.

85. Mich. Stat. Ann. § 14.800 (415) (1976 Supp.).

86. *Id.,* at § 14.800(417)(4).

87. *Id.,* at § 14.800(417)(6).

88. *Id.,* at § 14.800(417)(7).

89. Melville v. Sabbatino, 30 Conn. Sup. 320, 313 A.2d 886 (1973). The information and analysis presented here may also be found in H. Beyer & J. Wilson, *The Reluctant Volunteer: A Child's Right to Resist Commitment,* in *Children's Rights and the Mental Health Professions,* 133-148 (G.P. Koocher, ed. 1976).

90. Saville v. Treadway, C.A. No. 6969 (U.S.D.C., M.D. Tenn., Order of April 18, 1974).

91. In the Interest of Lee and Wesley, Nos. 68J(D) 1362, 66J(D) 6383, and 68J 15805, Cir. Ct. of Cook County, Dept. Juv. Div (Ill., Feb. 29 and Aug. 24, 1972).

92. Bartley v. Kremens, note 76 above. *But see* John S. v. Medical Director of Westwood Hospital, 135 Cal. Rptr. 893 (Ct. App. 1977).

93. *See* note 76 above. The Court has since agreed, however, to hear J.L. v. Parham, 412 F. Supp. 112 (M.D. Ga. 1976), a case presenting essentially the same issues. *See* note 98 below.

94. 402 F. Supp. at 1049-54.

95. *Id.,* at 1052-53 (footnotes omitted).

96. *Id.,* at 1047-48.

97. *Id.,* at 1053-54 n.26.

98. Parham v. J.L. and J. R., *prob. juris.* noted 427 U.S. 903 (1977); *leave to proceed in forma pauperis,* 97 Sup. Ct. 2647 (1977); *argued* Dec. 6, 1977, 46 U.S.L.W. 3386 (12/13/77); *reargument ordered* Jan. 16, 1978, 46 U.S.L.W. 3452 (1/17/78); *facts and opinion sub nom.* J.L. v. Parham, 412 F. Supp. 112 (M.D. Ga. 1976), 412 F. Supp. 141 (M.D. Ga. 1976).

99. "The Congress shall have the power to enforce, by appropriate legislation, the provisions of this article." U.S. Const. amend. XIV, § 5. "The Congress shall have Power . . . To regulate Commerce . . . among the several States. . . ." U.S. Const. art. I, § 8.

100. The Fourteenth Amendment applies only to the states, but elements

of equal protection guarantees applicable to the federal government have been found in the due process clause of the Fifth Amendment. *See* Bolling v. Sharpe, 347 U.S. 497 (1954); Buckley v. Valeo, 424 U.S. 1 (1976). Justice Stevens, in a majority opinion in Hampton v. Mow Sun Wong, 426 U.S. 88 (1976) notes that although the protections of the two amendments are substantially identical, they are not always coextensive. However, "when a federal rule is applicable to only a limited territory, such as the District of Columbia, . . . and when there is no special national interest involved, the Due Process Clause has been construed as having the same significance as the Equal Protection Clause." *Id.* at 100 (footnote omitted).

102. *See* Doe v. Bellin Memorial Hospital, 479 F.2d 756 (7th Cir. 1973); Moose Lodge v. Irvis, 407 U.S. 163 (1972).

103. *See, e.g.,* Wolman v. Walter, 97 S. Ct. 2593 (1977).

104. However, it should be noted that the U.S. Supreme Court has recently directed that the following question be briefed and argued: "Whether, where the parents of a minor voluntarily place the minor in a state institution, there is sufficient 'state action' including subsequent action by the state institution, to implicate the Due Process Clause of the Fourteenth Amendment?" Parham v. J.L. and J.R., note 98 above.

105. Jackson v. Metropolitan Edison Co., 419 U.S. 345 (1974).

106. 407 U.S. 163 (1973).

107. Mulvihill v. Julia Butterfield Memorial Hospital, 329 F. Supp. 1020 (S.D.N.Y. 1971); Ward v. Saint Anthony's Hospital, 476 F.2d 671 (10th Cir. 1973). *But see* text below at note 112.

108. Evans v. Newton, 382 U.S. 296, 299 (1966).

109. Jackson v. Metropolitan Edison Co., note 105 above, at 352.

110. "As of January 1972 there were approximately 471,800 psychiatric beds (30 percent of the total hospital beds) in the United States. Seventy-seven percent of these were still in State and county mental hospitals. At that 1972 date only 2 percent of the available beds were in federally funded community mental health centers. The latter, of course, have a more rapid turnover. . . .

"During 1971, of the 1,755,916 inpatient episodes: 745,259 were in State and county mental hospitals; 542,642 in psychiatric wards of general hospitals; 176,800 in Veterans Administration hospitals; 130,088 in community mental health centers; 97,963 in private mental hospitals; 28,637 in residential treatment centers for emotionally disturbed children; and 34,427 in other multiservice facilities. Although similar data is not available for all facilities in 1973, there is evidence indicating a diminishing reliance on State and county mental hospitals.

"All of the aforementioned data are derived from the statistical notes of the Department of Health, Education, and Welfare, Public Health Service, Alcohol, Drug Abuse, and Mental Health Administration, National Institute of

Mental Health, Office of Program Planning and Evaluation, Biometry Branch, "Survey and Reports Section." A. Stone, Mental Health and Law: A System in Transition, DHEW Publication No. (ADM) 75-176 (1975), at 42.

111. Marsh v. Alabama, 326 U.S. 501 (1946); Amalgamated Food Employee Union Local 509 v. Logan Valley Plaza, Inc., 391 U.S. 308 (1968); Central Hardware Co. v. NLRB, 407 U.S. 539 (1972).

112. Simpkins v. Moses H. Cone Memorial Hospital, 323 F.2d 959 (4th Cir. 1963), *cert. denied* 373 U.S. 938 (1964).

113. Text below, at note 145.

114. R. Burt, *Developing Constitutional Rights Of, In, and For Children,* 39:3 Law and Contemp. Prob. 118, 137 (Summer 1975).

115. Shelley v. Kramer, 334 U.S. 1 (1948).

116. U.S. Const. amend. XIV, § 1.

117. Railway Express Agency v. New York, 336 U.S. 106, 112-13 (1949) (Jackson, J., *concurring*).

118. Lochner v. New York, 198 U.S. 45, 58 (1905).

119. Williamson v. Lee Optical, 348 U.S. 483 (1955); Nebbia v. New York, 201 U.S. 502 (1934).

120. Chapter 5, text at notes 21-28.

121. Williamson v. Lee Optical, 348 U.S. 483 (1955).

122. Substantive due process analyses have not been entirely abandoned by the Court, however. *See, e.g.,* Moore v. City of East Cleveland, 97 S. Ct. 1932 (1977).

123. Railway Express Agency v. New York, 336 U.S. 106 (1949).

124. *See* Gunther, chapter 5, note 28, at 8.

125. Borden's Farm Products v. Baldwin, 293 U.S. 194 (1934).

126. Shapiro v. Thompson, 394 U.S. 618, 658 (1969) (Harlan, J., *dissenting*).

127. Note, *Mental Illness: A Suspect Classification?*, 83 Yale L.J. 1237, 1240 (1974) [hereinafter cited as Yale Note].

128. In re Gault, 387 U.S. 1 (1967).

129. *See* chapter 2 at notes 215 *et seq.*; and below, at note 184 *et seq.*

130. *Incarcerated Juveniles—Why? An Analysis of Partial Data Submitted by Defendants in Response to Interrogatories by Plaintiffs,* by David Ferleger, Esq., Next Friend and Attorney for the Plaintiffs in Bartley v. Haverford State Hospital, C. A. No. 72-2272 (E.D. Pa. 1973) at 3-4. (*See* text above at notes 76 and 92 *et seq..*)

131. *See, e.g.,* Wyatt v. Aderholt, 503 F.2d 1305 (5th Cir. 1974); Donaldson v. O'Connor, 493 F.2d 507 (5th Cir. 1974); Welsch v. Likins, 373 F. Supp. 487 (D. Minn. 1974).

132. San Antonio Ind. School Dist. v. Rodriguez, 411 U.S. 1, 28 (1973).

133. Loving v. Virginia, 388 U.S. 1 (1967).

134. Korematsu v. U.S., 323 U.S. 214 (1944).

135. Graham v. Richardson, 403 U.S. 365 (1971).

136. Frontiero v. Richardson, 411 U.S. 677 (1973); *but see* Greduldig v. Arello, 417 U.S. 484 (1974).

137. Michelman, *Foreword: On Protecting the Poor through the Fourteenth Amendment,* 83 Harv. L. Rev. 7 (1969).

138. *See, e.g.,* Shapiro v. Thompson, 394 U.S. 618 (1969) (fundamental right to travel); Harper v. Board of Elections, 383 U.S. 663 (1963) (fundamental right to vote).

139. Yale Note, note 127 above. *See also* The Mentally Retarded Citizen and the Law (M. Kindred *et al.* ed. 1976), at 43, 98, 174-79, and 226.

140. U.S. v. Carolene Products Co., 304 U.S. 114, 152 n.4 (1938).

141. *See* Sugarman v. Dougall, 413 U.S. 634, 657 (1973) (Rehnquist, J. *dissenting*); Ely, *The Constitutionality of Reverse Racial Discrimination,* 41 U. Chi. L. Rev. 723, 724-30 (1974).

142. Korematsu v. U.S., 323 U.S. 214, 243 (1944) (Jackson, J., *dissenting*).

143. Ely, note 141 above, at 732-33 (1974).

144. *See, e.g.,* Wyatt v. Stickney, 344 F. Supp. 373 at 387 (M.D. Ala. 1972), *affirmed sub nom.* Wyatt v. Aderholt, 503 F.2d 1305 (5th Cir. 1974).

145. A. Kleinfeld, *The Balance of Power Among Infants, their Parents and the State: Part III,* 5 Fam. L. Q. 64, 65-66 (1971).

146. Griswold v. Connecticut, 381 U.S. 479 (1965).

147. Harper v. Board of Elections, 383 U.S. 663 (1963).

148. Shapiro v. Thompson, 394 U.S. 618 (1969).

149. N.A.A.C.P. v. Alabama, 357 U.S. 449 (1958).

150. Skinner v. Oklahoma, 316 U.S. 535 (1942).

151. Griffin v. Illinois, 351 U.S. 12 (1956).

152. D. Chambers, *Alternatives to Civil Commitment of the Mentally Ill: Practical Guides and Constitutional Imperatives,* 70 Mich. L.R. 1107 (1972) at 1155-68.

153. San Antonio Ind. School Dist. v. Rodriguez, note 132 above. *But see* Serrano v. Priest, 18 Cal. 3d 728, 135 Cal. Rptr. 345, 557 P.2d 929 (1976) and Horton v. Meskill, 172 Conn. 615, 376 A.2d 359 (1977) (In California education is a "fundamental interest," and in Connecticut a "fundamental right," for purposes of interpreting provisions of the respective state constitutions.)

154. Note, *Developments in the Law—Equal Protection,* 82 Harv. L.R. 1065, 1130-32 (1969).

155. *Id.,* at 1130.

156. *See, e.g.,* Skinner v. Oklahoma, 316 U.S. 535 (1942).

157. Ely, note 141 above, at 735, *citing* Railway Express Agency v. N.Y., 336 U.S. 106, 111-13 (1949) (Jackson, J., *concurring*).

158. *See* chapter 2 at note 313 *et seq.*

159. Note 3 and text at note 61 above.

160. Note 62 above.

161. Cox, *The Supreme Court, 1965 Term, Foreword: Constitutional Adjudication and the Promotion of Human Rights,* 80 Harv. L. Rev. 91, 95 (1966).

162. Reed v. Reed, 404 U.S. 71 (1971); Eisenstadt v. Baird, 405 U.S. 438 (1972); James v. Strange, 407 U.S. 128 (1972).

163. G. Gunther, *The Supreme Court, 1971 Term Foreword–In Search of Evolving Doctrine on a Changing Court: A Model for a Newer Equal Protection,* 86 Harv. L. Rev. 1 (1972), at 10-20.

164. 407 U.S. 128 (1972).

165. 405 U.S. 438 (1972).

166. 404 U.S. 71 (1971).

167. Gunther, note 163, at 36.

168. Baxstrom v. Herold, 383 U.S. 107 (1966).

169. Note, *Recent Developments: Constitutional Law,* 12 Vill. L. Rev. 178, 181-82 (1966).

170. 387 U.S. 1 (1967).

171. 386 U.S. 605 (1967).

172. 405 U.S. 504 (1972).

173. 406 U.S. 715 (1972).

174. San Antonio Ind. School Dist. v. Rodriguez, 411 U.S. 1, 99 (1973) (Marshall, J., *dissenting*); *see also* Dandridge v. Williams, 397 U.S. 471, 519 (1970) (Marshall, J., *dissenting*).

175. U.S. Const. amend. XIV, § 1.

176. In re Gault, 387 U.S. 1, 20 (1967).

177. *See* notes 118-23 and accompanying text above.

178. 387 U.S. 1 (1967), at 7-8.

179. Goss v. Lopez, 419 U.S. 565 (1975).

180. *See* chapter 5, text at note 43; chapter 2, at note 133.

181. *Id.,* at 581.

182. *Id.,* at 579.

183. *Id.*

184. 387 U.S. 1 (1967), discussed in chapter 2, at note 215 *et seq.*

185. *Id.,* at 18.

186. *Id.,* at 24.

187. *Id.,* at 26.

188. *Id.,* at 27, citing Holmes's appeal, 379 Pa. 599, 616, 109 A.2d 523, 530 (1954) (Musmanno, J., *dissenting*) (footnote omitted).

189. *Id.,* at 27-28.

190. 397 U.S. 358 (1970).

191. Chapter 2, at note 221.

192. 403 U.S. 528 (1971).

193. Goss v. Lopez, note 178 above.

194. Morrisey v. Brewer, 408 U.S. 471, 481 (1972).

195. Kent v. U.S., 383 U.S. 541, 554 (1966).

196. Cafeteria Workers v. McElroy, 367 U.S. 886, 895 (1961).

197. *See* chapter 2, at note 215 *et seq.*

198. Lessard v. Schmidt, 349 F. Supp. 1078 (E.D. Wis. 1972); Bell v. Wayne County Hospital, 384 F. Supp. 1085 (S.D. Mich. 1974); Hawks v. Lazaro, 202 S.E.2d 109 (W.V. 1974).

199. Gomes v. Travisono, 490 F.2d 1209 (1st Cir., 1973).

200. Sniadach v. Family Finance Corp., 395 U.S. 337 (1969).

201. Bell v. Burson, 402 U.S. 535 (1971). *See also* Fuentes v. Shevin, 407 U.S. 67 (1971). *But see* Mitchell v. W.T. Grant Co., 416 U.S. 600 (1974). Hearings have also been required before termination of Welfare benefits, Goldberg v. Kelly, 397 U.S. 254 (1970); revocation of parole, Morrissey v. Brewer, 408 U.S. 470 (1972); and probation, Gagnon v. Scarpelli, 411 U.S. 778 (1973).

202. Goss v. Lopez, note 178 above.

203. Mathews v. Eldridge, 424 U.S. 319 (1976).

204. Goldberg v. Kelly, 397 U.S. 254 (1970).

7

The Right to Treatment of Adolescents in Institutions

The constitutional "right to treatment" is of recent origin, and its contours are still in the process of formation. First articulated in a seminal article by Dr. Morton Birnbaum in 1960,[1] the right was claimed as "the legal right of a mentally ill inmate of a public mental institution to adequate medical treatment for his mental illness."[2] Since then, three federal circuit courts (District of Columbia, Fifth and Seventh Circuits) and a number of federal district courts and lower state courts have recognized and enforced this right on behalf of litigants in numerous contexts: civilly committed mental patients[3] and mentally retarded persons,[4] criminal defendants committed as incompetent to stand trial[5] or after acquittal on grounds of insanity,[6] persons committed as sexually dangerous,[7] convicted criminals,[8] and youthful residents of juvenile detention facilities,[9] and reform schools.[10] A body of scholarship has also been produced on the right to treatment in the adult[11] and juvenile[12] contexts.

This chapter reviews the recent cases and other materials on the "right to treatment" to determine their applicability to the access of adolescents to mental health treatment. Although the "right to treatment" in some contexts is based on statutes, this discussion focuses primarily on its constitutional aspects. The issue of ultimate interest is: do adolescents confined in a state or private treatment facility have a constitutional right to mental health treatment? And, to the extent they have such a right, how is it defined, on what theories does it rest, and how may it be enforced?

The following discussion supports the view that adolescents who are confined in state hospitals, training schools or other state facilities, for purposes other than punishment for a criminal offense, have a constitutional right to treatment for their mental health needs. Depending, perhaps, upon the circumstances of commitment, the same right may extend to youths confined in private facilities. However, in 1975, in deciding the case of *O'Connor v. Donaldson*,[13] the United States Supreme Court had the opportunity to acknowledge (or deny) the existence of such a constitutional right, clarify its theoretical basis, and explore the extent of its protection. The Court declined to address the right to treatment issue, confining its discussion to the narrow facts of the case.[14] Pending further clarification by the Court, therefore, the future of a constitutional right to treatment for confined children and adults remains uncertain.

This chapter was contributed by Professor Stanley Z. Fisher, Boston University School of Law.

The Right to Treatment: Adults

Although courts holding that children have a right to treatment can to some extent draw upon an independent statutory and constitutional base,[15] for the most part they rely upon case precedents involving adult plaintiffs. For this reason, it is necessary to review as background the major outlines of the right recognized for adults.

Constitutional Bases of the Right

Although decided upon statutory grounds, *Rouse v. Cameron*[16] is regarded as the first case recognizing a constitutional right to treatment. Rouse had been committed to a mental hospital after being acquitted of criminal charges by reason of insanity. He petitioned the courts, complaining that he was being confined without psychiatric treatment. The District of Columbia Circuit Court of Appeals held that under applicable statutes Rouse had a right to treatment. Chief Judge Bazelon, writing for the court, hinted that in the absence of statutory right, the petitioner's confinement without treatment might be unconstitutional on any of three grounds: procedural due process, equal protection, and cruel and unusual punishment.[17] Later cases have expanded upon the application of these constitutional theories to the "right to treatment" and added to them. Currently, the right may be said to rest upon four theories, which have been defined variously by different courts. Each is described below.

Substantive due process. This has been appropriately described as the "core argument in the right to treatment cases."[18] Its basic premise is that a person is deprived of liberty without due process of law, in violation of the Fourteenth Amendment, when he is confined for the purpose of medical treatment and adequate treatment is not provided.[19] This substantive due process theory was fully elaborated by the United States Court of Appeals for the Fifth Circuit in *Donaldson v. O'Connor*,[20] a decision later vacated and remanded by the Supreme Court.[21]

The appeals court's analysis in *Donaldson* is based on the recognition that civil commitment entails a "massive curtailment of liberty" and stigmatizes the affected person.[22] This infringement of personal liberty by the state gives rise to a right to treatment under the due process clause on two grounds. The first is restricted to those commitments justified by considerations of *parens patriae* rather than public safety. It is supported by the Supreme Court's holding in *Jackson v. Indiana* that "due process requires that the nature and duration of commitment bear some reasonable relation to the purposes for which the individual is committed."[23] Because the commitment of a nondangerous person can only be justified by his need for care and treatment,[24] his constitutional rights are violated unless treatment is provided.

The second ground, which applies to all civil commitments, focuses on the lack of safeguards associated with nonpenal as compared to penal processes. When a person is confined without proof of specific criminal acts, in a proceeding not subject to rigorous procedural protections (such as jury trial and the "beyond a reasonable doubt" standard of proof), resulting in indefinite confinement, treatment is "the *quid pro quo* society [has] to pay as the price of the extra safety it derive[s] from the denial of [his] liberty."[25]

The Supreme Court, reviewing the appeals court's decision in *Donaldson,* approached the case more narrowly. Expressly refusing to decide:

whether mentally ill persons dangerous to themselves or to others have a right to treatment upon compulsory confinement by the State or whether the State may compulsorily confine a nondangerous, mentally ill individual for the purpose of treatment,

the Court[26] stated:

A finding of "mental illness" alone cannot justify a State's locking a person up against his will and keeping him indefinitely in simple custodial confinement . . . if [he is] dangerous to no one and can live safely in freedom.

The Court's holding, based on substantive due process, stops short of finding a "right to treatment" but is not inconsistent with the existence of such a right. However, in a concurring opinion Justice Burger sharply criticized the rationale and conclusions of the circuit court's opinion and expressed doubt that any constitutional right to treatment exists. The states, he argued, may validly confine mentally ill persons for the protection of society or themselves, without any requirement that they be treated or treatable.

Procedural due process. This argument is similar to arguments based on substantive due process, but focuses more narrowly on the absence in civil commitment of the procedural protections constitutionally guaranteed to criminal defendants. To confine a person without treatment is arguably akin to punishment, imposed without affording him the procedural protections enjoyed by persons similarly confined under the penal process.[27]

Cruel and unusual punishment. The United States Supreme Court recently stated, in *dictum*, that deliberate indifference by prison personnel to a prisoner's serious illness or injury constitutes "cruel and unusual punishment," contravening the Eighth Amendment.[28] The Court has not yet discussed the amendment's applicability to institutionalized mental patients. Some lower courts have, however. In the 1966 case *Rouse v. Cameron,*[29] Judge Bazelon of the District of Columbia Court of Appeals suggested in *dictum* that indefinite confinement of a patient[30] without treatment may be "punishment" for his mental illness or defect in violation of the Eighth Amendment. In support of this thesis, Judge Bazelon cited the Supreme Court's opinion in *Robinson v. California*[31] which held it was cruel and unusual to convict and imprison persons for being narcotics addicts. However, *Robinson* also contains *dictum* to the effect that a state may commit the mentally ill for "compulsory treatment, involving quarantine, confinement or sequestration."[32]

In its 1968 opinion in *Powell v. Texas*,[33] in which the Court refused to extend *Robinson* to invalidate statutes punishing chronic alcoholics for the crime of public drunkenness, the Court went on to suggest that such persons could constitutionally be civilly committed "without effective treatment." And it is doubtful, on the basis of other Supreme Court cases, that the Court would apply the Eighth Amendment to state actions, such as hospitalization of the mentally ill, which were not taken with an intent to punish.[34]

Nevertheless, the courts have invoked the Eighth Amendment as a source of the "right to treatment" in several situations. Some courts reason that state-imposed confinement for benign purposes is still "punishment" under the Eighth Amendment if such confinement affects patients similarly to imprisonment. On that reasoning, at least one lower court has held that confinement for mental illness without treatment may be unconstitutional.[35] Courts have also used the Eighth Amendment to invalidate certain poor institutional conditions and some forms of treatment.[36] Some commentators have criticized these cases on the ground that the Eighth Amendment should not be applied to restrictions imposed by the state for benign purposes.[37] Even if the criticism were accepted by the courts, the Eighth Amendment would still play a role in cases litigating the right to treatment of juvenile delinquents, whose confinement the Supreme Court has already construed as "punitive" for certain constitutional purposes.[38]

Equal protection. The right to treatment may be based upon the arbitrary denial of treatment benefits to civilly committed residents of an institution in comparison to residents of other state institutions who are civilly committed or confined for other purposes.[39]

Definition of the Right

In defining the right to treatment, the courts use both "subjective" and "objective" approaches.[40] Under a subjective approach the court attempts to determine whether the treatment plan for a particular patient is inadequate or inappropriate for that patient. Under an objective approach the court sets institution-wide standards for staff, facilities, expenditures, patient treatment plans, and so forth. A failure to meet these standards would imply a per se violation of the patient's right to treatment; and because it is difficult for courts to assess specific treatment modalities, further inquiry into the level of individual treatment is not pursued if objective criteria are satisfied.[41] A subjective approach was used by the court in *Rouse v. Cameron,*[42] and has been accepted in a number of juvenile court cases.[43] In *Wyatt v. Stickney* the court took the objective approach, as have most courts in dealing with adult and juvenile right to treatment cases.[44]

Regarding the *quality* of treatment to which patients are entitled, the D.C. Circuit Court's analysis in *Rouse* was to the effect that: (a) "The hospital need not show that the treatment will cure or improve [the patient] but only that there is a *bona fide* effort to do so;"[45] (b) "The effort should be to provide treatment which is adequate in light of present knowledge. . . . the possibility of better treatment does not necessarily prove that the one provided is unsuitable or inadequate;"[46] (c) "Continuing failure to provide suitable and adequate treatment cannot be justified by lack of staff or facilities" (or inadequate funds).[47] In the *Wyatt* opinion, the Alabama federal district court required that patients be provided (a) adequate staff and facilities; (b) a human psychological and physical environment; and (c) individual treatment plans.[48]

Some courts have accepted that the "right to treatment" includes the right to be treated by the "least restrictive treatment necessary to achieve the purposes of commitment."[49] This right has been construed to include the provision of noninstitutional, community-based alternatives to institutional programs.[50] In *Wyatt* the court specified that "least restrictive conditions" include the state's obligation to "make every attempt to move residents from (1) more to less structured living; (2) larger to smaller facilities; (3) larger to smaller living units within facilities; (4) group to individual residences; (5) living segregated from the community to living integrated into the community; and (6) dependent to independent living."[51]

The Right to Treatment: Juveniles

The different contexts in which an adolescent's right to treatment may arise are as various as the ways in which a juvenile can become confined in a mental hospital or other nonpenal "treatment facility." These include civil commitment by a court under the regular civil commitment statute, commitment by a specialized juvenile (or family) court, and "voluntary" admission. In some instances, discussed below, a given youth's confinement might be classified under more than one head, as when a civil commitment occurs with the consent of the youth's parent, or when the juvenile court gives custody of the youth to a public or private agency which then places the youth in a mental institution by a "voluntary admission" process.

Some familiarity with the jurisdiction and dispositional powers of juvenile courts is useful background to the discussion of the cases which follow. Most juvenile courts have jurisdiction over three classes of youths: "neglected" (or "dependent"), "PINS" and "delinquent." In neglect actions the court can intervene in situations in which children's needs are seriously neglected by their parents. In such cases the child is regarded as a victim in need of protection by the state. By contrast, PINS and delinquency actions base the need for state intervention upon the youth's misconduct. PINS, or "persons in need of supervision,"[52] are children whose actions consist of noncriminal deviance, such as truancy, incorrigibility, or running away from home. "Delinquents" are usually defined as children who have committed an act which, if performed by an adult, would be a crime. In some jurisdictions, the PINS category does not exist, and "delinquency" includes both criminal and noncriminal misbehavior.

The juvenile court's dispositional power varies according to the type of case but is ordinarily quite flexible. A neglected child may be returned under supervision to the custody of his parents or placed in the temporary custody of a private individual or a public or private child welfare agency, which may in turn place the child in foster care or another residential environment suited to his needs. A juvenile court may treat a PINS or delinquent child as it would a neglected child; in addition, the court may be permitted to commit PINS and delinquents to special training schools or to a state agency which administers such facilities. If commitment is to a state juvenile correctional agency, such as the Massachusetts Department of Youth Services or the Texas Youth Council, the agency may have the power to place the youth in private or state facilities outside its direct administration, such as mental hospitals, schools, or community-based residences or treatment facilities. Juvenile court commitments may be for a definite or an indefinite term but normally may not extend beyond the youth's majority.[53]

The power of juvenile courts to commit neglected, delinquent, and "in need of supervision" children directly to mental hospitals appears to vary from state to state. In some, the law gives the juvenile court concurrent jurisdiction to hear civil commitment petitions with respect to children and permits the court to cause such petitions to be filed in appropriate cases. In such cases the state's regular civil commitment procedures apply.[54] Other states expressly authorize the juvenile court to place children needing psychiatric treatment directly in treatment facilities, apparently without following normal civil commitment procedures.[55] The District of Columbia statute appears to authorize the juvenile court to choose whether to direct the initiation of ordinary civil commitment proceedings or to adjudicate children neglected, delinquent, or in need of supervision and itself commit them "for psychiatric . . . treatment at an appropriate facility on an inpatient basis. . . ."[56] Finally, in some states the statutes do not clearly describe the juvenile court's powers or obligations in cases when children appear to require inpatient mental health treatment.[57]

Purpose of Juvenile Court Commitments and the
Right to Treatment

Probably the most important factor affecting a committed youth's constitutional right to treatment is the purpose for which he was committed. If he was committed for benign, *parens patriae*[58] reasons—as opposed to commitment for the protection of the community—then arguably the Fourteenth Amendment due process clause requires that he be given needed treatment.[59] This argument builds in part upon the case of *Jackson v. Indiana,*[60] decided by the Supreme Court in 1972. Jackson was a mentally defective deaf mute declared incompetent to stand trial on a charge of robbery. Without following the procedures or criteria of the Indiana civil commitment law, the state committed Jackson to a mental institution for an indefinite period, until he should regain competency. Because the evidence showed that Jackson was unlikely ever to become competent to stand trial, the Supreme Court ordered the state either to release him from confinement or pursue the regular civil commitment procedures. Due process requires, the Court held, that the nature and duration of a person's confinement bear some reasonable relation to the purpose for which the individual is confined. In Jackson's case, confinement was not leading to the achievement of competence, and its indefinite continuance was therefore unjustified.

To determine the relevance of *Jackson* to juvenile court commitments, we must examine the purposes of such commitments. It is clear that court intervention in the lives of neglected dependent children is justified only by benign concerns—to promote the child's best interests. Viewed abstractly, there might be more debate about the purposes of restricting the liberty of PINS and delinquents, since both the latter classes of youths may, if unrestrained, threaten the well-being of themselves and the public. But for historical reasons the courts have thus far assumed a *parens patriae,* and not a "police power,"[61] justification for their confinement, and have on that premise based the constitutional right to treatment.[62] This perception of the purpose of juvenile court PINS and delinquency proceedings is drawn from two major sources, statutory and judicial. Each is described separately below.

1. Juvenile court statutes commonly contain a "purpose" clause requiring that after state intervention "the care, custody, and discipline of a child [should] approximate that which should be given by his parents."[63] Many courts have reversed juvenile court dispositional orders because they violated the juvenile's statutory right to a disposition which serves his best interests.[64] Such cases have successfully challenged the place of commitment,[65] the lack of psychiatric care for a youth in need of such treatment,[66] and the transfer for criminal prosecution of a juvenile who needed psychiatric treatment.[67] The lack

of "parental care" guaranteed by statute has been the basis for challenges to the conditions of pretrial detention as well as commitment[68] for all three classes of children within the jurisdiction of the juvenile court.

2. The pronouncement in statutes of a "rehabilitative purpose" underlying the juvenile court's jurisdiction over children, including those who commit dangerous criminal acts, has been adopted and stressed traditionally in the rhetoric of courts and scholarly commentators. The Supreme Court's 1967 decision in *In re Gault*[69] discussed and ratified the *parens patriae* function of juvenile courts, even while it found that the lofty goals of the juvenile justice system had not been met. One footnote passage of the *Gault* opinion has indeed been thought by some courts and commentators to recognize in *dictum* the juvenile's right to treatment after a delinquency commitment:[70]

While we are concerned only with procedure before the juvenile court in this case, it should be noted that to the extent that the special procedures for juveniles are thought to be justified by the special consideration and treatment afforded them, there is reason to doubt that juveniles always receive the benefits of such a *quid pro quo*. . . . The high rate of juvenile recidivism casts some doubt upon the adequacy of treatment afforded juveniles. . . .

In fact, some courts have recently indicated that appropriate treatment is essential to the validity of juvenile custody, and therefore that a juvenile may challenge the validity of his custody on the ground that he is not in fact receiving any special treatment. . . .

Cases Recognizing a Constitutional Right to Treatment for Children

A number of recent cases expressly recognize that children confined in mental institutions and other nonpenal facilities have a constitutional right to treatment. We shall review the cases according to three categories: children confined by order of a juvenile court in facilities other than mental hospitals; children who have been civilly committed to mental hospitals; and children who have been admitted "voluntarily" to such hospitals.

The Rights of Children Detained in or Committed to Facilities Other Than Mental Hospitals by Order of a Juvenile Court

Unlike the right to treatment cases involving patients in mental hospitals, these cases concern only children. In them, therefore, courts have been led to focus on how the right to treatment should reflect the special needs of all children, or of children committed by the juvenile court for particular reasons. For example, courts have recognized the special vulnerability of children to psychological harm from conditions which adults might be able to tolerate.[71] As a result, courts have curtailed the use of "solitary confinement" or "isolation" of children because the practice is "counterproductive to the development of the child."[72] Judicial recognition of the child's vulnerability may also help account for the fact that many juvenile right to treatment cases have been decided upon Eighth Amendment cruel and unusual punishment grounds rather than upon substantive due process or other grounds.[73] Also, the close connection between delinquency and criminal proceedings explains the greater use of the Eighth Amendment to attack conditions of confinement in facilities for delinquents rather than conditions in mental hospitals.

Courts reviewing the right to treatment of delinquent children who have been confined by order of the juvenile court have had to face another issue. Does a delinquent's commitment to an institution entitle him to individual therapeutic treatment for the "ill" of delinquency? Most courts wisely refrain from taking the view that every committed delinquent by definition has an illness which the state has an obligation to treat. Instead they confine the scope of the youth's constitutional right to treatment for specific physical, emotional or mental ailments.[74] But other problems arise in defining the right to "treatment" if the "problem" is not necessarily or principally defined in medical terms. For example, has the state an obligation to provide positive rehabilitative measures above and beyond the "floor" of minimal privileges implicit in the notion of a humane environment? Few courts have faced this issue.

Neglected children. Several courts have addressed the right to treatment of neglected children, some of whom were restrained in detention facilities or placed in private temporary residences where they lacked proper care.[75] The right has been based upon both statutory and constitutional grounds. In one case the due process clause and the Eighth Amendment's prohibition of cruel and unusual punishment were invoked to justify applying the right to a deaf mute child kept in a detention facility for an extensive period.[76] In another case,[77] the Oregon Court of Appeals upheld the juvenile court's statutory power to order a state agency either to provide residential psychiatric treatment to its neglected ward or to terminate its custody of the child.

Delinquents and PINS. Courts have also addressed the right to treatment of children in detention centers awaiting trial in juvenile court for delinquency or PINS misconduct. In two cases,[78] relief was granted principally on the basis of the "parental care" provision of the governing statute. Both the equal protection and due process clauses of the Fourteenth Amendment have been cited to justify court orders,[79] and in two cases the court also relied upon a constitutional right to treatment.[80] In one of these cases, *Martarella v. Kelley*,[81] the court held explicitly that children detained in poorly maintained maximum security facilities are constitutionally entitled to treatment in the form of therapeutic services and not merely "good will and kindness." The court also found conditions at some facilities to be so poor as to violate the Eighth Amendment.

Several other important "right to treatment" cases concern children committed to "training schools" or "reform schools" *after* adjudication by a juvenile court. Some of these cases take a "subjective" approach, in the sense that they involve an individual's claimed right to psychiatric or other special treatment, as opposed to cases taking an "objective" approach, which deal with a wide range of institutional treatment issues. Several "subjective" cases involve youths in need of psychiatric care who have been committed to facilities where such care is not available; in these situations, on the basis of a statutory "right to treatment," courts have ordered new hearings,[82] release on probation,[83] and placement in a private psychiatric hospital.[84] In one case[85] in which a right to treatment was derived from New York statutes and the New York Constitution, the court required the state to provide facilities for a delinquent, homicidal youngster, even though no suitable, secure rehabilitative facility existed at the time of the order. Said the court: ". . . [I]t is a fundamental right of these children to receive the necessary education and treatment required for their respective problems." Other courts have also interpreted the right to treatment to require the affirmative provision of rehabilitative facilities not in existence at the time of the order.[86]

The "objective" right to treatment cases frequently include discussion about the rights of specific individuals. Of the three principal cases,[87] the district court opinion in *Morales v. Turman*[88] (appealed and now remanded for reconsideration) goes the furthest in establishing a broad right to treatment. While parts of the opinion are based on the cruel and unusual punishment prohibition of the Eighth Amendment[89] and upon Fourteenth Amendment procedural due process,[90] most of the court's orders are based on the right to treatment under Fourteenth Amendment substantive due process and state statutes. The court ordered widespread reforms in the Texas institutions for delinquent children, two of which it closed due to their history of brutality. Its mandates included the right to preliminary psychological assessments,[91] academic[92] and vocational[93] education, numerous rights to ensure a humane physical and psychological environment,[94] and the availability of medical and psychiatric care (including minimum staff requirements, "individual or group psychotherapy for every child for whom it is indicated," and freedom from indiscriminate and excessive medication).[95] The court also set minimum standards for casework and child care, including a rejection of "milieu" or "environmental" therapy as insufficient. It specified required elements of individual treatment programs, staff ratios and training, and the formulation of individual treatment plans.[96] To enforce its orders, the court required the use of monitoring devices, including an ombudsman and a system for statewide monitoring.[97] Finally, the court suggested that the use of large, rural, secure institutions may be incompatible with the right to treatment,[98] and it ordered Texas to cease to institutionalize[99] any juveniles except those who are found by a responsible professional assessment to be unsuited for any less restrictive, alternative form of rehabilitative treatment. Additionally, the defendants must . . . create or discover a system of community-based treatment alternatives adequate to serve the needs of those juveniles for whom the institution is not appropriate. Those juveniles for whom close institutional confinement is necessary must *actually* be treated . . . [and] . . . must be surrounded by a staff trained to meet their special needs, in a virtually one-to-one ratio.

Children Who Have Been Civilly Committed to Mental Hospitals

Some cases, recognizing a "right to treatment" for adults who are in mental institutions as a result of involuntary civil commitment proceedings, have expressly stated that children similarly situated enjoy the same constitutional rights, as well as additional rights necessitated by reason of their youth. For example, as previously mentioned, the 1972 case of *Wyatt v. Stickney*[100] held that committed mental patients have a wide range of rights under the constitutional "right to treatment," including the right to a humane psychological and physical environment (for example, privacy, the least restrictive conditions necessary to achieve the purposes of commitment, access to visitors and attorneys, mail privileges, freedom from unnecessary or excessive medication, freedom from physical restraint and isolation, right to medical treatment for physical ailments, to exercise, religious worship, etc.), individual treatment plans, and qualified staff in numbers sufficient to administer adequate treatment.[101] Addressing itself specifically to young patients, the court also held:[102]

In addition to complying with all the other standards herein, a hospital shall make special provisions for the treatment of patients who are children and young adults. These provisions shall include but are not limited to:

a. Opportunities for publicly supported education suitable to the educational needs of the patient. This program of education must . . . be compatible with the patient's mental condition and his treatment program, and otherwise be in the patient's best interest.

b. A treatment plan which considers the chronological, maturational, and developmental level of the patient;

c. Sufficient Qualified Mental Health Professionals, teachers, and staff members with specialized skills in the care and treatment of children and young adults;

d. Recreation and play opportunities in the open air where possible and appropriate residential facilities [*sic*];

e. Arrangements for contact between the hospital and the family of the patient.

The same court, in a companion case concerning a state hospital for the mentally retarded,[103] also addressed the special education needs of "school-age" patients, who were held entitled to "a full and suitable educational program" for which the court established minimum standards.[104]

The Rights of Children Admitted "Voluntarily" to Mental Hospitals

The civil commitment cases establishing a constitutional right to treatment are mainly addressed to the situation of persons *involuntarily* confined for the purpose of receiving mental health care and treatment. A major issue requiring analysis, therefore, is the right to treatment of an adolescent placed in a mental institution by means other than civil commitment procedures. Typically, this is done by "voluntary admission" of the child by consent of his or her parent, guardian, or legal custodian, but without any requirement that the child consent.

Although few reported cases face this issue, the existing case law supports the view that a child "voluntarily" admitted by his parent or other custodian into a *state* institution for mental health treatment has the same constitutional right to treatment as does an adult committed to the institution involuntarily. No sources have been found dealing with the admission of a youth to a *private* hospital by consent of his or her parent. It is not clear whether "state action" theories might successfully be argued in such cases.

Admission by parent to state institution. Professor Charles Murdock presents three arguments for applying the constitutional right to treatment to a child admitted to a state hospital by "substituted consent" of a parent.[105] First, he argues, substantive due process is violated if the state "steps into the role of the parent and assumes custody of the child" without in fact providing adequate care and treatment. This theory is apparently grounded on the notion that the state's action (that is, receipt of the child into state-run facilities), taken in accord with *parens patriae* doctrines, can only be justified by the delivery of treatment.[106] The second argument is that the admission is often involuntary from the point of view of the child. In determining whether the child will be kept at home or admitted to a mental institution, the parents' and child's interests may conflict. In such cases, how can the parents' consent be validly substituted for that of the child?[107] (The commitment may also be involuntary from the parent's point of view, if the parents are acting under emotional and financial pressure to admit the child.) The third argument is based on the Fourteenth Amendment equal protection clause—that there is no rational basis for granting a right to involuntarily committed patients and withholding the right from patients voluntarily admitted, particularly if the terms of their voluntary admission preclude ready departure from the institution. Because children admitted "voluntarily" by their parents are typically not free to leave the institution, this argument has particular force for such children.

A few courts have treated the issue of children placed by their parents in state hospitals. *New York State Ass'n. for Retarded Children, Inc. v. Rockefeller*[108] was a suit to enforce the right to treatment for residents at a state facility for the mentally retarded. The court said,[109] regarding patients who had been admitted by consent of their parents:

There may be a fundamental conflict of interest between a parent who is ready to avoid the responsibility of caring for an abnormal child, and the best interests of the child ... A "voluntary admission" on the petition of parents may quite properly be treated as an "involuntary admission," in the absence of evidence that the child's interests have been fully considered. There may be occasions where a court should appoint a law guardian or a special guardian to represent a child before institutionalization.

Other courts have also focused on the possibility of parent-child conflicts of interest in voluntary admissions. In *Bartley v. Kremens,*[110] discussed in the previous chapter, a three-judge federal court invalidated a Pennsylvania voluntary admission statute because it did not afford children procedural safeguards adequate under the Fourteenth Amendment due process clause; and in *J.L. v. Parham,*[111] a similar case (presently before the Supreme Court) overturning a Georgia law, another federal district court issued orders designed to ensure to certain of the plaintiffs the right to be treated in a less restrictive nonhospital setting.

Admissions by consent of guardians who are not the parents. A child may become the ward of a state agency, such as the Department of Welfare, by several means, such as when a child's parent voluntarily surrenders custody of a child to an agency on a temporary basis, or when a court removes a child from his or her parents' custody as the result of a juvenile court proceeding and awards custody or guardianship rights to an agency. The agency having custody may then place the child "voluntarily" (without the normal civil commitment proceedings) in a public or private mental hospital. But the legality or conditions of hospital confinement for such children may be challenged in the context of right to treatment suits or other legal actions. *In the Interest of Mary L. and Pamela W.,*[112] an Illinois case in 1975, involved such children. This was a class action to implement the constitutional right to treatment of wards of the Illinois Department of Child and Family Services by the least restrictive methods appropriate for each child. The Illinois court said, in the resulting consent judgment granting relief to the plaintiffs:[113]

The *Donaldson* [v. O'Connor] case dealt with an adult who was involuntarily hospitalized. The distinction between "voluntary" and "involuntary" is not significant when we deal with the class of youngsters involved in this matter.

The constitutional limits on a state agency exercising parental powers were also emphasized in *dictum* by the United States Court of Appeals for the Seventh Circuit in *Vann v. Scott;*[114]

> ... the law is clear that a state may not act arbitrarily with children merely because they are children. And while a parent, as legal custodian of his child, may be able to restrict his child's liberty with impunity (subject, of course, to child abuse legislation), it does not follow that a state has the same unfettered rights as a parent merely because it becomes legal custodian of the child. The state, even when acting in a "private" capacity, is always subject to the limitations of the Fourteenth Amendment.

Similar questions regarding the juvenile court's power to confine its wards for mental health treatment were raised in two recent California cases. Both concerned the court's power to effect a ward's hospitalization without following normal procedures for involuntary civil commitment. In the case *In re L.L.,*[115] a juvenile court had declared a sixteen-year-old youth to be a "ward of the court" based on the commission of a PINS-type offense. Against the wishes of the boy and his parents, the juvenile court ordered its probation officer to place the youth in a state mental hospital for rehabilitative treatment; the ordinary civil commitment procedures were not followed. The appellate court held that the admission had been accomplished in effect by the juvenile court judge, was involuntary, and was in excess of the juvenile court's disposition powers. The second case, *In re Michael E.,*[116] concerned a delinquent ward also admitted to a California state mental hospital by the consent of a probation officer pursuant to the juvenile court's instructions. The California Supreme Court again invalidated the admission, ruling that the probation officer did not have "custody" over the youth so as to empower him to admit the youth "voluntarily" under the state civil commitment law.

"Voluntary" admission of children by parents to private hospitals. No authority has been found for the proposition that children "voluntarily" admitted to private institutions by consent of their parents have a constitutional right to treatment.[117] To find a constitutional right to treatment, there would first have to be a showing of "state action" in the child's confinement without treatment.[118] Although difficult to apply in this context, if it could be shown, for example, that coercion in the form of "PINS" jurisdiction might be used to prevent children "voluntarily" admitted to private facilities from leaving them, a child denied treatment in such a facility could support a constitutional claim by arguments based on substantive due process (right to treatment), or on equal protection (comparing children and adults, or parentally placed patients with civilly committed patients).[119]

    If it is not possible to demonstrate a constitutional right to treatment in this situation, other remedies might be sought in the areas of: (a) third-party beneficiaries to the contract between parent and hospital; or (b) a neglect action brought in juvenile court against the parent and the hospital to effect a release from custody, or an improvement in the conditions of custody, including the provisions of treatment.[120]

Conclusion

The above review of recent judicial decisions demonstrates the growing recognition of a constitutional right to treatment for juveniles confined in state hospitals, training schools and other nonpenal facilities. Many of the cases have arisen in the context of juvenile court proceedings regarding children who have committed delinquent and other deviant acts. Because in theory—if not always in fact—such proceedings serve benign rather than punitive goals, the courts have increasingly recognized the right to treatment as a proper restriction upon the nature of state-imposed confinement both before and after adjudication. Like the adult right to treatment cases, the juvenile cases focus primarily upon the right to treatment for physical, mental and emotional ailments. However, the doctrine is often invoked to challenge conditions of confinement which are inhumane—particularly in light of a juvenile's special vulnerability—and institutional programs which lack adequate rehabilitative components such as education, counseling, recreation, and programs for reintegrating the youth into his family and community. Although the Supreme Court has yet to recognize or define the right to treatment, for the time being the doctrine has an important role to play in determining the nature and conditions of confinement in juvenile detention facilities.

In mental health facilities, the major hurdles to be overcome in assuring this legal right to minors are the "voluntary" patient status of many, the questionable applicability of Fourteenth Amendment guarantees to "private" facilities, and, of course, the difficulties in defining specifically what constitutes appropriate treatment. Although these obstacles are not insubstantial, it is reasonable to expect that adolescent inpatients' legal right to treatment will continue to grow significantly in the next several years.

Notes

1. M. Birnbaum, *The Right to Treatment,* 46 A.B.A.J. 499 (1960).
2. *Id.*
3. Donaldson v. O'Connor, 493 F.2d 507 (5th Cir. 1974).
4. Wyatt v. Stickney, 344 F. Supp. 387 (M.D. Ala. 1972). *But see* N.Y. State Ass'n. for Retarded Children, Inc. v. Carey, 393 F. Supp. 715 (E.D.N.Y. 1975).

5. State v. Carter, 316 A.2d 449 (N.J. 1974); Jackson v. Indiana, 406 U.S. 715 (1972).

6. Rouse v. Cameron, 373 F.2d 451 (D.C. Cir. 1966). *Compare* James v. Wallace, 382 F. Supp. 1177 (M.D. Ala. 1974) (state must justify the reasonableness of providing rehabilitative services to some prisoners while denying such services to others).

7. Stachulak v. Coughlin, 364 F. Supp. 686 (N.D. Ill. 1973), Millard v. Cameron, 373 F.2d 468 (D.C. Cir. 1966).

8. State of Washington v. White, Nos. 67488 and 68250 (Superior Court of King County, Wash., Nov. 15, 1974); *reversed sub nom* State of Washington v. Damon and White, No. 4350-1 (Wash. Ct. App., Jan. 31, 1977), 1 Ment. Disabil. L. Rptr. 332 (1977). *Compare* James v. Wallace, 382 F. Supp. 1177 (M.D. Ala. 1974) (no obligation to provide rehabilitative services to prisoners, but the state may not impose cruel and unusual, or arbitrary, restraints to hinder prisoners' efforts to rehabilitate themselves).

9. Martarella v. Kelley, 349 F. Supp. 575 (S.D.N.Y. 1972).

10. Lollis v. N.Y. State Dep't. of Social Services, 322 F. Supp. 473 (S.D.N.Y. 1970).

11. *See, e.g.,* Comment, *Wyatt v. Stickney and the Right of Civilly Committed Mental Patients to Adequate Treatment,* 86 Harv. L. Rev. 1282 (1973); C. Murdock, *Civil Rights of the Mentally Retarded: Some Critical Issues,* 48 Notre Dame Law. 133 (1972); Symposium, *The Right to Treatment,* 57 Geo. L.J. 673 *et seq.*; Symposium, *The Right to Treatment,* 36 U. Chi. L. Rev. 742 *et seq.*; Note, *Civil Restraint, Mental Illness and the Right to Treatment,* 77 Yale L.J. 87 (1967); Note, *The Nascent Right to Treatment,* 53 Va. L. Rev. 1134 (1967).

12. Note, *Limits on Punishment and Entitlement to Rehabilitative Treatment of Institutionalized Juveniles: Nelson v. Heyne,* 60 Va. L. Rev. 864 (1974); P. Wald & L. Schwartz, *Trying a Juvenile Right to Treatment Suit: Pointers and Pitfalls for Plaintiffs,* 12 Am. Crim. L. Rev. 125 (1974); W. Bailey & J. Pyfer, *Deprivation of Liberty and the Right to Treatment,* 7 Clearinghouse Rev. 519 (Jan. 1974); Note, *A Right to Treatment for Juveniles?,* Wash. Univ. L.Q. 157 (1973); Note, *The Courts, the Constitution and Juvenile Institutional Reform,* 52 B.U. L. Rev. 33 (1972); A. Gough, *The Beyond-Control Child and the Right to Treatment: An Exercise in the Synthesis of Paradox,* 16 St. Louis U. L.J. 182 (1971); N. Kittrie, *Can the Right to Treatment Remedy the Ills of the Juvenile Process?,* 57 Geo. L.J. 848 (1969).

13. O'Connor v. Donaldson, 422 U.S. 563 (1975).

14. *See* text below, at note 26.

15. *See* section below, beginning after note 51.

16. Rouse v. Cameron, note 6 above.

17. *Id.,* at 453.

18. Wald & Schwartz, note 12 above, at 135.

19. *See* Wyatt v. Stickney, 325 F. Supp. 781 (M.D. Ala. 1971), at 784.

20. Donaldson v. O'Connor, note 3 above, at 521 *et seq.*

21. O'Connor v. Donaldson, note 13 above.

22. Donaldson v. O'Connor, note 3 above, at 520, *quoting* Humphrey v. Cady, 405 U.S. 504, 509 (1972).

23. Jackson v. Indiana, note 5 above, 406 U.S. at 738.

24. *But see* O'Connor v. Donaldson, note 13 above, 422 U.S. 578-85 (Burger, C.J. *concurring*), criticizing this theory.

25. Wyatt v. Aderholt, 503 F.2d 1305, 1312 (5th Cir. 1974); Donaldson v. O'Connor, note 3 above, at 522-24. *But see* O'Connor v. Donaldson, note 13 above, 422 U.S. 585-87 (Burger, C.J., *concurring*), criticizing this theory.

26. O'Connor v. Donaldson, note 13 above, at 422 U.S. 573-75.

27. *See* Rouse v. Cameron, note 6 above, at 453; Welsch v. Likins, 373 F. Supp. 487, 496 (D. Minn. 1974); S. Goodman, *Right to Treatment: The Responsibility of the Courts,* 57 Geo. L.J. 680, 688 (1969).

28. Estelle v. Gamble, 97 Sup. Ct. 285 (1976), *reh. den.* 97 Sup. Ct. 798 (1977).

29. *See* Rouse v. Cameron, note 6 above; Horacek v. Exon, 357 F. Supp. 71 (D. Neb. 1973).

30. Charles C. Rouse had been involuntarily committed to St. Elizabeths Hospital upon being found not guilty by reason of insanity of carrying a dangerous weapon. 373 F.2d at 452.

31. Robinson v. California, 370 U.S. 660 (1962).

32. *Id.,* at 666.

33. Powell v. Texas, 392 U.S. 514 (1968) (plurality opinion).

34. Note, *Developments in the Law: Civil Commitment of the Mentally Ill,* 87 Harv. L. Rev. 1190, 1259-64 (1974) [hereinafter cited as HLR Note]; Kennedy v. Mendoza-Martinez, 372 U.S. 144 (1963).

35. N.Y. State Assoc. of Retarded Children v. Carey, 393 F. Supp. 715 (E.D.N.Y. 1975).

36. *See* cases cited in HLR Note, note 34 above, at 1330-31, notes 62-67.

37. *Id.,* at 1331-33.

38. In re Gault, 387 U.S. 1 (1967).

39. Rouse v. Cameron, note 6 above; Nason v. Superintendent of Bridgewater Hosp., 233 N.E.2d 908, 913 (Mass. 1968); Goodman, note 27 above, at 690-91; Wald & Schwartz, note 12 above, at 135-36.

40. This terminology is used but defined differently in Bailey & Pyfer, note 12 above, at 526 *et seq.*

41. Bailey & Pyfer, note 12 above, at 527.

42. Rouse v. Cameron, note 6 above.

43. *See* the "subjective" juvenile cases discussed in text at note 82 *et seq.* below.

44. *See* sources cited in Bailey & Pyfer, note 12 above, at 526-27; *Wyatt* appendices at 344 F. Supp. 373, 379, 395.

45. Rouse v. Cameron, note 6 above, at 456. *Compare* R. Schwitzbagel, *Right to Treatment for the Mentally Disabled: The Need for Realistic Standards and Objective Criteria,* 8 Harv. C.R.-C.L. L. Rev. 513, 520 (1973) (proposing an "effectiveness" standard).

46. Rouse v. Cameron, note 6 above, at 456-57.

47. *Id.,* at 457.

48. 344 F. Supp. 373, at 379-85; discussed further in text at note 101 below.

49. *See* case citations and discussion in Murdock, note 11 above, at 151; Wyatt v. Stickney, 344 F. Supp. 373, 384.

50. *See* Welsch v. Likins, note 27 above, at 501-2; Dixon v. Weinberger, 405 F. Supp. 974 (D.D.C. 1975) (statutory interpretation).

In contrast to mentally ill patients, the *mentally retarded* have been accorded a constitutional right to "habilitation," or "protection from harm" rather than to "treatment." (*See* Wyatt v. Stickney, 344 F. Supp. 387 (1972); Welsch v. Likins, note 27 above; New York State Ass'n for Retarded Children v. Carey, note 4 above.) In both *Wyatt* and *Welsch,* the courts construed this right to include the "least restrictive treatment" appropriate to the patient's needs.

51. Wyatt v. Stickney, note 4 above, at 396.

52. In some jurisdictions, "minor in need of supervision" (MINS), or "child in need of services" (CHINS).

53. *See generally,* Uniform Juvenile Court Act, §§ 30-33 (1968); U.S. Children's Bureau, Legislative Guide for Drafting Family and Juvenile Court Acts, § 34 (1969).

54. *See* N. Mex. Stats. §§ 13-14-9, 13-14-32 (1972); Purdon's Pa. Stat. Ann. § 50-326 (1972); Uniform Juvenile Court Act, §§ 4, 35 (1968); U.S. HEW, Model Family Court Act §§ 7(b)(6), 40 (1975).

55. *See* Colo. Rev. Stat. Ann. § 22-8-11(i) (1963) (delinquent children); Fla. Stat. Ann. § 39.08 (1975 Supp.); Neb. Rev. Stat. § 43.210.02 (1974); R.I. Gen. Laws Ann. §§ 8-10-3, 14-1-51 (1969).

56. D.C. Code Ann. §§ 16-2320, 16-2321 (1970).

57. *See, e.g.,* Cal. Welf. & Inst. Code §§ 600(2), 705, 727, 730, 731; Mass. Gen. Laws Ann. ch. 119, §§ 26, 39G, 58; ch. 120 § 14; N.Y. Fam. Ct. Act, §§ 231, 232(b), 760, 1055; N.Y. Ment. Hyg. Law §§ 31.13, 31.27, 31.49 (McKinney's 1975 Supp.). *But see* clarifications of the California statutes in *In re Michael E.,* 123 Cal. Rptr. 103, 538 P.2d 231 (Cal. 1975); P. Roos & T. Ellison, *The Mentally Ill Juvenile Offender,* 27 Juv. Just. 25 (1976).

58. For a discussion of the *parens patriae* doctrine, see Hawaii v. Standard Oil Co., 405 U.S. 251, 257 (1972); Lessard v. Schmidt, 349 F. Supp. 1078 (E.D. Wis. 1972), *vacated sub nom* Schmidt v. Lessard, 414 U.S. 473 (1974), *reheard* 379 F. Supp. 1376 (E.D. Wis. 1974), *again vacated* 421 U.S. 957 (1975), *prior judgment reinstated* 413 F. Supp. 1318 (E.D. Wis. 1976); Hawks v. Lazaro, 202 S.E. 2d 109 (W.V. 1974).

59. *See* Donaldson v. O'Connor, discussed above at note 20 *et seq.*

60. Jackson v. Indiana, note 5 above.

61. *See* Donaldson v. O'Connor, at note 20 *et seq.* above.

62. *See* Morales v. Turman, 383 F. Supp. 53 (E.D. Tex. 1974) at 70-71; In re R.R. (Miss. Youth Ct., Hinds City 1st Dist. March 11, 1976), 2 Fam. L.R. 2381 (April 13, 1976). (*Compare* Kittrie, note 12 above, at 171).

63. Ind. L. 1903 ch. 237 amended 1905, as amended by ch. 203 of 1907, §§ 10-12, quoted in S. Dash *et al.,* Law, Mental Disorders and the Juvenile Process, vol. 2 of 4 (unpublished, Dec. 1971), at 312. *See also* U.S. Children's Bureau, Legislative Guide for Drafting Family and Juvenile Court Acts § 1 (1969); Note, *The Courts, the Constitution and Juvenile Institutional Reform,* note 12 above, at 38-42.

64. *See* P. Piersma, *Commitments to Juvenile Institutions,* 5 Clearinghouse Rev. 597 (Feb. 1972).

65. In re Hamill, 271 A.2d 762 (Md. Ct. Spec. App., 1970); C. v. Redlich, 32 N.Y.2d 588, 347 N.Y.S.2d 51, 300 N.E.2d 424 (1973).

66. In re C., 354 N.Y.S.2d 18 (App. Div. 1974); Creek v. Stone, 379 F.2d 106 (D.C. Cir. 1967); In re Elmore, 382 F.2d 125 (D.C. Cir. 1967); In the Matter of L., 546 P.2d 153 (Ore. 1976).

67. Kent v. United States, 401 F.2d 408 (D.C. Cir. 1968).

68. *See* In re Savoy, Docket Nos. 70-4808, 70-4714 (D.C. Juv. Ct., Oct. 13, 1970), discussed in Dash *et al.,* note 63 above, at 320 *et seq.*; Note *The Courts, The Constitution and Juvenile Institutional Reform,* note 12 above, at 38-42.

69. In re Gault, 387 U.S. 1 (1967). *See* discussion in chapter 2 above. *See also* McKeiver v. Pennsylvania, 403 U.S. 528 (1971).

70. In re Gault, 387 U.S. 1 (1967), at 22-23, note 30, *citing* Creek v. Stone, Elmore v. Stone, Rouse v. Cameron, and other "right to treatment" cases. This language of the Supreme Court was partially relied upon in Morales v. Turman, 383 F. Supp. 53, 71 (E.D. Tex. 1974) and Martarella v. Kelley, 349 F. Supp. 575, 599 (S.D.N.Y. 1972).

Note that many court decisions recognizing a "right to treatment" rely on a combination of local statutory rights and rights under the Federal Constitution. This is true, *e.g.,* of Morales v. Truman. *See also* In Interest of D.F., Camden Co. Juv. & Dom. Rels. Ct., J-5129-74 (1975), May 1976 *Juv. Ct. Digest* 278; In re R.R., (Miss. Youth Ct., Hinds Cty.; 1st Dist. March 11, 1976), 2 Fam. L.R. 2381 (April 13, 1976).

71. The attention which many juvenile right to treatment cases give to the right to education, including vocational training to suit individual needs and aptitudes (*see, e.g.,* Morales v. Turman, note 70 above, at 89-92), also illustrates the court's recognition of the special needs of children.

72. Lollis v. N.Y. State Dept. of Social Services, 322 F. Supp. 473 (S.D.N.Y. 1970) [hereinafter cited as Lollis], at 480; Inmates of Boys Training School v. Affleck, 346 F. Supp. 1354 (D.R.I. 1972) [hereinafter cited as Affleck], at p. 1371, note 5.

73. *See, e.g.*, N.Y. State Ass'n. for Retarded Children, Inc. v. Carey, note 4 above, stressing the distinction; Affleck, note 72 above; Morales v. Turman, note 70 above, at 70-79.

74. *See* Note, *The Courts, the Constitution and Juvenile Institutional Reform*, 52 B.U. L. Rev. 33, 45-49 (1972); Morales v. Turman, 383 F. Supp. 53 (E.D. Tex. 1974), at 102, 105-6, 121-26. *Morales* has been reversed and remanded for reconsideration by a three-judge court pursuant to 28 U.S.C. § 2284, Morales v. Turman, 535 F.2d 864 (5th Cir. 1976).

75. In re Harris, 2 Crim. L. Rptr. 2412 (Ill. Cir. Ct., Cook Cty., Juv. Div., 1967) discussed in Bailey & Pyfer, note 10 above, at 525; In the Matter of Application of D.C. Family Welfare Rights Organization, Docket No. 71-1150 (D.C. Super. Ct., Fam. Div., June 18, 1971), discussed in Dash, note 63 above, at 322 *et seq.*; Janet D. v. Carros, (Pa. Super. Ct. Mar. 29, 1976), 2 Fam. L.R. 2293 (Apr. 20, 1976); In the Matter of L., 546 P.2d 153 (Ore. 1976).

76. In re Harris, note 75 above.

77. In the Matter of L., note 75 above.

78. Creek v. Stone, 379 F.2d 106 (D.C. Cir. 1967); In re Savoy, Nos. 70-4808 and 70-4714 (D.C. Juv. Ct. Oct. 13, 1970). Both *Creek* and *Savoy* are discussed in Note, *The Courts, the Constitution and Juvenile Institutional Reform,* note 12 above, at 39-42. *See also* Tommy P. v. Spokane School District, No. 224974 (Wash. Super. Ct., Spokane County, June 22, 1976), 10 Clearinghouse Rev. 293 (Aug. 1976).

79. In re Savoy, note 78 above (equal protection requires the provision to detained youth of educational services equal to those provided to nondetained children in the community); City of Newport v. In re: Juvenile [sic], (R.I. Fam. Ct. April 9, 1976) 2 Fam. L.R. 2450 (May 11, 1976) (due process, the right to treatment and the "purposes" clause of Rhode Island's Family Court statute require that juveniles detained prior to delinquency trials be housed apart from adjudicated delinquents in quarters "designed to insure the child's security, privacy, and dignity.") *See also* Inmates of Judge Connelly Youth Center v. Dukakis, U.S.D.C., D. Mass., Civ. No. 75-1786-G (1975) (consent decree); Roe v. Pennsylvania, No. 74-519 (W.D. Pa. June 9, 1976), 10 Clearinghouse Rev. 294 (Aug. 1976).

80. City of Newport v. In Re: Juvenile [sic], note 64 above, and Martarella v. Kelley, 349 F. Supp. 575 (S.D.N.Y. 1972).

81. 349 F. Supp. 575 (S.D.N.Y. 1972).

82. In re Elmore, 382 F.2d 125 (D.C. Cir. 1967).

83. In re Ilone I., 316 N.Y.S.2d 356 (Fam. Ct. 1970).

84. In Interest of D.F., Camden Co. Juv. & Dom. Rels. Ct., J-5129-74 (1975), reported in Juv. Ct. Dig. (May 1976), at 278.

85. In re S., 78 Misc. 2d 351, 356 N.Y. Supp. 2d 768 (Fam. Ct. 1974).

86. Welfare of J.E.C. v. State, 225 N.W.2d 245 (1975), and In re Welfare of J.E.C., Case No. 75604 (Feb. 1975), Hennepin Co., Minn., Dist., Ct., Juv. Div.,

reported in Juv. Ct. Dig. (May 1975), at 459. In re R.R. (Miss. Youth Ct. Hinds Cty. 1st Dist., Mar. 11, 1976), 2 Fam. L.R. 2381 (Apr. 13, 1976) dealt with a similar situation. Based on the delinquent's statutory and constitutional right to treatment, the court ordered the state either to place the youth in a suitable out-of-state psychiatric treatment facility, or to release him. *See also* Morales v. Turman, note 74 above, at 125.

87. Inmates of Boys Training School v. Affleck, note 72 above; Morales v. Turman, note 74 above; Nelson v. Hyne, 491 F.2d 352 (7th Cir. 1974).

88. Morales v. Turman, 383 F. Supp. 53, note 74 above.

89. *Id.,* at 70-79.

90. *Id.,* at 78-85.

91. *Id.,* at 88.

92. *Id.,* at 89-90. The Court ordered the testing of inmates to detect retardation, minimum student-teacher ratios, and bilingual educational services.

93. *Id.,* at 91-92. The Court required individual employability plans and programs for on-the-job training.

94. *Id.,* at 100-01. These included rights relating to recreation, privacy, diet, mail and telephone communications, coeducational living, dress and hair styles, and adequate casework services.

95. *Id.,* at 105-06.

96. *Id.,* at 118-19. The Court also ordered family involvement in inmate therapy programs, and access to visits by friends and family. The most intensive treatment was ordered reserved for the most disturbed and antisocial children.

97. *Id.,* at 120-21.

98. *Id.,* at 121-26.

99. *Id.,* at 125-26.

100. 344 F. Supp. 373.

101. *Id.,* at 379-85.

102. *Id.,* Appendix A, ¶ 32, at 385-86.

103. Wyatt v. Stickney, 344 F. Supp. 387 (M.D. Ala. 1972).

104. *Id.,* at 396-97.

105. Murdock, note 11 above.

106. This argument is subject to criticism on the ground that the state is acting as *parens patriae,* but is providing services to parents in a proprietary role, often for a fee. Murdock, note 11 above, discusses this objection.

107. This argument has been developed in Strunk v. Strunk, 445 S.W.2d 145 (Ky. 1969) and other organ transplant cases. *See* C. Baron, M. Botsford & G. Cole, *Live Organ and Tissue Transplants from Minor Donors in Massachusetts,* 55 B.U. L. Rev. 159 (1975) and articles cited therein at 170 n.57.

108. 357 F. Supp. 752 (E.D.N.Y. 1973).

109. *Id.,* at 762. *See also* New York State Ass'n. for Retarded Children v. Carey, note 4 above; Horacek v. Exon, Memorandum and Order on Motion for Summary Judgment No. CV72-L-299 (June 4, 1974, U.S.D.C., D. Neb. 1973-74).

110. 402 F. Supp. 1039 (E.D. Pa. 1975) *remanded for exclusion of moot claims and reconsideration of class definition,* 97 S. Ct. 1709 (1977).

111. 412 F. Supp. 112 (M.D. Ga. 1976); *prob. juris. noted sub nom* Parham v. J.L. and J.R., 427 U.S. 903; *motion to proceed in forma pauperis granted* 97 S. Ct. 2647 (1977); *argued* Dec. 6, 1977, 46 U.S.L.W. 3386 (12/13/77); *reargument ordered* Jan. 16, 1978, 46 U.S.L.W. 3452 (1/17/78); *Accord.*

112. In the Interest of Mary L. and Pamela W., Memorandum Opinion and Order, Juvenile Division, Cook Co., Cir. Ct., Nos. 68J(d) 1362, 68J(D) 6383, 68J 15850 (March 5, 1975).

113. *Id.; see also* J.L. v. Parham, note 111 above.

114. 467 F.2d 1235 (7th Cir. 1972) at 1240, note 15.

115. 39 Cal. App. 3d 205, 114 Cal. Rptr. 11 (1974).

116. 123 Cal. Rptr. 103, 538 P.2d 231 (Cal. 1975).

117. *See generally* J. Ellis, *Volunteering Children: Parental Commitment of Minors to Mental Institutions,* 62 Calif. L. Rev. 840 (1974).

118. *See* discussion of state action in chapter 6 above.

119. *See* Murdock's discussion, mentioned in text above at note 107, regarding Strunk v. Strunk line of cases, and conflict of interest between parent and child in the commitment decision.

120. At least one court, however, has held that its jurisdiction does not extend to neglect allegedly committed by a state institution rather than by a natural person. In re D., 335 N.Y. Supp. 2d 638, 70 Misc. 2d 953 (Fam. Ct. 1972) (alleged child neglect by the N.Y. State Department of Mental Hygiene at the Willowbrook School).

8

The Rights of Privacy and Confidentiality Accorded Adolescents Receiving Mental Health Treatment

This section deals with the rights of privacy and confidentiality accorded minors receiving treatment for mental illness. It specifically excludes discussion of the rights of the mentally retarded[1] or of minors receiving drug or venereal disease treatment. Particular emphasis will be devoted to the confidentiality rights of minors vis-à-vis their parents, guardians, school officials, the juvenile court, law enforcement agencies, and others, including employers.

The general topic of confidentiality and privacy is divisible into four subject areas: the right of privacy, the right of confidentiality, the evidentiary or privilege doctrine, and the doctrine of waiver.[2] The concept of privacy encompasses a right to withhold information about oneself and one's personality from others. The right of confidentiality, on the other hand, assumes that certain information will be disclosed to another for a specific purpose, and that because of an express or implied agreement, this information will not be released to a third party. The testimonial privilege doctrine is concerned with confidential communications that cannot be divulged in a legal setting without the consent of the holder of the privilege (for example, the patient or client). Finally, all of the aforementioned rights may be waived by a minor (or his parent or legal guardian), provided the consent to waive is competent, informed, and voluntary.

Most writers justify the need for rights of privacy and confidentiality in this area as protection against the unfortunate stigmatization which accompanies the term "mental illness" and the concomitant discrimination against former mental patients.[3] A fifty-item survey conducted by the Institute of Communications Research, University of Illinois, revealed that public attitudes toward the mentally ill are largely negative.[4] "The mentally ill are regarded with fear, distrust, and dislike, and are thought to be unpredictable."[5] In a similar survey conducted by the National Opinion Research Center of the University of Chicago, 60 percent of the respondents stated "that they would not act or feel normally toward a former mental patient, even though they did not learn of his illness until they had known him for some time without noticing anything wrong about him."[6]

Members of the medical community advance an additional reason for the protections of confidentiality and privacy. Confidentiality, they urge, is a necessary factor in the formation of a therapeutic relationship.[7] The law should encourage confidence in this relationship, because those concerned will benefit from the full disclosure of all facts which may have a bearing upon the diagnosis and treatment of the patient.[8] Balanced against these rights, however, are the needs of others for information in certain contexts: family members who may be endangered or who wish to aid in treatment efforts, potential employers, juvenile authorities and the like. In years past, the resulting compromises have given less protection to the rights of the individual and more to the needs of these others, but this situation is gradually changing.

The Right of Privacy

Dean Roscoe Pound identified the claim to privacy as "the demand which the individual may make that his private personal affairs shall not be laid bare to the world."[9] Stated more specifically, for the minor receiving mental health treatment, the right of privacy means (1) the right to be left alone, and, more importantly, (2) the right to choose the time and circumstances under which, and the extent to which, his beliefs and behaviors may be shared with others or withheld from others.[10] However, this right, which is subjective and incorporeal, is difficult to identify and almost impossible to measure for the purpose of assessing damages in a legal action.[11] It has been suggested that privacy is actually a concept of human dignity and that its violation does not constitute a tort.[12]

In 1965, in *Griswold v. Connecticut*,[13] the United States Supreme Court declared privacy a fundamental right under the Constitution and suggested that its legal basis could be found in the penumbras of the First, Third, Fourth, Fifth, and Ninth Amendments. *Griswold* involved the use of contraceptive devices by married couples. Subsequently, in *Eisenstadt v. Baird*,[14] the Court upheld the privacy right of single persons to purchase and use contraceptives, and in 1977 it held this right applicable to minors under sixteen.[15] In two other recent opinions,[16] a majority of the Court apparently sanctioned a limited claim to the right by minors in the context of abortion, even in opposition to parental dictates. State court cases, such as *State v. Lowry*,[17] have held that the constitutional right of privacy should be applicable to the young and old alike.[18] And a lower federal court, in *Merriken v. Cressman*,[19] a case involving the use of a highly personal questionnaire as part of a proposed school drug abuse prevention program, sustained a privacy argument based on *Griswold*, which was advanced by a minor and his parent. There the court stated: "The fact that the students are juveniles does not in any way invalidate their right to assert their constitutional right to privacy."[20]

The dimensions of the constitutional right to privacy are still ill defined. More than thirty states, however, now recognize some form of privacy in their legislative enactments.[21] A sampling of these right to privacy laws will give an indication of their effectiveness. In some, the state law defines privacy narrowly to include a prohibition against the use of one's name or picture for advertising without consent.[22] This limitation seemingly affords a minor receiving mental health treatment few rights against an invasion of his private personality. In others—Arizona, for example—the right is broadly defined: "No person shall be disturbed in his private affairs, or his home invaded, without authority of law."[23] Under this provision, it appears that a minor has a right to withhold information as he or she pleases, but the Arizona courts have indicated that this section of its constitution should be generally interpreted as similar to the right to be secure against unreasonable searches and seizures in the Fourth Amendment to the United States Constitution.[24] Other states, such as Illinois, explicitly combine the right of privacy with the right against searches and seizures:[25]

The people shall have the right to be secure in their persons, houses, papers and other possessions against unreasonable searches, seizures, invasions of privacy or interceptions of communications by eavesdropping devices or other means.

The nature of the protection afforded mental health patients by the Fourth Amendment of the United States Constitution and similar provisions in state constitutions depends on a case-by-case determination. The case of *Merriken v. Cressman*,[26] mentioned earlier, upheld a student's and his parent's Fourth Amendment right to privacy with respect to the facts of that case. However, another federal case, *Winters v. Miller*,[27] has held that a New York statute providing for compulsory fingerprinting and photographing of state mental patients did not violate a mental patient's Fourth Amendment right to privacy. The court was swayed by the fact that these procedures are needed to aid in the identification of patients,[28] and that fingerprinting does not carry with it a stigma or any implication of criminality.[29] It is unclear, therefore, whether the right will be recognized in situations involving greater invasions of the minor's privacy than fingerprinting or photographing, although presumably its chances of being upheld are considerably greater if the invasion results in stigma.

Even in situations where a minor might exercise a right of privacy, it may be possible for the parent to waive the right.[30] Parents have control over the person of a child and over his or her possessions if either resides within the home owned by the parent, so many courts in search and seizure cases have approved a parental waiver of the minor's rights to privacy.[31] The right of waiver has also been extended to school officials who undertake a search of a student's room, locker or pockets.[32] In the *Merriken* case,[33] the federal court recognized the difficult question of "whether parents, as guardians of the children, can waive their children's Constitutional rights."[34] It concluded, however, that it need not decide the issue in that case, because the parents had not been provided with sufficient information to consent validly to a waiver, even if they possessed the right.

The Right of Confidentiality

As discussed in chapter 4,[35] recent enactments in several states have lowered the age at which minors, or at least "emancipated" minors, may consent to hospital care or treatment rendered by a licensed physician, surgeon, or dentist.[36] These laws must be considered generally to expand minors' privacy rights. Some of them, however, do not accompany this with strong confidentiality rights; a number give the physician the right to inform the parents of any treatment given or needed. California, for example, gives the physician the right to so inform the parents or legal guardian of the minor, with or without the consent of the patient.[37] Minnesota's act is more restrictive; it allows the physician to inform the minor patient's parents or legal guardian only if "failure . . . would seriously jeopardize the health of the minor patient."[38] In addition, Minnesota explicitly includes mental health services within the services that may be provided to an independent minor without the consent of his or her parents. Mental health care may well be implied in the phrase "hospital care" as used in the California statute, but this remains an open question.

In general, an issue of confidentiality may arise after a minor has disclosed information about his or her behavior, opinions, beliefs or personality to a professional and then wishes to limit dissemination of this information. There is no absolute right to confidentiality, however; the release of information depends in each case upon who is requesting the information and for what purpose.[39] The identity of the person disclosing the information may also be important. Arguably, the fact that minors are more vulnerable emotionally and may not know their own best interests may be a reason for affording their confidential communications greater protection than is accorded adults.

What is the legal basis for the right of confidentiality, and what actions may be brought for the breach of this confidentiality? Generally, a physician has an ethical duty to maintain the confidentiality of information obtained in the course of his professional employment. The American Medical Association has embodied this responsibility in its Principles of Medical Ethics:[40]

A physician may not reveal the confidence entrusted to him in the course of medical attendance, or the deficiencies he may observe in the character of patients, unless he is required to do so by law or unless it becomes necessary in order to protect the welfare of the individual or of the community.

In some states this ethical responsibility has been embodied in law, and betrayal thereof is grounds for suspension or revocation of a physician's license.[41] In the absence of statutory protection, the minor must rely upon his or her ability to bring an action for defamation based upon the breach of confidentiality. However, if the information disclosed is accurate, no liability will lie unless the disclosure is made to an excessive number of people (that is, excessive publication).[42] In addition, the defense of qualified privilege may immunize the professional from liability.[43] The weakness of this approach is compounded by the difficulty in assessing damages. How much is a person injured by the dissemination of truthful information? What is the cost of stigmatization?

Equitable relief to prevent further disclosure may also be an inadequate remedy. In *Garrison v. Louisiana*[44] the Supreme Court ruled that truth alone, without a showing of good motive, constituted a defense to a criminal libel action, when the alleged libel was directed against the conduct of a public official in the discharge of his or her public duties. The Court explicitly did not decide whether this defense would be appropriate in an action for a purely private libel,[45] and in more recent decisions it has limited itself to expanding the definition of a public person.[46] In view of the uncertainty of the law with respect to private libel, therefore, it is not clear whether truthful disclosure of confidential communications and records may be enjoined in the absence of statutory protection.[47]

Statutorily mandated confidentiality provides the minor receiving mental health care the greatest protection. Since most laws dealing with the issue of confidentiality are concerned with the confidentiality of records, the following discussion will be limited accordingly. Confidentiality of communications will be discussed in the section on privileges.

In determining what rights of confidentiality a minor receiving mental health treatment has to various records, problems arise concerning (1) the material included in the record, and (2) the ownership of the record. If the record contains only identification information, such as fingerprints or photographs in an arrest file, then the claim for confidentiality is weaker than if it contains evaluative or highly sensitive information. In the latter case, ownership becomes very important. Yet medical records which often contain very personal information are generally thought to be the property of the hospital or physician; similarly, school records are the property of the school, and court records the property of the court.[48] As the patient loses control over the contents of and access to these records, the need for confidentiality becomes all the more acute.

Balanced against the patient's need for confidentiality of records is the public's right to know, as embodied in the federal Freedom of Information Act.[49] This statute makes federal records and information accessible to the public, but it is subject to two exceptions which strengthen the argument for the confidentiality of a minor's mental health treatment records. The law does not apply to "personal and medical files the disclosure of which would constitute a clearly unwarranted invasion of personal privacy."[50] Similarly, the Federal Census Law,[51] which must be read in conjunction with the Freedom of Information Act, protects a minor's right of confidentiality and anonymity. This law provides that statistical summaries may be available to any person for a fee; however, no identifiable data on the individual may be released, and wrongful disclosure is subject to a criminal penalty.

Hospital Records

A majority of states have enacted statutes requiring all licensed hospitals and clinics to keep records of the treatments and medical histories of their patients. The Mississippi statute,[52] is typical:

All hospitals, their officers or employees and medical and nursing personnel practicing therein, shall with reasonable promptness prepare, make and maintain true and accurate hospital records complying with such methods and minimum standards as may be prescribed from time to time by rules and regulations adopted by the licensing agency.

Pursuant to this law, a minor's hospital record will indicate that he or she has been hospitalized and has received mental health treatment. Does the minor have a right of access to these records, and, more importantly, what right of confidentiality does he or she have to prevent indiscriminate dissemination of this record?

In some states, hospital records are considered public records, and thus they are open to inspection by anyone unless a specific statutory exemption makes the records confidential.[53] Iowa, for example, has a statute which makes certain public records confidential, including "[h]ospital records and medical records of the condition, diagnosis, care or treatment of a patient or former patient, including out-patient."[54] California exempts from public scrutiny "[p]ersonnel, medical, or similar files, the disclosure of which would constitute an unwarranted invasion of personal privacy."[55] In some states where confidentiality of general hospital records is required, however, it is questionable whether the records of a minor can legally be withheld from the minor's parents, even if the minor should so desire.[56]

Only three states guarantee patients the right of access to their records in general hospitals. In Massachusetts, for example, although the hospital record is owned by the hospital and not by the patient, the patient, or his or her attorney on written authorization from the patient, has the right to inspect the record.[57] Connecticut[58] and Illinois[59] have similar laws. This is an important right, especially if the records are open to inspection by other parties. The patient can review the contents of his or her record and contest their accuracy or completeness. And even though a minor's right of access to his or her hospital record may be controlled by the parents or guardian, the three states mentioned above—Massachusetts, Connecticut and Illinois—appear to accord the minor protection from total and indiscriminate disclosure. All three also afford him a chance to review the contents of the record for its accuracy.

If a minor is in a mental health facility, his or her rights of confidentiality are generally more complete. Over two-thirds of the states provide for the confidentiality of mental institution records. Some require either the patient's consent[60] or a court order[61] before any information may be disclosed. Others permit disclosure of the record to a court if necessary for the conduct of its proceedings, or disclosure of the patient's current medical condition to family and friends who request such information.[62] Still others allow disclosure of the record to attorneys, insurers, welfare departments and other federal and state law enforcement agencies.[63]

The majority of the states with explicit confidentiality statutes combine several of the above-mentioned prototypes.[64] The Alaska statute[65] is typical:

Sec. 47.30.260. *Disclosure of information.* (a) All applications, records and reports . . . together with clinical information relating to the patients, shall be kept confidential and shall not be disclosed by a person except insofar as

(1) the individual, or his legal guardian or, if he is a minor, his parent or legal guardian consents; . . .

(3) a court directs, upon its determination that disclosure is necessary for the conduct of proceedings before it and that failure to make the disclosure would be contrary to the public interest.

(b) Nothing in this section precludes disclosure, upon proper inquiry, of information concerning current medical condition to the immediate family of a patient. . . .

A statute such as the one above does not afford absolute privacy and confidentiality to a minor receiving mental health treatment. First of all, even if a minor could commit himself or herself without parental or guardian consent, the nature of his or her medical condition may not be withheld from the immediate family, even if expressly requested by the adolescent. In addition, a legal guardian may consent to disclosure. Minors are not regarded as competent to waive statutory provisions enacted for their benefit and protection, and there is a general assumption that the interests of a minor and his or her parents or guardian are identical.[66] The statute quoted above also may not prevent law enforcement agencies from obtaining a minor's records, if a court decides that the records are necessary in a juvenile court proceeding.

In addition to the exceptions to the general rule of confidentiality in the majority of states, several state statutes provide other exceptions. The states of Idaho[67] and California,[68] for example, provide that mental health records may be disclosed to insurance companies. California also provides that information and records may be made available to researchers.[69] Several states allow disclosure to other medical professionals for the purpose of aiding in diagnosis and treatment.[70] Other states provide a catch-all provision which allows disclosure to those persons "legitimately and properly interested in the . . . condition of the patient"[71] or if the "disclosure will be in the best interests of the patient."[72] Unless interpreted restrictively, such provisions could be damaging to the confidentiality rights of a minor receiving mental health care; employers, school officials and law enforcement agencies, among others, may gain access to highly sensitive documents without the minor's knowledge or consent.

The control over the dissemination of mental institution records may be most important to a minor in the area of employment, but only three states provide protection in this area. A few states, such as Massachusetts,[73] prohibit job discrimination against anyone solely on the grounds of having received treatment for mental problems. Some also prohibit employers from inquiring on employment applications about past admissions to mental institutions.[74] One author suggests that if an employer knows of past treatment, he or she may be able to circumvent such laws by asserting that he is denying employment "not because the applicant is a former mental patient but because, as a former patient, he is a greater risk for the future than non-patient applicants."[75] The California statute[76] similarly does not prohibit an employer from receiving mental health records; as a safeguard it provides that the patient must give permission, and the records will then be released unless "the physician or administrative officer responsible for the patient deems the release of such records contrary to the best interests of the patient."

As noted above, if a minor has been institutionalized, his or her hospital records will probably be available to the juvenile court and law enforcement officers. However, if he or she has not been hospitalized but has received mental health treatment on an outpatient basis (for example, from a private psychologist or a school counselor), it is not clear whether a court or its officers may obtain access to the records and communications. (This issue will also be discussed in the subsequent section on testimonial privileges.) In addition, once records are in the hands of the juvenile court and law enforcement officers, possibly supplemented with information about court-ordered mental examinations, it is important to determine who then may obtain access to them.

Juvenile Justice Records

In *In re Gault,*[77] the Supreme Court held that a juvenile defendant in a delinquency proceeding is entitled to most of the protections afforded adults in criminal trials.[78] However, by withholding the rights to trial by jury,[79] the Supreme Court has arguably continued the characterization of juvenile court procedures as noncriminal. As such, the juvenile justice system must maintain strict confidentiality of its records for the protection of its young clients.[80] One commentator[81] suggests that:

the promise of noncriminality and confidentiality is in the nature of a contract by the state with the juvenile wherein certain rights ordinarily accorded to a citizen in our judicial system are relinquished by a juvenile in return for the assurance of confidentiality and protection from a stigmatic record.

But just how confidential are the records in a juvenile proceeding? A few states, such as Minnesota,[82] define the court record as including any and all police records pertaining to juveniles; any rights of confidentiality are therefore extended to this entire record. Other states have different standards of confidentiality for four roughly defined classes of records: (1) identification data (fingerprints, photographs); (2) law enforcement or arrest records; (3) probation officer's reports; and (4) juvenile court records.

Fingerprinting and photographing, in the states which permit those procedures, are generally allowed only if the complaint or petition against a juvenile is for an offense which would be a felony if the juvenile were an adult. The majority of states which provide for these procedures demand that such records "be kept separate from records and files of adults and shall not be open to public inspection."[83] Florida, on the other hand, does not demand such absolute confidentiality and allows the records to be open to law enforcement officers, the court, the child, the legal guardians, their attorneys, and anyone "upon a showing of good cause."[84]

More crucial for the minor receiving mental health treatment is the confidentiality of law enforcement records and probation officer's records, which in many states are considered one and the same.[85] These records relate to (1) the taking of a minor into custody, (2) the investigation by law enforcement officers into the background of the juvenile, and (3) the recommendations for the disposition of the case. Such reports can contain highly stigmatizing information about the minor's mental health evaluations, diagnoses, and treatment, and should not be exposed to public scrutiny. Thus California[86] and Hawaii[87] allow law enforcement records to be disclosed only to persons with a legitimate need for the records for the purpose of official disposition of a case. Other states provide for the general confidentiality of these records without specifying who may gain access thereto.[88] Still others allow disclosure to the court, other law enforcement officers and agencies, counsel and the minor's family.[89] No state has made specific provision for a minor's right to review his or her arrest records, but a few, which differentiate between arrest records and probation officers' records, grant the minor a right of access to the latter.[90] This is an important right, because these reports may contain inadequate or misleading information which the minor should be able to rectify.

Social reports have been defined as:[91]

primary . . . reports of investigations concerning the child, including an investigation of the home and environmental situation of the child, his previous history, and the circumstances which brought him before the court, and reports about his conduct and condition while under supervision, if he had been confined or placed on probation.

Because the social records in a juvenile proceeding, whether compiled by a probation officer or other court personnel, contain highly sensitive material, they should be especially confidential. These reports could conceivably contain information about any mental health treatment or guidance a minor is receiving from friends, doctors or school officials. In fact, in two states, school records are available to law enforcement officers[92] and thus may form part of the social record. Connecticut law,[93] for example, provides:

Such investigation shall consist of an examination of the parentage and surroundings of the child, his age, habits, and history, and shall include also an inquiry into the home conditions, habits, and character of his parents or guardians. Where a child is or legally should be in attendance at school, it shall further contain a report of the child's school adjustment, which shall be furnished by the school officials to the court upon its request.

Several states provide generally for the confidentiality of social records or probation officers' reports.[94] For the District of Columbia, Congress has recognized (1) the difference between social records and the general records of the juvenile court and (2) the need for maintaining the confidentiality of the former.[95] There, attorneys possess a general right to see all juvenile court legal records, but they may inspect social records only in limited circumstances.[96] In Minnesota, the social history of a minor is open to inspection only "by the attorneys of record a reasonable time before it is used in connection with any proceeding before the court."[97] New York handles the problem by giving the court discretion to "withhold from or disclose [the record] in whole or in part to the law guardian, counsel, party in interest, or other appropriate person."[98] Of all the states which classify as confidential the social reports of law enforcement officers respecting minors, Oregon seems to have the most perceptive law. An Oregon statute[99] provides that:

[r]ecords and other material relating to the child's history and prognosis are privileged and, except at the *request of the child,* shall not be disclosed directly or indirectly to anyone other than the judge of the juvenile court, those acting under his direction and to the attorneys of record for the child or his parent or guardian. (Emphasis added.)

Persons with "alleged" legitimate interests are not, under this law, afforded access to the reports.

The use and disclosure of general juvenile court records are regulated more than identification data, law enforcement or arrest records, or probation officers' reports. As a part of juvenile proceedings, a court may require a physical and mental examination,[100] and a report of such examination becomes part of the juvenile record. Thus, even if a minor is not receiving mental health treatment, his or her record may contain psychological data which he or she would wish to keep confidential.

Close to one-half of the states have laws which withhold juvenile court records from indiscriminate public inspection.[101] Their usual format is to mandate the confidentiality of the records and then carve out certain exceptions. Common exceptions include review by court personnel, the parties to a proceeding and their counsel, a public or private agency or institution providing supervision or having custody of a child under order of the court, and other persons having a "legitimate interest."[102] Of the states which subject juvenile court records to a general right of confidentiality, only eight allow the record to be seen by the minor in question,[103] and South Dakota allows a child to inspect his or her own records only with the consent of the court.[104] Other states which recognize some right of confidentiality word their statutes so as to allow no publicity regarding juvenile court procedures.[105] On the other hand, a few states allow some decisions to be published.[106] Mississippi, for example, provides that:[107]

when any child for the second time or more shall be adjudged to be a delinquent child, his name and the name of his parents or the persons in whose custody he lives shall thereupon be published in a newspaper having a general circulation in the county of said child's residence, along with the fact of such adjudication.

Besides his or her parents and attorney, court personnel and some agencies, a minor may also worry whether school officials will learn of the contents of his or her juvenile record. In some states, these officials might possibly qualify as persons with a "legitimate interest." Illinois is unique in specifying that all courts and law enforcement agencies shall report to the principal of any public school the fact that a minor enrolled therein is involved in a juvenile proceeding:[108]

The information derived thereby shall be kept separate from and shall not become a part of the official school record of such child and shall not be a public record. Such information shall be used solely by the principal, counselors and teachers of the school to aid in the proper rehabilitation of the child.

Finally, most states which recognize a right of confidentiality in this area also provide for the sealing of juvenile court records. About half of these states[109] make sealing of court records mandatory if a petition is presented to the court, a certain length of time has passed since the date of discharge from the supervision of the juvenile court, and a subsequent proceeding has not been instituted against the minor. A minority of states provide that upon a showing of similar facts, the court, in its discretion, may order the records expunged.[110] This procedure may be especially crucial to the minor's potential employment. Louisiana is one of the few states which specifically provides that law enforcement records will not be disclosed to "a prospective or actual employer conducting a reference investigation."[111] This law, of course, does not concern itself with the more crucial juvenile court record, but it would seem logical to suggest that if a minor has stayed out of trouble for several years and is presumably rehabilitated, his or her court record, with its highly sensitive contents, should be automatically expunged. An alternative solution might prevent access by employers to these records or forbid employers to ask whether applicants have been involved in a juvenile court proceeding.

School Records

The state of Mississippi requires that the state Board of Education keep cumulative records for each student enrolled in the public schools of the state.[112] Besides statistical data regarding date of birth, attendance, and grades, this record includes information about "mental and scholastic abilities [and] personality traits and characteristics."[113] Other states require similar records, but, unlike Mississippi, not all provide for their confidentiality. Some state laws limit disclosure to such persons as the parent or guardian, a person designated by the pupil (if the pupil is an adult, or if not, by his or her parent or guardian) certain officials, law enforcement officers, education officials, and colleges and universities.[114]

In recent years there has been a significant trend toward making school records available to parents, although some states have granted parents such access only if assisted by a school official trained and qualified to interpret the data therein.[115] Viewing the scholastic records helps the parent evaluate his or her child's needs and check on the accuracy of the reports included in it. Generally speaking, a parent with access to a record may also consent to its disclosure to others, and such action may not always be in the best interests of the child. Delaware, addressing itself to this problem, has determined that "[a] minor having reached the age of fourteen shall be considered an adult" for the purpose of its law restricting disclosure of pupils' school records.[116] Upon reaching the age of fourteen, the minor has the right to designate the school, college, employer or physician who may be a recipient.

The right of a parent to gain access to his or her child's school record was, until recently, an issue on which little law existed. The most significant developments had occurred in New York in the early 1960s. There, the state Department of Education had directed that parents of public school children be permitted to inspect the records of their children.[117] Such records included communications between school psychologists and students, and a section of the New York Education Law made communications between a psychologist and his or her "client" confidential and privileged.[118] The department held, however, that because the students were minors, the parents or guardians were, in fact, the "clients," and were thus not precluded from receiving the information.[119]

This result was upheld by the New York courts in 1961 in *Van Allen v.*

McCleary.[120] The parent in that case had heard from faculty members that his son was in need of psychological treatment. He retained the services of a private physician and then requested his son's school records. This demand was refused. The court stated that adoption of compulsory education in New York State did not deprive a parent of his "natural rights in the vital area of the education of his child."[121] It cited the common law rule that, when not detrimental to the public interest, persons with sufficient interest have a right to inspect records of a public nature. Emphasizing the obvious interest which a parent has in the school records of his child, the court held as a matter of law that a parent is entitled to those records.[122] The paucity of other litigation suggests that, at the time, *Van Allen* represented the settled view.[123]

A major clarification of this area of law occurred when Congress enacted the Family Educational Rights and Privacy Act of 1974, commonly referred to as the "Buckley Amendment."[124] This law mandates that no federal funds be made available under any education program to any school, college, or educational agency which denies parents access to their children's records. Since the overwhelming majority of American educational institutions receive federal funds through some program or mechanism,[125] and extremely few choose to risk losing such funds, this law and its corresponding regulations[126] represent the current national standard on the subject.

Besides granting parents access to all of their children's school records, the Buckley Amendment and associated regulations give parents the right to challenge information which they believe is inaccurate, misleading, or otherwise in violation of a student's rights; it also sets forth hearing and appeals procedures to resolve conflicts over the amendment of records. The rules also provide that information from a student's record may, in general, not be shared with third parties without the written agreement of the parent. However, records may be released with such consent to other school officials and elementary or secondary school systems in which the student intends to enroll; to federal officials in connection with federally supported education programs; in response to judicial orders or subpoenas; to "state and local . . . authorities to whom information is specifically required to be reported or disclosed pursuant to State statute adopted prior to November 19, 1974";[127] for testing and accreditation purposes; and in health or safety emergency situations.[128]

Although the Act and regulations refer to students' rights, in practically all cases the exercise of those rights is accorded to parents until the students attain age eighteen or enter an institution of higher education, at which point the rights are accorded to the student.[129] Congress, however, did not necessarily deny such rights to the minors themselves. "[T]he Act and the regulations . . . shall not be construed to preclude educational agencies or institutions from according to students rights in addition to those accorded to parents of students."[130] Such rights can also be accorded to minor students through legislation in the individual states.

Testimonial Privilege

Privileges are evidentiary rules designed to protect the confidential nature of certain disclosures or communications which have been deemed less important to the fact-finding process than an individual's privacy. The word "privilege" stems from the Latin phrase *privata lex,* meaning a prerogative given to a particular person or class of persons.[131] Basically, there are three types of privileges: (1) those designed to protect the individual (for example, the privilege against self-incrimination); (2) those designed to protect the maintenance of government (such as the informer's privilege); and (3) those designed to encourage participation in relationships which are dependent for their effectiveness on full mutual disclosure by the participants and which are sufficiently important to merit state protection (for example, the attorney-client privilege).[132] To the minor receiving mental health treatment who wants to maintain the confidentiality of communications with a professional from whom he or she is seeking aid, a privilege may afford extra protection from unwanted disclosure. This is especially true if the privilege is not merely testimonial, preventing disclosure in a judicial setting, but extends to general disclosure of the minor's communications.

An adolescent with a mental health problem may wish to seek aid from a physician, a psychologist, a psychiatrist, a school teacher or counselor, or a social worker. Whether his or her communications with these professionals are privileged will be discussed below.

Physician-Patient Privilege

At common law neither the patient nor the physician possessed a privilege to refuse disclosing a communication of one to the other in a judicial setting.[133] In addition, neither could claim a privilege that would prevent disclosure to a third party. In 1828, New York passed the first physician-patient privileged communications law,[134] and since then over two-thirds of the states have enacted similar legislation.[135] These statutes prohibit a physician from disclosing information of a confidential nature acquired while attending a patient in a professional capacity. Without such statutory protection, the doctor's duty to refrain from disclosing the patient's communications is usually predicated upon his or her professional code of ethics,[136] an invasion of privacy,[137] or libel.[138] In these situations, however, if the doctor is acting in good faith and makes disclosure only to relevant parties[139] or is acting in the public interest,[140] he or she may escape liability unless the patient can show some malice on the doctor's part in disclosing the confidential information.[141]

In states where there is no physician-patient privilege, arguably there is no evidence that patients are more reluctant to divulge confidential information than in states which do provide this privilege.[142] However, as one author suggests, because mental illness bears so great a stigma, there is a "good deal more reason for supposing that a person who consults a psychiatrist intends to speak in confidence than the automobile-accident plaintiff [who consults a lawyer]."[143] In support of this conclusion, it should be noted that, according to the weight of authority, a physician-patient privilege can be used to prevent a physician from testifying as to a patient's mental condition, even when such mental condition was not the occasion of the patient's consulting the doctor.[144]

Generally, the physician-patient statutes are for the protection of the patient and cannot be claimed by the physician or by an adverse party.[145] (But query: as a legal guardian or parent is not an adverse party, may either be able to waive the privilege on behalf of the minor?)[146] Most of these statutes contain a common clause which prohibits the disclosure of communications which arise in the course of the professional relationship. If the minor is formally seeking medical aid, he or she should be deemed to have established such a relationship. Another recurring requisite of the privilege is that the communications be of a confidential nature.[147] The privilege may be eliminated in certain situations where there is a strong public policy in favor of disclosure, for example, venereal disease or narcotics addiction,[148] but a minor's confidential communications with respect to mental illness do not appear to trigger these public policy considerations.

One court in particular[149] has recognized the necessity of preserving the confidentiality of communications reflecting one's mental health:

The psychiatric patient confides more utterly than anyone else in the world. He exposes to the therapist not only what his words directly express; he lays bare his entire self, his dreams, his fantasies, his sins and his shames. Most patients who undergo psychotherapy know that this is what will be expected of them, and that they cannot get help except on that condition. . . . It would be too much to expect them to do so if they know that all they say . . . may be revealed to the whole world from a witness stand.

Unfortunately, in applying the privilege, a distinction has sometimes been drawn between treatment for physical and mental illness, with courts refusing to accord to the latter the privilege applicable to the former. As a psychiatrist holds an M.D. degree, it seems reasonable to assume that a mentally ill patient's communications would be covered by the physician-patient privilege.[150] Many courts do not accept this assumption, however, and if the state law does not provide for a specific psychotherapist-patient privilege, patients receiving mental health care may be entitled to less protection of their confidential communications than those who are being treated for a physical ailment.[151]

Psychotherapist-Patient Privilege

Psychotherapy as a term is meant to embrace:[152]

that relationship which exists between two persons (or more) where one (or more) is seeking help in the solution of a mental problem caused by psychological and/or environmental pressures from another whose training and status are such as to warrant other persons confiding in him for the purpose of such help.

The common law did not provide protection against disclosure of psychotherapist-patient communications. Even now, very few states have one privilege which covers all those who provide psychotherapy. Usually this privilege is extended only to persons in recognized professions, such as psychologists or psychiatrists, and it may differ in each case. Some states have a psychologist-patient privilege statute, but no psychiatrist-patient privilege statute, or vice versa, and courts have limited the extent of the privilege to the specific type of psychotherapist denominated therein.[153] For example, if the privilege is a psychiatrist-patient privilege, the court may not extend the privilege's protection to communications between a psychologist and patient.[154]

Perhaps surprisingly, psychologist-patient privileged communications statutes are more prevalent than those dealing with psychiatrist-patient communications. The former are generally of two types. The first equates the privilege with that of the attorney-client relationship.[155] A statute worded thusly will be broader in scope than the physician-patient privilege or other psychologist-patient privilege laws, because the attorney-client privilege protects any and all communications between attorney and client in the course of the professional relationship, unless they are in furtherance of a criminal or fraudulent act.[156] The second type delineates specific exemptions to the psychologist-patient privilege,[157] or, conversely, it specifically describes the subjects covered. The psychiatrist-patient privilege statutes likewise generally spell out the specific scope of the privilege.[158]

The Connecticut psychiatrist-patient statute is exemplary in its explicit instructions regarding consent for disclosure.[159] It speaks in terms of the consent of the "patient or his authorized representative," the word "patient" being defined as "a person, who communicates with, or is treated by, a psychiatrist in diagnosis or treatment."[160] Presumably, therefore, the statute confers no rights on a minor's parents to consent to disclosure without authorization. Under this statute, a patient's confidential communications may be revealed without his or her consent in only four types of circumstances: (1) to others engaged in his or her diagnosis or treatment, (2) when there is substantial risk of imminent physical injury by the patient to himself or herself or to others,[161] (3) for the collection of fees for services, or (4) in certain legal proceedings.[162]

Several authors have urged the adoption of a privilege which would protect the general function of psychotherapy rather than the specific therapies of one or two professions.[163] Many of the persons who treat the mentally disabled, such as those engaged in social casework, psychology, psychiatry, counselling, and guidance, provide separate but not distinct forms of treatment. Under the circumstances, a psychotherapist-patient privilege seems to afford the best, most comprehensive protection. In particular, this all-emcompassing privilege would be best for the minor receiving mental health treatment. Oftentimes he or she may be unaware of professional differences or unable to afford one type of professional over another; moreover, a social worker or a school counselor may be more available, and the minor's needs for confidentiality in these situations are as great as those of the patient of a licensed psychologist or psychiatrist.

In his treatise on evidence Dean Wigmore advanced four tests for determining whether a privilege should be adopted:[164]

(1) Does the communication in the usual circumstances of the given professional relationship originate in the confidence that it will not be disclosed?

(2) Is the inviolability of that confidence essential to the achievement of the purpose of the relationship?

(3) Is the relation one that should be fostered?

(4) Is the expected injury to the relationship through the fear of later disclosure greater than the expected benefit to justice in obtaining the testimony?

Professor Ralph Slovenko has analyzed the psychotherapist-patient privilege using Wigmore's formula:[165]

(1) Communicatons of this type are essentially of a confidential and secret nature.

(2) They are less likely to be made and far more difficult to obtain if the patient knows that they may be revealed during the course of some future lawsuit.

(3) The psychotherapist-patient relationship is one which should be fostered.

(4) This type of information if revealed would produce far fewer benefits to justice than it would injury to the entire field of psychotherapy.

Two states, California[166] and Massachusetts,[167] have statutory privileges which purport to apply to psychotherapists. The Massachusetts statute, however, limits its definition of psychotherapist to "a person licensed to practice medicine who devotes a substantial portion of his time to the practice of psychiatry."[168] Thus it affords no protection to a Massachusetts minor receiving therapy from a social worker or psychologist.[169]

The California statute provides what is truly a psychotherapist-patient privilege as that term is used herein. It applies not only to persons licensed to practice medicine, but also to psychologists, clinical social workers, persons who serve as school psychologists, and persons licensed as marriage, family or child counselors. The California privilege is limited by only a few exceptions, for example, it contains the patient-litigant exception, as do most privileges,[170] and no privilege exists if the patient is a child under the age of sixteen and the psychotherapist has reason to believe that the patient has been the victim of a crime.[171] Yet even this California law, which seems by far the most protective and comprehensive of any state, has its critics. They argue that the psychotherapist privilege should be extended further to require even nondisclosure of the patient's identity to prevent the patient from suffering any embarrassment associated with receiving mental health treatment.[172]

Social Worker-Client Privilege

California has recognized the importance of fostering and protecting the social worker-client relationship by incorporating it into its general psychotherapist privilege. Few other states have recognized the need for maintaining confidentiality in this area.[173] Yet the goal of the social work profession is to help people learn to live with the pressures of life, a task also performed by doctors, lawyers and clergymen,[174] all of whom are generally covered by some form of testimonial privilege. For the minor receiving mental health care and counselling from a social worker, the privilege is an equally necessary prerequisite to establishing the needed relationship between professional and client.[175] It is also needed because there is always the danger that a social worker's testimony or records may be incorrectly interpreted.[176] To protect a therapeutic relationship, it should even take precedence over the right of a parent to have all relevant information about a minor child.

School Official-Student Privilege

Often a minor in need of mental health treatment will turn to the nearest professional for help—usually a school official, a teacher, a school guidance counselor or psychologist, or a school nurse. As discussed previously, several states provide for the confidentiality of a student's school records. Several states also give student-school official communications the status of privileged communications. Michigan, for example, provides a very broad privilege to the confidential communications between a student and a teacher, guidance officer, school executive or other professional person engaged in character building.[177] The protections of the far-reaching Michigan privilege are, however, vitiated by the fact that parents of a minor under eighteen may consent to the disclosure of such communications.

Other states limit the scope of the privilege to communications between a student and a "school staff member,"[178] a "school counselor,"[179] or a "school psychologist."[180] Finally, one state, Wisconsin, recognizes that a student in a college or university may also need the communications privilege. Its law[181] provides that:

[n]o dean of men, dean of women or dean of students at any institution of higher education in this state, or any school psychologist at any school in this state, shall be allowed to disclose communications made . . . in the course of counselling a student. . . .

Conclusion

One commentator[182] has concluded that:

As long as mental illness carries with it a stigma which does not attach to other forms of disease, patients should receive legislative protection against possible social disgrace resulting from publicity.

For minors as well as adults, the problem of undue publicity can be partially met through laws affording present and former mental patients access to and authority over the dissemination of their records to anyone without a legitimate and vital interest therein. Confidentiality of certain records, with access strictly limited, is now assured in some jurisdictions; this right should be expanded in all jurisdictions to cover hospital and mental institution records, juvenile court records, law enforcement records, and school records.

The problem of undue publicity can also be met through a broad psychotherapist privilege. The theory behind testimonial and other communications privileges is that forced disclosure is justified only if society's interest in a communication outbalances the social utility of a professional relationship. For the minor receiving mental health care, confidentiality of communications is indispensable to a beneficial working relationship between minor and therapist. To maintain this relationship, the privilege should arguably require nondisclosure even to parents in the absence of the minor's consent.

Notes

1. For a discussion of the rights of the mentally retarded, *see* C. Murdock, *Civil Rights of the Mentally Retarded: Some Critical Issues,* 48 Notre Dame Law. 133 (1972).

2. W. Curran, B. Stearns & H. Kaplan, *Privacy, Confidentiality and Other*

Legal Considerations in the Establishment of a Centralized Health-Data System, 281 New Eng. J. of Med. 241 (1969).

3. *See* G. Melchiode and M. Jacobson, *Psychiatric Treatment: A Barrier to Employment Progress,* 18:2 J. of Occupational Med. 98 (Feb. 1976); J. Foreman, *Ex-Mental Patients Need Not Apply,* Boston Globe, May 25, 1976, at 21; *Public Rejects Former Patients, Study Shows,* N.Y. Ment. Hyg. News, May 7, 1976, at 7; Glassman v. N.Y. Medical College, 64 Misc. Repts. 2d 466 (N.Y. Supr. Ct., N.Y. Cnty., Sept. 29, 1970); Matthews v. Hardy, 420 F.2d 607, 610 (D.C. Cir. 1969), *cert. denied* 90 S. Ct. 1231 (1970).

4. U.S. Dep't. of HEW, Public Opinions and Attitudes About Mental Health 12 (1963).

5. *Id.*

6. *Id.,* at 8.

7. M. Lewis, *Confidentiality in the Community Mental Health Center,* 37 Amer. J. of Orthopsychiat. 946 (Oct. 1967). *See also* Weinhofen, Legal Services and Community Mental Health Centers (1969).

8. Berry v. Moench, 8 Utah 2d 191, 331 P.2d 814 (1958).

9. R. Pound, *Interests of Personality,* 28 Harv. L. Rev. 343, 362 (1915).

10. O. Ruebhausen & O. Brim, Jr., *Privacy and Behavioral Research,* 65 Colum. L. Rev. 1184 (1965).

11. *Id.,* at 1186.

12. E. Bloustein, *Privacy as an Aspect of Human Dignity: An Answer to Dean Prosser,* 39 N.Y.U. L. Rev. 962 (1964).

13. 381 U.S. 479 (1965).

14. 405 U.S. 438 (1971).

15. Carey v. Population Services International, 97 S. Ct. 2010 (1977).

16. Danforth v. Planned Parenthood Association of Central Missouri, 428 U.S. 52 (1976) and Bellotti v. Baird, 428 U.S. 132 (1976), discussed in chapter 6 at notes 3, 61, and 62.

17. 230 A.2d 907 (Sup. Ct. N.J., 1967).

18. *Id.,* at 911.

19. Merriken v. Cressman, 364 F. Supp. 913 (E.D. Pa. 1973).

20. *Id.,* at 918.

21. *See* W. Prosser, *Privacy,* 48 Calif. L. Rev. 383, 386-39 (1960).

22. Okla. Stat. Ann. 21, § 839.1 (1973 Supp.).

23. Ariz. Const. Art. 2, § 8.

24. Turley v. State, 48 Ariz. 61, 59 P.2d 312 (1936).

25. Ill. Const. Art. 1, § 6.

26. Note 19 above.

27. 446 F.2d 65 (2d Cir. 1971).

28. *Id.,* at 71.

29. *Id.,* at 72.

30. *Compare* parents' and minors' power to waive rights in the juvenile justice context, discussed in chapter 2, at note 223 *et seq.*

31. Consent by parent to search of son's room approved. State v. Kinderman, 136 N.W.2d 577 (S. Ct. Minn. 1965); State v. Vidor, 452 P.2d 961 (S. Ct. Wash. 1969). *Contra* People v. Flowers, 179 N.W. 2d 56 (Mich. App. 1970); Reeves v. Warden, 346 F.2d 915 (4th Cir. 1965).

32. State v. Stein, 456 P.2d 1 (Kan. 1969).

33. Note 19 above.

34. *Id.,* at 919.

35. Chapter 4 at note 95 *et seq.*

36. *See, e.g.,* Colo. Rev. Stat., § 41-2-13 (1971 Supp.); Alabama Code, tit. 22, § § 105 (15)-(18) (1973 Supp.); Mass. Gen. Laws Ann. ch. 112, § 12F (1976 Supp.).

37. Cal. Civ. Code, § 34.6 (1977 Supp.). For a discussion of the effects of this law, *see Medical Care and the Independent Minor,* 10 Santa Clara Law. 334 (1970).

38. Minn. S.A. § 144.346 (1973 Supp.).

39. Curran, Stearns & Kaplan, note 2 above.

40. A.M.A. Principles of Medical Ethics, § 9 (1957).

41. *See, e.g.,* Ohio Rev. Code Ann., § 4732.17(D) (1972 Supp.); Cal. Bus. and Prof. Code § 2960(g) (1974 Supp.).

42. K. Karst, *"The Files": Legal Controls Over the Accuracy and Accessibility of Stored Personal Data,* 31 Law and Contemp. Probs. 342, 347 (1966).

43. Simonsen v. Swenson, 104 Neb. 224, 177 N.W. 831 (1920).

44. 379 U.S. 64 (1964).

45. *Id.,* at 72 n.8.

46. *See* Curtis Publishing Co. v. Butts, 388 U.S. 130 (1967); Monitor Patriot Co. v. Ray, 401 U.S. 265 (1971); and Cox Broadcasting Corp. v. Cohn, 420 U.S. 469 (1975).

47. Karst, note 42 above, at 351.

48. C. Lister, M. Baker & R. Milhous, *Record Keeping, Access, and Confidentiality,* in Issues in the Classification of Children (N. Hobbs ed. 1975), at 544, 548.

49. 5 U.S.C.A. § 552.

50. 5 U.S.C.A. § 552 (b)(6).

51. 13 U.S.C.A. § 8.

52. Miss. Code Ann. § 41-9-65 (1972).

53. Alaska Stat. Ann. § 09.25.120 (1973 Supp.); Cal. Gov. Code § 6253 (1974 Supp.).

54. Iowa Code Ann. § 68A.7 (1973).

55. Cal. Govt. Code § 6254 (1974 Supp.).

56. Without an express statutory prohibition, the issue is unclear. In Oregon, for example, access to hospital records is limited by statute to "[a]ny party legally liable or against whom a claim is asserted. . . ." Ore. Rev. Stat. § 441.810 (1971).

A rare instance of judicial attention to this issue occurred recently in New Jersey. There, in 1976, a trial court refused to order that the mental hospital records of a 13-year-old involuntarily committed girl be made available to the mother who had applied for her commitment. The court ruled that information for the mother must come from the guardian *ad litem* whom the court had appointed to safeguard the child's interests. Matter of J.C.G., 366 A.2d 733 (N.J., Hudson Cnty. Ct. 1976).

57. Mass. Gen. Laws Ann. ch. 111, § 70 (1969). However, a 1974 survey of 16 Boston area hospitals by the Boston University Center for Law and Health Sciences found only one that unequivocally recognized the right of patient access upon request. The others indicated varying degrees of noncompliance with the law, including three which claimed never to grant access. Boston Globe, March 1, 1974, at 12.

58. Conn. Gen. Stat. Ann. § 4-104 (1969 Supp.)

59. Ill. Ann. Stat. 51, § 71 (1974 Supp.).

60. D.C.C.E. § 21-562 (1967).

61. Code of Ala. 22 § 336(1) (1971 Supp.); Gen. Stat. of N.C. § 122-8.1 (1973 Supp.).

62. Maine Rev. Stat. Ann. 34 § 2256 (1973 Supp.); Cal. Welf. and Inst. Code § 5328.1 (1972).

63. Ill. Ann. Stat. 91 1/2 § 12-3 (1974 Supp.); Rev. Stat. of Neb. § 83-109 (1971).

64. Alaska Stat. Ann. § 47.30.260 (1971); Fla. Stat. Ann. § 394.459(9) (1974 Supp.); Code of Ga. Ann. § 88-502.10 (1971); Haw. Rev. Stat. § 334-5 (1973 Supp.); Idaho Code § 66-348 (1969); Ind. Stat. Ann. § 22-1331 (1973 Supp.); Kan. Stat. Ann. § 59-2931 (1973 Supp.); Ky. Rev. Stat. Ann. § 210.233 (1972); N.J. Stat. Ann. § 30:4-24.3 (1973 Supp.); N.M. Stat. Ann. § 34-2-17 (1973 Supp.); N.D. Century Code § 25-03-22 (1970); Ohio Rev. Code Ann. § 5122.31 (1970); Code of Laws of S.C. Ann. § 32-1022 (1973 Supp.); Tenn. Code Ann. § 33-306(j) (1955); Tex. Civ. Stat. Ann. art. 5547-87 (1958); Utah Code Ann. § 64-7-50 (1955); Vt. Stat. Ann. § 7103 (1968); Wyo. Stat. Ann. § 25-74 (1967).

65. Alaska Stat. Ann. § 47.30.260 (1971).

66. Lister, *et al.,* note 48 above, at 552. This problem may be rectified to a degree by lowering the age after which a parent's consent may not be substituted for a minor's.

67. Idaho Code § 66-348(3)(b) (1969).

68. Cal. Welf. & Inst. Code § 5328(i) (1974).

69. Cal. Welf. & Inst. Code § 5328(e); Ann. Code of Md. art. 43, § 1-I (1971); Fla. Stat. Ann. § 394.459(9)(c)(d) (1974 Supp.).

70. Fla. Stat. Ann. § 394.459(c) (1974 Supp.).

71. La. Rev. Stat. Ann. § 44:7(B) (1974 Supp.).

72. Tex. Civ. Stat. Ann. art. 5547-87(a)(4) (1958).

73. Mass. Gen. Laws Ann. ch. 151(B) § 4 (1974 Supp.).

74. *Id.,* at § 4 (9A).

75. B. Ennis, *Civil Liberties and Mental Illness,* 7 Crim. L. Bull. 101, 123 (1971).

76. Cal. Welf. & Inst. Code § 5328.9 (1974 Supp.).

77. 387 U.S. 1 (1967). Discussed in chapter 2 at note 215 *et seq.,* in chapter 6 at note 31, and in chapter 7 at notes 69-70.

78. *Id.,* at 33, 36, 55 and 56.

79. McKeiver v. Pennsylvania, 403 U.S. 528 (1971).

80. C. Cashman, *Confidentiality of Juvenile Court Proceedings: A Review,* 24 Juv. Just. 30 (Aug. 1973). *See also* M. Altman, *Juvenile Information Systems: A Comparative Analysis,* 24 Juv. Just. 2 (Feb. 1974). A question beyond the scope of this discussion is whether the ever-increasing amount of information collected and recorded on each juvenile offender actually contributes in any way to his, her, or society's welfare. *See* E. Czajkoski, *Computer Backfire on the Ethical Mission of Juvenile Justice,* 24:4 Juv. Just. 24 February 1974).

81. *Id.,* at 31.

82. Minn. Stat. Ann. §§ 260.161 and 260.211 (1973 Supp.).

83. Wyo. Stat. Ann. § 14-115.41 (1973 Supp.). *See also* Code of Ga. Ann. § 24A-3503 (1972); Haw. Rev. Stat. § 571-84 (1973 Supp.); Ill. Ann. Stat. ch. 37, § 702-8 (1972); La. Rev. Stat. Ann. § 13:1586.1 (1974 Supp.); Nev. Rev. Stat. § 62.265 (1973); N.D. Century Code § 27-20-53 (1973 Supp.); Vt. Stat. Ann. 33, § 664 (1973 Supp.); Wyo. Stat. Ann. § 14-115.41 (1973 Supp.).

84. Fla. Stat. Ann. § 39.03(6)(1) (1974 Supp.).

85. *Compare* N.Y. Family Court Act § 784 (1963) (arrest records) and § 746 (1973 Supp.) (probation officer's reports).

86. Cal. Welf. & Inst. Code § 828 (1974 Supp.).

87. Haw. Rev. Stat. § 571-84 (1973 Supp.).

88. Ill. Ann. Stat. ch. 37, § 702-8 (1972); La. Rev. Stat. Ann. § 13:1586.1 (1974 Supp.); Ann. Code of Md. art. 26, § 70-24 (1973 Supp.); Minn. Stat. Ann. § 260.161 (1971); Mo. Ann. Stat. § 211.321 (1973 Supp.); Code of Va. Ann. § 16.1-163 (1960); Wisc. Stat. Ann. § 58.26 (1957).

89. Code of Ga. Ann. § 24A-3502 (1972); Ky. Rev. Stat. Ann. § 208.340; N.Y. Family Court Act § 784 (1963); N.D. Century Code § 27-20-52 (1973 Supp.); Pa. Stat. Ann. § 50-335 (1973 Supp.); Tex. Civ. Code Ann. (Family Code) § 51.14 (1973 Supp.); Vt. Stat. Ann. ch. 33, § 663 (1973 Supp.).

90. Cal. Welf. & Inst. Code § 827 (1974 Supp.); Ky. Rev. Stat. Ann. § 202,340 (1972); Rev. Code of Wash. Ann. § 13.04,230 (1973 Supp.).

91. Watkins v. U.S., 343 F.2d 278 n.1 (D.C. Cir. 1965).

92. Cal. Ed. Code § 10751(d) (1974 Supp.); Conn. Gen. Stat. Ann. § 17-66 (1973 Supp.).

93. Conn. Gen. Stat. Ann. § 17-66 (1973 Supp.).

94. Haw. Rev. Stat. § 571-84 (1974 Supp.); Ohio Rev. Code Ann. § 2151.14 (1968); S.D.C.L. § 26-8-33 (1967).

95. D.C.C.D. § 11-1586(b) (1966).

96. *Id. See also* Kent v. U.S., 343 F.2d 247 (D.C. Cir. 1965).

97. Minn. Stat. Ann. § 260.161 (1971).

98. N.Y. Family Court Act § 746 (1973).

99. Ore. Rev. Stat. § 419.562(2) (1971).

100. Conn. Gen. Stat. Ann. § 17-66 (1973 Supp.); Wyo. Stat. Ann. § 14-115.22 (1973 Supp.).

101. Code of Ala. ch. 13, § 353 (1958); Alaska Stat. Ann. § 09.25.120 (1973 Supp.); Conn. Gen. Stat. Ann. § 17-57(a) (1973 Supp.); D.C.C.E. § 11-1586 (1966); Code of Ga. Ann. § 24A-3501 (1972); Haw. Rev. Stat. § 571-84 (1973 Supp.); Maine Rev. Stat. Ann. ch. 15, § 2606 (1973 Supp.); Mass. Gen. Laws Ann. ch. 119, § 60A (1969); Minn. Stat. Ann. § 260.161 (1971); Mo. Ann. Stat. § 211.321 (1973 Supp.); Nev. Rev. Stat. § 62.270 (1973); N.H. Rev. Stat. Ann. § 169:22 (1964); Gen. Stat. of N.C. § 7A-287 (1969); N.D. Century Code § 27-20-51 (1973 Supp.); Ore. Rev. Stat. § 419.567 (1971); Pa. Stat. Ann. § 50-334 (1973 Supp.); Code of S.C. Ann. § 15-1209 (1962); S.D.C.L. § 26-8-33 (1967); Tex. Civ. Code (Family Code) § 51.14 (1973 Supp.); Code of Va. Ann. § 16.1-162 (1960); Wyo. Stat. Ann. § 14-115.40 (1973 Supp.).

102. Pa. Stat. Ann. § 50-334 (1973 Supp.).

103. Code of Ala. ch. 13, § 353 (1958); D.C.C.E. § 11-1586 (1966); Mass. Gen. Laws Ann. ch. 119, § 60A (1969); Gen. Stat. of N.C. § 7A-287 (1969); N.D. Century Code § 27-20-51 (1973 Supp.); Ore. Rev. Stat. § 419.567 (1971); Pa. Stat. Ann. § 50-334 (1973 Supp.).

104. S.D.C.L. § 26-8-33 (1967).

105. Colo. Rev. Stat. § 22-8-1(4) (1963); Rev. Code of Mont. § 10-633 (1968); N.H. Rev. Stat. Ann. § 169:27 (1964).

106. Conn. Gen. Stat. Ann. § 51-21 (1973 Supp.); Miss. Code § 43-21-19 (1972); Code of Va. Ann. § 16.1-162 (1960).

107. Miss. Code § 43-21-19 (1972).

108. Ill. Ann. Stat. ch. 122, § 22-26 (1974 Supp.).

109. Ariz. Rev. Stat. Ann. § 8-247 (1973 Supp.); Cal. Welf. & Inst. Code § 781 (1974 Supp.); Conn. Gen. Stat. Ann. § 17-72a (1973 Supp.); Fla. Stat. Ann. § 39.12 (1974 Supp.); Code of Ga. Ann. § 24A-3504 (1972); La. Rev. Stat. Ann. 13:1586.1 (1974 Supp.); N.D. Century Code § 27-10-54 (1973 Supp.); Tex. Civ. Code (Family Code) § 51.16 (1973 Supp.); Vt. Stat. Ann. ch. 33, § 665 (1973 Supp.); Rev. Code of Wash. Ann. § 13.04.250 (1973 Supp.).

110. Colo. Rev. Stat. § 21-1-11; Ind. Stat. Ann. Code Ed. § 31-5-7-16 (1973 Supp.); Ann. Code of Md. art. 26, § 70-21 (1973 Supp.); Mass. Gen. Laws Ann. ch. 276, § 100B (1972); Mo. Ann. Stat. § 211.321 (1973 Supp.); Nev. Rev. Stat. § 62.275 (1973); N.J. Stat. Ann. § 2A:4-39.1 (1973 Supp.); Ohio

Rev. Code Ann. § 2151.36 (1972 Supp.); Wyo. Stat. Ann. § 14-115.42 (1973 Supp.).

111. La. Rev. Stat. Ann. § 13:1586.1(C) (1974 Supp.). One of the dilemmas posed by such statutes was highlighted recently by an incident in Boston, where police charged a school bus driver with the rape of two retarded children, passengers in his vehicle. The suspect's past criminal record reportedly includes more than twenty years of moral offenses against juveniles. (M. Barnicle, *An Individual's Privacy vs. Children's Safety,* Boston Globe, July 11, 1977, at 21). The bus company employer maintains that it is unable to learn of such past offenses while screening prospective employees because of a Massachusetts statute (Mass. Gen. Laws Ann. ch. 6, § 172) which prohibits dissemination of criminal record information to all but authorized parties.

112. Miss. Code § 37-15-1 (1972).

113. Miss. Code § 37-15-1 (1972); *see also* Iowa Code Ann. § 68A.7 (1973 Supp.).

114. Cal. Ed. Code § 10751 (1974 Supp.); Del. Code Ann. ch. 14, § 4114 (1970); Maine Rev. Stat. Ann. ch. 20, § 805 (1973 Supp.); Ore. Rev. Stat. § 336.191 (1971).

115. *E.g.,* Oregon's school records law provides: "student behavior records shall be released only in the presence of an individual qualified to explain or interpret the records." Ore. Rev. Stat. § 336.195(2) (1971).

116. Del. Code Ann. ch. 14, § 4114(b) (1970).

117. A. LoGatto, *Privileged Communications and the Social Worker,* 8 Cath. Law. 5, 11 (Winter 1962).

118. N.Y. Ed. Law, § 7611.

119. *Id.,* at 11 and 12, *citing* In the Matter of Thibadeau, N.Y. Dept. of Educ. No. 6849 (Sept. 22, 1960).

120. 27 Misc. 2d 81, 211 N.Y.S.2d 501 (Sup. Ct. 1961).

121. *Id.,* at 511.

122. *Id.,* at 513.

123. Comment, *Parental Right to Inspect School Records,* 20 Buffalo L. Rev. 255, 265 (Fall, 1970). *See also* Johnson v. Bd. of Educ. of City of N.Y., 31 Misc. 2d 810, 220 N.Y.S.2d 362 (Sup. Ct. 1961).

124. P.L. 93-380 (Aug. 21, 1974).

125. The act applies even to institutions which may receive funds from students who have themselves received those funds for educational purposes under a federal grant or loan program. 45 C.F.R. 99.1, 41:118 Fed. Reg. 24670 (June 17, 1976).

126. *Id.,* at 41:118 Fed. Reg. 24662, *et seq.*

127. *Id.,* at 45 C.F.R. 99.31(5), 41:118 Fed. Reg. 24673.

128. *Id.,* at 45 C.F.R. 99.31, 41:118 Fed. Reg. 24673.

129. P.L. 93-380, § 438(d). Prior to this point, the student appears to be accorded only one personal right: if he or she has applied for admission to an

institution of higher education, only the student, (regardless of age) and not his or her parent, may waive his or her right to review confidential letters and statements of recommendation concerning such admission. 45 C.F.R. 99.7(d), 41:118 Fed. Reg. 24672. For a discussion (by the brother of the author of the federal act) of the dilemma underlying this waiver provision, *see* W. Buckley, *A Classic Dilemma on Records of College Students,* Boston Globe, Nov. 29, 1974, at 19.

130. 45 C.F.R. 99.4(c), 41:118 Fed. Reg. 24671.

131. D. Coburn, *Child-Parent Communications: Spare the Privilege and Spoil the Child,* 74 Dick. L. Rev. 599, 601 and 602 (1970).

132. R. Fisher, *The Psychotherapeutic Professions and the Law of Privileged Communications,* 10 Wayne L. Rev. 609, 610 (1964).

133. Randa v. Bear, 50 Wash. 2d 415, 312 P.2d 640 (1957); In re Koenig's Estate, 247 Minn. 580, 78 N.W.2d 364 (1956).

134. N.Y. Rev. Stat., 1828 II, 406, Part III, ch. VII, art. 8 § 73.

135. Ariz. Rev. Stat. Ann. § 12-2235 (1956) (civil) and § 13-1802(4) (1972) (criminal); Cal. Evid. Code § 994 (1974 Supp.); D.C.C.E. § 14-307 (1966); Haw. Rev. Stat. § 621-20.5 (1973 Supp.); Idaho Code § 9-203 (1972); Ill. Ann. Stat. 51, § 5.1 (1966); Ind. Stat. Ann. § 2-1714 (1968); Iowa Code Ann. § 622.10 (1973 Supp.); Kan. Stat. Ann. § 60-427 (1973 Supp.); La. Rev. Stat. Ann. 15:476 (1967) and 13:3734 (1974 Supp.); Maine Rev. Stat. Ann. ch. 32, § 3295 (1973 Supp.); Minn. Stat. Ann. § 595.02 (1970); Miss. Code § 13-1-21 (1972); Mo. Ann. Stat. § 491.060(5) (1952); Rev. Stat. of Neb. § 25-1206 (1964); Nev. Rev. Stat. § 49.225 (1973); N.H. Rev. Stat. Ann. § 329:26 (1972); N.J. Stat. Ann. § 2A:84A-22.2 (1973 Supp.); N.Y. Civ. Proc. Law § 4504 (1973 Supp.); Gen. Stat. of N.C. § 8.53 (1973 Supp.); N.D. Century Code § 31-01-06 (1973 Supp.); Ohio Rev. Code Ann. § 2317.02 (1954); Okla. Stat. Ann. 12, § 385; Ore. Rev. Stat. § 44.040(d) (1971); S.D.C.L. § 19-2-3 (1967); Utah Code Ann. § 78-24-8(4) (1967); Code of Va. Ann. § 8-289.1 (1972 Supp.); Wisc. Stat. Ann. § 885.21 (1966); Wyo. Stat. Ann. § 1-139 (1957).

136. Note 40 above.

137. Griffin v. Medical Society of New York, 7 Misc. 549, 11 N.Y.S.2d 109 (1939).

138. Berry v. Moench, 8 Utah 2d 191, 331 P.2d 814 (1958).

139. *Id.,* at 819.

140. Simonsen v. Swenson, 104 Neb. 224, 177 N.W. 831 (1920) (concerned with syphilis).

141. Schwartz v. Thiele, 242 Cal. App. 2d 799, 51 Cal. Rptr. 767 (1966). *See also* Iverson v. Frandsen, 237 F.2d 898 (10th Cir. 1956).

142. M. Guttmacher & H. Weinhofen, Psychiatry and the Law 271 (1952).

143. *Id.*

144. *Anno: Physician-Patient Privilege,* 100 A.L.R.2d 648, 649.

145. *Privilege, In Judicial or Quasi-Judicial Proceedings, Arising From Relationship Between Psychiatrist or Psychologist and Patient,* 44 A.L.R.3d 24 (1973) [hereinafter cited as 44 A.L.R.3d].

146. For a discussion of waiver of minors' rights in another context, *see* chapter 2 at notes 223-49.

147. Milano v. State, 44 Misc. 2d 290, 253 N.Y.S.2d 662 (1964).

148. Guttmacher & Weinhofen, note 142 above, at 274.

149. Taylor v. U.S., 222 F.2d 398 (D.C. Cir. 1955).

150. *See* People v. English, 31 Ill. 2d 301, 201 N.E.2d 455 (1964); Newell v. Newell, 146 Cal. App. 2d 166, 303 P.2d 839 (1956).

151. R. Allen, E. Ferster & J. Rubin, Readings in Law and Psychiatry 156 (1968).

152. Fisher, note 132 above, at 617.

153. 44 A.L.R.3d, note 145 above, at 50.

154. Elliott v. Watkins Trucking Co., 406 F.2d 90 (7th Cir. 1969).

155. Code of Ala. § 297(36) (1971); Ariz. Rev. Stat. Ann. § 32-2085 (1973); Ark. Stat. § 72-1516 (1957); Del. Code Ann. 25, § 3534 (1970); Code of Ga. Ann. § 84-3118 (1970); Idaho Code § 52-2314 (1972); Ky. Rev. Stat. Ann. § 319.111 (1972); Rev. Code of Mont. § 66-3212 (1973 Supp.); Rev. Stat. of Neb. § 71-3826 (1971); N.H. Rev. Stat. Ann. § 330-A:19 (1966); N.Y. Civ. Pract. Law § 4507 (1973 Supp.); Okla. Stat. Ann. 59, § 1372 (1971); Pa. Stat. Ann. ch. 62, § 1213 (1973 Supp.); Rev. Code of Wash. Ann. § 18.83.110 (1973).

156. Allen, Ferster & Rubin, note 151 above, at 157.

157. Conn. Gen. Stat. Ann. § 52-146c (1973 Supp.); Colo. Rev. Stat. § 154-1-1 (1967 Supp.); Fla. Stat. Ann. § 490.32 (1974 Supp.); Ill. Ann. Stat. ch. 91 1/2, § 406 (1966); Ind. Stat. Ann. § 63-3617 (1973 Supp.); Ann. Code of Md. art. 35, § 13A (1973 Supp.); Mich. Stat. Ann. § 14.677(18) (1973 Supp.); Miss. Code § 73-31-29 (1972); N.M. Stat. Ann. § 67-30-17 (1973 Supp.); Gen. Stat. of N.C. Ann. § 8-53.3 (1973 Supp.); Ohio Rev. Code Ann. § 4732.19 (1972); Ore. Rev. Stat. § 44.040(h) (1971); Utah Code Ann. § 58-25-9 (1967).

158. Conn. Gen. Stat. Ann. § 52-146d and 146e (1973 Supp.); Fla. Stat. Ann. § 90.242 (1974 Supp.); Code of Ga. Ann. § 38-418 (1972); Ill. Ann. Stat. ch. 51, § 5.2 (1974 Supp.); Ky. Rev. Stat. Ann. § 421.215 (1972); Maine Rev. Stat. Ann. ch. 16, § 60 (1973 Supp.); Ann. Code of Md. art. 35, § 13A (1973 Supp.).

159. Conn. Gen. Stat. Ann. § 52-146d-f (1973 Supp.).

160. Conn. Gen. Stat. Ann. § 52-146d (1973 Supp.).

161. *See, e.g.,* Tarasoff v. Regents of Univ. of Cal., 529 P.2d 553, 118 Cal. Rptr. 129 (1974); 551 P.2d 334, 131 Cal. Rptr. 14 (1976); criticized in A. Stone, *The Tarasoff Decisions: Suing Psychotherapists to Safeguard Society,* 90 Harv. L. Rev. 358 (1976).

162. Conn. Gen. Stat. Ann. § 52-146f (1973 Supp.).

163. Note, *The Psychotherapists' Privilege*, 12 Washburn L.J. 297, 311 (Spring 1973) [hereinafter cited as *Psychotherapists' Privilege*] ; Fisher, note 132 above, at 612.

164. J. Wigmore, 8 *Evidence* § 2285 (McNaughton rev. 1961). *See also* R. Morris & A. Moritz, Doctor and Patient and the Law 282 (5th ed. 1971).

165. R. Slovenko, *Psychiatry and a Second Look at the Medical Privilege,* 6 Wayne L. Rev. 175, at 202 n.87 (Spring 1960). *See also* Dubey, *Confidentiality as a Requirement of the Therapist: Technical Necessities for Absolute Privilege in Psychotherapy,* 131 Am. J. Psychiat. 1093 (1974).

166. Cal. Evid. Code § § 1010, 1012 (1974 Supp.).

167. Mass. Gen. Laws Ann. ch. 233, § 20B (1973 Supp.).

168. Mass. Gen. Laws Ann. ch. 233, § 20B (1973 Supp.).

169. S. Fox, *Psychotherapy and Legal Privilege,* 53 Mass. L.Q. 307, 312 (1968).

170. In re Lifschutz, 2 Cal. 3d 415, 467 P.2d 557, 85 Cal. Rptr. 829 (1970). Cal. Evid. Code. § 1016 (1974 Supp.).

171. Cal. Evid. Code § 1027 (1974 Supp.).

172. *Psychotherapists' Privilege,* note 163 above, at 301. There would be a statutory exception in the case of a patient dangerous to himself or others. Cal. Evid. Code § 1024 (1974 Supp.). In the case of danger to others, there might even be a duty to warn. Tarasoff v. Regents of Univ. of Cal., note 161 above.

173. La. Rev. Stat. Ann. 73:2714 (1974 Supp.); N.Y. Civ. Pract. Law § 4508 (1973 Supp.).

174. Note, *The Social Worker-Client Relationship and Privileged Communications,* 1965 Wash. U. L.Q. 362, 363 (1965) [hereinafter cited as *Social Worker-Client Relationship*].

175. *See* Biestek, The Casework Relationship 121 (1957).

176. *Social Worker-Client Relationship,* note 174 above, at 380.

177. Mich. Stat. Ann. § 27A.2165 (1973 Supp.). *See also* Pa. Stat. Ann. ch. 24, § 13-1319 (1973 Supp.).

178. Ore. Rev. Stat. § 44.040(i) (1971).

179. Ind. Stat. Ann. § 28-4537 (1970); Maine Rev. Stat. Ann. ch. 20, § 806 (1973 Supp.); Nev. Rev. Stat. § 49.290 (1973); Gen. Stat. of N.C. § 8-53.4 (1973 Supp.); N.D. Century Code § 31-01-06.1 (1973 Supp.); S.D.C.L. § 19-2-5.1 (1967). *See* W. Robinson, *Testimonial Privilege and the School Guidance Counselor,* 25 Syracuse L. Rev. 911 (1974).

180. Idaho Code § 9-203(6) (1972); Ohio Rev. Code Ann. § 4732.19 (1972).

181. Wisc. Stat. Ann. § 885.201 (1973 Supp.).

182. H. Ross, *Commitment of the Mentally Ill: Problems of Law and Policy,* 57 Mich. L. Rev. 945, 998 (1959).

Model Admission Procedures

This chapter contains proposed model procedures for the admission of juveniles to mental health facilities. Based upon the findings in the preceding chapters, these procedures are meant to constitute the basis for the enactment of juvenile admission statutes throughout the United States. Like any proposed legislation in the form of a model code, they should be read as a whole to be fully understood, as many sections relate to others. Unlike draft legislation, however, the procedures have to an extent been written in narrative style rather than in the terse economy of language typical of statutory draftsmanship. It is hoped thereby that they will be more readable and more readily understood by those who are not accustomed to reading statutes. At the same time, each provision can be converted easily into a section or subsection of a new juvenile admission code.

Proposed Model Procedures for Juvenile Admissions to Mental Health Facilities

1. Applicability

The following procedures shall be followed for any admission (other than involuntary civil commitment) of any person under the age of sixteen to inpatient status at any mental health facility (as defined by state statute or regulation). For persons sixteen or over, the procedures for adult voluntary admission or involuntary civil commitment are applicable.

2. Initiation of Juvenile Admission Process

Upon request for admission by the juvenile, his parent, guardian, or legal custodian, and a decision by the admitting officer of a mental health facility that the juvenile should be admitted to inpatient status, the admission procedure described herein in initiated.

3. The Juvenile Advocate Office

The Juvenile Advocate Office shall be located at or near the mental health facility, but not affiliated with or under the control of the hospital or the state department of mental health. The office shall be staffed by one or more Juvenile Advocates (J.A.) assisted by qualified mental health professionals. The number of J.A.'s and other staff members shall be determined by the size of the mental health facility and the number of juveniles to be served. The J.A.'s shall be attorneys licensed to practice in the state.

4. The Juvenile Advocate's Role in the Admission Process

A. After the admitting officer of a mental health facility has decided to admit a juvenile to inpatient status at a facility, he shall notify the Juvenile Advocate's Office of the proposed admission. The office shall assign a J.A. to represent the juvenile throughout the process. As soon as possible following the initiation of the admission process, the J.A. shall interview the juvenile; his parent, guardian or legal custodian; the admitting officer; any examining mental health professional; and anyone else who may have information about the circumstances of, the desirability of, or the necessity of the proposed admission. The J.A. shall advise the juvenile and his parent, guardian or legal custodian of the right of any of these parties to obtain review of the appropriateness of the admission and of the juvenile's right to the least restrictive treatment alternative.

The J.A. shall inform the juvenile that he or she will assist the juvenile in finding less restrictive alternatives to hospitalization (see § 12 below) and will represent him or her in challenging the admission or seeking an admission against the desires of his or her parent, guardian or legal custodian. Throughout the admission process, the J.A. shall advance the juvenile's professed desires, regardless of the J.A.'s personal opinion of the advisability of the proposed admission. The J.A. shall provide a thorough explanation of all relevant facts concerning the admission, including: a description of the living conditions within the facility, the treatments provided by the hospital which may be administered to the juvenile, any significant restrictions which may be imposed on his or her freedom and privacy, and the regulations and policies with which he or she will be required to comply as an inpatient. In addition the J.A. shall advise the juvenile that if he or she is admitted to the facility he or she will be discharged only upon the consent of a parent, guardian, or legal custodian, (see § 13 below) or upon order of the review board following a discharge hearing (§ 14 below), and that requests for discharge hearings will be honored only at specified intervals (§§ 14 & 15 below). The J.A. shall advise the juvenile that his or her case will be reviewed periodically by the J.A. (see §§ 15 & 16 below), and that mandatory review hearings will be scheduled if no discharge hearings are requested (§ 14D below).

B. If, after being fully informed as described above, the juvenile consents to be admitted to the mental health facility, the J.A. shall assess the validity of that consent and judge whether it is competent, knowing, and voluntary. For purposes of this assessment, the consent of any child less than twelve years of age shall be conclusively presumed to be not competent.

5. First Decision: Is An Admission Hearing Required?

A. If the hospital refuses to admit the juvenile the process is not initiated and no hearing is required; the child is not admitted.

B. If the party or parties proposing the admission decide to withdraw their request after meeting with the J.A. (*e.g.,* because less restrictive treatment alternatives are found), the process is not initiated; the child is not admitted.

C. If the facility's admitting officer; the parent, guardian, or legal custodian; *and* the juvenile (after being advised of his or her rights by the J.A., as required by § 4A above) consent to the juvenile's admission, *and* the J.A. determines that the juvenile's consent is competent, knowing, and voluntary (§ 4B above), no admission hearing is required; the juvenile is admitted and the J.A. sends the admissions review board a written report of the admission and the reasons therefore.

D. If the facility's admitting officer agrees to the proposed admission, but the juvenile *or* his or her parent, guardian, or legal custodian withhold their consent to admission, *or* the J.A. finds that the juvenile's consent is invalid (§ 4B above), *or* it is not possible for the J.A. to conduct an interview with the juvenile, an admission hearing (§ 9 below) is required. This hearing must be held within three days of admission if the juvenile is hospitalized prior to the hearing (§ 6 below) and within ten days if he is not hospitalized.

6. Second Decision: Is Emergency Hospitalization Required?

A. When an admission hearing before the admissions review board is required (§ 5D above), a decision shall be made as to whether the juvenile will be hospitalized pending the hearing. The director of each mental health facility shall designate one or more mental health professionals whose duty it shall be to decide whether a juvenile shall be hospitalized; such designated mental health professional shall permit emergency hospitalization only when he finds it *more probable than not* that the following standard has been met:

B. Emergency Hospitalization Standard

(1) The juvenile has a mental disorder; and
(2) Because of this mental disorder the juvenile is in imminent danger of causing serious harm to himself or others, as evidenced by recent overt acts or repeated, continuing, and credible threats of such acts; and
(3) No less restrictive alternative is available.

C. The designated mental health professional may order emergency hospitalization before the J.A. can meet with the juvenile in facilities where, because it may not be possible to staff the J.A. office twenty-four hours a day, the admission may be decided upon during the J.A.'s absence. In such a case, the J.A. shall meet with the juvenile within sixteen hours of the admission. A situation may also arise in which the J.A. decides that the juvenile is so mentally or emotionally disturbed that no interview (as described in § 4A above) can be reasonably conducted. In such a case the J.A. shall interview the juvenile as soon as possible. But no juvenile shall ever be hospitalized prior to an interview with the J.A. unless the designated mental health professional has found it to be more probable than not that the emergency hospitalization standard (§ 6B above) has been met.

7. Emergency Hospitalization Restrictions

Pre-hearing hospitalization, or hospitalization prior to meeting with the J.A., shall be for the shortest possible period commensurate with the § 6B standard. No juvenile shall be retained in the hospital for over three days (including any detention prior to the J.A.'s meeting with the juvenile) without either an interview by the J.A. or an admission hearing before the admissions review board pursuant to § 5D. All juveniles so hospitalized shall be reexamined by a mental health professional between twenty-four and thirty-six hours after entrance to determine whether such hospitalization shall be continued.

Any juvenile so hospitalized shall be kept in a ward separate from the general patient population. Neither shall medication be administered nor restraints used except where there is the occurrence of, or serious threat of extreme violence, personal injury, or attempted suicide. Any medication administered shall be prescribed by a qualified physician and shall be of the mildest type and minimum dosage required to prevent violence, injury, or suicide. Any restraints used shall similarly be the minimum necessary under the circumstances. The use of any medication or restraints shall be reviewed at least once every eight hours by a qualified physician to determine whether it should be continued, reduced, or discontinued. A report of all medication administered to the juvenile shall be made to the admissions review board prior to an admission hearing.

8. Admissions Review Board

The admissions review board shall be composed of three persons: a licensed attorney, a licensed psychiatrist, and a person with knowledge of the alternative treatment resources available. The third person shall not be a lawyer or a medical doctor. None of the three shall be affiliated with the hospital involved in the proposed admission. (It would also be preferable if none was affiliated with the state department of mental health, but this may be too stringent a requirement for the psychiatrist, except in very large cities).

A pool of board members shall be appointed for staggered terms of four years by the governor or his or her designee. The three board members to sit at a particular hearing shall be chosen from the pool in a manner determined by the administrative needs of the jurisdiction, but insuring the proper mix of professional disciplines and designed to include on each board (after a two-year start-up phase) at least one member with a year or more of experience in the conduct of such hearings. The board shall conduct hearings at a place or places to be determined by the board.

9. The Admission Hearing

A. An admission hearing shall be held before the admissions review board in all cases specified in § 5D above. At each hearing the board shall consider all relevant testimony and other information relating to the juvenile's case, and shall determine whether the particular facts of the case justify an admission in accordance with the standard set forth in subsection D below.

Commensurate with the circumstances, admission hearings shall be conducted informally. Strict conformity with the rules of evidence shall not be required. However, all witnesses will be sworn. A hospital mental health professional who has personally examined the juvenile shall testify as to his mental disorder and shall present at least a preliminary treatment plan for the child.

B. At the hearing the juvenile will be represented by the J.A. unless he or she presents counsel of his or her own choosing. Neither the child nor the parents may waive the child's right to counsel at the hearing. However, for good cause shown and upon approval of the review board, the juvenile, with the concurrence of the J.A., may waive his right to be personally present at the hearing.

The juvenile shall not be compelled to testify. If he or she does testify, he or she may refuse to answer specific questions. However, to encourage openness and a full disclosure of all relevant information, the juvenile shall be granted "use" and "derivative use" immunity from prosecution in criminal court and any procedure in juvenile court for any information disclosed by any person at the hearing. The juvenile shall have the right to offer evidence and present witnesses on his or her own behalf and to confront and cross-examine adverse witnesses. Further, the juvenile shall have the right to a psychiatric examination, by a psychiatrist of his or her choosing, and at the expense of the state.

C. The admissions review board shall be required to make an audio tape recording of the hearing to facilitate later appeal to a court, but a tape shall be transcribed only when required. In addition, the board at its discretion may grant to any party permission to make a record (audio or written) of the proceedings. Maintenance of strict confidentiality shall be required for all records of the hearing. If the board concludes that the juvenile shall not be admitted to the facility, all records of the hearing and of any pre-hearing hospitalization will be expunged. A juvenile shall be admitted only when at least two of the three members of the board find that the need for hospitalization has been proven by *clear and convincing evidence* according to the following standard:

D. The Admission Standard

(1) The juvenile has a mental disorder; and
(2) a. The juvenile needs treatment for this disorder, and the specific treatment modalities proposed for this juvenile are available at the facility, have been shown to be effective, and will substantially benefit him or her; or
     b. By reason of this mental disorder the juvenile is in imminent danger of causing serious harm to himself or herself or others, as evidenced by one or more recent overt acts or repeated, continuing, and credible threats of such acts; and
(3) No less restrictive alternative is available.

10. Statement of Findings by Admissions Review Board

To facilitate any later appeal to a court, the admissions review board shall state how the facts in a particular case either satisfy or fail to satisfy the admission standard (§ 9D above).

11. Appeal

The juvenile, or his or her parent, guardian, or legal custodian may request judicial review of the board's decision. However, admission of the juvenile shall not be delayed pending completion of the appeal process.

12. Alternative Living Arrangements

When the juvenile is not hospitalized before a hearing (§ 6 above), or when the juvenile is not admitted to the hospital following an admission hearing, it may be advantageous to locate alternative living arrangements for the juvenile so that he or she need not be sent home to unsatisfactory living conditions. Upon the concurrence of the juvenile and his or her parent, guardian, or legal custodian, the J.A. will attempt to find, or have social agencies find, such alternative placements outside of the facility. The third member of the admissions review board may also possess helpful knowledge of such alternative placements.

13. Automatic Discharge from Mental Health Facility

Where the juvenile is admitted to a mental health facility (either with or without a hearing) and subsequently he or she *and* his or her parent, guardian, or legal custodian concur by signed statement that the juvenile should be released from the facility, the juvenile shall be discharged immediately. Should a facility mental health professional believe that continued hospitalization is necessary for such a juvenile, his or her sole recourse shall be to provisions of the state involuntary civil commitment statute.

14. Discharge Hearings, Mandatory Hearings

A. Discharge hearings shall be conducted by the admissions review board in a manner identical to admission hearings (§ 9 above). The juvenile shall be discharged unless at least two of the three members of the board are satisfied that there is clear and convincing evidence of the need for continued hospitalization, as articulated in the admission standard (§ 10 above).

B.

(1) If the juvenile is admitted to a mental health facility *without* an admission hearing pursuant to § 5C above and, subsequently, either the juvenile *or* his or her parent, guardian, or legal custodian request discharge, but do not obtain the other party's concurrence (compare § 13), a discharge hearing shall be conducted before the admissions review board within three days of the request (excluding Sundays and holidays). The J.A. shall represent the juvenile at such a hearing.
(2) Where the juvenile is admitted *pursuant* to an admission hearing, a discharge hearing may not be demanded until fifteen days after the admission unless

the admissions review board specifies at the hearing that the parties have a right to demand an earlier discharge hearing.

(3) The J.A. may request a hearing at *any time* following admission for good cause shown.

(4) The juvenile shall have the right to petition a court of law for a writ of *habeas corpus* at any time.

C. After an initial discharge hearing is held pursuant to subsections B(1) or B(2) above, the juvenile, or his parent, guardian or legal custodian may demand a second discharge hearing thirty days after the first; a third forty-five days after the second; a fourth three months after the third; a fifth six months after the fourth; and successive discharge hearings at one year intervals thereafter.

D. In all cases where no discharge hearing is demanded pursuant to subsection B above, a mandatory discharge hearing shall be conducted before the admissions review board three months after admission. Subsequent, mandatory discharge hearings shall be held annually thereafter unless discharge hearings are requested more frequently by one of the parties pursuant to subsection C above.

E. The admissions review board may at any discharge hearing grant to the juvenile or his parent, guardian, or legal custodian the right to call for other discharge hearings at times earlier than those specified in the above schedules.

15. Periodic Review

Regardless of whether or not the juvenile or other party requests a discharge hearing, a hospital mental health professional and the J.A. shall review the juvenile's condition, treatment, and progress fifteen days after his admission, thirty days after the first review, forty-five days after the second review, and every three months thereafter. This review shall include a personal interview of the juvenile by the J.A. and mental health professional. If, upon such review, either reviewer decides that the juvenile should be discharged, he will so inform the other reviewer, the juvenile, and the parent, guardian, or legal custodian. If all concur, the juvenile shall be discharged. If all do not concur, the reviewer favoring discharge may demand a discharge hearing. (The J.A. shall demand such a hearing only if the juvenile desires to be discharged.)

16. J.A.'s Role After Admission

In addition to participating in periodic reviews (§ 15 above) and discharge hearings (§ 14 above), the J.A. shall monitor the juvenile's condition and progress and the facility's conformity with the treatment plan. He or she shall present suggestions and requests to the appropriate members of the facility staff, as he or she and the juvenile think appropriate, to improve the juvenile's treatment or condition, and shall call for an admissions review board hearing if such recommendations fail to rectify unsatisfactory conditions.

17. Intrusive Treatments

Explicit recognition shall be accorded to important rights of bodily integrity. The administering to juveniles of highly intrusive, irreversible treatment modalities shall be prohibited absolutely, and the use of less intrusive modalities shall be restricted to those cases in which there has been a convincing showing that such use is warranted.

A. The state legislature shall explicitly define which treatment modalities are intrusive and subject to the prohibitions or restrictions of this section, and shall determine in which of the following two categories each intrusive treatment shall be placed:

(1) Treatment modalities which are highly intrusive and may never be administered to juveniles (e.g., psychosurgery, certain nontherapeutic medical experiments involving inpatients as subjects, and possibly electroconvulsive therapy (ECT));

(2) Less intrusive treatment modalities which may be administered in specific cases where parental consent and admissions review board approval is obtained in conformity with § 17C below. (E.g., aversive conditioning, dosage of drugs for specific conditions higher than a defined maximum, therapeutic experimental modalities, possibly ECT if not included in category 1 above.)

B. When an intrusive modality (as defined in § 17A(2)) is proposed for use on a juvenile inpatient, the director of the mental health facility shall notify in writing the juvenile; his or her parent, guardian, or legal custodian; the juvenile's J.A.; and the admissions review board. Upon receipt of such notice the board shall conduct a hearing (no waiver shall be permitted) within three days (excluding Sundays and holidays) to determine whether the proposed treatment may be administered. The following standard shall be employed:

C. Intrusive Treatment Standard
§ 17A(2) intrusive treatment may be administered if, and only if, the juvenile's parents, guardian or legal custodian consent and the admissions review board *unanimously* finds by *clear and convincing evidence:*

(1) That the juvenile has been shown to have a mental disorder;
(2) That other less intrusive treatment modalities have been tried but have not satisfactorily alleviated the juvenile's mental disorder;
(3) That the proposed intrusive treatment is available at the hospital and has been shown to be effective in treating disorders of the type afflicting the juvenile; and
(4) That there are no less intrusive alternative treatments available.

D. Nontherapeutic Experimentation

Generally, nontherapeutic experimentation may not be conducted on inpatients under sixteen years of age, but such experimentation may be conducted in limited cases where all of the following conditions are met:

(1) The proposed experimentation is only minimally intrusive (*e.g.,* a blood sample) and does not involve any health risk to the juvenile;
(2) The purpose of the experimentation is to obtain significant medical or behavioral science research information;
(3) The experiment conforms with the highest ethical standards applicable to medical research, including approval by the institutional review board for the protection of human subjects (where the potential risks of such experimentation cannot be safely ascertained, such experimentation is prohibited); and
(4) The juvenile has knowingly and voluntarily consented to participate in the research after an interview with the J.A. The J.A. shall assess the validity of the juvenile's consent and judge whether it is competent, knowing, and voluntary. For purposes of this assessment, the consent of any child less than twelve years of age shall be presumed to be not competent.

18. Commitments Directly From Juvenile Court Prohibited

No Juvenile Court may commit a person under sixteen years of age directly to inpatient status at a mental health facility, but it may deliver the juvenile into the custody of a state agency (such as a Department of Youth Services or a Division of Family and Child Services) to have such agency apply for the juvenile's admission to a mental health facility in accordance with the procedures herein. The procedures set forth herein shall represent the only means other than the state's civil commitment process, which is applicable to adults as well as to juveniles, by which a person under the age of sixteen may be admitted to inpatient status at a mental health facility.

19. Definitions

§ 1 *Mental Health Facility* - any public or private hospital, clinic, or residential mental health treatment center which admits juveniles for inpatient mental health diagnosis or treatment.

§ 2 *The Admitting Officer* - the mental health professional authorized by the director of a mental health facility to determine whether juveniles should be admitted for inpatient diagnosis or treatment.

§ 6 *Designated Mental Health Professional* - a staff psychiatrist authorized by the director of a mental health facility to decide whether a juvenile shall be admitted pursuant to § 6B above prior to an interview by the J.A. or an admission hearing.

§ 9 *Use and Derivative Use Immunity* - a prohibition against the use of any information contained in or derived from testimony given at a hearing against the possessor of the immunity (here the juvenile whose admission is being considered at the hearing) in any criminal or juvenile justice action.

§ 11 *Less Restrictive Alternatives* - available mental health treatment modalities, including psychotherapy, counseling, care at outpatient centers, assignment to halfway houses, etc., which do not involve inpatient hospitalization at a mental health facility.

20. Regulations

The state Department of Mental Health [Mental Health and Retardation, Mental Hygiene, or other agency responsible for administering the state's mental health system] is authorized to adopt, amend, and repeal rules and regulations to effect the implementation of these procedures and to insure that the highest practicable standards of professional care are maintained.

Appendix A
Age of Majority in Each
State

State	Age of Majority	Relevant Statutes
Alabama	21	Alabama Code, Recompiled 1958, tit. 47 § 154(1)(a), (m) (1973 Supp.). (Definition of minor under Uniform Gift to Minors Act.)
Alaska	18	Alaska Stat. § 25.20.010 (1977 Supp.). But minor attains age of majority at time of marriage, if 18. Alaska Stat. § 25.20.020 (1977 Supp.).
Arizona	18	Ariz. Rev. Stat. Ann. § 1-215(2), (4), (14) (1974).
Arkansas	18	Ark. Stat. § 57-103 (1975 Supp.). (Except drinking age retained at 21.)
California	18	California Civil Code § 25.1 (1975 Supp.).
Colorado	21	Colo. Rev. Stat. 1973 § 2-4-401 (6) (1974). (Definition of minor person under 21.) However, an 18-year-old is competent to make contracts, sue and be sued, and make decisions in regard to his own body; a minor can consent to medical treatment and acquire birth control supplies and information. Colo. Rev. Stat. 1973 §§ 13-22-101 to 13-22-105.
Connecticut	18	Conn. Gen. Stat. Ann. § 1-1(d) (1976 Supp.).
Delaware	18	Del. Code Ann. 1 § 302(1), (12) (1974).
District of Columbia	21	D.C. Code § 16-2301 (1973).
Florida	18	Florida Stat. Ann. § 743.07 (1978 Supp.).
Georgia	18	Ga. Code Ann. § 74-104 (1973).
Hawaii	18	Hawaii Rev. Stat. § 577-1 (1975 Supp.).

State	Age of Majority	Relevant Statutes
Idaho	18	Idaho Code § 16-2002(b) (1977 Supp.).
Illinois	18	Ill. Rev. Stat. ch. 3 § 11-1 (1976 Supp.).
Indiana	18	Burn's Indiana Stat. Ann. (Code Edition) § 34-1-67-1(6) (1977 Supp.).
Iowa	18	Iowa Code Ann. § 599.1 (1976 Supp.). (Except all minors attain majority by marriage.)
Kansas	18	Kansas Stat. Ann. § 38-101 (1973).
Kentucky	18	Kentucky Revised Stat. § 2.015 (1971). (Except age for drinking is 21 and for treatment of handicapped children it is 18-21.)
Louisiana	18	La. Rev. Stat. Ann. Civil Code, Art. 37 (1976 Supp.).
Maine	18	Me. Stat. Ann. tit. 1 § 72 (1973 Supp.).
Maryland	18	Ann. Code of Maryland art. 1 § 24 (1976 Supp.).
Massachusetts	18	Mass. Gen. Laws Ann. ch. 4 § 7-51 (1976 Supp.).
Michigan	18	Mich. Stat. Ann. § 25.244 (51-52) (1974).
Minnesota	18	Minn. Stat. Ann. § 645.45 (14) (1978).
Mississippi	21	Miss. Code Ann. § 1-3-27 (1972).
Missouri	21	Mo. Stat. Ann. § 475.010 (4) (1972).
Montana	18	1972 Const. of Mont. art. II § 14 (1975 Supp.).
Nebraska	19	Neb. Rev. Stat. § 38-101 (1971). (Unless person marries before 19.)
Nevada	18	Nev. Rev. Stat. Ann. § 129.010 (1975).

State	Age of Majority	Relevant Statutes
New Hampshire	18	N.H. Rev. Stat. Ann. § 21:44 (1973 Supp.).
New Jersey	18	N.J. Stat. Ann. § 9:17b-1 (1976 Supp.). (General legislative finding that persons 18 or over may enter binding contracts, but persons 18-21 may still be defined as minors for other purposes.)
New Mexico	18	N.M. Stat. 1953 Ann. § 13-13-1 (1976 Supp.). (Except drinking age retained at 21.)
New York	18	McKinney's Consolidated Laws of New York Ann. Domestic Relations § 2 (1977).
North Carolina	18	Gen. Stat. of North Carolina § 48A-2 (1976).
North Dakota	18	North Dakota Century Code § 14-10-01 (1977 Supp.).
Ohio	18	Page's Ohio Rev. Code Ann. § 3109.01 (1977 Supp.).
Oklahoma	18	Okla. Stat. Ann. tit. 15 § 13 (1972).
Oregon	18	Ore. Rev. Stat. § 109.510 (1975).
Pennsylvania	21	Pennsylvania Consolidated Statutes, Title 1, § 1991 (1977 Supp.). (Minor means an individual under the age of 21, but minors 18-21 have full contractual rights. Purdon's Penn. Stat. Ann. tit. 73 § 2021 (1976 Supp.)).
Rhode Island	18	Gen. Laws of Rhode Island § 15-12-1 (1975 Supp.).
South Carolina	21	Code of Laws of South Carolina § 62-402 (11) (1975 Supp.).
South Dakota	18	S.D. Codified Laws § 26-1-1 (1976 Supp.).
Tennessee	18	Tenn. Code Ann. § 1-313 (1977 Supp.).

State	Age of Majority	Relevant Statutes
Texas	18	Vernon's Texas Civil Stat. Ann. art. 5923(b) (1976 Supp.).
Utah	18	Utah Code Ann. § 15-2-1 (1977 Supp.).
Vermont	18	Vt. Stat. Ann. tit. 1 § 173 (1976 Supp.).
Virginia	18	Code of Va. 1950 § 1-13.42b (1976 Supp.).
Washington	18	Rev. Code Wash. Ann. § 26.28.010 (1975 Supp.).
West Virginia	18	West Virginia Code § 2-2-10 (aa) (1976 Supp.).
Wisconsin	18	Wis. Stat. Ann. § 990.01 (20) (1975 Supp.).
Wyoming	19	Wyo. Stat. § 8-18.1 (1975 Supp.).

Appendix B
State Statutory Provisions Relating to Admission of Minors to Mental Health Facilities

State	*Statutory Provisions*
Alabama	"Any citizen may be admitted . . . on his own application." Code of Alabama Recompiled 1958, tit. 45 § 205(*1*)-(*1*) (1973 Supp.). (No mention of parental consent or control.)
Alaska	Minor under 19 may apply for admission, but must have parental consent. Alaska Stat. § 47.30.020 (1975 Supp.). For release minor may need parental consent if discharging authority so requires. Alaska Stat. § 47.30.050 (1975 Supp.). (No mention of whether parent may admit minor unilaterally without minor's consent.)
Arizona	Parental consent is needed for both admission and release of minors under 18. Arizona Revised Stat. §§ 36-518(B), 36-519 (1974).
Arkansas	Parental consent necessary for admission. Arkansas Stat. § 59-405(B) (1971).
California	Only parents can admit, and they must approve release. California Welfare & Institutions Code § 6000(b) (Supp. 1975).
Colorado	Minor 15 years or older may apply for admission without parental consent. Apparently parents may also apply on the minor's behalf; in these cases the minor's consent is not needed, and he or she apparently cannot veto the parental application. Colo. Rev. Stat. 1973, §§ 27-10-103(2), (3) (1974).
Connecticut	"Any person" may request admission in writing and can obtain release 10 days after a request for release. Conn. Legislative Service 1976, Public Act No. 76-227 (1976). (No mention of parental authority.)
Delaware	Minor 16 or over may apply for admission. However, "[i] f applicant is under 18, the application shall also be signed by his parents." (May imply that parents may not act unilaterally for their children 16 or over.) Release of minors under 18 may be conditioned on parental consent. Del. Code Ann. tit. 16 § 5123(a), (c), (3) (1974).
District of Columbia	Parental consent required for both admission and release. D.C. Code Ann. § 21-511, § 21-512 (1973).

State	*Statutory Provisions*
Florida	Parents may apply for admission of persons aged 12-18. Minors 12-18 may apply for admission, but parents may then apply for discharge. Florida Stat. Ann. § 394.465 (1975 Supp.). (No mention of procedures for minors under 12.)
Georgia	Parental consent required for admission of minors, Ga. Code Ann. § 88.503.1 (1971), and for release. Ga. Code Ann. § 88.503.3 (1971).
Hawaii	Parental consent necessary for both admission and release. Hawaii Revised Stat. tit. 19 §334-52(e) (1968).
Idaho	A minor 14-18 may apply for admission, but parents may seek release 5 days after such admission. Idaho Code § 66-318 (1976 Supp.). (No mention of parents' right to admit minor child, but § 66-320(a)(2) states that, by reason of age, a patient can be admitted by another person.) For release, persons under 16 need parental or guardian consent if the minor was admitted on the application of another person. Idaho Code § 66-320(a)(2) (1977 Supp.).
Illinois	Parents, guardian, Department of Corrections, Department of Children and Family Services, or person *in loco parentis* may apply for admission of minors under 18. Ill. Rev. Stat. ch. 91 1/2 § 5-2(3) (1977 Supp.). If hospital intends to keep a patient after 60 days, it must apply to a court for approval, and the patient may request a hearing. Ill. Rev. Stat. ch. 91 1/2 § 6-6 (1977 Supp.). A voluntary admittee may seek release in 5 days. Ill. Rev. Stat. ch. 91 1/2 § 5-3 (1978 Supp.). (No mention of necessity for parental consent.)
Indiana	Parents may apply for admission of minors under 18. Burn's Indiana Stat. Ann. (Code Edition) § 16-14-9.1-2(2) (1977 Supp.).
Iowa	Parents may seek admission, but if the minor objects the parents must petition the juvenile court for approval of admission. Iowa Code Ann. § 229.2 (1977 Supp.).

State	Statutory Provisions
Kansas	Parental consent required for admission and release of minors. Kansas Stat. Ann. §§59-2905, 59-2907 (1975 Supp.).
Kentucky	Parents must consent to admission and release unless minor is emancipated. Kentucky Rev. Stat. § 202A.020(1), (2) (1977 Supp.).
Louisiana	"Any mentally competent person who is mentally ill" may apply; if person is incompetent, parent or spouse may consent for him or her for admission or discharge. La. Rev. Stat. Ann. § 28:51 (1975 Supp.). (No definition of the age of mental competence.)
Maine	Parents must consent to admission of minors under 16. Any voluntary patient is free to leave at any time. Me. Rev. Stat. tit. 34 § 2290 (1974 Supp.). (No mention of age for release.)
Maryland	Persons under 18 must have consent of one parent for admission. Parent requesting admission may demand discharge. Ann. Code of Maryland art. 59 § 11(g) (1972).
Massachusetts	Parents may apply for admission of minors under 18. Minors 16 or over may apply for admission without parental consent. Mass. Gen. Laws Ann. ch. 123 § 10 (1976 Supp.). "Any person" may apply for release, including parents if they applied for child's admission. Mass. Gen. Laws Ann. ch. 123 § 11 (1972).
Michigan	Parent may apply for admission of a minor under 18 as a "formal voluntary patient." Mich. Stat. Ann. § 14.800 (415) (1976 Supp.). (But a minor 13 or over may challenge admission and obtain a hearing. Mich. Stat. Ann. § 14.800 (417) (1976 Supp.)).
Minnesota	No age distinction for admission. (A 1973 amendment specifically deleted previous language permitting parents to admit minors.) Minn. Stat. Ann. § 253A.03 (1976 Supp.).
Mississippi	Parent may apply for admission of unmarried minor under 18. Miss. Code Ann. § 41-21-103 (2)(c) (1977 Supp.).

State	Statutory Provisions
Missouri	Parents may apply for admission of minor under 16. Minor 16 or over may apply for admission without parental consent. Mo. Stat. Ann. § 202.783 (1972). Parents must apply for release of minors under 16. Ann. Mo. Stat. § 202.790 (1972).
Montana	Minor 16 or over may apply for admission. Parents may admit minors (apparently including those 16 or over) for a 30 day period; longer periods authorized only through involuntary civil commitment. Mont. Rev. Code § 38-1303 (1977 Supp.). If the minor opposes the parents on admission, the admission is treated as an involuntary commitment. Mont. Rev. Code § 38-1303(9) (1977 Supp.).
Nebraska	No age distinctions for making application for voluntary admission. Rev. Stat. Neb. § 83-324 (1976).
Nevada	Parental consent necessary for admission of minors under 18. Nev. Rev. Stat. § 433A.1401 (1975).
New Hampshire	Eligibility of minors to apply for admission is to be governed by regulations to be prepared by Division of Mental Health of Department of Health and Welfare. N.H. Rev. Stat. Ann. ch. 135–B:11 (1973 Supp.). (No mention of parental authority.)
New Jersey	A person 18 or over, or (for a minor under 21) a parent, guardian, grandparent or adult brother or sister may apply for voluntary admission. N.J. Stat. Ann. § 30:4-46 (1977 Supp.). Discharge may be obtained on the certificate of the medical director or chief of staff. N.J. Stat. Ann. § 30:4-48 (1977 Supp.).
New Mexico	Parents can admit minor under 16. N.M. Stat. 1953 Ann. § 34-2-2 (1954).
New York	Parents must consent to admission of minors under 16. A minor 16-18 may apply, and director of hospital may accept the minor's application or may require parental consent. McKinney's Consolidated Laws of N.Y. Ann., Mental Hygiene § 31.13 (1976 Supp.).

State	*Statutory Provisions*
North Carolina	Parents must consent to admission and release of minors. Gen. Stat. of North Carolina § 122-56.3, .5 (1975 Supp.).
North Dakota	Parents or guardians must apply for admission of minors under 16. Minors 16 or over may apply for admission without parental consent. North Dakota Century Code § 25-03.1-04 (1977).
Ohio	Parents must consent to admission of minors under 18. Persons over 18 may make written application for voluntary admission. Page's Ohio Rev. Code Ann. § 5122.02 (1977 Supp.).
Oklahoma	Only parents can admit minors. "Patients admitted voluntarily" may obtain release unless a physician intends to commence court certification proceedings to commit the patient. No age limitation or parental consent requirement is included in the release provisions of the statute. Okla. Stat. Ann. tit. 43A § 184 (1977 Supp.).
Oregon	Parents must consent to admission and release of minor under 18. Ore. Rev. Stat. § 426.220 (1975 Supp.).
Pennsylvania	Any person 14 or over may apply for admission. Parents may request hearing to challenge admission of minor 14-18. Minor 14-18 may apply for release at any time. 1976 Purdon's Penn. Leg. Service, Act. No. 143, S.B. No. 1025, art. II §§ 201 to 206.
Rhode Island	Parental consent necessary to admit minor under 18, but the minor must also consent to be admitted. Gen. Laws of Rhode Island § 40.1-5-6 (1975 Supp.).
South Carolina	Minor 16 or over may apply for admission; a parent may apply "on behalf" of a minor under 16. Code of Laws of South Carolina § 44-17-310 (1976).
South Dakota	Parents may apply for admission of minor. S.D. Codified Laws § 27-4-12.1 (1976 Supp.). The minor may challenge the admission and request a hearing. S.D. Codified Laws §§ 27-4-12.3, 27-4-12.8. (1976 Supp.).

State	*Statutory Provisions*
Tennessee	Minor 16 or over may request admission or release. If patient cannot file written request for admission or release, a spouse, parent, or guardian may file in patient's behalf, but patient must consent to such action. Tenn. Code Ann. § 33-601 (1977 Supp.). (It is not clear what procedures, if any, apply to minors under 16.)
Texas	Parents and minor must consent to admission. Vernon's Texas Civil Stat. Ann. art. 5547-23 (1958). Parents and minor must consent to release. Vernon's Texas Civil Stat. Ann. art. 5547-23, 5547-25 (1958).
Utah	Parents may apply for admission of minors under 16, but "[n]o person over sixteen years of age may be hospitalized . . . against his will" unless he is involuntarily committed. Utah Code Ann. § 64-7-29 (1977 Supp.).
Vermont	Minor 16 or over may apply for admission. Vt. Stat. Ann. tit. 18 § 7503 (1968). (No mention of whether parents may admit minor under 16.) Minor under 16 must have parental consent for release. Vt. Stat. Ann. tit. 18 § 8001 (1968).
Virginia	"Any person" may be admitted for voluntary mental health care. Code of Va. 1950, § 37.1-65 (1976 Supp.). (No mention of age or parental authority.)
Washington	Parental consent required for admission of minors 13 or under. For a minor over 13, parents may apply, but minor must also consent. If minor over 13 refuses to consent, he may only be involuntarily committed. Minor over 13 does not need parental consent for release. Rev. Code Wash. Ann. § 72.23.070 (1976 Supp.).
West Virginia	Parental consent necessary for admission, but minor must consent also if he is 12 or over. West Virginia Code § 27-1-1 (1976 Supp.). Minor under 12 needs parental consent for release; minor 12 or over can refuse to be released on parental application. West Virginia Code § 27-4-3 (1976 Supp.).

State	*Statutory Provisions*
Wisconsin	Parental consent required for admission of minors. Wis. Stat. Ann. § 51.10 (1957).
Wyoming	Parental consent required for admission and release of minors. Wyo. Stat. §§ 25-54, 25-56 (1975 Supp.).

309

The author is grateful for permission to quote from the following:

John Janeway Conger, *Adolescence and Youth: Psychological Development in a Changing World*, (Harper & Row, Publishers, Inc., 1973), pp. 5, 20, 94, 95, 101, 108, 127, 140, 155, 160-61, 185, 185, 195. Copyright © 1973 by John Janeway Conger. By permission of Harper & Row, Publishers, Inc.

B. David Hinkle, Intrafamily Litigation—Parent and Child, 542 *Insurance Law Journal* 133 (March 1968), pp. 137, 146. Reprinted with permission.

U.S. Dept. of HEW, National Institute of Mental Health, *Public Opinions and Attitudes about Mental Health* (1963). Reprinted with permission.

A. Stone, *Mental Health and Law: A System in Transition*, NIMH, DHEW Publication No. (ADM) 75-176 (1975). Reprinted with permission.

D. Kirp, *Student Classification, Public Policy and the Courts*, 44 Harv. Ed. Rev. 7 (1974), copyright © 1974 by President and Fellows of Harvard College, reprinted with permission in edited form from D. Kirp, *Schools as Sorters: The Constitutional Policy Implications of Student Classification*, 121 *U. Pa. L. Rev.* 705 (1973). Copyright © 1973 by University of Pennsylvania Law Review.

W. Buss, Procedural Due Process for School Discipline: Probing the Constitutional Outline, 119 *U. Pa. L. Rev.*, no. 4 (February 1971). Copyright © 1971 by University of Pennsylvania Law Review. Reprinted with permission.

Note, "The Vestiges of Child-Parent Tort Immunity, 6 *Calif. L. Rev.* (1973), pp. 195, 196, 197, 204, 204-5. Copyright © 1973, California Law Review, Inc. Reprinted by permission.

Tussman and tenBroeck, The Equal Protection of the Laws, 37 *Calif. L. Rev.* 341 (1949), p. 344. Copyright © 1949, California Law Review, Inc. Reprinted by permission.

Note, Legislative History of Title III of the Voting Rights Act of 1970, 8 *Harv. J. on Legislation* 123 (1970), p. 139. Reprinted with permission.

R. Mnookin, Foster Care—In Whose Best Interest? 43 *Harv. Ed. Rev.* (1973), p. 601. Copyright © 1973 by President and Fellows of Harvard College. Reprinted with permission.

Note, Parental Consent Requirements and Privacy Rights of Minors: The Contraceptive Controversy, 88 *Harv. L. Rev.* 1001 (1975), pp. 1003-1004. Copyright © 1975 by The Harvard Law Review Association, Reprinted with permission.

Note, Recent Cases: Constitutional Law—Schools and School Districts—Prohibition of Long Hair Absent Showing of Actual Disruption Violates High School Students' Constitutional Rights, 84 *Harv. L. Rev.* 1702 (1971). Copyright © 1971 by The Harvard Law Review Association. Reprinted with permission.

B. Grumet, *The Plaintive Plaintiffs: Victims of the Battered Child Syndrome, in the Youngest Minority: Lawyers in Defense of Children*, ABA Press (S. Katz, ed. 1974), p. 151. Reprinted with permission of Sanford N. Katz, Editor-in-Chief.

The Relation to the State, 5 *Fam. L.Q.* (1971), pp. 66, 97, 98. Reprinted with permission of Sanford N. Katz, Editor-in-Chief.

Parental Power, 4 *Fam. L.Q.* (1970), pp. 412-414, 418, 434. Reprinted with permission of Sanford N. Katz, Editor-in-Chief.

Black's Law Dictionary, West Publishing Co., St. Paul, Minn. (rev. 4th ed. 1968), pp. 70, 834, 1392. Reprinted with permission from *Black's Law Dictionary*, Revised Fourth Edition, copyright © 1968 by West Publishing Co.

J. Ziskin, *Coping with Psychiatric and Psychological Testimony*, Law and Psychology Press, 202 South Rexford Drive, Beverly Hills, Cal. (2d ed. 1975), pp. 38, 39. Reprinted with permission.

J. Nunnally, *Psychometric Theory*, McGraw-Hill, New York (1967), p. 226. Copyright © 1967 by McGraw-Hill, Inc. Used with permission of McGraw-Hill Book Company.

R. Fisher, The Psychotherapeutic Professions and the Law of Privileged Communications, 10 *Wayne L. Rev.* 609 (1964). Reprinted with permission.

R. Slovenko, Psychiatry and Second Look at the Medical Privilege, 6 *Wayne L. Rev.* 202, n. 87 (Spring 1960). Reprinted with permission.

J. Tanner, Sequence Tempo, and Individual Variation in the Growth and Development of

310

Boys and Girls Aged Twelve to Sixteen, 100 *Daedalus* (1971), pp. 907-908. Reprinted by permission of the American Academy of Arts and Sciences, Boston, Massachusetts.

Bakan, Adolescence in America: From Idea to Social Fact, 100 *Daedalus* (1971), p. 979. Reprinted by permission of the American Academy of Arts and Sciences, Boston, Massachusetts.

L. Kohlberg and C. Gilligan. The Adolescent as a Philosopher: The Discovery of the Self in a Postconventional World, 100 *Daedalus* (1971), pp. 1065, 1067-1068, 1072. Reprinted by permission of the American Academy of Arts and Sciences, Boston, Massachusetts.

News Briefs, Divorce Rate, 1 *Fam. L. Rptr.* 2070 (November 26, 1974). Reprinted with permission.

Henkins, Morals and the Constitution: The Sin of Obscenity, 63 *Colo. L. Rev.* 391 (1963), p. 413. Reprinted with permission.

J. Adelson, A Disappointing Sample, 21 *Contemp. Psychol.* (1976), p. 120. Copyright © 1976 by the American Psychological Corporation. Reprinted by permission.

E. Erikson, *Childhood and Society*, W.W. Norton & Company, Inc., New York (1950), p. 261. Reprinted with permission.

E. Erikson, *Identity: Youth and Crisis*, W.W. Norton & Company, Inc., New York (1968), pp. 128, 156. Reprinted with permission.

H. Ginsburg and S. Opper, *Piaget's Theory of Intellectual Development: An Introduction*, Prentice-Hall, Englewood Cliffs, N.J. (1969), pp. 181, 203-4, 204-5. Reprinted with permission.

Waite, "How Far Can Court Procedure be Socialized without Impairing Individual Rights," 12 *J. Crim. L. & Criminology* (1922), pp. 339, 340. Reprinted with permission.

L. Shapiro, Ladies Last, *The Real Paper* (June 9, 1976), p. 8. Reprinted with permission.

C. Hall, *Financing Mental Health Services through Insurance*, 131 *Am. J. Psychiat.* 1079 (1974), p. 1080. Copyright © 1974, the American Psychiatric Association. Reprinted by permission.

J. Tanner, Growing Up, 229:3 *Scientific American* (September, 1973), pp. 36, 42. Copyright © 1973 by Scientific American, Inc. All rights reserved.

J. Gossett, S. Lewis, J. Lewis, V. Phillips, Follow-Up of Adolescents Treated in a Psychiatric Hospital: A Review of Studies, 43 *Amer. J. of Orthopsychiat.* Reprinted, with permission, from the American Journal of Orthopsychiatry; copyright 1973 by the American Orthopsychiatric Association, Inc.

C. Cashman, Confidentiality of Juvenile Court Proceedings: A Review, 24 *Juv. Justice* (August, 1973), p. 31. Reprinted with permission.

Robert Audette, Massachusetts Associate Commissioner for Special Education, "Parental Consent to Core Evaluations" (memo written on May 19, 1975). Reprinted with permission.

Children Out of School in America, A Report by the Children's Defense Fund of the Washington Research Project, Inc. (October, 1974). Reprinted with permission.

John Larkin Thompson, President, Massachusetts Blue Cross/Blue Shield, Inc. (letter written to Henry A. Beyer December 21, 1973). Reprinted with permission.

R. Mnookin, Child Custody Adjudication: Judicial Functions in the Face of Indeterminacy. Reprinted with permission from a symposium on Children and the Law appearing in *Law and Contemporary Problems*, vol. 39, no. 3 (Summer 1975), published by the Duke University School of Law, Durham, N.C. Copyright © 1975 by Duke University. Article copyright © 1976 by R. Mnookin.

R. Roth and J. Lerner, Sex-Based Discrimination in the Mental Institutionalization of Women, 62 *Calif. L. Rev.* 789 (1974), p. 793. Reprinted with permission.

J. Gossett, S. Lewis, J. Lewis, and V. Phillips, Follow-Up of Adolescents Treated in a Psychiatric Hospital: A Review of Studies, 43 *Amer. J. of Orthopsychiat.*, 602 (1973), p. 603. Reprinted with permission from the *American Journal of Orthopsychiatry*, copyright © 1973 by the American Orthopsychiatric Association, Inc.

Hard Times for Kids Too. Reprinted by permission from *Time*, The Weekly Newsmagazine; Copyright Time Inc. 1975.

John Ely, The Constitutionality of Reverse Racial Discrimination, 41 *U. Chi. L. Rev.* 723, 735 (1974). Reprinted with permission.

The Boston Globe: Ken Botright and Walter Haynes, NAACP: School Discipline Code "Very Fair" (December 9, 1975), p. 5; Robert B. Carr, Child Abuse: A Growing National Tragedy (March 31, 1976), pp. 1, 8; Jean Dietz, Ward of State Sues Welfare Department (June 6, 1975); Ron Hutson, School Suspensions: 1092 Minority, 550 White (December 9, 1974), p. 40; Martin F. Nolan, Clergymen and Politics (May 20, 1974), p. 2; R.H. Stewart, West and East: The Two States of Massachusetts (November 30, 1975), pp. 22, 44. (Courtesy of The Boston Globe)

Index

About the Author

John P. Wilson is associate dean and director of the Legal Studies Institute at the Boston University School of Law. He received his A.B. degree from Princeton University in 1955 and his L.L.B. degree from Harvard Law School in 1962. Prior to law school, Mr. Wilson worked for a year in the Bureau of the Budget, Executive Office of the President, Washington, D.C., and he served for approximately 3-1/2 years in the United States Navy. Following law school, after a brief stint in private practice in his home state of New Jersey, he returned to Harvard Law School as assistant dean. He came to Boston University in 1968. Mr. Wilson is a former member of the Health Facilities Appeals Board, and presently serves on the Board of Overseers of the Boston Hospital for Women and on the Board of Directors of Greater Boston Legal Services. He has written articles on the subjects of law and mental health, fetal experimentation, and legal education.